Citizen Jane

Citizen Jane

The
Turbulent Life
of
Jane Fonda

CHRISTOPHER
ANDERSEN

VIRGIN

First published in Great Britain in 1990 by
Virgin Books
A division of W. H. Allen & Co Plc
26 Grand Union Centre
338 Ladbroke Grove
London W10 5AH

First published in 1990 by Henry Holt and Co., Inc., New York

British Library Cataloguing in Publication Data
Andersen, Christopher
    Citizen Jane: the turbulent life of Jane Fonda.
    1. Cinema Films. Acting. Fonda, Jane, 1937–
    I. Title
    791.43028092

ISBN 1-85227-353-4

Typeset by Medcalf Type Ltd, Bicester
Printed and bound by Butler and Tanner Ltd, Frome, Somerset

For Valerie and Kate

'What do I think of Jane?
First I have to find out who
the hell she is today!'

—Henry Fonda

'I am many people.'

—Jane Fonda

CONTENTS

ILLUSTRATIONS

ACKNOWLEDGEMENTS

Over the course of the past fifteen years, I have had the privilege of interviewing all the famous Fondas – starting with Henry and ending, appropriately, with Jane. A tremendous amount of research is necessary for any thorough biography, and such was the case with *Citizen Jane*. Even more time was spent tracking down sources: co-workers, acquaintances, friends, employers, employees – and, yes, ex-friends and critics as well. For those of you who requested anonymity, I have respected your wishes and withheld your names. To all those who spoke to me, my heartfelt thanks.

I am also indebted to my agent, Ellen Levine, and Ellen's associate, Diana Finch. For their support and encouragement, my love and gratitude to my wife, Valerie, and our daughter, Kate.

Additional thanks to the late Joshua Logan, the late Bette Davis, Katharine Hepburn, the Lincoln Center Library for the Performing Arts, the Academy of Motion Picture Arts and Sciences, Homer Dickens, the Bettmann Archives, Pictorial Parade, Wide World, the Federal Bureau of Investigation, Campaign California, John Puzzo, Robert McColley, Dan Pitzer, John Harvey, the Waterbury *Republican*, Joseph Mankiewicz, Captain Eugene 'Red' McDaniel, the Greenwich Academy, the Emma Willard School, Vassar College, and the American Film Institute.

Donald Hutter did not live to see its publication, but *Citizen Jane* would not have been possible without his vision, passion and editorial brilliance. For these I am truly grateful, as are all authors who had the good fortune to work with him.

PART ONE
Lady Jane

I was in awe of my father. As a girl I would do naughty things just to gain his attention.

There are two sorts of people in this world. The dead — even if they think they're living — and the survivors. We're survivors. All the Fondas are.

Being a movie star is not a purpose.

If you're a strong, famous woman, it's not easy to find a man who isn't threatened.

1

SHE WOULD come to rue the day she had ever decided to make a film in Waterbury, Connecticut. Yet how was Jane Fonda – or anyone, for that matter – to know that a firestorm awaited her behind the placid façade of this middle-American mill town? After all, it had been half a century since Waterbury's halcyon days as the nation's 'Brass City', manufacturer of more candlesticks, fireplace screens and bullet casings than any other city in the world. The old Union Station, with its two hundred-foot-tall Romanesque clock tower, modelled by the legendary architect Stanford White after the campanile in Siena's Palazzo Pubblico, still stands as a reminder of Waterbury's past glory. But the overall impression created by largely abandoned Dickensian factories and crumbling tenements is unmistakably that of a working-class community sadly gone to seed.

All of which made Waterbury the perfect setting for *Stanley and Iris,* MGM's topical blue-collar tale of an illiterate cook (played by Robert De Niro) and the factory worker who teaches him how to read. The announcement that Fonda and De Niro would be making the film, then tentatively called *Union Street,* appeared on the front page of the *Waterbury Republican* on 11 November 1987 – Veterans Day. The cast and crew, said the movie's producers, would arrive sometime in May 1988 to begin filming.

Initially, the city fathers were thrilled. The film would not only mean a $3 million windfall for Waterbury, it would also give the city a much-needed public relations boost. One who was not thrilled was Gaetano 'Guy' Russo, a World War II veteran and retired major general in the National Guard. As far as Russo was concerned, Fonda's activities during the Vietnam War – specifically her controversial 1972 Hanoi trip, during which she had cheerfully posed for pictures riding a North Vietnamese anti-aircraft gun and made broadcasts for Radio Hanoi denouncing American soldiers as war criminals – constituted an act of treason for which she had unjustly escaped punishment.

Russo dashed off a letter to the *Waterbury Republican,* promising to campaign 'vigorously against her presence in Waterbury' and exhorting 'all Waterburians

3

who feel as I do to stop being a silent majority and write or call our mayor to let him know the extent of our feelings'. Russo went on to accuse Fonda of giving 'vocal comfort and support to the regime in North Vietnam that killed and maimed so many of our young sons and brothers'. Later, flanked by local Vietnam veterans who shared his outrage at Fonda's intention to film in Waterbury, Russo appeared on the front page of the paper displaying a black-and-white bumper sticker he had printed. It read 'I'm Not Fonda Hanoi Jane'. The sticker was an immediate success, and drivers honked in support of one another whenever they spotted this emblem of anti-Fonda sentiment.

An Associated Press story soon followed. 'Patriotism runs deep in this predominantly working-class city,' the article began, 'where veterans' groups are vocal, the newspaper is named the *Republican*, and the Elks Club is one of the most popular lunch spots.'

The AP piece clearly struck a nerve, and what had begun as Guy Russo's one-man crusade exploded overnight into a national *cause célèbre*. Jane Fonda versus the people of Waterbury became a prime talk-show topic, and switchboards at radio stations from Manhattan to Honolulu lit up as callers phoned in to offer support for the anti-Fonda movement or, in fewer cases, defend the actress's wartime activities. All three television networks carried the story, each running the old fifteen-second footage of Jane mounting the anti-aircraft gun to the obvious delight of her Communist hosts.

For weeks the controversy raged in letters-to-the-editor columns everywhere, and in Waterbury, both daily papers were flooded with mail from around the country. Typical of the anti-Fonda letters was one from Vietnam veteran James William Taylor of Linden, Michigan. 'I just watched the evening news with Tom Brokaw,' wrote Taylor, 'and was disgusted after seeing a piece on Jane Fonda. After all the years that have gone by, I still have a deep gut-wrenching feeling when I hear her name.' Taylor went on to say that twelve of his friends were killed in Vietnam, and that Fonda was responsible for 'beefing up the war effort through motivation for the Vietcong'.

'Thank you! Thank you! Thank you!' wrote one vet's mother, Barbara T. Stellings of Beloit, Wisconsin. 'For years I have voiced my opinion that Hanoi Jane should be tried for treason.' 'Hooray for Waterbury,' agreed John Anderson of Bemus Point, New York. 'It's about time Jane Fonda got what she deserved.' Chicago's Jess Rodriguez suggested 'Hanoi Jane' be 'sent packing. That woman does not belong in this country!' Several chapters of the Vietnam Veterans of America joined the fray, calling for Fonda to be 'held accountable' for 'her traitorous actions'.

The letters were running 5–1 against Fonda, but there were two famous names among her defenders. 'If we are willing to forgive experienced political leaders who mistakenly sent American men to Vietnam,' pleaded former United States senator and 1972 Democratic presidential candidate George McGovern, 'can't we forgive a passionate young actress whose distress over the war led her to a form of protest which she herself now says was ill-advised?' Former first lady Rosalyn Carter, referring to her own daughter Amy's highly publicised civil disobedience against South Africa's apartheid policies, also defended Fonda's right to free speech.

Millions of Americans under the age of 35 had known Jane Fonda only as an Academy Award-winning actress, Hollywood producer, and taut-bodied ruler of her Workout empire. These were the adoring fans who bought more than $500 million worth of her fitness videos, books and tapes and always put her near the top of annual polls of America's most admired women. Now they were getting a glimpse of a very different Jane Fonda – one that the star had been trying to bury for years.

Indeed, the last thing Fonda needed now was a public crisis after the gruelling months she had just spent on location in Mexico filming *Old Gringo*. It had taken eight years for her to get the film based on Carlos Fuentes's novel into production, and by the time shooting began she was an emotional wreck. When co-star Gregory Peck kissed her for the first time on screen, neither she nor her director Luis Puenzo was satisfied with the result – a problem Fonda, the hard-driven perfectionist, quickly ascribed to her own professional shortcomings. 'We were supposed to finish the scene on Saturday and we didn't,' she later recalled. 'There was something wrong and we didn't know what. So we were held over until Monday – and I had my nervous breakdown on the weekend.' When her husband, Tom Hayden, arrived on the set that Sunday, he found Jane lying on top of the bed in her hotel room 'in the foetal position. What he doesn't know,' she added, 'is that I cried all night and I was . . . dysfunctional.'

Fonda's self-doubt over the kiss on the set of *Old Gringo* may have had all the markings of a manufactured movie star 'crisis', but Waterbury was the genuine article. Both Haydens had long been resigned (if not entirely accustomed) to encountering occasional placard-waving protesters wherever they appeared. But Waterbury marked the first time that Fonda's political critics had banded together to prevent her from shooting on location. Movies, after all, were not only the foundation of her empire, they were a Fonda family birthright. This time, she could not simply look the other way.

Jane Fonda turned 50 on 21 December 1987. She had three exercise videos on *Billboard* magazine's 'Top Twenty' and could look back on a film career that included two Oscars (for *Klute* and *Coming Home*) and seven nominations; but, back home in Santa Monica, Jane saw little reason to celebrate. Not since the mid-1970s had she been the target of such invective. By way of launching a counterattack, her production company, Fonda Films, commissioned the

5

California firm of Fairbank, Bregman & Maullin to conduct a poll of Waterbury residents. The results offered encouragement: while 13 per cent favoured barring Fonda from the city, 73 per cent said she should be allowed to film there.

Even if things were not as bad as they had seemed in Connecticut, anti-Fonda sentiment had spread to neighbouring Massachusetts. In Holyoke, where MGM had intended to shoot for two days, the town's aldermen voted 11–4 in February to bar Fonda from filming in their city. Two months later, aldermen in nearby Chicopee, Massachusetts, also voted to declare her *persona non grata*.

Before a similar resolution could be brought before Waterbury's board of aldermen, the Fonda forces moved quickly to sway public opinion. Tom Hayden flew to Hartford, then took a 45-minute ride to Waterbury for a hastily called meeting with the editors of the *Republican* and the *American*. The one-time radical leader, now a buttoned-down California assemblyman with his eye on higher office, had more riding on this mission than his wife's film career. Hayden described his wife to the Waterbury editors as 'a strong-willed patriotic American taught by her father to speak out. She feels particularly terrible because she is so pro-GI. She was sympathetic to the agony the country went through, sympathetic of the divisions of families. She didn't kill anybody . . .' But, he added, 'Jane's a strong person. She stands up for what she believes. Not everybody is going to love you.'

On 25 April, the Waterbury board of aldermen voted 11–2 not to ban Fonda from filming in the city. Nonetheless, Russo and the anti-Fonda forces pledged to picket the actress when she arrived to begin filming. 'She had the right to come here,' he explained, 'so we have the right to protest.'

In fact, Russo had accomplished far more than he realised. Old wounds had been reopened, and with Tom back in California the Haydens worried that irreparable damage had been done not only to Fonda's public image but to Tom Hayden's political future. Then, too, the renewed controversy had put added strain on their already fragile marriage. But the more practical, immediate problem was filming *Stanley and Iris* in Waterbury that summer. It was too late now to back out, and the prospect of battling protesters during three weeks of shooting was costing Jane more sleepless nights.

To put Vietnam behind them once and for all, Jane told her husband that she wished to make a public statement of contrition – if only to allow veterans, denied victory over the enemy, at least some measure of satisfaction for having defeated Jane Fonda. Hayden opposed the idea. Why should they apologise when those who conducted the war never had? He worried that anything she said now on the subject would be misinterpreted as an admission of guilt.

Typically determined to do *something*, Jane picked up the telephone and called her old friend Barbara Walters, whose husband Merv Adelson, happened to own the company that distributed Fonda's videotapes.

On 17 June, Walters's interview with Fonda, titled 'Healing the Wounds', was broadcast as the lead-in segment on ABC's '20/20'. Fonda had not slept at all the night before the taping; she was, as she recalled later, exhausted, numb, desperately hoping the inspiration would come, that the words would 'really say it'. She would have to, in other words, give the performance of her life.

The interview was conducted in the Haydens' high-ceilinged living room, and, though she tried to look relaxed, Fonda's face was etched with tension.

WALTERS: Why do you think it is that when so many people protested the war . . . why are your actions today still being criticised? Why is it so painful?

FONDA: The war was a very divisive and very confusing tragedy for all of us, but because I don't think we've ever resolved what the war meant, there are still festering wounds and a lot of pain, and for some I've become a lightning rod.

WALTERS: What lingers in people's minds, what angers many people, was the trip that you took to Hanoi in 1972. There is that famous picture of you aboard the North Vietnamese anti-aircraft gun. Tell us how that happened. Did you realise the effect that it would have?

FONDA: No.

WALTERS: What were you doing climbing on that gun?

FONDA: That was a thoughtless and careless thing to have done. For someone like me, who's – I'm in the communication business. I know the power of images. To have put myself in a situation like that was a thoughtless and cruel thing to have done. It was quite normal for visitors to North Vietnam to visit military sites, anti-aircraft guns – you're given a helmet to put on –

WALTERS: They give you – the North Vietnamese give you the helmet.

FONDA: Yeah.

WALTERS: Did they encourage you to get on the gun?

FONDA: I'm not sure. I take full responsibility for it. I was not a kid, you know. The responsibility is mine.

WALTERS: Do you feel you were duped by the North Vietnamese for propaganda purposes?

FONDA: No, I don't. I really don't . . . I don't remember being led to this gun. I mean, you know, I'm a strong woman. I'm naïve and I make mistakes, but it was my fault that I sat there, you know. I mean, I was a big girl. I could have said no, I can't do this. It was my fault.

Walters then zeroed in on Fonda's broadcasts over Radio Hanoi. Had she called American soldiers war criminals? No, said Jane. An excerpt, obtained by ABC through the Freedom of Information Act, was then played.

7

This is Jane Fonda speaking in Hanoi. And I'm speaking particularly to US servicemen who are stationed on the aircraft carriers in the Gulf of Tonkin. I don't know what your officers tell you, those of you who load the bombs on the planes, but one thing that you should know is that these weapons are illegal and the use of these bombs, or the condoning the use of these bombs, makes one a war criminal.

'You asked American soldiers to disobey their orders,' Walters persisted. 'You called their officers . . . war criminals.'

Fonda was taken aback by this. She had not heard her own broadcasts since making them sixteen years earlier. 'I wanted to say to them,' she tried to explain, 'let's think about what we are doing, all of us, because it's as much an American tragedy as it is a Vietnamese tragedy.'

Fonda was in for another rude surprise when Walters asked her to watch a taped interview with retired Navy captain Eugene 'Red' McDaniel, a former POW. McDaniel remembered how he felt when Fonda's words were played over and over on loudspeakers in the streets of Hanoi. 'It was kind of hard to keep going,' he said. 'I felt betrayed and hurt . . . I don't think the right to dissent extends to the capital city of the enemy in time of war.'

'I understand that he has his point of view,' Fonda responded coolly. 'But we did what we all felt we had to do . . . I am proud of most of what I did and I am very sorry for some of what I did.'

But what of the returning POWs who claimed they were tortured when they refused to greet Fonda on her Hanoi trip? John McCain, the Republican senator from Arizona, was a prisoner of war in May 1972 when his captors informed him that Fonda was in Hanoi. The North Vietnamese ordered McCain to have his picture taken with her and make statements condemning the war. When he refused, both his arms were broken and he was confined to a six-by-three-foot box for five months.

Walters introduced another embarrassing news clip.

'What about these men now that are commenting back home [a reporter asks a 35-year-old Fonda], saying that when you came to Hanoi they were tortured?'

'I think they're lying [she replies point-blank]. I think they're lying and I think they're not only going to have to live with the fact that they were carrying out acts of murder for the rest of their lives, they're also going to have to live with the fact that they're lying on their consciences. It was not — it was not a policy of the North Vietnamese to torture prisoners.'

'I was angry,' Fonda conceded to Barbara Walters. 'I popped off and I shouldn't have done it.' She stopped noticeably short, however, of retracting her statement

8

altogether. 'It's beside the point. They [the POWs] suffered. They suffered enough. They didn't need to hear from me.'

Clearly, this was not enough for Walters. 'Jane, you wanted to do this interview because there were some things that you wanted to set straight . . . There are still people who, I guess, feel you have never apologised. Would you like to just say something to them now?'

'I would like to say something,' Fonda replied. Her speech was deliberate, measured. 'Not to Vietnam veterans in New England, but to men who were in Vietnam who I hurt or whose pain I caused to deepen because of things that I said or did. I feel that I owe them an apology. My intentions were never to hurt them or make their situation worse. It was the contrary. I was trying to help end the killing, end the war, but there were times when I was thoughtless and careless about it and I'm very sorry that I hurt them. And I want to apologise to them and to their families.'

After the taping, Fonda worried that she might have made a fatal error by choosing as her forum a prime-time television show over which she had no control. She was also dissatisfied with her performance. Her lack of sleep the night before had made her look somehow distant, wooden, and, worst of all, *insincere*. She wanted to shoot the scene again.

Predictably, Fonda's harshest critics were unconvinced. Ben Wattenberg, a scholar at the American Enterprise Institute and a syndicated columnist, noted that Fonda's statements were 'more in the nature of conversational remarks' and not a political apology. 'We do indeed believe in political redemption in this country, and properly,' he wrote. 'But from what I heard, that was a well-intentioned apology for being in favour of a victory over American forces. That was different than the goal of the peace movement, which was simply to get America out of the war.'

Back in Waterbury, many shared Wattenberg's view of Fonda's '20/20' appearance that Friday night as a cynical attempt to expedite the filming of *Stanley and Iris*. 'Too little, too late,' said one veteran interviewed on the local news. 'She must toss and turn in her sleep,' said another, 'and I hope she does until her dying day.'

Joseph Griggs, a leader of the Veterans Coalition Against Hanoi Jane, saw an opportunity in Fonda's apology. 'It's been our position for some time now that efforts have to go along with the words.' Specifically, Griggs stressed, the veterans wanted Fonda either to become actively involved in the MIA issue, or to help with the plight of children born with birth defects that might have been caused by their fathers' exposure to the defoliant Agent Orange.

Less than twelve hours after the '20/20' broadcast, Fonda made another characteristically bold and risky move, quietly boarding a plane that would take her into the heart of the enemy camp. At the invitation of the Reverend John McColley, she met secretly at St Michael's Church in Naugatuck,

Connecticut – the town neighbouring Waterbury – with more than a hundred of her most vocal critics.

For three emotion-charged hours, these men – many clad in fatigues and defiantly displaying their 'I'm Not Fonda Hanoi Jane' stickers and buttons – listened as Fonda tried to explain why she became active in the anti-war movement, and what she had hoped to accomplish in Hanoi. For the first time, she also offered a new explanation as to why she appears to be almost giddy in the infamous film clip of her riding the anti-aircraft gun. Her North Vietnamese escorts had just sung their national anthem for her, and she was responding by belting out an equally stirring American song for them. Fonda told the assembled veterans that, rather than cheering on the enemy gun crew, she was in fact delivering an animated, arm-waving rendition of 'Yankee Doodle'.

Face-to-face with the woman whom they had come to view as a traitor, several of the vets were overcome with emotion. Others seemed merely starstruck. 'To some of the guys,' said one of those present, 'it was like, "Gee, I'm talking to a real live movie star!" They forgot why we were there.'

Whether they were impressed by her sincerity or simply taken in by the talents of a first-class actress, Fonda's audience of Vietnam veterans gradually softened. To win them over completely, she promised to appear at a special fund-raiser for the children suffering birth defects that might have been caused by Agent Orange.

After four hours, one of the veterans pulled a card out of his pocket and held it up. It was the ace of spades. 'This is what we'd leave on the bodies of the VC,' he said, tearing up the card he had saved all these years for Fonda. 'I guess I won't be needing it any more.'

Jane emerged from St Michael's Church into the glare of television lights. To her obvious displeasure, someone had tipped off the local press to her 'private' meeting with the veterans. Still, she could not help but feel satisfied. She had not only cleared away whatever obstacles blocked the path to her next movie, she had also succeeded – for the moment at least – in putting Vietnam behind her. In a quick sequence of carefully planned, artfully executed public relation moves, Jane Fonda had shown the world once again that, when it came to achieving her goals, she was capable of whatever it takes.

2

IF BLOODLINES are a valid indication, Jane Seymour Fonda was destined to become a high-strung thoroughbred. On her mother's side, she was descended from a distinguished Norman–Welsh line, and in fact was named after the clan's most historically significant member – Jane Seymour, the third of Henry VIII's six ill-fated wives.

At about the time of Jane Seymour's untimely demise, Henry Fonda's Italian ancestors were fighting on the losing side of the Reformation. They escaped to Amsterdam and, after a century in Holland, made their way to the New World. They settled in the Hudson Valley north of Manhattan and, by the time Washington Irving arrived to immortalise the region in 'Rip Van Winkle' and 'The Tale of the Headless Horseman', had established the town of Fonda, New York.

After distinguishing himself at Gettysburg, Jane's great-grandfather moved the family to Nebraska, and it was there that his son William Brace Fonda – Henry's father – started out in the printing business. Eventually, the family put down roots in Omaha, where the sidewalks were still made of wood and where Henry had what he was to recall as 'a Norman Rockwell childhood – straight off the cover of *The Saturday Evening Post*'. For the most part, his memories would be of ice cream sodas, family picnics, and Sunday rides in their father's Hupmobile. The Fondas, devout Christian Scientists, scrupulously avoided physicians. Whenever a family member was sick, 'there were always enough relatives around to come pray for you until you recovered'.

In 1910, at the age of five, Henry was rustled out of bed one night by his mother to witness the arrival of Halley's Comet. His younger sisters, Harriet and Jayne, were allowed to sleep undisturbed. His mother said it would not be back for another 76 years. Henry wondered if he would be around to see it again.

To the generation who came to know him as one of Hollywood's lankiest leading men, it is hard to imagine that Henry Fonda was small as a boy. At the age of seventeen, he would shoot up almost overnight to a full six foot, one and a half inches. But in the meantime, he was the family runt – shorter than his sisters and most of the girls he went to school with in Omaha. Shy and introverted, he turned to writing, and in the fifth grade won a short-story contest. The story was published in the local paper, and the family agreed that young Henry was destined for a brilliant career in journalism.

Not long after, Henry witnessed an event that would have a profound and lasting effect not only on him but also, ultimately, on his daughter. 'When I was about eleven,' he recalls, 'there was a race riot one night in Omaha. My father's business was on the third floor of a building overlooking the courthouse square. He took me there and lifted me up to the window. A young black man had been accused of rape, and now there was an angry mob below, waving torches and demanding that he be killed. I saw them drag him from the courthouse jail, string him up to a lamp-post, and, while his body still twitched, riddle him with bullets. Then they tied the body to a car and dragged it along the streets. The mayor rode up on his horse to calm them down, but the mob almost lynched him too.'

William Fonda, never an overtly affectionate or particularly communicative father, remained silent. 'All the while, my father never spoke, never said a word. He didn't have to. He just wanted to make sure I saw it, that's all.' Shaken, Henry could not sleep that night 'and a lot of other nights. That is something I will never forget.'

Henry became an Eagle Scout and earned a letter in basketball at Omaha Central High School in 1923. By the time he graduated, he had decided he would major in journalism at the University of Minnesota, though the question remained of just how he would pay for it on a $10 weekly allowance from Dad. Henry had worked after school hours as a printer's 'devil' (apprentice) in his father's shop, and had held a variety of odd jobs around town. So the prospect of working his way through college did not bother him at all.

In Minneapolis, Henry landed two jobs – as a part-time troubleshooter for the Northwestern Bell Telephone Company and as a social worker at the Unity Settlement House. 'Right after classes at three in the afternoon, I'd take a streetcar across town to Unity House,' he remembered. 'Then I'd work my tail off for eight straight hours coaching softball, basketball, football, swimming . . . I always fell asleep over my homework. Then it was up bright and early the next day to be in class by eight.'

An exhausted Fonda dropped out halfway through his second year. Soon after his return home, Henry and several buddies went out drinking and wound up at a local house of ill repute; Fonda recalled that his introduction to sex was so 'repulsive' that he swore off it for 'quite a while'.

Now that he was no longer headed for a college degree and a writer's life, Fonda turned his energies to finding a job – if for no other reason than to appease his increasingly impatient father. But what kind of job? It was then that Dorothy ('Do') Brando, a friend of Henry's mother and herself the mother of a newborn infant named Marlon, stepped into the picture. An actress and co-founder of Omaha's Community Playhouse, Do Brando told Henry that the company was mounting a production of Philip Barry's *You and I*, and that the director was looking for a juvenile actor.

Actually, the director, a cocky, Cagneyesque redhead named Gregory Foley, was desperate to find someone to play the part. The fact that Fonda had never before seen a script, had no idea what a reading was, and at first kept saying the name of his character as if it were part of the dialogue ('Ricky: But why not? Other people . . .') made no difference. He *looked* right for the role and, Foley reasoned, he would learn as he went along.

From that first terrifying moment when he stepped on stage on 10 September 1925, Fonda knew he was irretrievably hooked. For the next nine months, until May 1926, Henry immersed himself in the work of the Omaha Community Playhouse, building sets, painting scenery, and, of course, acting.

It was an exhilarating experience, but it did not pay the bills. Henry was still living at home, and his father worried about the boy's future. At Dad's urging, Henry searched through the job ads and took a respectable $30-a-week position as an accountant with the Retail Credit Company. But then Greg Foley called him at his office to offer him the title role in the Playhouse's season opener, *Merton of the Movies* by George S. Kaufman and Marc Connelly. Henry couldn't refuse.

When Henry broke the news to his family at the dinner table, Dad flew into a rage. This acting business had gone too far. It was time to grow up, to start living in the real world. But Henry was adamant. He insisted that he could keep his job at Retail Credit and still study for the lead in *Merton of the Movies*. In the end, father and son did not speak for six weeks.

The entire Fonda family, including Dad, turned out for Henry's debut in a lead role. Young Fonda received a standing ovation. That night, he returned home to the unstinting praise of his mother and sisters. William Fonda sat silently, reading the evening newspaper. The praise continued unabated, but after ten minutes or so, Harriet allowed that she had one 'teeny-tiny' suggestion. 'Shut up,' boomed Dad's voice from behind the newspaper. 'He was perfect!'

After two more years balancing his love for the theatre and his career with the Retail Credit Company, Henry headed with a friend for New York. There he feasted on all that Broadway had to offer, catching nine shows in a single week. It was on this trip, while staying with a friend in Princeton, New Jersey, that the painfully shy Nebraskan double-dated one of two sisters named Davis and worked up the nerve to give her a backseat kiss. The next day, he headed back home to Omaha. In time, Bette Davis, who would win an Academy Award opposite Fonda in *Jezebel*, never missed an opportunity to kid him about their whirlwind romance.

In April 1927, Fonda hooked up with George Billings, an actor who was making a name for himself touring the country as Abraham Lincoln. Fonda played the role of Lincoln's secretary for several months, but after Billings's chronic drinking led to an abrupt end of the tour, he was once again left to his own devices.

Henry heard that summer stock was flourishing on Cape Cod, so in June 1928 he hitched a ride to Provincetown. There he happened upon the University Players, a group of Ivy League undergraduates who were honing their skills on the Cape. One member of the group, an aspiring director named Joshua Logan, hardly knew what to make of this gangly, stooped Midwesterner dressed in white trousers, black socks, and a black sweater. He was not a student like the rest of them, but there was a sensitivity in what Logan recalled as 'that beautiful male face' and an endearing aw-shucks Midwestern earnestness that convinced Logan, James Stewart, and the other collegians that he belonged with them. After a bumpy start as an Italian Marquis (stick to painting scenery, someone advised), Fonda redeemed himself playing a cocky fighter in *Is Zat So?* The audience response was so warm, in fact, it persuaded him that he not only had the makings of an actor but was in fact leading-man material.

At the end of that first summer season, the rest of the University Players returned to campus life, leaving Fonda to have a go at the Broadway theatre alone. At a time when a quirky Katharine Hepburn was starting to attract notice in such plays as *Art and Mrs Bottle* and *Holiday*, Fonda was knocking on agents' doors, hanging around producers' offices, and religiously reading *Variety*. But a job in the theatre never materialised. So after a brief stint with the National Junior Theater in Washington, DC (where he got his first taste of Shakespeare playing in *Twelfth Night* with a seventeen-year-old Mildred Natwick), Henry returned the next summer to the Cape and the University Players.

It was during that summer of 1929 that Henry began his tumultuous affair with a headstrong Virginia girl named Margaret Sullavan. From their first moments together on stage when she slapped his character for getting fresh, Henry knew she would be a handful. 'When this girl slapped me,' he would recall, 'every time in rehearsal and every performance, it was a solid-rock slap – you would have thought I could only say, "Who is this bitch? Get her out of my sight." But it didn't work that way, see. She intrigued me.'

And many others, it seemed. With very little training but plenty of natural star appeal, Sullavan landed a job as an understudy in a touring production of *Strictly Dishonorable*. When the star fell ill, she stepped in and, as chance would have it, caught the eye of producer Lee Shubert. He was impressed enough to cast her in a Broadway comedy, *A Modern Virgin*, but despite Sullavan's dazzling performance, the play flopped.

Now that Logan, Stewart, and the others had graduated, the University

Players took up residence in Baltimore. There, Sullavan rejoined them – and a delighted Hank Fonda. Peggy and Hank shared the same birthday – 16 May – and a burning acting ambition, but they were woefully mismatched temperamentally. She was as fiery-spirited and flamboyant as he was reticent and shy; her offstage rages, often directed at poor Hank, became legendary.

Tipped off on Christmas Eve, 1931, that Fonda and Sullavan had taken out a marriage licence, a *Baltimore Post* reporter showed up at the hotel where the company was staying and demanded to know the truth. 'Him?' said a startled Peggy, pointing at Hank. '*Him??* You must be kidding. Who in his right mind would want to marry Henry Fonda?' Then she marched out of the room. It was a solid performance – convincing enough to send a bewildered Fonda scurrying after her.

The next day, they were married at noon in the dining room of Baltimore's Kernan Hotel. His wedding present to her was a used Stutz Bearcat, with lots of chrome and a bad battery. In March they moved into a small flat in Greenwich Village. Instantly, they were at each other's throats. She would explode into a rage over the slightest provocation, or with no provocation at all. He responded in kind. As he would recall, 'I never even knew I had a temper until I married Peggy.'

Three months later, Fonda moved out. He learned soon after that his wife was in the middle of a torrid affair with the theatrical producer Jed Harris. Considered to be the 'wizard' of Broadway, the lean, dark, anxious-looking Harris had an uncanny knack for making enemies. Laurence Olivier remembered Harris as 'the most loathsome man I'd ever met', and later based his characterisation of Richard III on the producer. Harris was also the model for Walt Disney's Big Bad Wolf. Sullavan, like many other leading actresses of the day, found the vaguely sinister Harris irresistible.

'I'd lean against the fence,' Fonda recalled in his autobiography, 'and I'd stare up at our apartment with the lighted windows on the second floor. I knew Jed Harris was inside . . . I couldn't believe my wife and that son-of-a-bitch were in bed together . . . Never in my life have I felt so betrayed, so rejected, so alone.'

In the autumn of 1932, Hank moved into a two-room apartment on West 64th Street with three fellow Cape Cod alumni – Logan, Myron McCormick (who would eventually become a major radio star), and James Stewart. Surrounded by these friends, Fonda could not hide the fact that he was devastated by the breakup with Sullavan – her betrayal made all the more painful by her sudden success. Continuing her early rise, Sullavan won over the critics in *Dinner at Eight*, and Universal signed her to a movie contract. On her 24th birthday, the estranged Mrs Fonda arrived in Hollywood to pursue screen stardom.

It would be some time before that invitation was tendered to her ex-husband,

15

who spent his birthday that year making ends meet by lugging huge pots in a flower shop on East 72nd Street. Even when he couldn't land a decent part, he managed to put his artistic talents to work designing sets and painting scenery for small theatre groups.

Fonda jumped at the chance to ham it up on Broadway opposite another eager unknown, Imogene Coca, for $35 a week in Leonard Sillman's *New Faces* revue. The critics were smitten with the all-American Fonda and Coca, the engaging clown, just as they were with each other. Their brief love affair ended with the show.

Fonda's performance in *New Faces* caught the eye of Katharine Hepburn's hot young agent, Leland Hayward. Within days after the closing of *New Faces*, Hayward had arranged a meeting for Fonda with film producer Walter Wanger in Hollywood. Wanger was riding high in the summer of 1934; his *Queen Christina* starring Greta Garbo was an enormous hit, and now he was searching for actors to put under personal contract. (Wanger would go on to make such films as *Stagecoach* and *The Long Journey Home*. Married to actress Joan Bennett, Wanger would become notorious in the 1950s for shooting his wife's lover, Jennings Lang, in the groin, a bit of retribution that landed him in the state penitentiary.)

'I was visiting Omaha,' Fonda recalled, 'when I got a two-page telegram from Hayward in Hollywood, telling me to come on out. I sent a one-word telegram saying no. But nobody can keep saying no to Leland for very long.' Fonda relented, and when he arrived in Los Angeles Hayward gave him the full star treatment. He met his new client at the airport, then took him to a suite in the Beverly Hills Hotel. 'Half an hour later, as I stepped out of a cold shower, there was Hayward with a man whose name I had heard often. Dripping wet, I shook hands with Walter Wanger, and that's how I signed for two pictures a year, a thousand dollars a week.'

For the time being, however, Wanger had no screen roles for Fonda, so he was free to return to New York and the title role in Marc Connelly's *The Farmer Takes a Wife*. It was during rehearsals for the play that Hank learned his mother had died from a fall. It was the first of many personal tragedies that he would cope with by burying himself in his work.

After seven hand-to-mouth years, Fonda was an 'overnight sensation' in *The Farmer Takes a Wife*. When the film version was made, Fonda was summoned to Hollywood to repeat his performance opposite Janet Gaynor. Before the film's release, Hank's father died suddenly. It would always trouble Fonda that neither of his parents lived to see his success.

Meantime, Margaret Sullavan had married director William Wyler. The remarriage of his ex-wife did not come as the emotional blow Fonda expected it to be. Besides, MGM had invited Jimmy Stewart to Hollywood, and Hank was pleased to have his old room-mate back again. This time, the venue was decidedly more elegant – a tile-roofed hacienda right next to the Brentwood estate of Greta Garbo. As bachelors-about-town, Fonda and Stewart cut quite a swath, escorting the up-and-coming likes of Lucille Ball and Ginger Rogers to such legendary establishments as the Brown Derby, the Coconut Grove, and the Trocadero.

Fonda's success as an actor was beginning to approach that of Sullavan. In the span of sixteen months, he made six movies – including *The Trail of the Lonesome Pine*, the industry's first Technicolor western and the film that firmly established him as a major box office draw.

Whether it was due to the long, hard struggle for recognition or the emotional upheaval wrought by his ill-fated first marriage, success seemed to change Henry Fonda. He could still turn on the Midwestern charm when it suited him, but now he was a man of strong opinions about how things should be done and a man not at all reluctant to express himself. Fonda quickly became known around the business as an implacable perfectionist. Analysing the nuances of every gesture, every line of dialogue, Universal's lanky leading man was employing the same nitpicking skills that had made him a valued employee of the Retail Credit Company. Perhaps because success had eluded him for so long, he was not about to let it slip away.

In April 1936, Fonda and Sullavan were thrown together again, this time snowbound in Lake Tahoe to film a comedy, *The Moon's Our Home*. Already divorced from Wyler, Sullavan was intrigued by her newly confident co-star. Fonda, now on more or less an equal footing with his ex-wife, felt he was up to the challenge. Stewart and Logan were not at all surprised that she would make a play for their roommate, nor that he would fall for her again. Her Southern charm, Logan later said, 'was intoxicating. She was extremely flirtatious in that Scarlett O'Hara way of hers.' What did astonish those who knew them was that they now seriously talked about retying the knot.

Their friends need not have worried. Before filming on *The Moon's Our Home* was completed, Sullavan erupted in a jealous rage when she saw Fonda dancing with another woman at a party. Any thought of remarriage was off.

This time, however, Fonda wasted no time in regret. He and Sullavan managed to remain civil on the set – both appeared to be resigned to the fact that their union wasn't meant to be – and as soon as filming was over Fonda set sail aboard the *Ile de France* for England. At Denham Studios outside London, he was set to star in Europe's first Technicolor feature, *Wings of the Morning*.

It was there, on the set at Denham Studios, that the lives of Jane Fonda's parents intersected. While Henry filmed a scene, a dozen American tourists

17

watched silently from the wings. One of them was the recently widowed American socialite, Frances Seymour Brokaw.

The Seymour family pedigree was exceptional even by social register standards. Making their way down from Canada in the early part of the eighteenth century, the Seymours intermarried with several other first families of New York. Through her paternal grandmother, Frances Gabrielle Ford of Morristown, New York, Frances Brokaw was related to the Stuyvesants, Fishes, Howlands, and Pells — not to mention the Biddles of Philadelphia.

Frances's great-great-uncle Horatio, then governor of New York, ran (and lost) as a Democrat against incumbent president Ulysses S. Grant in the election of 1872. That defeat did little to tarnish the clan's fortunes; by the turn of the century, the Seymours' Wall Street and real-estate investments made them as wealthy as they were socially correct — all the Seymours, that is, with the exception of Frances. Her father, Eugene Ford Seymour, an alcoholic with a violent temper, squandered much of his inheritance. While she certainly never knew anything approaching poverty, Canadian-born Frances was, by comparison with her Park Avenue cousins, a classic 'poor relation'.

This singular indignity was one that young Frances did not suffer lightly. While her peers went on to such upper-crust women's colleges as Radcliffe, Vassar, Sarah Lawrence, and Bryn Mawr, Frances attended the Katharine Gibbs Secretarial School for a year, then went straight to work as a secretary in the loan department of Morgan Guaranty Trust. From the outset, her intention was not to succeed in business but to marry someone who already had.

George T. Brokaw certainly qualified. An immensely wealthy Wall Street lawyer and self-styled 'sportsman' who had served a term in Congress, Brokaw was 52 and newly divorced from the celebrated playwright *(The Women)* Clare Booth. (Later, as the wife of Time Incorporated founder Henry Luce, Clare Booth Luce would become one of the most influential women of her time, serving both in Congress and as US Ambassador to Italy.) What Brokaw saw in Frances Seymour was obvious: Frances was only 22 — tall, slender, and elegant, with flowing auburn hair and intelligent brown eyes.

The fact that Brokaw was 30 years Frances's senior, older than her own father, mattered not at all to the young socialite turned secretary. She was drawn to Brokaw because he was rich and also because, as she later confided, she found older men sexually attractive. And, as she was the first to admit, he reminded her of her father. The resemblance was *too* close, it would turn out.

Frances was so determined to become Mrs Brokaw that, after several frustrating months of rather blatant hinting, she came right out and popped the question. Some five hundred people turned out for their wedding on 10 January 1931, and the couple took up residence in Brokaw's sprawling, 25-room French Regency town house on Fifth Avenue.

While the rest of the country struggled through the worst of the Depression,

18

the Brokaws appeared to lead the sort of charmed existence one saw only in the movies – penthouses and parties, flowing champagne and glittering evenings at the theatre.

Yet, out of the public eye, Frances paid a heavy price. When George Brokaw drank too much – as he often did – he turned abusive, even violent. She would learn too late that her predecessor, Clare Booth, had miscarried no fewer than four times before managing to carry a pregnancy to term – each miscarriage the direct result of a savage beating by Brokaw. (The only child of Clare Booth and George Brokaw, a daughter named Ann, was killed in a freak car accident at the age of nineteen. It seems no small irony that Jane Fonda, whose name would later become synonymous with radical politics, should share this tenuous step-family connection with the archconservative Republican Clare Booth Luce.)

Very soon, Frances was pregnant, and managed to keep out of harm's way long enough to give birth to a daughter, Frances de Villers Brokaw. The baby girl was nicknamed Panchita, a Spanish variation of Frances, and finally, 'Pan'.

By the spring of 1934, George's drinking had got so out of hand that he grudgingly agreed to be admitted to a sanatorium near Greenwich, Connecticut. Much like the lead character later portrayed by Ray Milland in *The Lost Weekend*, Brokaw cleverly concealed alcohol in various strategic spots on the clinic grounds – tucked under lampshades, in window boxes, even in hollowed-out tree trunks. Though he thus managed to thwart his keepers, Brokaw paid the ultimate price. On the morning of 10 May 1935, his bloated body was found floating facedown in the sanatorium pool.

The New York Times dutifully reported the news that Brokaw had died from an apparent heart attack. There was no mention of the real circumstances surrounding the millionaire's demise, or of his alcoholism.

For all she had suffered at her husband's hands during their four years of marriage, his death evidently came as a blow to Frances. The $1 million in cash she inherited may have helped soften it considerably; still, a full year of mourning would pass before she felt it was appropriate to embark on a European holiday. Four-year-old Pan was left in the care of her loving grandmother, Sophie Seymour.

On that afternoon of their first meeting at Denham Studios, both Hank and Frances had recently risen from the ashes of personal disaster. Although he was instantly struck by her beauty (Frances was considerably more attractive than Margaret Sullavan) and engaging personality, it was once again up to Frances to make the first move. She invited Hank to dinner at the Savoy Grill, and he accepted.

Their courtship moved quickly on to Paris and then to Berlin, where Frances had previously arranged to attend Hitler's Olympics. Quickly put off by the menacing atmosphere, the couple hired a car and drove to romantic Budapest before returning home.

New York bluebloods may have frowned on one of their own marrying a Hollywood actor, but they nevertheless turned out at Park Avenue's Christ Church on the afternoon of 16 September 1936, to see Frances Seymour Brokaw and Henry Jaynes Fonda wed by the Reverend Ralph W. Sockman.

The event might just as well have been the film-studio version of a high-society wedding. Decked out in top hat and tails, Henry was, by his own admission, 'straight from central casting'. The urbane Leland Hayward, who always seemed utterly at home at these affairs, was Henry's usher. Best man Josh Logan bore the brunt of the responsibility for keeping Fonda from bolting at the last minute.

The bride was escorted by her brother, Ford de Villers Seymour, and her only attendant was her sister, Miss Marjory Capell Seymour. Five-year-old Pan was flower girl. Frances, wearing a sky-blue taffeta gown and matching hat, carried a bridal bouquet of pink roses and delphiniums.

A crowd had gathered outside the church on the corner of Park Avenue and 60th Street, waving as limousines drove the wedding couple and their party three blocks to the reception at the roof garden of the Pierre Hotel.

The story in the next morning's *New York Times* reflected Fonda's general place in the social scheme of things. Beneath a sizeable headline, 'MRS F. S. BROKAW BECOMES A BRIDE', was the modest subhead, 'She Is Married in Christ Church Here to Henry Fonda of Motion Pictures'.

That Thursday, the Fondas hopped on to the first plane bound for California. At dawn the following day, Henry slipped out of their honeymoon bed in the Beverly Hills Hotel and headed for the studio to begin shooting *You Only Live Once* with Sylvia Sidney.

While looking for suitable land to build on in the Hollywood hills, the newlyweds took up temporary residence at a house in Pacific Palisades. Meanwhile, Frances adjusted as best she could to life among the wide-hipped, vacant-eyed starlets, cigar-chomping moguls, and fast-talking agents of Lotusland. She never really missed life in the East; she just brought it along with her. Eschewing the California casual look, she stuck to tailored clothes, white gloves, and hats. She was not interested in stars or movies but rather in the political and economic issues of the day. Hank read the trades and the columns; Frances's taste ran to *The Wall Street Journal*. Her role, she decided, would not be to throw parties for her husband's cronies; she would use her background in finance to manage her husband's investments. In short, she was to be anything but the typical Hollywood wife.

Within weeks of moving into their temporary Pacific Palisades house, the Fondas welcomed as their new neighbours Leland Hayward and his new wife, Margaret Sullavan. From this point on, the lives of the Fondas and the

Haywards – Henry's agent-friend and his former wife – would be linked in a way that seemed almost predestined. 'The Fondas went back forever in time as we knew it,' recalled the Haywards' eldest child. 'Our families were united in the most abstract but intricately woven pattern.'

One spring evening in 1937, Frances announced over dinner that Pan would soon have a sibling. Predictably, Henry was both thrilled and terrified at the prospect of becoming a father for the first time. Yet his wife's pregnancy would not keep him from returning to New York, first to star in a Westchester Theater production of *The Virginian*, then in a Broadway turkey, *Blow Ye Winds*.

When he returned home to California, Henry was asked to play opposite his former blind date Bette Davis in *Jezebel*. The Civil War costume drama, in which Davis played a Scarlett O'Hara-type heroine, was studio mogul Jack Warner's attempt to pre-empt David O. Selznick's long-delayed and much-ballyhooed screen version of *Gone with the Wind*. With Bette, who had already won an Academy Award for *Dangerous*, in the central role, *Jezebel* was almost certain to be a success. Henry wanted the part, but there was a major complication. Pan had been delivered by Caesarean section, and since their child would be too, Frances wanted it delivered by her trusted New York obstetrician. She also wanted her husband to be there. Henry's contract stipulated that, should his wife go into labour, he would be allowed to drop everything and join her in New York.

Frances, now seven months pregnant, journeyed to New York that October and busied herself disposing of the furniture from the town house she had shared with George Brokaw. Her outstanding collection of eighteenth-century French antiques included a Louis XV inlaid kingwood *bombé* commode with marble top signed by the master cabinet-maker Ellaume, a Louis XVI carved, lacquered, and gilded trumeau mirror, a pair of Louis XVI chairs with fan-shaped backs, and another pair upholstered in Aubusson tapestry. In Thanksgiving week, dealers and collectors jammed the Anderson Galleries auction house to bid for the furniture, and Frances – though she hardly needed the extra income – walked away $20,000 richer.

Frances's determination to put her affairs in order before the birth of Henry's child was accompanied by a mounting obsession with the sex of the child. She already had a daughter, and now she wanted a son. Another girl, she told Henry, would only serve to complicate matters and would blur Pan's role in the family. Besides, Frances planned to use her business acumen to build Henry's fortune, and she felt it was time they produced a male heir. Henry professed no preference as to gender. Neither did he object when Frances became more and more forceful in asserting hers.

Midway through one day's shooting on *Jezebel*, Henry got the long-awaited call. Frances had checked herself into Doctors' Hospital. Henry wasted no time invoking the special clause in his contract and boarding the first available flight for New York.

On Sunday, 21 December 1937, Henry paced in the waiting room with the other expectant fathers while his first child was delivered by Caesarean section. They named her Jane – Jane Seymour Fonda.

Frances did not attempt to conceal her disappointment. Jane would later say that she never felt a strong emotional bond with her mother – a lack of intimacy that clearly had its roots in Frances's desire for a boy. Before long, that wish was granted, but in the meantime, during Jane's first two formative years, she was denied the requisite measure of unconditional maternal love. This would be a major factor in her own early emotional development. Frozen out by her mother from infancy, Jane would turn increasingly to her father for love and approval. Neither would be easily – if indeed ever – won.

The Fondas remained in New York while Frances recuperated from Jane's birth, seeing in 1938 from her hospital bed. But in the first week of January, Henry, Frances, and 'Lady Jane', as the newest Fonda quickly came to be called, were back house-hunting in California. They settled on a two-storey, ten-room dwelling at 255 Chadbourne Street, surrounded by acacias and towering pines. Again the Haywards followed, moving with their newborn daughter, Brooke, into a white colonial just around the corner on Evanston Street. A block in the opposite direction was the house shared by Jimmy Stewart and another old University Player, John Swope. Jane would come to rely on them, along with Josh Logan, as her unofficial godfathers.

As it turned out, Lady Jane (or, more often, just 'Lady') would need all the affection she could get from outside the home. Frances, determined to raise her children according to the rules of the Eastern elite, hired a governess in a starched white uniform to care for Lady.

If either Mother or Father wanted to look in on their baby, they first had to make certain that it was acceptable to the governess. Most of the time, Frances insisted that anyone coming in contact with Lady wear a surgical mask. Holding the baby was discouraged, kissing strictly forbidden. Such coddling, declared the governess, would serve only to make the child emotionally dependent. Frances was in complete agreement. Jane Fonda spent the first year of her life in this sterile, hospital-like atmosphere of sensory and emotional deprivation.

Decades later, Henry would look back on his acquiescence to the governess's rules with tearful regret. At the time, however, it suited him perfectly. He was building a career and did not need the distraction of fatherhood.

Jezebel earned Bette Davis her second Oscar, and further fuelled the demand for Henry's talents. Before Jane turned two, her father had acted in ten more pictures, including *Young Mr Lincoln*, *Jesse James* and *The Story of Alexander Graham Bell*. Then, in 1939, along came *The Grapes of Wrath*. Fonda recognised

22

the saga of a poor farm family making its way from the Dust Bowl to a new life in California as the masterpiece it was. He would have sold his soul for the part of Tom Joad, and in a sense he did. Twentieth Century-Fox's dictatorial chief Darryl Zanuck agreed to give Fonda the role only if he would sign a seven-year contract with Fox. Fonda did, grudgingly, and under the direction of John Ford turned in what is widely regarded to be his greatest performance. Yet the Academy Award that year went to Fonda's buddy James Stewart for *The Philadelphia Story*. (Stewart, a member of the Academy, actually voted for Fonda. 'Of course, I also voted for Alfred Landon, Wendell Willkie, and Thomas E. Dewey,' Stewart cracked.) No matter. With *The Grapes of Wrath*, Fonda took his place in the first rank of screen actors.

There was another reason to celebrate. Once again, the Fondas journeyed to New York – this time for the birth of their second child. It would also, Frances's obstetrician informed her, probably be the last she would be able to have. On the morning of 23 February 1940, Frances went into labour. Three hours later, she delivered – again by Caesarean section – a son, Peter Henry Fonda. Had it not been a boy this time, Frances told her mother, she would have insisted they go ahead and adopt one.

While Frances had never got around to christening Jane, now that Peter had arrived it seemed the right thing to do. Henry, who had long since given up his Christian Science beliefs, consented to having both children christened when Peter turned four months old. Their godfather, Frances's friend J. Watson Webb, Jr, duly recorded the event on film. Although Jane would later maintain that her mother favoured Peter, it was of little consequence. Like his sister, Peter spent his infancy starved of affection.

Henry, meanwhile, seethed over the mediocre movies he was being forced to make under his contract with Zanuck, who loaned Fonda out to other studios whenever he didn't have the actor grinding out pictures for Fox. Among these were such eminently forgettable films as *Lillian Russell* (in which he was one of no fewer than ten actors courting Alice Faye), *That Certain Woman, Spawn of the North, Slim* and *The Magnificent Dope*. Notable exceptions were the well-received Revolutionary War epic *Drums Along the Mohawk, The Male Animal, The Lady Eve* (with his favourite leading lady, Barbara Stanwyck) and *The Ox-Bow Incident*. There was no one at home to commiserate with him, no one to help diffuse his smouldering rage and frustration; the very attributes that had made Frances such a standout among the other wives – her aristocratic bearing, her seeming indifference to show business – now prevented him from confiding in her. As Joshua Logan recalled, 'Frances was not really interested in acting, so she was always embarrassed to talk about it. She'd talk of children, operations, jewellery, the stock market. I often wondered what she and Henry talked about, because these were the only subjects Henry couldn't talk about.'

One thing they could talk about was their long-standing plan to build the house of their dreams on a hilltop parcel of land high above Los Angeles at 600 Tigertail Road. After years of prodding, the land development company that owned the property was at last willing to sell the Fondas nine acres for $27,000.

They cleared the land of the manzanita scrub that had made it all but impenetrable and set to work. With Frances commanding an army of contractors, the Pennsylvania Dutch farmhouse they had always wanted – a Currier & Ives confection of fieldstone and wood shingles – went up in record time. Tigertail had a winding gravel drive, clay tennis courts, a free-form pool designed to resemble one of the swimming holes from Hank's Nebraska youth, and a 'playhouse' with a walk-in hearth. But hardly a children's playhouse. One was just as likely to find Hank, John Wayne, John Ford, and Jimmy Stewart playing cards there in a cloud of cigar smoke.

Tigertail also boasted orange groves, flower beds, a vegetable garden – 'I was gardening organically thirty years before it became fashionable,' Fonda would claim – chicken coops, and a barn for the horses. 'We were in the middle of nowhere. You could hear the coyotes howling at night, but what we really worried about was skunks.' On more than one occasion, he was nailed by one of these animals and had to be subjected to the time-honoured cure – a nice long bath in tomato juice.

Once inside the main house, it was obvious that Frances had left her taste for French antiques back in Manhattan. Now there were exposed beams in the panelled living room, random-width plank flooring, overstuffed sofas, wing chairs, rockers, and large ceramic pitchers overflowing with roses from the garden. The brightly furnished ground-floor master bedroom had its own corner fireplace and was safely out of earshot from the children's rooms upstairs. Lady's room was every little girl's fantasy: her canopied bed was strewn with embroidered pillows, and there was a cosy window seat from which she could gaze out over the rough mountain terrain.

With Hank revelling in the life of a gentleman farmer, Lady's early memories are of her father hoeing and watering the garden, baling hay, and sweating behind the wheel of his tractor on the tract of land they called the North Forty. When the mood struck him, Hank even hitched up his two mules Pancho and Pedro to plough the fields the way they did in the movies.

It was one of her own such rustic episodes that introduced Lady Jane to the subject of sex. 'Pancho was actually a girl,' remembered Jane, 'and I was riding her bareback and leading Pedro because you couldn't separate them. We were going across one of these hills and Pedro mounted Pancho – with me on her. It was one of the most frightening things!'

As far as her image of her father was concerned, Lady Jane just assumed he was a farmer – until she asked her mother why he was always growing beards and shaving them off. One of the first times she saw Hank on the screen, in *Drums Along the Mohawk*, she cried as tomahawk-waving Indians stalked Daddy.

While Hank sweated on soundstages and out in the fields those first few months at Tigertail, Frances was consolidating her control over the household. She turned a bedroom into her office, hired a secretary, and personally supervised a staff that included the governess, two maids, a gardener, a cook, a laundress, and a chauffeur.

Yet she was showing signs of strain. While the Brokaw inheritance continued to grow – making the Fondas wealthy even by Hollywood standards – the real-estate and stock investments Frances had made using her husband's money did not. To finance the building of Tigertail, she had sold off some of Hank's holdings at a considerable loss. As the self-appointed holder of the family purse strings, Frances was devastated by her seeming inability to manage Hank's finances. Remorse turned to obsession, as Frances kept track of every penny that went in and out of the family household. Although her office was adjacent to the master bedroom, Frances began keeping her ledgers and balance sheets on the bedside table. When Henry returned at 2 a.m. from the studio, Frances would be sitting up, poring over the figures, oblivious of his arrival.

Money was not Frances's only obsession. Since Peter's birth, she had suffered from a variety of physical ailments – from loss of appetite and weight loss to headaches and fever. Frances spent three weeks at the Scripps Clinic near La Jolla, but the doctors doubted whether there was anything medically wrong with her. She skipped from one doctor to another and from one medication to another. Henry, meanwhile, lost himself in his gardening and his work.

Pearl Harbor offered an avenue of escape for Hank Fonda. After finishing *The Ox-Bow Incident* and a piece of wartime propaganda called *The Immortal Sergeant*, Navy Apprentice Seaman Fonda boarded a bus for San Diego and basic training before shipping out on the destroyer *Satterlee*.

With Henry away, Frances was in complete command of life at Tigertail. She went over the correspondence, paid the bills, managed the stock portfolio, dictated each day's menu, and subjected both the staff and family to a white-glove inspection: no dust on the mantel, no jacket carelessly tossed over the back of a chair, no dining room chair the least bit out of alignment.

Frances soon added to her growing list of neuroses a morbid fear of growing old. Only in her mid-thirties, she nonetheless dreaded the prospect of looking older than her eternally youthful husband. To stave off the effects of ageing, she wore chin straps and triangles of adhesive tape at the corners of her eyes.

Feeling increasingly lonely, isolated, and insecure, Frances decided to get more involved in the war effort. She worked at the Hollywood Canteen, helped sell war bonds, and visited hospitals. Eventually (according to Henry in his later years), she sought solace and reassurance in the arms of other men.

Lady, despite few memories of affection from her father – she'd been invited to sit on Hank's lap for publicity purposes (though was hardly ever kissed by him) – missed Dad. But not enough to interfere with her performance at exclusive Brentwood Town and Country Day School. Miss Fonda's teachers reported that Lady (the name tag sewn inside her school uniforms read 'Lady Fonda') was a studious, well-adjusted, courteous first-grader. But back home at Tigertail, Lady acted, for the most part, like anything but. Perhaps because of her mother's ill-disguised preference for Peter, Jane would later admit, 'I always had a deep-rooted psychological need to be a boy.' Dressed in her snappiest Hopalong Cassidy getup, Lady instructed her little brother in the art of building forts and defending them against the onslaught of imaginary Indians.

Reinforcements came in the form of a car full of Haywards: Brooke, who was precisely Jane's age; her sister, Bridget, one year older than Peter; and the youngest, little Bill Hayward. A natural alliance formed between the boys and the girls. As Brooke Hayward would later concede, she and Lady saw themselves as the ringleaders for various nefarious activities. On one occasion, Jane rounded up her cohorts in crime and, with the precision of an artillery captain, ordered them to pelt passing cars with rocks and gravel. When one of the rocks finally found its mark, the car's infuriated driver, Brooke recalled, 'got out and chased us across the field, but we were too nimble for him – all except Peter, who was nabbed in a clump of beeches. Whereupon Jane and I, overflowing with adrenaline and bravado, wheeled around and went back for him, screaming at the man to let go of him that minute.' At that point, Frances emerged from the house to placate the offended motorist. The Hayward brats were sent home, and their fellow felons were packed off to bed.

Flamboyant children's birthday parties were a Hollywood tradition, and for these Jane (as she now insisted on being called) wore petticoats and lace. The guest list always included the three Hayward children, and more often than not Joan Crawford's daughter Christina, Gary Cooper's daughter Maria, Laurence Olivier's son Tarquin, and the Mankiewicz, Schary, and Selznick children. These round-robin occasions had mostly to do with competition between the parents over who could throw the most lavish affair. Shunning ostentation, Frances kept things simple – a clown and some party treats, birthday cake, and maybe a pony ride around the grounds. One of the other mothers, on the other hand, went so far as to employ a small circus – complete with elephants and a small ferris wheel – for the tots' amusement.

Pan was away at summer camp when Hank Fonda returned home in 1945 with lieutenant's bars and a bronze star, but the rest of the family was there to greet him with news of all that had transpired in their lives over the last three years. So much had changed – and so little. Peter barely recognised his father; on their first meeting the boy confused Hank with one of the characters he had played, Chad Hannah. Jane was now an accomplished horsewoman with a roomful of blue ribbons to prove it.

Frances looked 'more beautiful than I remembered', Hank recalled; but the chasm between them had grown even wider. 'She made it crystal clear,' says a friend, 'that she still ran things as far as the house was concerned. The rules she had laid down were more rigid than any Hank had encountered in the military.' She was now working in bed on a more or less full-time basis, withdrawing to her columns of figures, placing phone calls to brokers and accountants. To the outside world, she remained Henry Fonda's beautiful and charming wife. To her husband, she was indifferent. Their sex life ground to a halt.

Baffled by his wife's attitude, Hank responded by doing what he always did in times of personal crisis: he buried himself in his work. This time it was a labour of love – the role of Wyatt Earp in John Ford's classic western *My Darling Clementine*.

In avoiding his wife, Hank also all but ignored his children. Peter made his first obvious play for attention when he introduced Jane and the Hayward kids to smoking with cigarette butts he had methodically collected from unemptied ashtrays. Frances literally got wind of their little experiment and, after once again dispatching the Haywards, took out two packets of cigarettes and handed them to her children. Jane and Peter were told to go right ahead and light up – and to keep smoking until they turned green and threw up, which they both did.

Not long after, Peter was playing with matches again, setting fire to Dad's precious North Forty just to see what would happen. When the flames started to spread through the dry grass, Jane joined him and together they grabbed two tennis-ball cans, ran to the pool, and tried to douse the blaze with water. The fire department was summoned, one of the firefighters was bitten by a rattlesnake, and Hank came home from the studio to find half his property blackened. Peter was so shaken by the terrifying experience that his father didn't have the heart to punish him.

That was, to be sure, an uncharacteristically charitable reaction. Already famous for his explosive temper on the job ('Hank could be a real bastard at times,' Joshua Logan told me), Fonda quickly became the terror of Tigertail Road. 'We were all afraid of Jane's father in those days,' one of Jane's Brentwood School classmates recalls. 'We always felt he was a time bomb ready to explode. But it was years before we actually saw him lose his temper over some forgotten trivia. It was the only time I was ever privileged to see what may have been a constant for Lady Jane.'

'He was trouble,' says Brooke Hayward. 'We were all scared of him.' When the family's pet dalmatian killed one of Hank's chickens, he chained the chicken to the dog's collar. 'The carcass was dragged around for weeks until it just disintegrated. Hank terrified everyone.'

27

'My father was not a demonstrative person,' Jane told her father's biographer, Howard Teichmann. 'In those days his major emotion was rage . . . His rages,' she continued, 'were terrifying.'

Peter, in particular, gave his father plenty of reason to erupt. In addition to setting the North Forty on fire, the little boy bit one of the Haywards' nannies on the leg hard enough to draw blood, lost his Dad's bronze star, and flushed a pet goldfish down the toilet. No matter how great his father's anger, however, none of these incidents provoked a spanking.

Frances's overprotectiveness towards her only son was part of the problem; she was convinced that Peter, like her, was delicate, even sickly – so much so that when Hank went on location to film *Fort Apache*, she spirited the boy away to John Hopkins Hospital to be examined by a team of world-class diagnosticians. They concluded that he was perfectly healthy. While at John Hopkins, Frances also took her doctors' advice and underwent a hysterectomy. When Henry returned home from his location shoot, he found Frances back at home where he had left her, going over her business ledgers in bed.

Much of Peter's mischievousness, his mother's smothering attentions aside, stemmed from his father's indifference. 'Peter's childhood was one loud cry for attention,' says a friend, 'but Hank always seemed to be somewhere else – even when he was right in the room. He didn't know how to show love towards his family, or maybe he just didn't want to.'

Jane, meanwhile, was forced to deal with the indifference of both parents. 'I didn't like her to touch me,' she says of her mother, 'because I knew she really didn't love me.' She did believe her father loved her, though in truth he was no more capable of expressing affection than Frances.

By now Jane had begun to fantasise that her father was married to someone else. 'I used to look at Katharine Hepburn up on the screen and think, Wow,' she says. 'I had no idea at all back then of becoming an actress, but I did want Katharine Hepburn in my life. I used to imagine that she and Dad would fall in love and she would be my mother.'

On the surface, Jane seemed to handle this sorry state of family affairs well. To all outward appearances, she was the most well-adjusted Fonda. 'We were all sort of in awe of Jane,' observed Brooke Hayward. 'Nothing seemed to throw her. She was very athletic, very self-reliant, very tough. Like tempered steel.' At the age of ten, she had learned that she could depend on only one person – herself.

3

'AS A young girl,' Jane Fonda once reflected, 'most of my dreams evolved from the basic need of being loved, and being frustrated in fulfilling that need. I would often dream of myself in a large banquet hall faced with mountains of food but unable to reach it. I also dreamed of pursuing beautiful objects which seemed to elude my grasp.' As her childhood dreams suggest, Jane had always wanted nothing so badly as her father's love and approval. Daddy, however, was far too preoccupied to notice . . .

Fed up with movies in general and Darryl Zanuck in particular, Henry Fonda completed the last picture he owed Fox in February 1947. He immediately began to cast about for a project that would take him back to his first love – the theatre. Fonda did not have to look far. His old friend Joshua Logan and writer Thomas Heggen had just collaborated on a stage adaptation of Heggen's novel about Navy life in the South Pacific during World War II. To make it really a family affair, the play's producer would be Leland Hayward.

Fonda jumped at the opportunity. He could memorise lines after a single reading, and by the time he packed to leave Tigertail for rehearsals in New York, he had already mastered the dialogue. Peter, not exactly thrilled at the prospect of Father abandoning the family yet again, made a half-hearted attempt to run away from home. Jane internalised her feelings of confusion and abandonment. She adored her father, but she was also intimidated by him. She concentrated on her riding and pretended not to notice.

When it opened at Broadway's Alvin Theater in February 1948, *Mr Roberts* was more than just a critically acclaimed hit. In the title character of the quietly heroic naval officer Doug Roberts, Hank Fonda had discovered not only the proverbial role of a lifetime but also his fictional alter ego. Standing up for his men in defiance of a tyrannical captain, Mr Roberts represented a sort of all-American, good-humoured hero-despite-himself; a man essentially passive yet drawing others to him for the inner strength he embodied. Henry dug in for a very long run.

Hank had no difficulty convincing Frances that a new life waited for them in the East. Like a general called out of retirement, she relished the challenge of organising the family's relocation – settling accounts with characteristic military precision, determining what would be shipped east and what would be stored, arranging to sell the house. As soon as the school year ended that June, Frances and the children boarded a plane for La Guardia Airport.

Though they had both been born in New York City, Peter and Jane regarded themselves as diehard Californians. With its sweeping views of the Pacific and its canyon-rim ruggedness, Tigertail had been a magical place for the Fonda children. Peter, nine, felt he was being 'booted out of paradise' and made no secret of his anger. Eleven-year-old Jane, informed that their new home in Greenwich, Connecticut, would be just a few blocks from a stable, began to view the whole experience as an adventure.

To be sure, the rented estate into which they moved had much to offer a child. There were ponds full of frogs; lush, sprawling fields of emerald grass; plenty of heavy-limbed elms, maples, and hemlocks for climbing; and stone walls perfect for crouching behind and ambushing an enemy. The main house had its own lift and a walk-in safe, where Peter could pretend he was the world's richest man – a fantasy that undoubtedly had rubbed off from his money-obsessed mother. Still, these diversions did not deter Peter from scrawling 'I HATE THE EAST' on every wall in their new house.

For well-heeled WASPs like Frances, Greenwich was another kind of paradise. A half-hour train ride from Manhattan, this was not just a suburb but the prototype for all suburbs. At its heart, Greenwich retained much of its Connecticut picture-postcard quaintness. Steepled churches abounded, of course, and along Greenwich Avenue there were the New England small-town requisites – ice-cream parlour, hardware store, dress shop, bakery, barber, the post office. But just a few blocks from its epicentre one began to encounter the real Greenwich – one baronial mansion after another in every conceivable architectural style from Tudor to Southern plantation house, each separated by a broad carpet of carefully tended lawn.

The social fabric of the town was made up of a network of private clubs – the Round Hill Club and the Greenwich Country Club foremost among them. All were, in the genteel parlance of the time, 'restricted'. As, for that matter, was all of Greenwich property. For Jane, who had absolutely no idea what the word 'Jew' meant, even though many of her childhood playmates back in Brentwood had been Jewish, Greenwich marked her introduction to virulent anti-Semitism. Within a few weeks, she was aping the bigoted remarks of her new playmates. Jane's stunned father promptly set her straight. Prejudice of any sort, he said sternly, was not to be tolerated in the Fonda household.

For Jane, that first summer in Greenwich was memorable for being miserable. At the age of eleven she was going through something of a chubby stage.

30

Predictably, her model-sleek mother was showing her usual lack of compassion, taking every opportunity to criticise Jane's weight gain. Jane began biting her nails. She then contracted an ear infection from the country club pool, got blood poisoning when a cut became infected, and, finally, fractured her arm while scrapping with a boy. To make matters worse, Sophie Seymour was insisting that her granddaughter swap her scruffy jeans for attire more suitable for a proper young lady. Jane had no choice but to comply.

Hank took little notice. Instead, he channelled all his prodigious energies into his stage role while fuming over Frances's continuing indifference. She still skipped meals with the family to work alone in her bedroom, and looked up from her ledgers only long enough to admonish the children for their minor infractions. The household keys were neatly arranged on rows of coloured hooks in the kitchen, each key corresponding to a particular colour. She became increasingly agitated whenever the keys were not placed on their proper hooks.

Although he want through the motions of fatherhood – taking the kids to the circus, ferrying them to and from the stable for their weekly riding lessons, even fishing with them – Hank's brooding silences spoke volumes. Jane was terrified to speak up for fear of igniting one of his purple-veined tantrums. What preoccupied Hank, of course, was his disintegrating marriage. 'He resented his wife's domestic tyranny,' says Brooke Hayward. 'He was sensing a loss of control.' He was also looking for a way out.

Frances, meanwhile, stayed locked in her room – terrified that she was growing old and obese, certain that her mismanagement of the family's investments would bring financial ruin, and convinced that the servants were spying on her. A psychiatrist might suggest today that, in addition to hypochondria and paranoia, Frances suffered from agoraphobia.

Her husband countered by withdrawing into a world of his own. When he wasn't on stage, Fonda was painting in a realistic style strongly reminiscent of Andrew Wyeth. He even tried his hand at sculpture, completing a lifelike bust of Peter. Almost immediately (and prophetically), it cracked.

Without consulting Hank, Frances again checked into a clinic, this time the Austen Riggs Foundation in Stockbridge, Massachusetts. She left Sophie in charge of getting the kids properly launched in their new schools.

If blacks and Jews were nowhere to be seen in and around Greenwich, 'show people', as the local dowagers still disdainfully referred to movie stars and Broadway actors, were just as scarce. The Fondas were the first to be readily accepted, certainly to some extent because of Frances's own impeccable social credentials. With her pick of Greenwich's best schools, Frances chose the Greenwich Academy for Jane and Brunswick for Peter.

The presence of a movie star's daughter in their midst created quite a stir among the students at Greenwich Academy. 'Our fathers were all lawyers and investment bankers,' says one. 'One of our classmates was the daughter of a congressman, and that's about as interesting as it got. But suddenly here was *Henry Fonda's* daughter. Everybody wanted to be her friend.'

Jane, who had been just another celebrity's child at Brentwood Town and Country Day in California, quickly discovered she enjoyed being the centre of attention. But she would not have the spotlight all to herself for long; after only a few weeks at school, Brooke Hayward arrived. Margaret Sullavan had decided that her own brood needed civilising. To her mind, that meant leaving California, and, since Brooke's father, Leland Hayward, was in New York producing *Mr Roberts*, it only made sense that they follow the Fondas to Connecticut.

With Frances away at Austen Riggs, Jane and Brooke wasted no time noting that Margaret's face lit up whenever Hank came by to pick up the kids or drop them off. He still called her Peggy, and they still performed endless headstands for the kid's amusement. 'We children would eye each other reflectively,' said Brooke; 'they were still madly in love!'

One could hardly blame the children for such flights of fancy. What else but fate could explain this strange series of coincidences that had brought them together in towns a continent apart? It would not be evident until years later that both families were headed on parallel tracks towards tragedy.

The movie stars' daughters soon distinguished themselves as troublemakers. 'We were not allowed to read comics, listen to the radio, or watch TV,' Brooke Hayward said of the stern upbringing she shared with Jane. 'We had to invent what we did, and it was wild.' As for Jane, 'She was a tomboy, great at athletics, very *alive*.'

Looking deceptively prim in their olive-green schoolgirl uniforms, Jane and Brooke routinely marched into the principal's office to be scolded for throwing paperclips. Jane was singled out for storytelling abilities. 'There was this shed on the school grounds,' said Brooke Hayward, 'where we all used to go to listen to Jane tell her dirty travelling-salesmen stories.' Not that her audience understood them. 'We were eleven years old,' says a sixth-grade classmate, 'so of course we didn't really understand the jokes. She seemed awfully advanced to us, but I'm not at all sure she understood the stories, either. But it didn't matter. We all loved it. We laughed our heads off.' Behind her back, they also sniggered at rumours that her father was having an affair.

When she returned from yet another visit to the Riggs Sanitarium in the spring of 1949, Frances set out to plan a June wedding for Pan and her art teacher, Kress dime-store heir Bun Abry. Hank donned white tie and tails to give the bride away, and everyone agreed that Jane, an adorable flower girl in her lacy pink dress and wide-brimmed straw bonnet, already bore a striking similarity to her dad. To all outside appearances, the Fonda clan showed not the slightest sign of trouble.

Two months later, Henry asked his wife for a divorce. He had met and fallen in love with Susan Blanchard, the 21-year-old stepdaughter of composer Oscar Hammerstein. Without a trace of anger or sarcasm, Frances, who – whether consciously or unconsciously – had been pushing her husband away for years, wished him luck. The next morning, as Jane headed out of the door for school, Frances stopped her and matter-of-factly informed the eleven-year-old that her parents were getting a divorce. No explanation or elaboration. Jane spent the rest of the day in a daze.

Dad moved out of the house and into a one-bedroom flat in a town house on East 67th Street. He would visit the children at weekends, but these sojourns were fraught with even more tension than before. For Jane, the silences were deafening.

Sophie Seymour, accustomed as she was to filling the void left by her emotionally unstable daughter, moved in to help out with the children and the running of the house. Grandma Sophie, then 64, had always provided Jane and Peter with the parental warmth both Hank and Frances seemed constitutionally incapable of giving. Now the kids would rely on her almost exclusively to preserve whatever sense of family harmony remained.

At first it appeared to Sophie as if her daughter were taking the dissolution of the twelve-year union with Fonda well. But within a matter of weeks, Frances was sobbing quietly at the dinner table while the rest of the family behaved as if nothing out of the ordinary was happening. In a house full of alienated souls, Jane learned, 'polite suffering' was the order of the day.

When she was not crying or fretting about some meaningless detail such as the way the towels were folded in the guest bathroom, Frances now concentrated on ways to repay Hank for his infidelity. In October, she summoned her lawyers and secretly ordered them to redraft her will. She cut Hank out completely, dividing what would have been his share of her sizeable personal fortune among the children. She did not, it turned out, have the fortitude to fly to Reno and take the final step of filing for a Nevada divorce.

A breakdown sent Frances back to Riggs shortly before Thanksgiving. There were occasional signs of improvement, but for the most part her mental state continued on its downward spiral into the spring of 1950. That February, for the first time, she began to talk of taking her own life. Frances's doctors were concerned enough to call Henry and suggest she be transferred to a sanatorium better equipped to handle potentially violent mental patients. Specifically, they recommended she be sent to Craig House.

Sitting on three hundred acres overlooking the Hudson River in upstate Beacon, New York, Craig House was a sanctuary for mental patients with means. Founded by vanguard psychiatrist Clarence Slocum in 1915, by 1950 it included riding stables, swimming pools, even a golf course. There were several Victorian cottages scattered about the grounds, and in one of these

Frances took her first tentative steps towards recovery – or at least so her psychiatrists fervently hoped.

Frances did show encouraging signs of improvement during her first few weeks but then sank back into depression. She sat rocking back and forth, staring straight ahead, expressionless. On those rare occasions when Frances was well enough to pay a short visit to the family in Greenwich, Jane was not impressed. The little girl had always doubted her mother's love, and now, perhaps not understanding the seriousness of her mother's condition, she viewed Frances's more or less permanent absence as abandonment.

It had been three weeks since she had seen Jane and Peter when, on the second Saturday in April, Frances was driven down from Beacon. Jane heard the crunch of the gravel as her mother's car pulled into the driveway, and watched as her mother got out with two white-uniformed nurses. 'I didn't want to speak,' Jane recalls. 'I was frightened and angry.'

Peter was with his sister, and when he heard his mother call for her children, he started for the door. Jane held him back. For the next hour, Frances called for her children, but they would not move. 'Finally one of the nurses told my mother it was time to go back. "Oh, no," my mother said. "Not yet, I must talk to her." And she cried out my name again.' Jane then watched from her bedroom window as the car carrying her mother pulled out of their courtyard and disappeared into the night.

Several days later, shortly before dawn on 14 April, nurse Amy Gray brought a breakfast tray to Frances's room at Craig House as she did every morning. The bed had already been perfectly made, and there was light shining from beneath the closed bathroom door. Out of the corner of her eye, Nurse Gray spotted a note on the floor. 'Mrs Gray,' it read, 'don't enter the bathroom, but call Dr Bennett.'

She hurried to fetch the doctor, and when she returned with him she looked the other way as he slowly opened the door. What Dr Bennett saw was Frances lying face down in a pool of blood. She had slashed her throat from ear to ear. There was a glint from the tiny razor blade that lay on the floor near her right hand. She had managed to smuggle it out of the house in Greenwich during a visit home. There was a faint pulse, but she had already lost too much blood.

'When I heard the news I thought I was going to faint, my heart was pounding so hard,' recalled Henry Fonda. 'But when I arrived in Greenwich I was amazingly calm. It came as a total shock to me. Suicide was something I didn't really consider a possibility. But I think her death did not come as a complete surprise to Sophie.' The two said nothing on their winding and wretched drive together up the Hudson to Beacon. Dr Bennett told them that there was nothing they or anyone could have done – that she'd been determined to take her own life and she had. In the hours before she died, he continued, Frances had apparently written six notes – one for her doctor, one for her nurse, one for Sophie, and one for each of her children. He handed the four notes intended for the family to Sophie. Frances had pointedly left no parting words for her husband.

On the return trip, Sophie and Hank agreed that Jane and Peter were too young to be told the circumstances of Frances's death. When they returned from riding at the stables down the road, the children were informed that their mother had died of a heart attack. Frances had doted on Peter to the point of smothering him; he burst into sobs at the news of her death. Jane went to her room and sat on the edge of her bed, waiting for the tears. They never came.

Sophie had instructed the servants to keep Jane and Peter away from television, radio, and the newspapers. They did their job well. Despite the furore in the press, for months both children continued to believe that their mother had died of natural causes.

The curtain went up on *Mr Roberts* the night after Frances Fonda's death just as it had 882 times before. Over the objections of Josh Logan and Leland Hayward, Hank had decided to go on as if nothing had happened. Those few in the audience who had not yet heard the news saw nothing in Fonda's performance to indicate that anything out of the ordinary had transpired, much less that the star's wife had just slit her throat. There would always be those who saw Fonda's business-as-usual approach as callous. Yet for a man so emotionally crippled, losing himself in the character of the compassionate Doug Roberts was, Fonda said, 'the only way I could keep from going crazy'.

Back at home in Greenwich that night, a little girl lay in bed thinking that she would never see her mother again – and wondering why she couldn't cry.

4

'HANK CAN be rough,' Joshua Logan said. 'We've had some knock-down drag-outs [fights]. Growing up in the shadow of such a demanding man must have been terribly hard, but it has made Jane and Peter do extraordinary things they would not have done otherwise.'

Brooke Hayward and the other girls at Greenwich Academy were not entirely surprised at the apparent ease with which Jane adjusted to her mother's death. At twelve, Jane still appeared to be the most resilient and unflappable of the Fondas. If there was anguish or turmoil there, she had already learned to conceal it behind a mask of indifference.

That May, Jane and Brooke were surreptitiously reading fan magazines in class when they came upon a capsule biography of Henry Fonda. Brooke tried to rush past it, but Jane turned the page back and for the first time learned that her mother had killed herself. 'I watched her face when she learned,' recalls Brooke. 'She did not say a word.' Tempered steel. At least so Brooke thought at the time. But that same afternoon, a nurse who had been caring for Jane's ailing grandmother confirmed for the child that her mother had committed suicide. Jane's mind, as she later recalled, was swimming with confusion, despair, anger, and, increasingly, guilt. Over and over again she replayed that awful day she and Peter huddled upstairs while their mother cried out for them. Had she pushed her mother over the edge?

Jane kept her feelings to herself. She did not admit to anyone that she knew the terrible truth. Like her father, she was an expert at concealing her emotions. That summer at camp, however, Jane was plagued by nightmares. Camp counsellors would scramble to her bunk to comfort Jane, but, according to Brooke, her 'wild screaming went on for hours' during the night.

'I've been criticised by the kids for not telling them of their mother's suicide,' Fonda admitted years later. 'Their grandmother and I talked it over at length. We thought it would be harder to explain her suicide and harder for them to grasp it than if we said, "Your mother, who was in the hospital for a long time, won't be coming home. She died there." It seemed easier on the kids not to tell the whole truth. The stories about how they did discover the truth were varied. I wasn't there when either did. But the bottom line of it all is: I wasn't telling the truth.'

After a letter from Craig House medical director Dr Robert Knight had assured Hank once again that he could have done nothing to stop his wife from killing herself, he returned to life among the living. He was more open now about his affair with Susan Blanchard. At the Sunday softball games in the park between casts of the various Broadway shows, it was Susan who cheered Hank and his *Mr Roberts* team on.

During one of these softball games, Hank injured his knee sliding into second base and wound up in hospital. Susan was fluffing up his pillows when Jane walked into the room, unannounced. They hit it off instantly. Susan was a high-cheekboned, blonde beauty and terribly chic, just as the gossipmongers at Greenwich Academy had said. But, just as important, she was warm, animated, giving. For a little girl who had grown up around people who were rather stingy with their affections, her father's outgoing, affectionate fiancée was a godsend. From the outset, Jane would regard Susan, who was only ten years her senior, as more of a big sister and role model than a stepmother. Susan was, Jane would later say, 'everything I wanted to be'.

Peter did not share his sister's enthusiasm for the new woman in their lives. Susan's attempts to win the boy over were unsuccessful, and he returned to his prank-playing, obstreperous ways. Jane was fed up with what she perceived as her little brother's juvenile behaviour; not unlike other siblings, she got back by teasing him. 'Oh, I was very mean to my brother,' she recalls. 'But he was terrible back then.'

Three days after Christmas, 1950, Hank and Susan were married in Oscar Hammerstein's town house – nine months after Frances's suicide. Thirteen-year-old Jane beamed from the sidelines; Peter sneered. Within hours, Hank and his new wife were honeymooning at Caneel Bay on St John in the Virgin Islands. Two days later, they were summoned back. Peter had shot himself.

As his dad would later tell the story, 'Peter had always liked guns. He had wanted a gun very badly, and I said okay if it was only used when I was at home. We got him a .22-calibre rifle so that he could shoot at tin cans. When I was in the Virgin Islands, he cajoled his grandmother, which he could always do, into letting him take the rifle out of its case and carry it around. He told her he didn't want any bullets.' Then, Hank continued, Peter 'went off to his grandfather's estate with a chauffeur driving the car. He had two friends with him. Between them, they had a shotgun and an antique pistol – and all the bullets they could use.'

The chauffeur waited by the car while the boys went over a hill to throw things in the air and shoot them. 'No none had fired the relic pistol. Peter tried to load the .22 bullets into the gun, but they wouldn't go. Eventually, he pointed it into his belly while trying to load it and it went off. He ran down the hill towards the car and fell down. The chauffeur saved his life. He didn't panic. He drove straight for the hospital . . . rather than all the way back to the house in Greenwich. In five minutes, Peter was in the hospital.'

The bullet ripped through the boy's liver and a kidney before lodging next to his spine. A prison surgeon from nearby Sing Sing with plenty of experience of treating gunshot wounds came in from a hunting trip to treat Peter. The doctor managed to remove the bullet, but not, as he later told Grandma Sophie and Jane, before Peter's heart had stopped beating. But then it had revived, and now it looked as if he was going to make it.

'That was the first time in my life I remember praying,' recalls Jane ' "Dear God," I whispered, "if you let him live, I'll never be cruel to him again." ' He teetered on the edge of death for four more days. By the time it was clear he was going to pull through, Jane had forgotten her promise.

Hank was distraught – and enraged. 'He came into the hospital room,' Peter remembers, '*very* angry that I ruined his honeymoon. Gee, big fucking deal!'

Peter would later suggest that the shooting might have been a suicide attempt aimed at frightening his father. Whether or not it was intentional, there is no doubt that from the moment the gun went off Peter fought to stay alive.

Not long after, Henry Fonda was honoured as Father of the Year. 'I hope,' he said in his acceptance speech, 'Jane and Peter will be impressed.'

What impressed Peter was Susan's motherly concern. Finally won over, he even went a step further than his sister and started calling his dad's new wife Mom.

By the summer of 1951, Susan and Hank were ensconced in a brick town house on East 74th Street just off Lexington Avenue. On one side was the canopied entrance to a large apartment building; on the other, the Mannes School of Music. Each morning, the Fondas breakfasted to the strains of Vivaldi and Mozart wafting over from the neighbours next door.

Now that Susan was in charge, both Fonda children began to drift away from Grandma Sophie and the Seymour side of the family in Greenwich. It especially rankled the Seymours that Peter, and Jane now, were calling Susan Mom.

Both indeed found her enthralling, and as the time approached for them to be sent away to boarding schools – Peter to the Fay School in Massachusetts and Jane to Emma Willard in upstate New York – it was Susan they turned to for guidance. 'She put in a lot of time with us,' Jane has pointed out, 'and when I think of how young she was . . . I love her deeply for it.'

For young women of breeding and means, few boarding schools could match the cachet of Emma Willard. Located in the western Berkshires outside the drab Albany suburb of Troy, Emma Willard catered to those families who wanted to see their daughters go on to such top-flight women's colleges as Vassar, Radcliffe, Wellesley, and Bryn Mawr.

As she drove up with Susan to the school for the first time, Jane could not help but be impressed. Sitting on a plateau four hundred feet above the town, the thirty-five acre campus looked every inch the fortress of privilege it was. The school's neo-Gothic libraries and medieval-looking dormitories boasted turrets, crouching gargoyles, and mullioned windows choked with ivy. Each building was linked by a series of tunnels, making it possible to attend class in the middle of a blizzard without ever having to don an overcoat.

By way of recreation, Emma Willard was particularly proud of its hockey fields, tennis and basketball courts, Olympic-size pool, riding ring, and bridle paths (the latter two appealing particularly to the still-horse-crazed Jane). For the then-not-insubstantial sum of $2,000 a year, the young Emma Willard student could enjoy all these amenities, and a private room.

At first Jane, whose Greenwich upbringing had been nothing if not rigid, was eager not to disappoint. Although she once again found herself the only movie star's child on the premises, Emma Willard proved to be 'the great leveller', in the words of one fellow student. Jane was a head taller than most of her classmates, and she had yet to shed the baby fat that had plagued her back at Greenwich Academy. Not that the school's gingham shirtwaist uniforms helped matters much, or the regulation short hairstyle that accentuated her chipmunk cheeks. In short, like most adolescent girls, she hated the way she looked.

'As a child,' she would later point out, 'I was your basic klutz – awkward, plump, and self-conscious.' In Technicolor dreams ('always colour, never black-and-white,' she insists) fraught with Freudian overtones, the adolescent Jane began to see herself differently – usually dressed in frilly, white clothes on a four-poster bed. More often than not, the bed was in a desert, in a swamp, or floating on the sea.

It was during her holiday jaunts with Susan to Manhattan department stores and designer salons that Jane's eyes opened to the world of fashion and the painfully slender models that inhabited that world. Susan was one of these beautiful creatures – all eyes and bone structure. When she came to visit her at school, Jane burst with pride. Now, more than ever, Jane wanted to emulate her.

By her junior year, Jane hit upon a way to shed unsightly pounds. After dinner, she would go to the bathroom, turn on the tap so no one could hear, then stick her finger down her throat to induce vomiting. Thus, in 1954, long before everyone knew the word bulimia, Jane began the dangerous binge-and-purge cycle that would continue for another 'twenty-three years of agony'. At Emma Willard, Jane and her friends ate coffee ice cream by the gallon and cake by the pound. 'We bought bagfuls of brownies and gobbled them down.' Then they took turns waiting to go into the bathroom and throw up.

However potentially damaging to her health, bulimia did help her achieve the svelte exterior she wanted – though, she says, 'I was so conditioned to thinking of myself as fat that . . . I could never convince myself that I was thin enough.' Still, the change was sufficient to afford Jane a newfound self-confidence. For the first time, she was not ashamed to slip into a revealing leotard and attack her ballet classes with fearsome Fonda single-mindedness. Nevertheless, she remembers, 'they said I would never make it because I was too tall. This was in the days before Maria Tallchief. But it didn't matter, I just ignored them and practised like crazy.'

This streak of independence manifested itself in other ways. 'Jane was a leader,' says one Emma Willard classmate, 'and she was not afraid of the spotlight.' At Emma Willard there was a standing rule that students should wear high heels and pearls to dinner. One day, Fonda showed up wearing high heels and pearls – and nothing else.

'I know there are legends about me,' says Jane, denying that she recalls the incident despite the fact that several classmates insist that it happened. 'I *wish* I had been that kind of person.'

Whatever Jane's thirst for attention then, it did not yet extend to a theatrical spotlight. The teaching staff and her fellow students, sensing that Jane might have inherited some of her famous father's talent, urged her to participate in school dramatics. It was for precisely that reason, she insists, that she declined. She knew that because she was Henry Fonda's daughter she would be expected to live up to her classmates' high expectations, while in fact she doubted if she had any acting ability at all. 'Acting was something I never wanted to do as a young girl,' Jane says. 'Not at all.'

Late in her junior year she relented, auditioning for the title role in Christopher Fry's *The Boy with the Cart*. Like her idol Katharine Hepburn, who had made her acting debut at Bryn Mawr College in the role of a young man, Jane pulled on a pair of trousers, slicked back her hair, and threw herself into the part.

To no one's surprise except perhaps her own, Jane proved to be a natural. She went on stage again in her senior year and played the lead role of Lydia Languish in *The Rivals* by Richard Sheridan. Her father, who had gone straight from a national tour of Herman Wouk's *The Caine Mutiny Court Martial* to filming the movie version of *Mr Roberts* in Hollywood, was too busy to attend.

Nor was he paying much attention to his son's theatrical efforts. At prep school, Peter wrote and acted in his own satire, *Stalag 17½*. 'I produced and directed it, and took a supporting role,' Peter says. 'It was an instant success. They loved it. We were just a bunch of fourteen- and fifteen-year-old kids, but I argued that everything had to be real. There we were, smoking on stage

– a great revelation to the faculty. I don't think you could see what was going on for the smoke. Our next was a takeoff of *Mr Roberts*, but I graduated before I could get through writing the first act.'

Jane, meantime, was the picture of deportment. By the spring of 1955 she had already been accepted by Vassar and was following her father's example as an amateur painter.

Determined to pay for her father's birthday present with her own money, she did some modelling for print ads for several weeks to earn the necessary cash. When she proudly presented him with the gift she had picked out, 'he said "Thanks" but forgot to open the package,' she recalled. 'Like a fool, I cried all night in my bedroom.'

As spring went on, the most pressing question became how she would spend the summer. None too soon, a call came from Hank's sister, Jane's Aunt Harriet. Involved with the Omaha Playhouse ever since her brother made his debut there, Harriet asked if Jane would be interested in playing Hank Fonda's daughter in a benefit production of Clifford Odet's play about an alcoholic actor and his long-suffering wife, *The Country Girl*. Jane did not hesitate to accept.

Her father was a good deal less enthusiastic. For one thing, he had never talked to Jane about acting, so if she was at all interested in pursuing the profession it was news to him. But more important for Hank was the strain his daughter's presence in the same production might put on him. After all, he could not be expected to give a first-rate performance *and* worry about his daughter.

There was no cause for concern, as it turned out. 'In one scene,' Henry later recalled, 'Jane had to enter crying. That isn't easy – walking on at the height of an emotional breakdown. I didn't think she could do it . . . But she came on wailing and wet-eyed. I couldn't believe she was acting!'

In truth, she wasn't. Backstage, Jane had instructed a stagehand to strike her hard across the face seconds before she went on. The tears and wailing were very real indeed.

Neither Fonda noticed the buzz that went through the audience as playgoers got their first glimpse of Hank's daughter. The resemblance now was quite striking – the same long jaw, sensuous mouth, and, as one reviewer would put it, those 'pale, enquiring eyes of hunted animals'.

Their week-long run in *The Country Girl* over, all the Fondas – including Hank and Susan's newly adopted infant daughter, Amy – boarded a plane for Rome. There the family went sightseeing and lolled about the pool at their rented villa off the Via Attica while Dad played opposite Audrey Hepburn in Dino De Laurentiis's *War and Peace*.

The stay in Rome proved less than idyllic for the state of the union between Hank and Susan. His icy indifference – she once greeted him with a red fright wig as a gag, and he didn't notice – was something Susan could no longer tolerate.

Having been more of an older sister to the children than a mother, Susan also found it difficult to comprehend Henry's seeming lack of interest in his own flesh and blood. '[I would] drive him crazy talking to him until four in the morning about Jane and Peter,' Susan says. 'He used to clam up. He didn't know how to deal with it.' Admittedly, adds the third Mrs Fonda, 'no one in the family was easy. But none of them was boring, either.'

Once again, the famous Fonda silent treatment prevailed. Hank brooded, while Jane, who had known that a break-up was pending for some time, did not choose to confide in her little brother. 'Everyone in the family sort of exited stage left,' recalls Peter, 'but at least Susan came down and told me about the [impending] divorce.'

Susan scooped up the kids and returned with them to New York, leaving Hank to lick his wounds alone in the imperial splendour of their Roman villa. He would not be alone for long.

The prospect of a divorce hit Peter – so badly shaken by the disintegration of his parents' marriage and his mother's recent death – hardest. At his new prep school in Westminster, Connecticut, his behaviour became nothing short of manic. He started popping barbiturates to calm down, but they didn't do the job. 'At Westminster I was involved in art,' he says. 'I did cartoons for the school magazines and paper, always at the expense of faculty members. They were not very well received, except by the students.' Later he got together six classmates to form the Wampus Players. 'A "Wampus"', he explains, 'is a mythical cat, very large like a dragon, and he doesn't do anything but eat fair maidens and soak up the fruits of society. That was quite a good simile for what our group was like at the time.'

Looking back at her Emma Willard experience years later, Jane would describe life there as 'awful. All girls, no boys. Very unnatural.' Not surprisingly, then, she found conditions at Vassar nothing short of intolerable. From the moment she arrived with kindred spirit Brooke Hayward in the autumn of 1955, Fonda complained loudly to her father that she wanted to leave.

Located in Poughkeepsie, not far from the sanatorium where Jane's mother had committed suicide, Vassar was widely regarded as the epitome of a women's college in the mid-1950s. Not only did a Vassar girl stand a good chance of landing a wealthy young Yale or Harvard man as a husband – which at the time was still viewed as the primary reason women attended college – but she received a first-rate education into the bargain.

Hank was more than willing to pay the then-substantial sum of $2,500 a year to send his daughter to Vassar, and her ingratitude angered him. He was accustomed to such rebellious behaviour from Peter, but he felt he could always count on Jane's co-operation.

He was mistaken. Jane fought back. 'Jane was not a great student,' recalls Brooke in a stroke of understatement. 'Her entire freshman year was spent out of the classroom.' As Jane would later concede, when she discovered that she was attractive to boys, 'I went wild.'

Her first sexual experience, it turned out, was not with a boy at all. 'I was quite envious of her,' says Brooke, 'because she lost her virginity before I did' – to 'a much older, divorced man, an Italian or other European'. Jane unhesitatingly shared the details with her jealous classmates, describing how educated and 'instructive' her lover had been. '*Much* better,' says Brooke, 'than some callow youth.'

Jane's reputation as something of a libertine was not entirely unwarranted. 'She basically did what she wanted,' says another Vassar student. 'She led everybody to believe – and there was no reason to doubt it – that she played around a lot.' Or, as still another graduate put it, Jane was thought to be so 'socially promiscuous – so easy it was almost a joke'.

Hank Fonda's daughter missed curfews, even disappeared for days at a time, and her grades plummeted. Word filtered back to Rome that she was running with a 'loose' crowd, to use the parlance of the time. Hank even heard that a whooping, leather-jacketed Jane had sped on a Harley Davidson down a dormitory hallway.

Dad did not budge, though admittedly his own behaviour in Rome did not exactly make him the perfect role model for his children. His divorce from Susan Blanchard had not yet become final, but that did not prevent him from conducting a secret romance with Afdera Franchetti, the free-spirited 24-year-old daughter of a Venetian nobleman. To make matters worse, the blonde, willowy Afdera was engaged to someone else at the time.

With Dad in Europe and Susan trying to carve out a new life for herself with her daughter, Amy, Peter called Jane whenever his anxieties and problems got too much for him. 'At Vassar I got a call from him that he was flipping out,' relates Jane. 'So I drove to his school and he was hiding behind a bush, with dyed hair, calling himself Holden Caulfield. I didn't know what to do, so I put him on a train to my aunt [Harriet] in Omaha. I always thought Peter was much more neurotic than I was. Now I know neither of us was neurotic at all. Just schizophrenic.'

Despite the emotional wreckage that surrounded him, Peter had turned into something of a romantic. To Jane and his closest friend Eugene 'Stormy' McDonald, he now unabashedly professed his undying love for their old childhood playmate Bridget Hayward, who had grown into an ethereal beauty.

Jane somehow made it through that first year at Vassar and in July joined her father and brother on Cape Cod. A Yale student working as stage manager of the Dennis Playhouse caught her eye, and they began dating; his name was James Franciscus. The Fondas had been in residence only a couple of weeks when the house manager of the Dennis Playhouse called Henry with the idea that he star in their production of *The Male Animal*. Interrupting his vacation seemed out of the question – until it was suggested that Jane could play a small part.

With Henry Fonda's enormous star power as a draw, the curtain went up on a packed house. Dad watched from the wings as Jane did her scene; his entrance cue came as she stormed down a flight of stairs, through a door, and offstage. 'He just stood there for a moment,' recalls Jane, 'his face shining with pride and joy. It was beautiful.' It was at precisely that moment that Henry realised his daughter might just have a future in acting.

By Christmas of 1956, the divorce was final. Susan moved out of the 74th Street town house and into a Park Avenue apartment paid for by Hank, who now felt free to announce his engagement to Afdera. Peter was at the Westminster boarding school when the news that there would soon be a fourth Mrs Fonda came over the radio. After some gentle ribbing from his friends, Peter was summoned by one of the masters. The teacher lambasted young Fonda for his poor grades and general bad behaviour, then topped it off by comparing Peter to his father. 'And anyone,' Peter's teacher concluded, 'who's been married as many times as he has has got to be a son-of-a-bitch!' Without hesitating, Peter knocked the man cold. (The teacher was eventually dismissed.)

Afdera fared no better than Peter's teacher had. In Rome, her older brother beat her up for jilting the man he had selected for her and 'daring to marry an actor'. Not merely an actor, but a thrice-divorced, non-Catholic actor.

All obstacles aside, that March the first-floor drawing room of the East 74th Street town house was the site of the marriage of 'Countess' Afdera Franchetti (in fact, Afdera's sister inherited the title, not Afdera) to Henry Fonda. Peter, his father's best man, scowled as a New York State Supreme Court justice performed the brief ceremony. Jane looked on expressionless. Like the elder Fonda, she had learned to move through a room as if no one else was in it.

Back in Poughkeepsie, Jane seemed determined to outdo her brother as a troublemaker. Her late nights now were fuelled by gallons of black coffee and Dexedrine. She was also continuing to binge and purge.

Tipped off by a friend on one AWOL occasion to the fact that Vassar administrators were looking for her, Jane telephoned the college, sobbing. 'But before I got a chance to apologise, to say I was sorry, the professor said he understood that my father had just married for the fourth time and that I was emotionally upset. I wasn't. I'd just gone away with a boy for the weekend.'

After two years at Vassar, Jane felt she had reached the end of her rope. It was a sentiment shared by school officials. 'I guess,' she later observed with a shrug, 'they thought I was a misfit.' Speculation that she was leaving either to have a baby or an abortion ran rampant among her schoolmates; in truth, Jane merely felt she had 'wasted' enough of her time and her father's money. She pleaded with her father to let her drop out of Vassar and study painting at the Sorbonne in Paris. As an artist of sorts himself, Henry Fonda could appreciate the dream of studying in Paris. It was too late for him, he reasoned, but not for his daughter.

Jane was enrolled in the Beaux Arts school (even Henry Fonda could not pull enough strings to get his daughter into the Sorbonne at the last minute), and moved into the fashionable Right Bank apartment of a down-on-her-luck French countess who took in the young daughters of wealthy Americans. The view across the Seine to the Eiffel Tower was breathtaking, but inside the furniture was covered in plastic and, Jane later recalled with disdain, 'everything smelled. I hated it.'

She soon hooked up with a group of American expatriate intellectuals comprising the staff of the *Paris Review*; their leader at the time was an aspiring author named George Plimpton. With Plimpton and his friends smoothing the way, Jane overcame the language barrier – at the time her Vassar-girl French was abysmal – and quickly became a fixture on the party scene. Days were spent hanging out, chatting, and drinking coffee in the *Paris Review* offices, nights cavorting with freewheeling jet-setters and bohemians in Left Bank *boîtes*.

Jane, just nineteen, proceeded to extend her sexual horizons. Her celebrated Vassar exploits turned out to be tame compared with her adventures in Paris. When Papa, none too happy over the commercial failure of his critically acclaimed production of *Twelve Angry Men*, got word of Jane's antics, he exploded. Jane was ordered home immediately. 'I went to Paris to be a painter,' she remarks, 'but I lived there for six months and never even opened my paints.'

The night before flying home to America and her father's wrath, Jane went to one last party at Maxim's. That evening, as if to prepare for returning to her role as Daddy's little girl, Jane wore her reddish-blonde hair up à la Grace Kelly and a modest calf-length dress cinched at the waist. Her escort was French actor Christian Marquand. Had she not been dancing with Marquand, Roger Vadim, as he would one day admit, would have paid her no attention.

Vadim, a roguish film director already famous for discovering and marrying Brigitte Bardot, and who was about to wed actress Annette Stroyberg, slipped a note into his friend Marquand's jacket pocket as he and Jane twirled by. Assuming that the note was about her, Jane, who would recall incorrectly years later that Stroyberg was very pregnant with Vadim's child at the time, regarded Vadim cautiously. She had heard 'only bad things' about him. 'How he was a cynical, vicious, immoral, Svengali-type character.'

Once back at his table, Marquand read the note, then tossed it into an ashtray. When no one was looking, Jane retrieved it. 'Have you seen her ankles?' it read. That night, Jane's ankles were noticeably swollen. Vadim winced as she looked, quizzically, in his direction. They would not meet again for another three years.

5

IF HENRY Fonda was angrier than usual in early 1958, Jane was not the only reason. It had begun to dawn on him that in marrying Afdera he had made a calamitous mistake. Towering like a tall desert cactus in the middle of her chattering *dolce vita* crowd of short Italians and Spaniards, he felt painfully ill at ease. Yet, despite the appalling disparity in style and temperament between Fonda and his inexhaustibly social bride, Hank managed to fool even his close friends for a time. To them, he seemed happily (if unrecognisably) corrupted. Leland Hayward, among the guests at a birthday party for one of Afdera's friends, recalled, 'For dessert they had ice cream and chocolate sauce. There was dancing, and all of a sudden those nutty Italians began throwing ice cream and sauce on the walls. I thought Hank would commit murder. But he just stood there and smiled and enjoyed it.' What Hayward had witnessed was another splendid performance. Hank was miserable.

Whether or not Jane sensed her father's misery, she seemed determined this time to gain his approval. She signed up for piano lessons at the Mannes School of Music, resumed her art studies in earnest at the Art Students League, and even picked up where she had left off with the *Paris Review* – this time doing secretarial work and soliciting subscription orders at the paper's cramped Manhattan offices. But there was a cloud over her. The fact that she'd never finished what she started at Vassar ('I still dream that I'm back there,' she admits today) or in Paris left her feeling unworthy of the Fonda name. 'I tried to act like a lady,' says Jane. 'I bought Balenciagas and never wore them because I was a slob at heart. I did all kinds of things I didn't believe in because I didn't want to disappoint my father.'

Hank paid little attention anyway. He was too busy at night acting with newcomer Anne Bancroft in the Broadway hit *Two for the Seesaw* and in the day filming *Stage Struck*, a remake of *Morning Glory*, the 1932 film that earned Katharine Hepburn her first Academy Award.

Two for the Seesaw was an enormous success, but Hank was never totally satisfied with the way his character had been written, and he let his dissatisfaction be known by periodically throwing his by-now trademarked apoplectic tantrums. *Stage Struck*, though destined to be both a critical and commercial flop, was the more pleasant of the two jobs. Hank quickly hit it off with his co-star Susan Strasberg, a young actress who had already gained attention on Broadway in *The Diary of Anne Frank*.

Susan was Jane's age, and the two young women developed an instant rapport. Jane was particularly intrigued by what Susan had to say about the work being done by *her* father, Actors Studio artistic director Lee Strasberg.

An apostle of Stanislavsky and the controversial father of 'the Method', Lee Strasberg was peerless among acting teachers. Under his tutelage, such Actors Studio graduates as Bancroft, Marlon Brando, Paul Newman, Geraldine Page, Maureen Stapleton, James Dean, and Marilyn Monroe rose to stardom. (Not until his late seventies did Strasberg throw his own acting beret into the ring, winning critical acclaim in 1974 playing a takeoff of mobster Meyer Lansky in *The Godfather, Part II*.)

In the summer of 1958, Jane's father invited her to stay at his rented beach house in Malibu while he worked on his new television series, 'The Deputy'. Just down the beach the Strasbergs were psyching up Marilyn Monroe, over whom they seemed to exert total personal and professional control, to shoot *Some Like It Hot*. Susan Strasberg had to work harder than she had anticipated persuading Jane to consider seriously an acting career.

Then came an offer from another Malibu neighbour, producer Mervyn LeRoy, to play Jimmy Stewart's daughter in *The FBI Story*. LeRoy had been impressed with Jane's natural grace and the unmistakable 'El Greco shanks' that made her instantly recognisable as Henry Fonda's daughter. When she offhandedly ran the idea past her father, he sarcastically replied, 'If you want to be an actress, you don't want it to be as Jimmy Stewart's daughter.'

She was inclined to agree with her father. Despite her few school and summer turns on the stage, and her interest in the Strasberg Method, Jane was reluctant to commit herself as an actress. 'In fact, I actively wanted *not* to act,' she insists. Mainly it was a question of being compared with her legendary dad. 'When it came to thinking about it as a career, I got scared. After all, my father was a famous actor. I wondered whether I was good enough. Could I act well enough?'

After some gentle prodding by Susan and Paula Strasberg, Jane worked up the courage to audition for one of Lee Strasberg's private acting classes – the first step towards membership of the prestigious Actors Studio itself. For $35 a month, aspiring actors could study with the master, even perform with established stars such as Monroe and Brando who frequently dropped in to brush up on what was euphemistically referred to as 'the craft'.

'The only reason I took her,' Lee Strasberg recalled, 'was her eyes. There was such panic in her eyes.' That panic turned to jubilation when Strasberg praised her acting the first time she played a scene before the class. 'Lee Strasberg for some reason stopped me,' she recalls, 'and I don't know what he said, but he was complimenting me and said he saw a tremendous amount of talent, which totally changed my life. Nobody had ever told me that I was ever good at anything.'

At least, not the person most important to her. 'Henry was warmth and kindness personified on the screen and on the stage,' observes Josh Logan, 'but he could be utterly unfeeling towards those closest to him.'

For Jane, that first day at the Actors Studio was 'like a light bulb going on. I was a different person. I went to bed and woke up loving what I was doing. It was as if the roof had come off my life!' Yet no matter how many times she tried to convey her newfound sense of purpose to her father, he continued to look the other way. One afternoon she ran into Hank on the street, and the two decided to share a cab downtown. 'Panting with excitement,' she tried to tell him about the scene she had just played at the Studio. 'I could see his curtain come down. He smiled, but I just didn't get through.'

Henry Fonda remembered the incident somewhat differently. About a year before Jane started taking acting classes 'she was with a young beau of hers [James Franciscus], who was just getting started in the theatre, and he and I were talking about using an emotion, having to feel an emotion on stage. I told a story about the process I go through, likening it to a seaplane taking off. When the plane starts its takeoff, it is very slow in the water, very sluggish, but as it picks up speed it starts to skim across the water before lifting off. I used to feel that if I could get myself going, nothing could stop me. . . I was soaring. Anyway, about a year later, I found myself in a cab with Jane going downtown, and Jane said, "Do you remember the story that you told about soaring?" And she said, "Now I know what you mean. It happened to me today." Well, I can get emotional right now remembering Jane tell it, and probably the curtain came down to hide the emotion.'

There were other moments when, more than just bringing down the curtain, he would abruptly cut her off rather than listen to her extol Strasberg's genius. 'My father would say, "Shut up. I don't want to hear about it," ' Jane recalls. Hank's reaction probably had less to do with his daughter's interest in acting than the contempt he shared with many established stars for the Method. His seaplane metaphor aside, Fonda generally subscribed to Spencer Tracy's advice to 'just say the lines and try not to bump into the furniture'.

'There was a time,' Henry Fonda later confirmed, 'when Jane would have bored the hell out of anybody talking about the Method.' (Hank had, in fairness, once looked in on the Actors Studio himself. A few years earlier, he'd taken his place on a bench in the audience and waited for something to happen. For a long time nothing did. 'Finally one of the girls wandered slowly on to the acting area, sort of walked around. You've never seen anybody as aimless in your life. At last she stopped and started to pantomime. I don't know whether she was washing dishes or peeling potatoes, but every now and then she would look up and say, "Hello four o'clock, hello four o'clock." She said it about twenty times. I don't know how I kept from falling off the bench.')

Jane was determined to graduate from the Actors Studio whether her father approved or not, even as it became apparent to her that she had more to overcome than her father's thinly veiled contempt. 'I discovered because I was a Fonda everybody expected me to fall on my face. You'd think it'd be the other way around, but it wasn't. I found incredible resentment from other actors, and I remember one terrible, agonising audition when Tyrone Guthrie said to me, "What else have you ever done besides be Henry Fonda's daughter?" So instead of doing a scene a month in class, I'd do two a week, compensating for being a Fonda by working twice as hard as everybody else. Then if I got a part I could say it was because I worked for it.'

Sensing that her fragile self-confidence could not survive, much less flourish, under her father's cynical eye, Jane moved out of the Fondas' town house into a three-bedroom flat two blocks away on East 76th Street. One of her roommates was Susan Stein, whose father, Jules Stein, was founder of MCA (Music Corporation of America), the huge talent agency that represented, among many other top stars, Henry Fonda.

Jane was still reluctant to admit to outsiders that the acting classes were anything more than 'therapy', but she did proceed to make the sort of calculated business move for which she would become famous. Without consulting her dad, she signed with MCA's rival, Famous Artists. It was a way of announcing her serious intentions, distancing herself from her famous father, and teaching him a lesson, all in one stroke.

Yet, for all that, her first professional job offer would be the result of family connections. Nedda Harrigan Logan, Josh Logan's wife, was also from a distinguished theatrical family and prided herself on knowing raw talent when she saw it. Of all the Fondas, she had often told her husband, the fire burned brightest in Jane. No stranger to the Actors Studio crowd, having already guided Marilyn Monroe through her first serious role, in *Bus Stop*, Josh Logan learned from his wife that Jane was now one of Lee Strasberg's dedicated disciples.

To assess the seriousness of Jane's intentions, the Logans invited her to dinner one Sunday and asked her point-blank if she was now committed to being an actress. 'Jane just sat there,' Logan recalled, 'tossing her lovely head about and making long pronouncements about how she would never go on stage or have anything to do with the theatre.'

Playing it coy at the Logans' dinner table was one thing, but by late 1958

Jane was feverishly searching for work. She told Ray Powers at Famous Artists that she was eager to do commercials, print layouts, *anything*. Jane even made an appointment to see modelling agent Eileen Ford, despite continuing insecurity about her looks. To her astonishment, Ford signed her to an exclusive modelling contract on the spot.

Jane's appeal, in addition to her famous name, was that of the Eisenhower-era ingenue. With her long, dark-blonde hair, pert features, and neatly proportioned figure, Fonda's look was definitely all-American – in perfect counterpoint with the sophisticated European fashions she was modelling. Almost immediately, she was being paid $50 an hour (a handsome fee then) to twirl about in Chanel suits and Givenchy gowns before the lenses of the world's top fashion photographers.

When Nedda Logan flashed a copy of the July 1959 *Vogue*, with Jane on the cover, in front of her husband, he studied it carefully. For someone who had insisted only months before that she had no intention of pursuing a show-business career, Jane was certainly doing a deft job of skirting along its perimeters. 'I was suspicious of her career at first,' said Logan, 'as one always suspects newcomers who have successful parents. But as she matured, she became so beautiful I didn't care. I asked her why she didn't seriously try the theatre. She said, "Not interested." I had to wait for her to make up her mind.'

Logan decided to put her to the test. He had purchased the rights to *Parrish*, a *Peyton Place*-type best-seller by Mildred Savage about the melodramatic intrigues among wealthy tobacco growers in the Connecticut Valley. Logan had been searching for two unknowns to play the star-crossed young lovers. He had already cast Shirley MacLaine's unknown little brother, Warren Beatty, in the title role, and when Jane agreed to be screen-tested along with four other actresses, Logan, not surprisingly, gave her the other part.

Logan could not deny the public-relations appeal of introducing Henry Fonda's daughter and Shirley MacLaine's brother in the same picture, but, publicity value aside, he'd been impressed with Jane's understated delivery (a trick learned from watching her father) and the way the 'Fonda magic' had now manifested itself in female form. 'The camera loved her,' he said. 'And I'm not just talking about looks, or even acting ability. If somebody's home, if the lights are inside a person, the camera picks it up every time. Never fails. In her case, the lights were blazing.'

Taking his cue from Hank's old nemesis Darryl Zanuck, Logan signed his new discovery to a five-year, five-picture contract at $10,000 a year. She had yet to prove herself in a single professional performance, but already Jane Fonda was being given a sizeable boost up the ladder to stardom.

6

JANE HAD read the script and was memorising her lines when word came from Josh Logan that he had decided to drop *Parrish* because of casting problems. Though he had found his 'unknowns' to play the young lovers, he had failed to attract name-over-the-title stars for the adult leads. (Three years later, *Parrish* would be released with Troy Donahue, Connie Stevens, and Claudette Colbert in the lead roles.)

Logan reassured Jane that this was only a temporary setback. He was already searching, he promised, for the vehicle that would carry her to movie stardom. Meanwhile, Jane's modelling career was going strong, and so was her love life. Now a regular on the party circuit and in the society columns, Jane jettisoned longtime boyfriend James Franciscus — his patrician good looks, Ivy League loafers, and Brooks Brothers blazers reminding her too much of her own Emma Willard and Vassar days — and aggressively played the field.

Her brother, meanwhile, having scored so high on an IQ test administered by a psychologist as to be classified a genius, promptly enrolled as a second-year student at the University of Omaha. There, with his wealthy friend Stormy McDonald, Peter proceeded to cause his usual measure of trouble. He argued incessantly with his instructors, continued taking speed and barbiturates, and for kicks emptied the Greyhound Bus Depot with a phoney bomb scare. And, while writing intimate letters to Bridget Hayward, he managed to get the daughter of a prominent local family pregnant, then pay for an abortion.

While Hank was dealing via long distance with his son's delinquent behaviour — not to mention his own disintegrating fourth marriage — Jane received a telephone call that would change her life. Joshua Logan had kept his word and found a project for her to star in. He had purchased the film rights to *Tall Story*, the hit Broadway comedy adapted from a Howard Nemerov novel by the legendary Broadway team of Howard Lindsay and Russel Crouse. A romantic comedy about a naïve college basketball player caught up in a betting scandal and the cheerleader he falls in love with, it again offered two roles tailor-made for Jane and Warren Beatty. But once again the studio, this time

Warner Brothers, was not willing to risk all on two newcomers. One of the parts would have to be played by an established star. Gangly Anthony Perkins, who had already starred in *Desire Under the Elms, The Matchmaker* and *Friendly Persuasion*, was cast as the callow basketball star. Jane, who 'saw the play and hated it', rejoiced when Logan sent her the film script; it had been rewritten to expand her part, so much so that the cheerleader emerged as the central character. For now, the working title was to be *The Way the Ball Bounces*.

Her father, busy in Hollywood wrapping up the first season of his first television series, 'The Deputy', was cautiously optimistic about Jane's first film role. While still harbouring serious doubts about his daughter's abilities, Hank trusted his crusty old roommate's instincts. He was also pleased she would be acting opposite Perkins; the men had appeared together two years earlier in the western *Tin Star*, and Hank had been impressed by Perkins's dedication. He may also have been impressed by seeing so much of himself in the young actor. Audiences of the 1950s had by then grown accustomed to watching Perkins's Adam's apple bob up and down as he bashfully dealt with the opposite sex; the bony, stoop-shouldered Perkins could not avoid comparison to both Henry Fonda and Jimmy Stewart in their early days.

That July, reporters scrambled to be the first with the news of Jane's impending arrival. Although she had pointedly asked Logan and the Warner publicity department to soft-pedal the fact that she was Henry Fonda's daughter, the press, predictably, cared about little else. 'Attention, Hollywood! Another Fonda is headed your way,' proclaimed UPI's Jack Gaver. 'Next Tuesday a moderately tall, slim 21-year-old girl, with large, compelling dark-blue eyes and a shock of shoulder-length golden hair, will step off a plane in the movie capital to seek a screen career as her father did almost 25 years ago. She is Jane Fonda, daughter of Henry. You can't mistake her; her features are just like her dad's.'

At first Jane, whose alienation from Hank made it difficult for her to see the obvious resemblance, was taken aback by such comparisons – 'Dad has fine features for a man, but *really*' – but, eventually, growing more secure as both an actress and an individual, she came to regard the comparison as a compliment.

Associated Press columnist James Bacon would be among the first to note a special smouldering sensuality beneath the squeaky-clean surface: 'Jane is one of those girls who exude sex appeal on screen – and off – without trying. That asset is helped immeasurably by a curvaceous, high-breasted figure. She's 5 feet 7½ inches tall, weighs 112 pounds. Her body is what the trades call lissom and her face, which is a womanly version of her father's, is photogenic. She packs all that with a 132 IQ.'

At a story conference in the director's apartment, a studio photographer asked if, in the spirit of the film, Perkins and Fonda could neck on the couch for some publicity stills. 'Jane turned pale,' recalls Perkins. 'It was her first encounter with one of the absurdities of this business, and it was as if she said to herself, "My God, is this what being an actress means?" You could see her take a deep breath and say to herself, "Well, I guess it is, so okay, let's get it over with."' Jane was careful not to sound over-confident when interviewed about the prospect of making her first movie. This was not too difficult. She was terrified. 'It's wonderful, of course, but it's also very frightening,' Jane said in an interview that September. Frightening perhaps, but also a clear opportunity. To illustrate the piece, she got on the floor in front of a bookcase, lifted her backside in the air, and smiled prettily for the camera.

'Girls generally don't get a part like this until they've had lots and lots of experience,' she went on in the article. 'And I know I wouldn't have got it if I didn't have the father I have, and if Josh Logan hadn't known me all my life. It's a fearful responsibility, and of course I'm nervous about it. Everybody tell me that if such experienced people as Josh Logan and the Warners didn't think I would do a good job, they never would use me, no matter who my father and my grandfather were, because there's too much at stake – reputation, money, and all that – to take a chance on an unknown inexperienced person. I tell myself that, too, but I'm still nervous about it.'

Jane's first day on the job was not exactly designed to inspire confidence. 'I was at Warner Brothers,' she recalled, 'and they started examining my face. It was a bunch of make-up artists looking me over and it wasn't what they wanted. When they got finished with me. I didn't really know who I was. My eyebrows were like eagle's wings, and my mouth was all over my face. My hair was not the right colour, and it had to be changed. Then Jack Warner, the head of the studio, sent a message to the set that I had to wear falsies because you couldn't become a movie star unless you were full-breasted.' More to the point, Warner had said, 'She's got a good future if you dye her hair blonde, break her jaw and reshape it, and get her some silicone shots or falsies.'

'It seems silly today,' Jane would later reflect, 'given the consciousness that exists, that I would accept that. But I just assumed these men were experts. So I allowed myself to be changed . . .What it does is completely alienate you from yourself, and you spend your whole time pretending to be somebody other than yourself – not just on the screen, but because that is the standard that is being laid out for you as a woman as to what you're supposed to look like all the time.'

Whatever her anxieties at the time, and with the same fanatical zeal that would characterise every phase of her adult life, Jane plunged into preparation for the role. She visited college campuses in the Los Angeles area, dogged the footsteps of cheerleaders, and slavishly mastered their routines to lend authenticity to the role.

But the mounting sense of panic that she was able to disguise during the daytime came out in her dreams. In one recurring nightmare, she was left alone in a freezing house, unable to escape. In another, she had to defend herself against allegations of insanity. It was during this period that she also began sleepwalking. One night, she was startled awake only to realise that she was standing in the street outside her house, naked.

Things were not that much better during the day on the set. Working on a 35-day shooting schedule, Jane became less and less confident of her acting skills and increasingly paranoid about the other cast and crew members; she was convinced that they were sniggering about her behind her back (in fact they *were* sniggering – not about Fonda nepotism, but about the clumsy script).

What she had learned at Lee Strasberg's knee was proving of little value before the camera. 'I always thought that you go on and pretend the camera isn't there when you shoot a scene,' she would explain years later, 'when in fact, you relate to it in a certain way, with consciousness of the lights and all sorts of technical matters. You learn such fascinating things – like the fact that the audience's eyes tend to go to the right side of the screen, so you try to get over to the right side of the set. That's a subtle form of scene-stealing.'

Indeed, Jane learned fast. At first, whenever Perkins cued her for her close-ups, he just read the lines flat, without feeling. With essentially nothing to react to, Jane could not work up the requisite emotions. On the third day of shooting, she went to Perkins and threatened to deliver her lines in the same lifeless manner when the time came for *his* close-ups. From then on, Perkins read all his cue lines to Jane *con brio*.

Tall Story (the final title) was Jane's baptism by fire in more than one sense. Warner's publicity department wasted no time getting her name into the papers, hosting a cocktail party to introduce her to the Hollywood press. No sooner did she walk into the room than Jane burst into tears. She spotted Afdera, who slipped her a sedative, which, Jane recalled, 'relaxed me'. Why so nervous? Jane did not think she was glamorous or interesting enough to warrant the attention. 'If you're Marilyn Monroe, a press party is great,' said Jane. 'Her strap can break, or she can just stand there. . . . But who cares if *my* strap breaks?'

Jane managed to overcome her sense of insecurity enough to woo and win the industry's two most important columnists – Louella Parsons and Hedda Hopper. Parsons wrote for the powerful Hearst chain and was a woman to be both feared and courted. With one tiny item, the queen of the columnists could obliterate reputations, make or break careers, drive down the stock of entire studios.

Jane, properly coached by the Warner publicity man, brought 'Lolly' a token of affection. 'I shall never forget the way she looked when she breezed into my house from the beach where she had spent the day trying to get a suntan,' wrote Parsons. 'She was wearing a white blouse and yellow skirt, with her hair wrapped in a tight turban, which she called her "babushka". In her hand she carried a bright blue balloon which she found on the kerb outside my home – the colour effect was most becoming.'

A corny and obviously calculated gesture, it was precisely the kind Parsons would most appreciate. 'The second generation is often a disappointment because it's so difficult to follow in the footsteps of a celebrated father or mother,' Parsons went on. 'But I am willing to make a sizeable wager that Jane Fonda is going to be an exception.' The columnist described Jane as 'a pretty edition of Hank. She has the same soft brown [sic] eyes, light brown hair, and her profile is amazingly like that of her father . . . Quite a girl, my old friend Henry Fonda's daughter – beautiful, talented and charming. I invited her to come and see me again soon, and she promised she would.'

'When I was in Vassar,' Jane told Parson's crazy-hatted rival, Hedda Hopper, 'I thought that girls who want to be happily married and have families did not become actresses. I didn't know if I had any ambition to act or any talent.' As for *Tall Story*, Jane told Hopper, 'Well, it couldn't be more fun. It's like a big game, really.'

In truth, the making of *Tall Story* turned out to be a dismal episode in the professional life of Jane Fonda. Although continuing to keep up a brave front, she mistook the movie's inadequacies for her own. And all the while, she longed to be back in the bosom of the Strasbergs. The day after filming ended, she rushed back to New York.

Logan's heartfelt reassurances did not alleviate Jane's persistent feelings of not being up to the demands of the profession her father had mastered. Again she immersed herself in acting classes before taking a three-week break to star in *The Moon Is Blue* at a small theatre in Fort Lee, New Jersey. For the most part, she talked about acting almost as much as she did it. 'Some people say, "I don't want to study. It will hurt my quality." I wonder about this "quality" business,' she told a reporter. 'Initially, you're hired because you have something an audience likes. But it's essential that you change or else you become stale and pretty soon the people who loved you are starting to be bored by you. It seems to me that one of the actor's primary necessities is to expand.

'I know many superb actors,' she continued, 'whose motto appears to be "Why study?" I guess it works for them. But this is something that is part of my whole philosophy about work. I know that if I didn't study, I would be in bad shape.' Jane went on to cite 'a case in point: I had a very, very proper upbringing. And I had to counteract this facet of my personality in playing the part of a street tramp. It reached the point where I simply didn't know how to look another actor in the eye and deliver the crude, violently insulting dialogue that I was called upon to say in the script. Every time I played one of those scenes I wound up apologising to the actor.

'Eventually, through work in class and with my own coach, I've been able to overcome this built-in ladylike reticence and really let loose with the lines.' As for comedy, 'You need even more technique and timing. Making people laugh requires an elusive quality. It calls for perfect timing and pacing. The fully prepared actor has that slight edge that can make the difference between success and mediocrity. When I give up studying,' she concluded, 'it will be because I've given up acting.'

Speaking with the total self-assurance of a seasoned expert, newcomer Jane gave the press a hint of what was to come in her later incarnations as political activist and fitness guru. But these early pronouncements concerning the acting profession barely concealed the self-doubt that gnawed inside. Then, in Timothy Everett, one of the young actors attending her class, Jane found a kindred spirit. Together they worked on scenes and, what was more important, bolstered each other's self-esteem. Inevitably, Everett recalled, in the middle of one session 'I got consumed by this wave of tenderness and desire, and so did she. We ran upstairs to the bedroom, tore our clothes off, and stayed in bed for three days.'

Everett, who had in fact already made it on Broadway as one of the leads in William Inge's *Dark at the Top of the Stairs*, was as excitable as the Fondas were controlled. Hank found him irritating from the start, but Jane, having run through a series of brief affairs, wanted everyone to know that Everett was now the only man in her life. On weekends in the country, it was not unusual for a visitor to come upon Everett and Fonda lolling about unselfconsciously in the nude. Everett takes credit for Fonda's self-liberation: 'I taught her about emotions, I think, and I taught her about lovemaking and how to show love.'

Jane's sexual appeal had not eluded the press. Proclaiming the 'Inevitable Discovery of Jane Fonda,' *Look* magazine ran a provocative shot of her frolicking in the surf. The caption likened her 'kittenish quality' to that of Brigitte Bardot – a comparison that would recur and take an ironic twist when Jane wound up marrying Bardot's ex-husband.

What Jane needed now, she was convinced, was the respect of her peers – the kind only a Broadway drama could bestow. Again, Joshua Logan answered her prayers. His Christmas present to her was the lead in *There Was a Little Girl*, the provocative story of an upper-class girl who is raped and wonders if she may have invited it. *There Was a Little Girl* was certainly ahead of its time, and its lurid content troubled her father. Despite old buddy Josh Logan's involvement, Hank urged Jane not to take the role. 'My father thought the play and the part weren't right for me,' says Jane. 'He wanted to protect me from what he thought would be a disaster. But I thought, Who am I to turn down such a part – the leading role in a Broadway play? It was a great opportunity. I knew every young actress in New York would have given her eye teeth for the part.'

Jane recalls that, just three days before she signed the contract with Logan, her father 'called me and begged me to turn it down. I didn't.' Jane's mood had turned defiant. As she explained in an interview: 'I used to say I wouldn't go into acting because in it you must be the best or nothing. I had no confidence. Now I'm going to fight.' For the role of the rape victim in *There Was a Little Girl*, 'I'll murder anyone who gets in my way for the part.'

Hank suspected rightly that Everett, whom he distrusted and disliked, had persuaded her to take the part. 'What my father didn't realise was that if I refused the role I'd have a hard time getting other jobs. I'm not a star. But once I took it, he said nothing.' Hank had other things on his mind. On New Year's Day, he learned with the rest of the world that Margaret Sullavan, the first Mrs Henry Fonda, had taken her own life with an overdose of sleeping pills.

During rehearsals, Logan was tough on his star. 'I don't think you can do it,' he shouted at her in a moment of exasperation. 'You're going to fall behind your old man. When the curtain goes up, there'll be a ghost of your father sitting in the chair.'

'I got so mad,' Jane admitted at the time, 'but I know he's using every trick to make me do my best.' From the darkened wings, Henry quietly watched his daughter rehearse a romantic scene. 'Oh, youth, youth, youth,' he murmured to Logan, standing next to him. 'God! That's the exciting time. Oh, to have it all to do over again!'

On opening night in Boston, Jane brought the audience to its feet. 'The Boston critics said I was fragile, when I'm really strong as an ox. They said I was coltish, febrile, virginal, translucent – me! I realised I had created something that moved an audience. From there on I wanted to do nothing in life but become the greatest stage actress there ever was.'

The play opened in New York on 29 February 1960, at the Cort Theater, and the critics tore it apart, but for Jane, they, like their out-of-town counterparts, had nothing but praise. 'Although Miss Fonda looks a great deal like her father,' wrote *The New York Times*'s Brooks Atkinson, doyen of theatre critics, 'her acting style is her own. As the wretched heroine of this unsavoury melodrama, she gives an alert, many-sided performance that is professionally mature and suggests that she has found a career that suits her.'

Tall Story was released at about the same time, and again she managed to walk away from a disaster relatively unscathed. 'Nothing could possibly save the picture,' said *Time*, 'not even the painfully personable Perkins doing his famous awkward act, not even a second-generation Fonda with a smile like her father's and legs like a chorus girl.' *Films in Review* critic Ellen Fitzpatrick chimed in, 'The film wouldn't be reviewed in these pages but for the fact that Henry Fonda's daughter Jane makes her screen debut in it. She is a good-looking lass and she can act.'

On 17 May, Jane, wearing a demure sleeveless black cocktail dress and a diamond pin in the shape of a butterfly, was presented by actor Laurence Harvey with the *Theater World* award as 'one of the promising personalities of the 1959–60 season'. She picked up the same prize from the New York Drama Critics Circle. A *Time* magazine profile followed, then the cover of *Life*. Yet many inside the business wondered if she might be a flash in the pan. 'I have a hunch that Jane Fonda will do OK in pictures for about four years,' one correspondent cabled to his editors. 'Then as soon as she gets Hollywood out of her system she'll settle down with a nice, handsome husband, make babies, and that will be it. By 1965, I think she'll be more often on the society pages than the entertainment pages.'

It was not long before Jane was invited to do guest spots on 'The Jack Paar Show', 'What's My Line?' and CBS's 'Person to Person'. She was in the process of redecorating her apartment when the 'Person to Person' crew showed up. 'There's a tremendous amount of nervousness involved,' she said of the experience. 'No furniture. Paint cans. You know essentially the kinds of questions they'll ask, but I was just so scared I didn't know what I was saying. I was so scared, I was dizzy.'

Jane's bizarre response to all the attention was to make appointments for both herself and Timmy Everett to see a psychiatrist. Now that both of their careers were on track (Everett had just been chosen by Otto Preminger to play the important role of a young Israeli in the film *Exodus*), they were more passionately committed to each other than ever. But Jane had some unresolved feelings about her mother's suicide, her father's apathy, and what she perceived as an inherent inability to connect with her own emotions. Since the Method as interpreted by Lee Strasberg was intensely Freudian in its approach, Jane also believed that seeing a psychiatrist (the profession then was still largely Freud-oriented) might make her a better actress. If 'sense memory' – drawing on one's own experiences to summon up the necessary emotion for a scene – was at the core of Method acting, Jane reasoned, then she had better get in touch with those memories. 'I began to see that the problems of Jane Fonda the person were the same as those of Jane Fonda the actress. Acting, when you're serious about it, is tough. It hurts. It has to hurt; otherwise, you're not acting.'

7

WHEN MEL BROOKS was looking for precisely the right person to play the obsequious homosexual in *The Producers*, he picked Andreas Voutsinas. The London-educated son of Greek parents, Voutsinas fancied himself Lee Strasberg's lieutenant. He was also an aspiring producer and occasional actor who managed to insinuate himself into the life of anyone who might be of help to his career. In appearance, he was almost a caricature of the theatrical poseur of the late 1950s and early 1960s, a period of flamboyance and experimentation in the theatre. He adopted Strasberg's slightly bohemian uniform – black trousers, turtlenecks, and berets – and was prone to making sweeping gestures with his cigarette holder. He was seven years older and an inch shorter than Jane.

Voutsinas had already played Svengali to Anne Bancroft and a number of other New York actresses by the time he set sights on Jane. At first, she was bemused – certainly there could be nothing physical between them. She and Everett had just celebrated their second year together, and she found nothing attractive in the dissipated, serpentine Voutsinas.

Yet there was a certain unctuous assurance about the man. He told the 22-year-old actress what she wanted to hear – that there were great depths to her emotions that she had yet to plumb, that she was destined for greatness as an actress, that she was definitely not just Daddy's little girl. Still, Jane was suspicious of Voutsinas, and it seemed to Everett that Voutsinas's very presence made her feel strangely uneasy. But then all protestations ceased almost overnight, and soon, wherever Jane went Voutsinas was at her elbow, whispering in her ear. 'It was like the *Invasion of the Body Snatchers* or something,' says a friend from that time. 'It almost seemed like a joke at first, I mean you had to laugh at the guy, he couldn't be serious. Before you knew it, you were hanging on his every word. Andreas cast a lot of people under his spell, but with Jane it was more complete than with anyone I'd ever seen. I'm not so sure she would go to the bathroom if he had told her not to.'

That July, Voutsinas directed her in a summer-stock production of *No Concern of Mine* at Connecticut's Westport Playhouse. The play had been turned down by several theatres, and apparently with good reason. For one thing, it lacked a plot. 'It's not the kind of play you can understand just by reading it,' Voutsinas tried to explain.

'It took a lot of guts to do this play,' said Jane in an interview then, fiercely defending her new mentor. 'The funny thing now is that people are coming up to Andreas – some of the same people who turned it down – to congratulate him.'

No Concern of Mine ran for one week. By then Jane was reading for the part of Emily in a Circle-in-the-Square production of Thornton Wilder's *Our Town*. 'I had her come back twice,' recalls the director, José Quintero, 'as I was impressed, first by her looks, which as everybody knows are quite staggering, but then I was deeply moved by her vulnerability. I did not cast her in the role: she was too individual; Emily had to be everybody. The events were the important thing in *Our Town*. With Jane we see life as it happens to her. We see it through her perspective. I think she is unafraid to see it all.'

It was not long, however, before Jane came across *Invitation to a March* by Arthur Laurents. From the moment she got her hands on a copy of the play, Jane was determined to do the lead role of Norma Brown. 'The minute I read it, something clicked in my mind. Here was a script just labelled "Jane". Of course, I had to work pretty hard to convince the rest of the world about that.' She telephoned her father and told him, 'There's a play written for me, but they don't know it yet.' She waited two weeks for the call from Laurents to come, and when it didn't she telephoned her agent. He told her that the rest of the cast included Shelley Winters, Eileen Heckart, Madeleine Sherwood, and James MacArthur. In the company of such high-powered females as Winters and Heckart, her agent cautioned, a relative neophyte was sure to suffer. She disagreed. 'I told him much less experienced girls would be reading and there was no harm in letting me try out.' After a single reading, Laurents gave Jane the part.

For now, feeling positive about herself, she could afford to be magnanimous towards her father. When a veteran Broadway observer suggested to her that being Henry Fonda's daughter might be a professional hindrance, Jane appeared to be nonplussed. 'Hindrance? If I weren't his daughter it would have taken me years to push through the doors. Just his example helps. I watch him, and see why I should do something a certain way. It's a professionalism he has you just can't define. His stage presence, it's never excessive or unnecessary; it's a complete use of himself without whipped cream.'

As far as Hank was concerned about her new role, almost anything was an improvement over her rape-victim debut. *Invitation to a March* was a kind of contemporary 'Sleeping Beauty', dealing with a well-bred college girl whose existence is so monotonous that she can barely stay awake through it – until she's awakened by the kiss of a 'prince' who happens to be even younger than she. The prince in this case, MacArthur, had something in common with his leading lady – a famous parent, or actually two famous parents: playwright Charles (*The Front Page*) MacArthur and Helen Hayes.

As previous warnings had suggested, in the company of such first-rate stage actors Jane once again felt her sense of confidence begin to unravel. It didn't help that Voutsinas, who was originally supposed to serve as assistant director, wound up not getting the job because of a clash with Laurents, leaving Jane to fend for herself. 'In the beginning,' she would say later, 'when I first went on stage, I felt like apologising to the audience.' During previews, she would go up to the balcony just before the curtain and check out the audience, hoping not to find any 'mean' faces. And once on stage, 'I walked down to the footlights and all I hear are whispers. They're whispering, "She looks just like her father." This bothers me and I don't know why. I guess everybody wants their own identity.' Backstage, she overheard an actor say, 'She got the part because she's Fonda's daughter.'

'It made me feel awful,' Jane told a reporter, perhaps wondering why no one said the same thing about Helen Hayes's son. 'I know intellectually, that I got the part on merit – I read for it just like everyone else. But still they resent me. I know some other actors resent me because of my father. I don't mind being resented by people with no talent, but it hurts when they are people with talent.' The liabilities of having a famous father, Jane was coming to believe, had started to outweigh the assets.

By way of hedging her bets, Jane began to downplay her commitment to acting. 'I don't want to be a career woman,' she said during try-outs in Detroit. 'I hope that's not too ambiguous. What I'm trying to convey is that while I definitely do want a career professionally speaking, I also want a career as a woman. I want to marry and have children and devote sufficient time to a normal existence. They frighten me, these people who are so obsessed by business or art or whatever they've chosen that they leave no time for just living.'

But then everything was put in perspective by a tragic event in the lives of Jane's dear friends the Haywards. The week before Jane was to open on Broadway, Bridget Hayward, the Fondas' childhood playmate and the love of Peter's life, killed herself with an overdose of sleeping pills at the age of 21. Bridget had been institutionalised previously with psychiatric problems, and in Brooke Hayward's book, *Haywire*, Jane recalled the last time she had seen her – not ten months before – as they both took the train into New York from Connecticut: 'She was like someone who'd had shock treatment. Talking to her was like talking to someone through gauze, through heavy filters. There was the same attempt to reveal only the minimum . . . don't open those floodgates; don't let very much out; be as calm as you can; don't rock the boat . . . Bridget was trying to fit into a mould that had nothing to do with her. Her spirit had nowhere else to go.'

Jane received the news of Bridget's death during tryouts of *Invitation to a March* in Boston, and it hit her hard. Arthur Laurents recalled seeing Jane in her dressing room under sedation, sobbing and unable to go on.

'You're afraid you may kill yourself too, aren't you?' said Laurents.

'Yes.' Later, she would admit to frequent thoughts of suicide. 'Yeah, yeah. I always think about it, but I never would do it. I'm telling you I value my life too much. I think I'm too important.'

Peter was devastated. He had dropped out of the University of Omaha in his senior year and, intent on pursuing his own theatrical ambitions, returned to New York. He was auditioning for a play, *Blood, Sweat and Stanley Poole*, when he was told of Bridget's suicide. Dad did little to comfort his son; his main concern was for his friend Leland Hayward, who had now suffered through two suicides in less than a year. Peter, angered by his father's inability to perceive his own son's pain, ran back to his psychiatrist in Omaha.

The senior Fonda did not break stride. While his irrepressible social-butterfly wife, Afdera, fluttered from one party to the next, Hank squeezed more Broadway plays (*Silent Night, Lonely Night*; *Critic's Choice*) between starring roles in such blockbuster films as *How the West Was Won* and *Advise and Consent*.

Hank had also managed to campaign hard that autumn for his friend, Massachusetts Senator John F. Kennedy. Among all the Fondas, Hank, a lifelong liberal Democrat, was the only one up to then who had expressed any interest in politics. Peter was immersed in his own neuroses, Jane in how she would be received in her second starring role on Broadway.

Jane needn't have worried. As far as the critics were concerned, Henry Fonda's daughter owned the stage. Exulted Kenneth Tynan in *The New Yorker*, 'Jane Fonda can quiver like a tuning fork and her neurotic outbursts are as shocking as the wanton, piecemeal destruction of a priceless harpsichord.' Wrote *Newsweek's* George Oppenheimer, 'Here is surely the loveliest and most gifted of all our young actresses.'

On the strength of Jane's performance (and, undoubtedly, the Fonda mystique), *Invitation to a March* ran for three months. The critical raves were not enough for Jane, however, who walked away from the experience complaining that she had been forced to play her character as some sort of 'slick Ginger Rogers ingenue'.

This uncharacteristically cynical tone had the ring of Voutsinas. Apparently he was convinced that, rather than trying to be an American Audrey Hepburn, Jane should seek to be cast against type in gritty, earthy, *meaty* roles. He encouraged her to stay in therapy, and to reinforce their relationship he started seeing Jane's psychiatrist himself.

This may, in fact, have been excellent advice, but the fact remained that nearly all who knew him viewed Voutsinas as transparently ambitious, and manipulative in the extreme. 'If Svengali ever existed,' says one Actors Studio graduate, 'he was Voutsinas, and Jane was his willing Trilby.'

Gradually, insidiously, Voutsinas had supplanted Everett as Jane's mentor. Yet Everett maintains that Voutsinas's influence unleashed the rage that had smouldered inside Jane since childhood. While Everett had shown Jane how to admit to her doubts and fears, Voutsinas taught her how to transform those feelings of helplessness into anger. 'Now she could be mean and ugly and not feel guilty about it,' Everett explained.

It was, in a sense, a highly effective crash course in assertiveness. Yet the fact remained that, no matter how loudly she proclaimed her independence, Jane was still under contract to Josh Logan. He not only had the power to put her in more of his films but he could also loan her out to other studios at a handsome profit.

That January, Jane decided she had been in Strasberg's class long enough and was ready to graduate to the Actors Studio itself. For her audition before the Actors Studio board, she picked *Butterfield 8*, the role that brought Elizabeth Taylor her first Academy Award. When her father asked her why she chose the role of a high-class prostitute, Jane responded, 'Because I identify with her. Not the call-girl kind of life, but the guilts, the desperations, the emotions.' The audition was a success.

This interest in 'bad girl' parts may well have stemmed from Jane's natural desire to shock her upstanding father – and in the process win his attention if not his respect. Yet there was more to it than that. Jane was instinctively drawn to the role of the exploited woman, and that fascination with woman as victim would in turn lead to some of her finest work on screen.

Immediately after *Invitation to a March* closed, Jane made her television debut opposite George Grizzard in Somerset Maugham's 'A String of Beads'. Jane played Gloria, a young, naïve secretary who goes to a jewellery shop to buy a gift for the rich matron who employs her. While she is in the shop, Gloria buys herself a little string of inexpensive cultured pearls. They turn out to be worth $60,000, and when Gloria gets invited to her boss's dinner party as a last-minute substitute for a guest, she gets an enlightening new perspective on her life vis-à-vis the lives of the idle rich.

When reporter Harry Harris arrived at her flat to interview her about the programme, he was surprised by the actual Jane Fonda. 'You'd expect to find, behind the door of her practically unfurnished apartment, a glamourpuss – all frills and fuss. Instead, what confronts you is a cross between a beatnik and a Charles Addams eerie dearie – dishevelled, make-upless, in black tights, black blouse, only partially anchored, and black sunglasses.'

Throughout Harris's visit, Jane munched constantly. 'I have to be eating something all the time,' she told him. 'I can't sit still without doing anything . . . Do I have a weight problem? Oo! Ee! I try to stop eating. I do ballet sometimes four hours a day. I don't do any exercises *per se*. They have to be in terms of something. Like I lie down to do exercises and I end up chewing my fingernails. I forget why I'm there.'

When she arrived at the NBC studios to start rehearsals, Jane suddenly became terrified at the prospect of performing in a new medium with people who obviously knew far more about it than she did. 'Everyone but me was quite experienced in TV,' she said later. 'Very relaxed. I went into a panic.' With only four days of rehearsals and one day to shoot, she 'felt it was sort of a secret society I wasn't quite initiated into.

'Out of nerves, I become ridiculous . . . quite a tomboy. I have to chew gum, stick it on walls. I start laughing hysterically for no reason. I get very kind of silly. It's hard to describe, but I throw myself into a frenetic peak of hysteria.' One of her co-stars, Roland Winters, did not find her behaviour all that amusing. 'No one,' he told her, 'can reach twenty-three and be quite as repulsive. It's not possible.'

Not long after 'A String of Beads' aired to generally favourable reviews, Jane tried out for the lead in *Period of Adjustment*, Tennessee Williams's only comedy. Jane did not get the role ('At that time it was Greek to me – I didn't understand it at all'), and it was just as well. A far cry from *The Glass Menagerie* or *Cat on a Hot Tin Roof*, *Period of Adjustment* was about two marriages – one brand new, the other established – over the course of a single day. The critics dismissed it, and urged the playwright to stick to more familiar terrain.

At about this time, Josh Logan exercised his option and loaned Jane to Columbia for Charles Feldman's production of *Walk on the Wild Side*. Jane would almost surely have rebelled had it not been for the controversial nature of the film and Voutsinas's belief that it could alter the direction of her career. Based on the steamy Nelson Algren best-seller about a young Texan who goes looking for his lost love only to find her working in a bordello, *Walk on the Wild Side* offered Jane the chance to shatter her hitherto wholesome persona. 'What I want to do in terms of my career,' she said at the time, 'is to get away from things I'm identified with. It's easy for me to play the victimised sweet young thing. I'm almost twenty-four now and want to play my own age.'

Amoral, hell-raising teenage prostitute Kitty Twist would do nicely. Director Edward Dmytryk, in the Hollywood tradition of choosing English actors to play Southerners, had already picked Laurence Harvey to play the lovelorn

Texan Kitty falls for. Anne Baxter and Capucine were cast as Kitty's co-workers. Old Fonda family friend Barbara Stanwyck played a lesbian madam.

With something of a chip on her shoulder and Voutsinas at her side as dialogue coach, Jane began shooting *Walk on the Wild Side* at Columbia's Hollywood studios. From the start she was boasting about her Actors Studio experience and talking loudly about 'the morons in the film business'. When asked later about her behaviour on the set, Jane explained, 'There was a lot of stir because I had Andreas working with me. But I feel you have to learn as much as you can; if you're not good, people turn against you. But if you try to be good in a way that to them doesn't seem necessary, they lash out at you. I don't like people turning against me, but I've gotten over the feeling that everyone has to love me.'

Jane thought it would lend authenticity to her character not to wear underclothes; when director Dmytryk politely instructed her to put some on, she refused. In a fight scene with actress Sherry O'Neil, Jane got a little carried away and O'Neil walked away with a bloody nose and assorted bruises.

Laurence Harvey did not fare much better. At 34, Harvey had already helped two of his co-stars win Academy Awards – Elizabeth Taylor in *Butterfield 8* and Simone Signoret in *Room at the Top*. Among British actors, Harvey had the advantage of being able to pass as an American (most memorably in the role of the programmed assassin in *The Manchurian Candidate*, which was released the following year). Jane was upset to find that the man whose work she so admired on screen appeared to have a too-casual attitude towards his part and a thinly veiled contempt for his fellow actors. 'It's like acting by yourself,' complained Jane, who was not amused by Harvey's penchant for 'making faces' while others delivered their lines. 'No, it's *worse* than acting by yourself.'

Harvey had a few words to say about Jane: 'What a strange girl! She seems to be suffering from the Hollywood disease – Get yourself a big name and there's no need to live up to it.' She was, he concluded, a major know-it-all. 'She has a few things written about her and she comes to the conclusion she's the biggest star in the movie business. You can't tell her anything. Two hours on the set and she's playing director and running the outfit.'

Harvey did give her points for not being overly obsessed with her appearance – 'She *knows* she's sexy, and she also knows when to turn it off' – but he also noted that she seemed 'uncomfortable with touching or displays of affection'. There were no such constraints regarding Voutsinas – with whom, it was pointed out, Jane displayed a considerable amount of physical affection.

Jane had an entirely different problem with Stanwyck. Her father's favourite co-star still fondly called Hank's little girl 'Lady'. When Jane was called upon in a scene to confront Stanwyck's lesbian madam character with some pretty raw language, she could not bring herself to say the lines. Eventually, the scene was rearranged so that she would not have to look at Stanwyck while she delivered the offending dialogue.

Off the set – and again at Voutsinas's urging – Jane was talking frankly for publication. In fact, she adroitly used the Hollywood press to get out the message that she was, as she put it, no longer Hank Fonda's reliable 'goodie goodie girl'.

'She has more to say,' wrote columnist Sidney Skolsky, 'in 25 minutes than Henry Fonda has said for publication in 25 years.'

The most explosive of Jane's press encounters was her interview with Hedda Hopper, in which she declared that marriage was 'obsolete' – a rather radical notion in 1961, certainly one designed to ruffle middle-class feathers. Hopper claimed to be 'rocked back on my heels' by Jane's 'outspoken ideas' as she eagerly imparted them to her millions of readers. ' "I think marriage is going to go out, become obsolete," she said. "I don't think it's natural for two people to swear to be together for the rest of their lives." '

It seems incomprehensible almost three decades later, but these and similar statements were enough to ignite a blaze of indignant reaction. Hopper received letter from thousands of irate readers condemning Fonda's anti-wedlock stance. This was, of course, precisely the reaction she and Voutsinas had hoped for. Never again would she be typecast as the new Sandra Dee.

When the smoke from all these brushfires had cleared, Jane was quite happy with the way her second film turned out. If nothing else, she'd discovered that she enjoyed living on the edge. 'I knew that playing Kitty Twist would make me look very ugly,' she tried to explain. 'I thought my career might be ended because of it, but I went and did it anyway.' For Jane, *Walk on the Wild Side* had been an altogether satisfying experience, one that left her confident that she could take risks and still not forfeit her future in the movies.

When *Walk on the Wild Side* was released early in 1962, the critics were not kind. 'It is incredible that anything so foolish would be made in this day and age,' wrote Bosley Crowther in *The New York Times*. 'Laurence Harvey is barely one-dimensional and Barbara Stanwyck is like something out of mothballs. Jane Fonda is elaborately saucy and shrill – a poor exposure for a highly touted talent.' After agreeing with Crowther that the movie bore little resemblance to the sizzling book on which it was based, the *New York Herald Tribune*'s Paul V. Beckley did say that 'Jane Fonda, as a bouncy, wiggly, bratty little thief and prostitute, seems more like a Nelson Algren character than anyone else in the picture.'

Jane was eager to remain in Hollywood and do another movie, but Logan was having difficulty finding her another project. Jane tried out for *Fanny*, and when she didn't get it (Logan gave the part to Leslie Caron) she asked to be let out of her contract. Logan informed Jane that producer Ray Stark had offered to buy her contract for $125,000, and that she could buy herself out for a price barely lower than that.

Jane was livid. 'All that baloney about being my godfather,' she said, 'that was just for publicity . . . He's just a friend of the family who was not enough of a friend to let me pay less money to get free.' It cost Jane $100,000 to buy out her contract with Logan, and the experience left a bitter aftertaste. When Hank read Jane's comments in the papers, he was enraged at what he perceived to be his daughter's lack of manners in publicly attacking a family friend.

No matter. The omnipresent Andreas Voutsinas notwithstanding, Jane was now a free agent. She weighed her options carefully. Convinced that she'd been on the right track with Kitty Twist, Jane turned down a chance to return to Broadway as a womanising airline pilot's virginal sister in Garson Kanin's fluffy comedy, *Sunday in New York*. Instead, she wanted to audition for *The Chapman Report*, yet another film based on a racy best-seller. Irving Wallace's novel about a Kinsey-type sex-research study was widely considered at the time to be too hot for adaptation to the screen, and the property bounced from Twentieth Century-Fox to Warner's before Darryl Zanuck and his son Richard were given authority to proceed.

The most compelling consideration was the fact that the legendary George Cukor had been hired to direct *The Chapman Report*. By then Cukor was long established in the Hollywood pantheon as the greatest of the 'women's directors', responsible for some of the finest screen performances of Greta Garbo, Jean Harlow, Katharine Hepburn, Bette Davis, Joan Crawford, Ingrid Bergman, Marilyn Monroe, Judy Garland, and Audrey Hepburn – to name but a few.

Ostensibly, *The Chapman Report* delved into the sex lives of four 'typical' women living in small-town America. It was instantly apparent to Jane that the part with the juiciest potential was that of an insatiable nymphomaniac. She showed up at Cukor's office to audition for the role in full streetwalker regalia, looking much the same as she had in *Walk on the Wild Side*. 'Cukor looked at me and laughed,' she recalls. '"You are going to play the frigid widow," he said. But if I'd gone in my frigid widow clothes and make-up, I don't think he'd have hired me.'

In reality, the director all along had had Jane, with her still unmistakable traces of a finishing-school upbringing, in mind for the role of the frigid widow who eventually falls for the sex researcher (Efrem Zimbalist, Jr). The wildly diverse likes of Shelley Winters, Glynis Johns, and Claire Bloom were handed the remaining three dysfunctions.

Jane was disappointed, but she also had to admit, 'it was George Cukor, and you can wait a lifetime to work with him, so I took the part.'

Through retake after retake, Cukor proved to be a tough taskmaster.

Towards the end of the filming, he invited Jane to his house and told her point-blank: 'I've let you do certain things now that if you did them three years from now, I'd knock your teeth in.' Jane could only feel honoured to be learning at the hand of the master; Cukor taught his actresses discipline, he 'protected' them with his 'impeccable taste and a sense of subtlety'.

Cukor's main criticism of Jane was that she tended to overact – that, as he more delicately put it, she had such an 'abundance' of talent, she'd best learn to 'hold it in'. Later, he recalled being 'extraordinarily impressed with this young lady. I always had a terrible prejudice against children of famous stars. It is not difficult to believe they get where they do simply because of parental influence. This was definitely not so with Jane Fonda.' She was, he proclaimed, 'an American original'.

The Chapman Report and its director were lambasted by the critics, and the Harvard Lampoon named Jane 'Worst Actress of the Year' for her performance. If nothing else, Jane was proving repeatedly that she could rise above her material.

In the autumn of 1961, Jane arrived back in New York with Andreas Voutsinas in tow. Much had changed in her absence. At last fed up with la dolce vita, Hank had moved out of his town house on East 74th Street and into a hotel until he could set Afdera up in her own Park Avenue apartment. Once he did, he returned to discover that she had cleared out not only her own belongings but also Jane's antique canopied four-poster. To do this, workmen had had to remove the two window casings, lower the bed three storeys to the street on ropes, then reinstall the windows. Livid, Fonda angrily demanded that Afdera return Jane's bed. She agreed, and the next day a stunned Hank Fonda stood outside his house and watched workers go through the whole laborious process in reverse: they tore the windows out again, used pulleys to lift the bed back up to the third floor, then replaced and resealed the windows.

Peter was overjoyed by Afdera's departure. 'She never had any use for me,' he says, 'and I had even less for her.' There were other reasons for celebration. Peter had been called back to audition once again for Stanley Poole, and this time he got the part. Jane and Hank were both in the audience when the play opened on 5 October 1961, to mediocre reviews. But, like his sister, Peter was hailed as a rising new star. 'Now,' he said, 'I can stand on my own two feet and dispense with anybody who comes up to me and says, "You are here because of who you are and not because of your talent."'

Jane was doubly thrilled with her brother's success. She was happy for him, and also relieved that now he would share the burden of being compared constantly to Dad.

Three days after the opening, Peter married Sarah Lawrence graduate Susan Brewer, stepdaughter of longtime Howard Hughes confidant Noah Dietrich.

The wedding, which took place at St Bartholomew's Episcopal Church on Park Avenue, was a virtual replay of the Fonda–Brokaw nuptials 24 years before. Peter had picked Stormy McDonald to be his best man, and the bride's family made sure the guest list glittered with plenty of social register names.

A long green canopy stretched to the kerb where, after the ceremony, limousines waited to whisk the wedding party to the reception at the Pierre. There, the bride and groom drank champagne in the same room where Frances Seymour Brokaw and Henry Fonda had danced to 'The Way You Look Tonight'. In less than a year, Peter had come into his share of his mother's estate, triumphed in his first professional role (on Broadway, no less), and married a beautiful, wealthy, intelligent girl. For Jane Fonda's little brother, it looked as if things couldn't get much better.

They didn't. Exactly one month after his opening, one of the worst fires in California's history swept through Bel Air and Brentwood. Hundreds of estates were destroyed, including Tigertail. Sophie Seymour's house was also razed, and the contents completely destroyed – including family photographs and the three letters which Frances had written to her children just before she killed herself.

After the close of *Stanley Poole*, Peter went out to the old Fonda homestead and found only three stone chimneys remaining. He offered to buy the scorched acreage (including the North Forty that he had set ablaze as a boy) from the current owner, but she held out for $1 million – twice what he could afford. Eventually, the property was sold to a developer and carved into eighteen building lots. By 1990, each of the houses that stood on those lots was worth more than $2 million.

That Christmas was not a cheerful one. For both Jane and Peter, Tigertail represented the happiest part of their childhood – the time before their mother's death. With her memories literally up in smoke, Jane turned even more to the Actors Studio, psychotherapy – and to Voutsinas.

Jane's singular devotion to Voutsinas enraged Henry Fonda. He viewed the Greek as a preening opportunist. 'Don't mention Andreas when you talk to my father,' she told friends. 'It will bring your conversation to an abrupt end.' By comparison, the unstable but harmless Timmy Everett didn't look so bad to Hank. But then, that Christmas, Everett showed up drunk at Jane's now elegantly decorated apartment to stake his claim. He wound up grabbing a kitchen knife and, in a jealousy frenzy, started slashing at his wrists. Jane wrapped a dish cloth around the wounds to stop the bleeding, then took Everett across town to Roosevelt Hospital. She waited for him in casualty, and when it was clear his self-inflicted injuries were not serious, returned home.

Everett and Jane bumped into each other at the Strasbergs' New Year's Eve party, but it was over between them. 'Afterwards, I mean for about three or four years,' said Everett, 'life was pretty rough for me. I drank pretty heavily and finally ended up with a nervous breakdown. I just couldn't get her out of my system . . .'

Few men could. 'Jane approached the opposite sex the way she approaches everything,' says a friend from that period. 'If she fell in love, it was an all-consuming thing. Somebody said she "swallowed you whole". She doesn't do anything halfheartedly.'

What troubled both father and daughter right now was a paucity of roles worthy of their commitment. After travelling to France for a cameo appearance in the World War II epic, *The Longest Day*, Hank was sent the script for *A Gift of Time*, a play written by Garson Kanin from a book by Lael Wertenbaker. The true story of a woman who helps her cancer-stricken husband, a *Time* magazine writer, kill himself, *A Gift of Time* co-starred two-time Academy Award winner Olivia de Havilland. 'It was a great play, first-rate,' Fonda told me years later. 'We got tremendous reviews, but I guess the audiences just weren't ready to sit through an evening of cancer and suicide. No question about it, the story was pretty harrowing. But it was also beautifully written. You know, this was the only play I'd ever been in where people were too upset to applaud at the end. They just sat there in stunned silence, then quietly left. It got to everybody, I think. Which is the whole point of doing a play, isn't it?' *A Gift of Time* closed after a few weeks – Henry Fonda's first stage failure in 35 years.

Frustrated, Fonda switched from MCA to CMA (Creative Management Associates) in early 1962 – only to have them pass on Edward Albee's *Who's Afraid of Virginia Woolf?* without even telling their client. Albee had written the play with Henry Fonda in mind, but Hank's new agents felt the 'no-balls character' was not for him.

Hank found some solace in the refreshing new turn his private life had taken. After weeks of cruising New York singles bars and a brief affair with a photographer's leggy assistant, he met and promptly fell in love with Shirlee Adams, an airline stewardess 25 years his junior. In the meantime, CMA tried to compensate for *Virginia Woolf* by landing him the lead in *Spencer's Mountain*. From Jackson Hole, Wyoming, Hank ran up a sizeable phone bill chatting long-distance with Shirlee. When the movie, a cloyingly wholesome family feature, was released, it cleaned up at the box office. For the first time in a long while, Hank felt he could afford to relax.

Conversely, Jane was gradually being overcome by panic – a word she would use often in the ensuing years to describe her state of mind – as she waited for her next job offer. Ironically, when the phone call finally came, it was from director George Roy Hill asking if Jane would be interested in his new MGM film version of Tennessee Williams's *Period of Adjustment*.

Back in California with Voutsinas, she headed straight for Tigertail. Like her brother, she was deeply upset by seeing the charred remains of what had once been their childhood refuge. After sifting through the ashes, literally and figuratively, Jane returned to her work. She was now ready to take another giant step towards becoming a full-blown sex symbol. As Jim Hutton's hysterical bride, Jane wore low-cut, hip-hugging dresses, Minnie Mouse eyelashes, and platinum blonde ringlets. This time, Jane felt comfortable with her part. 'In *Adjustment*,' she later said, 'I felt I finally got hold of my character and . . . well, I liked what I did.

'Somehow making movies gets to you,' she added. 'It's ego-battering – you're up one day and down the next – and it's much much tougher work for an actor, because with all the various things involved it's harder to create a performance. When I did *Adjustment*, I finally began to feel like an experienced film actress, and I decided movies were for me.'

The critics seemed to agree. 'Jane Fonda,' said Crowther in *The New York Times*, 'is appropriately shallow and jittery. Her vague emotions and wispy feelings seem no deeper than her goose pimples which are revealed in some strangely familiar acting. Could it be the late Marilyn Monroe that Miss Fonda seems to resemble? She surely won't mind our saying so.'

One reviewer, Stanley Kauffmann of *The New Republic*, saw in Jane the promise that Cukor recognised: 'A new talent is rising – Jane Fonda. Her light is hardly under a bushel, but as far as adequate appreciation is concerned, she might as well be another Sandra Dee. I have now seen Miss Fonda in three films. In all of them she gives performances that are not only fundamentally different from one another but are conceived without acting clichés, and executed with skill. Through them all can be heard, figuratively, the hum of magnetism without which acting intelligence and technique are admirable but uncompelling . . . Not conventionally pretty, she had the kind of blunt, startling features and generous mouth that can be charged with passion, or the cartoon of passion, as she chooses. Her slim, tall figure has thoroughbred gawky grace. Her voice is attractive and versatile. Her ear for inflections is secure. What lies ahead,' he pondered, 'for this gifted and appealing young actress?'

What, indeed?

8

JANE HAD not given up on Broadway. Voutsinas, eager to launch his career as a director, dug up a comedy called *The Fun Couple* and persuaded Jane that it was the stage vehicle they had both been waiting for. Before she could make another try for Broadway stardom, however, Jane had to pay off her debt to Josh Logan. To do so, she took the first film project that came her way.

In the Cool of the Day appealed to Jane on a number of counts. The money being offered by MGM was substantial; the film's producer was one of the most respected figures in show business, John Houseman; and, since much of the movie was to be shot on location in Greece, Jane and Voutsinas could treat it like a busman's holiday – their first vacation in three years.

No sooner had Jane signed the papers than Voutsinas was informed that, since he had never served in the Greek military, he would be drafted the minute he landed in Athens. Jane ordered her agents to get her out of the deal, but Houseman refused to budge. Legally bound to do the film, Jane finally admitted defeat and flew to Athens alone.

The story of a terminally ill woman who has one last fling vacationing in Greece, *In the Cool of the Day* was the kind of soap opera that only Susan Hayward could pull off. Peter Finch, more than a decade away from the role in *Network* that would earn him a posthumous Oscar, played Fonda's lover in the film, while Angela Lansbury was cast in the familiar role of a menacing harridan.

Her hair dyed brown and lopped off in a severe fringe, Jane looked bad and felt worse. She did not need Voutsinas around to tell her that Houseman and director Robert Stevens were floundering. Finch harboured the same misgivings. 'I did the damned film mostly for the money, also for the chance to work with Jane and go to Greece,' he said. 'I accepted too hastily, trusting in the good taste of Mr Houseman. Romantic soap operettas can sometimes be turned into good trash and please large segments of the public, but *In the Cool of the Day* wasn't even good trash.'

After a month in Greece, the cast flew to London for some final location shots. There, Jane rendezvoused with Voutsinas, who resumed his role as *éminence grise*. Word of Voutsinas's presence in London got back to Henry, who again voiced his displeasure at the relationship. Voutsinas was trying to manipulate his daughter, Hank said, and he was increasingly concerned that she was 'going to get hurt' in the process.

Voutsinas responded to Henry's undisguised hostility by playing the wounded victim. 'I can't be that much of a Svengali, I really can't,' he protested at the time. 'And I'm hurt, very hurt by Jane's father's rejection of me. And so is Jane.'

Although she could easily have ended this public squabbling with a few soothing words, Jane merely sat back and enjoyed the show. Annoying her father was the object of this particular game, and by playing Voutsinas off against Hank, she was able to accomplish that rather nicely.

As soon as she returned to New York, Jane was notified by Washington that the Pentagon had named her 'Miss Army Recruiting of 1962'. Draped in a red, white and blue ribbon emblazoned with her new title, Jane Fonda gave an impassioned acceptance speech to officers and enlisted recruiters, praising the armed forces and defending the need for a well-prepared military to discourage America's communist enemies.

At Voutsinas's urging, Jane turned her attention back to *The Fun Couple*. Blinded by loyalty, she endured rewrite after rewrite, rehearsal after rehearsal. The farce, co-authored by a novice playwright and a moonlighting dentist, involved newlyweds who fear adult responsibilities will turn them into tiresome bores. She could not bring herself to admit that neither the play nor its director was up to Broadway standards. *The Fun Couple* premiered on 26 October 1962, to catcalls from an opening night audience of backers and friends. After a thorough drubbing from the critics, it closed after three performances. Jane, it appeared, had trusted in Voutsinas once too often.

Right after *The Fun Couple* bombed, *In the Cool of the Day* hit cinema screens across the country. The Greek dreadnought quickly sank from sight, but not before being broadsided by the critics: 'Soap opera cliché – one part schmaltz, one part travelogue, and one part nothingness. Most of the characters seem to be sleepwalking.' 'The only interesting moments occur in a museum inhabited by classical nude statues.' Again, *The New Republic*'s Stanley Kauffmann leapt to his favourite young star's defence: 'If such matters were legally actionable, Jane Fonda would have grounds for suit . . . Originally I suppose it was Miss Fonda's fault for having accepted her role in this John Houseman production. Houseman's name is practically synonymous with compromised quality; a producer whose ambitious conscience does not let him rest until, in his commercial pictures, he has tampered with something or someone serious. One sees [Fonda] struggling intelligently to give life to the lumber, and one also sees her consistently defeated.'

None of which, to Jane's astonishment, seemed to matter at all to the powers in Hollywood. Within twenty months' time, five Jane Fonda films had been released – making her one of the most visible, talked-about, and sought-after commodities around. Despite the dismal fate of most of her films, she continued to be deluged with offers.

The one that stood out among them was the screen version of *Sunday in New York*, the Norman Krasna sex farce that Jane had turned down the year before. With newcomer Robert Redford and Pat Stanley in the starring roles, it had become a respectable hit on Broadway. Now that Rod Taylor, Cliff Robertson and Robert Culp were set to star in the movie, Jane felt secure in accepting the assignment. Its commercial success was almost assured. For once, she would play it safe.

Before she could start work on *Sunday in New York*, however, she was given a rare opportunity to show her gratitude to Lee Strasberg – and one final chance to prove to herself that she still had it in her to become a stage actress. Utilising the formidable talents of its leading members, the Actors Studio occasionally mounted a piece worthy of commercial production. Shortly before Christmas 1962, José Quintero asked Jane if she would read for the Actors Studio's limited-run revival of Eugene O'Neill's Pulitzer Prize-winning *Strange Interlude*.

The central character, Nina Leeds, was played by Geraldine Page, a profoundly gifted actress whose speciality was playing middle-aged women on the verge of a nervous breakdown. Rounding out the superb Actors Studio cast were one-time screen heart-throb Franchot Tone, veteran character actress Betty Field, Ben Gazzara, William Prince, Pat Hingle, Geoffrey Horne, and a promising actor, Richard Thomas, who would find fame more than a decade later as John Boy in television's 'The Waltons'.

The revival opened on 12 March 1963, to critical acclaim. Page, whose talent intimidated Jane, garnered the lion's share of the praise, though reviewers were careful not to neglect the other cast members. *The New York Times*'s Howard Taubman offered a single comment about Jane's performance – that she 'happily contributed her vivacity and beauty to the final two acts'.

Acting alongside Geraldine Page had proved to Jane that she would never be a great stage actress. In truth, she had never been comfortable in the company of the Actors Studio crowd, and with the flowering of her movie career she had come to feel even more like an outsider. It was a feeling she shared with Marilyn Monroe, who seemed actually more insecure than Jane in the rarefied Strasberg atmosphere. Once, Jane turned to Monroe and, with the classic stage repertoire in mind, said, 'Think of all the wonderful parts you can play when you're older.'

Monroe looked startled. 'No, no!' she said. '*You* play them!'

Like Marilyn Monroe, Jane felt an imposter in the realm of serious

75

dramaturgy. Here she was, turning down lucrative offers while other, clearly more deserving, actors waited on tables or scraped by in off-Broadway productions. Yet what she lacked in pure acting ability, she more than compensated for in sheer presence. Translated to the screen, that meant star quality. 'What I have is obvious,' she said to a reporter. 'It's like a commodity and it's in demand.' Artistic purity aside, it was time to take advantage of the demand for her commodity.

If anything, *Sunday in New York* demanded that Jane be *less* of an actress than she was. Playing the virginal sister of a libidinous New York-based airline pilot (Cliff Robertson), Jane gets involved with a guileless journalist played by Rod Taylor. In the role of Eileen Tyler, Jane, pouty-lipped and crowned with a red-blonde bouffant, was required to react with wide-eyed innocence as naughty innuendo was heaped upon naughty innuendo. She managed to accomplish this without being cloying, and as a result *Sunday in New York* turned out to be one of the more brightly risqué screen comedies of the early 1960s.

That June, both Hank and Peter were working just a few blocks away – Dad in *Fail Safe* and brother in *Lilith* – so there was time for all the acting Fondas to converge on the set of Jane's picture for a family reunion of sorts arranged by their respective publicity departments.

It would not be a happy meeting. The photos show Henry, Jane, and Peter gamely clutching their bound scripts so the titles of their projects are clearly visible to the cameras. Their faces are etched with tension; the Fondas are definitely not having a good time. And indeed, soon afterwards Jane was telling reporters that her unhappy childhood had sent her into therapy. She suggested that the man responsible could himself have benefited from professional help. 'Daddy,' said Jane, 'should have been analysed forty years ago. Any man who is fifty-seven years old and has gone through four wives must be very unhappy.'

Hank did not respond at first, but her public attack upset him deeply when he read it in the press. As he later told a writer, 'I'm between planes somewhere, and a reporter has a clipping that says Jane Fonda thinks her parents led a phoney life. Or she thinks her father should have been psychoanalysed thirty-five years ago. Now it's all right for her to think it, but I don't think it's all right for her to say so in interviews. After all, I *am* her father, I mean, that's disrespectful. And some of the things she's been saying – well, they're just not true.'

Jane had also taken some pot shots at Peter. 'It was a time when we weren't very close,' she said. 'Peter had very short hair and insisted on getting married in a big church ceremony. I didn't understand his life and he didn't understand my friends.'

For his part, Peter conceded that he had been seeking his father's approval, and that he figured the best way to get it was to lead a solid, social-register life-style. 'I was registered Republican,' he recalled. 'Very conservative. I was trying to grab all the straight paraphernalia – the country club, fur coat for the wife, nice cars, have a silver pattern registered at Tiffany's.' Dad remained as distant as ever. 'I dig my father,' Peter insisted. 'I wish he could open his eyes and dig me.'

While their father's acting ability was never in question, brother and sister could not resist continuing to lob insults at each other. 'I could bite my tongue sometimes,' Jane said coyly. 'Peter is a performer of great charm, but he's not an actor yet.' Replied Peter: 'Jane was simply great, in that bomb [*Walk on the Wild Side*].'

Apart from the exterior shots filmed on location in Manhattan, most of *Sunday in New York* was shot on an MGM soundstage in Hollywood. Knowing what this movie could mean to her career after her string of turkeys, Jane couldn't have been more eager to please, more of a trouper. There was one scene, for example, in which the phone rings while Jane is dressing upstairs. She has to dash down a circular staircase, then fifty feet across the living room set before picking up the phone – all while trying to button her jacket. It turns out to be an urgent call for her brother (Cliff Robertson), who has just left, so she runs to the window to call down to him. In the process, she gets tangled in the phone cord. The whole scene was to last less than a minute on screen, but it would take four hours and ten takes for director Peter Tewksbury to be satisfied.

'I've just discovered something,' she said to the director, panting between takes. 'If a girl wants to stay in this business, she'd better stay healthy. Tomorrow I join the Y!' Would she do it just one more time, Tewksbury asked. 'I'm game,' she replied, 'as long as I hold out.' Jane cheerfully did the scene once again, but this time she tripped on the cord and fell flat on her face. It was not in the script, but cast and crew roared with laughter. 'Print it!' yelled a delighted Tewksbury.

If Jane delighted the cast and crew, the same could not be said for her ubiquitous mentor. Tewksbury resented Voutsinas's presence on the set, and several times the director ordered him to leave. Voutsinas would huffily retreat to Jane's dressing room and wait for her return.

Perhaps as part of an effort to save face and re-establish his authority over Jane, Voutsinas assumed even more control over her life after the filming of *Sunday in New York* – thereby justifying Henry Fonda's longlasting enmity. Jane was stricken with a bad case of flu, and, hearing that his daughter was sick in bed and unable to eat, Hank called her. Voutsinas refused to let him speak to his daughter. Hank then cooked up a homemade soup and carried it to Jane's apartment. 'That son-of-a-bitch answered my knock,' recalled

Fonda, 'snatched the package out of my hands, and said, "Oh . . . thank you very much," and closed the door in my face. He wouldn't even let me see my daughter . . .'

But it wasn't just Voutsinas. As she'd indicated all too clearly in her remarks following the publicly staged Fonda 'family reunion', Jane had come to resent what she saw as her father's interference in her life. At one point during this time, actress Shelley Winters invited both Jane and Henry to a party in New York. 'But shortly before the party my phone rang and it was Jane,' recalls Winters in her book, *Shelley II*.

'Do you consider yourself a good friend of mine, Shelley?' Jane asked.

'Of course.'

'If you are a good friend of mine, you'll uninvite my father.'

'I'll think about it,' Shelley answered, and hung up. 'In those days,' Winters writes, 'Jane would love her father intensely for some months, then hate him for other months.' She decided to go along with Jane's request. Once Henry answered the phone, all Winters managed to utter was 'Do you mind if . . .' before he broke in.

'I understand, Shelley,' said Henry. 'Jane doesn't want to be in the same room with me. It's okay. I understand.'

Winters goes on: 'He sounded as though he was weeping. It was one of the most heartbreaking feuds I ever witnessed.'

After playing a teenage sexpot in *Walk on the Wild Side*, a frustrated bride in *Period of Adjustment*, and a frigid widow in *The Chapman Report*, Jane could not deny that her film roles had one thing in common – lots of sex. 'So I guess sex is here to stay,' she told a reporter at the time. 'But the overemphasis on it *is* pretty silly. In *Sunday in New York* the girl I play is an absolute bore. She talks so much about her virginity; and you know the more she talks about it, the more you know it's on her mind. I mean, for God's sake, let her make up her mind one way or the other – and stop all that talking.'

When asked by the reporter if this meant she endorsed promiscuity, Jane was taken aback. 'Who said anything about being promiscuous? A man will marry a girl if he loves her. The sex incident has nothing to do with it. Sex is part of love; but love is a lot more than sex.'

If not a blockbuster, *Sunday in New York* turned out to be Jane's first money-making film. While the movie received lukewarm reviews, the critics were again won over by Jane's charms. *Time* called the film a 'glossy, glittering package of pseudo-sex that scores on style. Jane, in a plain blue wrapper, looks so honey-hued and healthy that her most smouldering invitation somehow suggests that all she really has in mind is tennis.' Another reviewer, echoing her own analysis of her role, dubbed her 'a consummate tease. Her roles insinuate sex but yield only a knowing wink; now that she has mastered this role, perhaps it is time for her to move on to more challenging stuff. Unlike most of her co-stars, she has the raw material to develop, if she's willing to give it a try.'

Whether or not it was sufficiently satisfying to be reminded yet again of her potential, her 'raw material', Jane must have been aware that the vehicles she and Voutsinas had chosen were themselves too limited to challenge her development as an actress. Though *Sunday in New York* was a hit, she was still playing the shallow ingenue of most of her other films. Perhaps that was, for now, not only safe but fulfilling – especially when the critics continued to point out that Henry Fonda's charming daughter lacked depth. It would be several years, and a good many more films, before Jane would dare to 'move on to more challenging stuff' – not just beyond Voutsinas's influence, but beyond that of the next father figure cum lover in her life.

9

SHE HAD left five years earlier as a self-perceived failure and disappointment to her father. But when Jane Fonda returned to Paris in September 1963, her arrival was greeted with all the hype and hoopla reserved for long-established movie stars. Cameras whirred, flashbulbs popped, and reporters pressed in with their microphones to ask 'just one more' question. This time determined to speak only French, Jane had brought a linguist to help her over the rough spots, and she promptly captivated her hosts with her generally correct but not quite conversational French. Voutsinas was also along, but clearly Jane's triumphal re-entry into France was casting him as little more than a spear carrier.

Jane had been dispatched to Paris by MGM to star in a film by the celebrated French director René Clément. France's 'New Wave' filmmakers, led by such *auteur* directors as François Truffaut and Clément, had begun to influence young international theatregoers to regard 'the cinema' as a true art form. Characterised by murky black-and-white cinematography, nudity, explicit dialogue, and existential themes, these art films (no longer just 'movies') bridged the gap between coffeehouse bohemianism and the coming counterculture. In *Joy House* – also at different times called *The Love Cage* and *Neither Saints nor Saviors* – MGM hoped to cash in on this latest trend in cinematic tastes.

Fonda's *Joy House* co-star was Alain Delon, the French matinée idol whose sleek looks and mysterious ties to the underworld made him perfect copy for the French tabloids. Even before shooting began, Jane got things going. 'I will undoubtedly fall in love with Alain Delon,' she declared. 'I can only play love scenes well when I am in love with my partner.' No idle prediction. Within weeks of her arrival, Jane had broken up Delon's longstanding affair with actress Romy Schneider.

In this new setting, a different, even more outrageous Jane emerged – much to the delight of MGM publicists. Back to blonde, Jane wore her lush hair cascading over her shoulders. Still bingeing and purging to keep her weight down to a svelte 7 stone 12 lbs, everything about her nevertheless seemed generous – from her pouty Fonda lips to her well-rounded, often bikini-clad figure. Likening her to France's sexual icon of the 1950s, Brigitte Bardot, the press started calling her *la BB Américaine*. She landed on the cover of *Cahiers du Cinéma*, France's prestigious film magazine, and one of the country's leading pop singers recorded a song comparing her to a gazelle, while a popular journalist compared her to a 'caged animal. I watched her move and thought in a flash of the black panther I used to watch in the zoo.'

For all the publicity, Jane had been cast in another turkey – and she knew it. In *Joy House*, Delon plays the character of a petty crook hiding out from the mob. He seeks refuge in a soup kitchen run by Lola Albright and her cousin, played by Jane. It turns out Albright is a wealthy eccentric, and soon she moves Delon into the Gothic mansion she shares with Jane. There is plenty of bed-hopping, although Delon is somewhat distracted by the shrunken human head Albright keeps in a jar. Rounding out the cast is Albright's insane lover, who roams about in the mansion's labyrinth of secret passageways, popping up periodically to menace the trio.

Solely on the basis of the tremendous publicity generated by the Fonda–Delon affair, *Joy House* was moderately successful on its home ground. In America, audiences and critics alike were left speechless. Even Fonda's most ardent defender, Stanley Kauffmann of *The New Republic*, seriously questioned whether she would ever overcome her taste in material: 'The question of Jane Fonda's development into an extraordinarily good actress, which I still think quite possible, is beclouded by her poor choice of vehicles. Her latest film is absurd . . . No summary of the silly plot is needed.' But the last laugh was left to Judith Crist. 'Miss Fonda has some mysterious hold over Miss Albright,' Crist wrote in the *New York Herald Tribune*. 'It's not all Miss Fonda has – or at least so she attempts to indicate by alternately impersonating the Madwoman of Chaillot, Baby Doll, and her father, Henry; she's a sick kid, this one.' Crist would later put *Joy House* on her list of the ten worst films of the year.

'There was no script and very little organisation,' Jane would offer in her own defence. 'It sort of threw me because I'm used to working within a structured framework. There was just too much playing it by ear for my taste. But Clément is still a wonderful director.'

France soon had more on its mind than the progress of Jane Fonda's film career. The French had become particularly enamoured of America's handsome, urbane young president and his stylish wife, and when John F. Kennedy was assassinated on 22 November 1963, Parisians wept in the streets. Whether Camelot existed or was a carefully orchestrated deception hardly mattered. For anyone old enough to comprehend the news, that moment would be frozen in time.

For the young all over the free world to whom Kennedy had seemed half messiah and half movie star, his death would usher in a decade of violence, sociopolitical upheaval, and cultural change. Vietnam, the anti-war movement, campus unrest, the assassinations of Robert Kennedy and Martin Luther King, riots, the Democratic Convention in Chicago, the Black Panthers, LBJ and Richard Nixon, hippies, yippies, free sex, Woodstock, Altamont, acid heads and acid rock, the Manson Family – these are the clashing images of the turbulent 1960s and early 1970s. Few people would be as closely identified with this age of discontent and institution-smashing rebellion as Jane Fonda.

Yet that eventual incarnation, if predicted in 1963, would have been laughed away. For the moment, *la BB Américaine*, whose grasp of current events was virtually nonexistent, remained devoutly apolitical. She felt fully appreciated in France, and, sensing that she could forge a new reputation for herself, embraced the French as they had embraced her. 'Perhaps,' she told a friend, 'I'll be able to discover a real identity in France. Everyone told me that I was crazy, that I was ruining my career. Nobody's ever heard of an American actress making a name for herself by taking off for Europe . . . We'll see.'

Jane continued her fling with Delon – they were photographed towelling each other down on a boat on the Côte d'Azur – though those who knew them thought the languid playboy and the highstrung American thoroughbred were ill matched. 'He was a classic pretty boy,' says an acquaintance from that period. 'Women thought he was beautiful, and he knew it. Delon didn't have an inquisitive mind. He wasn't a questioning sort of person, and he certainly didn't give a damn about the psyche. These were, of course, the very things that Jane thrived on. I can see the sexual attraction between them, but in the end they really didn't have that much to talk about.'

There would be no public denials, but to close friends Jane played coy. 'How can you prove that you've never been to bed with a man who has been holding you half naked in his arms on the set in front of sixty people? Alain is an extremely seductive man, and he's good to work with, but I just can't communicate with him.'

Whether or not the stars could communicate verbally, their body language was apparently explicit enough to send Voutsinas flying back to New York in a huff. Jane – praised daily in the French press as a 'revelation', 'a cyclone of femininity', 'the perfect American' – no longer required a mentor. Or at least so she thought.

Enter Roger Vladimir Plemiannikov, better known as Roger Vadim. Born in 1928, Vadim was the son of a White Russian émigré and a native-born Frenchwoman. When Vadim was nine, his father, who had become a French consul, died of a sudden heart attack at the age of 34. Young Roger's new stepfather, an urban planner and collaborator of Le Corbusier, was ten years younger than Vadim's mother and became a major influence on his life.

Vadim had hoped to follow in his father's footsteps as a diplomat, until the Nazi occupation forced a change of plans. After the war, Vadim tried

Henry Fonda and Margaret Sullavan in
1935. UPI/BETTMANN NEWSPHOTO

Frances Brokaw and Henry arrive from
Europe aboard the SS *Bremen*, 1936. They
were married twelve days later. ACME

Jane Fonda at eighteen months.
SPRINGER/BETTMAN FILM ARCHIVE

Henry Fonda with Peter and Jane,
1940. SPRINGER/BETTMANN FILM
ARCHIVE

Jane and Dad play leapfrog, 1945. SPRINGER/BETTMAN FILM ARCHIVE

The Fondas at Tigertail, 1947.
(*From left*): Frances, Peter, Pan, Jane,
and Henry. SPRINGER/BETTMAN FILM
ARCHIVE

Henry and family about to leave for
Rome and the set of *War and Peace*,
1955. Third wife Susan (holding
adopted daughter, Amy) left him a
month later. UPI/BETTMANN
NEWSPHOTO

The publicists' tense 'reunion' of
Fondas, all happening to be in New York
to film different movies. SPRINGER/
BETTMANN FILM ARCHIVE

Jane made her screen debut opposite
Tony Perkins in the 1960 comedy
Tall Story. MOVIE STAR NEWS

With Ruth Matteson, Jane impressed
Broadway critics playing a rape victim in 1960's
There Was a Little Girl. MOVIE STAR NEWS

A steamy Jane with Laurence Harvey in *Walk on the Wild Side*, 1962. MOVIE STAR NEWS

Before her own war with *Playboy*, Jane scans a copy as Rod Taylor looks on, in *Sunday in New York*, 1964. MOVIE STAR NEWS

The evening of Jane and Roger Vadim's wedding: Jane admires her ring at the Dunes Hotel in Las Vegas.
UPI/BETTMANN NEWSPHOTO

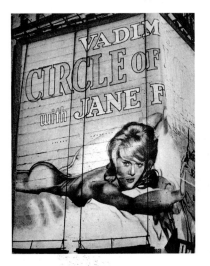 

The scandalous *Circle of Love* hoarding, before and after the cover-up. PICTORIAL PARADE

Jane faces the hangman's noose in *Cat Ballou*, 1965.

Jane teamed with Robert
Redford for the hit film
version of Neil Simon's *Barefoot
in the Park*.

With John Phillip Law in
Barbarella. MOVIE STAR NEWS

Mr and Mrs Roger Vadim
attend the 1967 Venice Film
Festival. UPI/BETTMAN NEWSPHOTO

Fonda's 1968 poster, an international
best-seller. GLOBE PHOTOS

They Shoot Horses, Don't They?
A turning point for Jane. MOVIE STAR NEWS

acting, but he soon realised that he was better suited for work behind the camera. It was while working as an assistant director that he spotted a picture of a striking, voluptuous brunette in the fashion magazine *Elle*. He saw great possibilities in the fifteen-year-old girl, and by way of moulding her talent, talked her parents into letting him move in with them. Vadim waited until she came of age, then married the girl. Her name was Brigitte Bardot.

In the mid-1950s Bardot, now a blonde sexpot, appeared in sixteen films. Yet, despite Vadim's skilful manipulation of the press, real stardom eluded her. Vadim decided to take matters into his own hands, and directed her in the steamy *And God Created Woman*. Overnight, the movie made Brigitte Bardot a global phenomenon and Vadim one of the most sought-after directors in Europe.

It also destroyed their marriage. Vadim was so intent on having his wife give a convincing performance of a woman in love that he directed her right into the bed of co-star Jean-Louis Trintignant. From Trintignant, BB, still married to Vadim, moved on to a number of other men, including actor Jacques Charrier and singer-guitarist Sacha Distel. An outspoken champion of the New Morality, Vadim, it appeared to many, had been hoist with his own petard.

'I did not invent Brigitte Bardot,' Vadim later wrote. 'I simply helped her to blossom.' He wasted no time finding another garden to tend. The day after his divorce from Bardot became final, Danish model Annette Stroyberg gave birth to Vadim's daughter Nathalie. Bardot, who had actually developed a sisterly affection for Annette, asked to be Nathalie's godmother.

Nathalie was seven months old when her parents got around to marrying in June 1958. Annette, now billed as Annette Vadim, starred *sans* wardrobe in *Les Liaisons Dangereuses*. The film was banned for two years, and Vadim was forced to hire a lawyer to pry the film out of the censors' hands. The lawyer's name: François Mitterrand.

Again, Trintignant had been cast by Vadim as his leading lady's love interest. Annette would become involved not with Trintignant but with another old rival of Vadim's. When the director discovered that his wife was conducting a clandestine affair with Sacha Distel, just as Bardot had done, Vadim filed for divorce. Cuckolded twice by the same man, Vadim convinced a sympathetic French judge to give him custody of three-year-old Nathalie.

Vadim quickly replaced Stroyberg with another beauty: Catherine Deneuve, eighteen-year-old younger sister of French film star Françoise Dorléac. As with Brigitte, he went about transforming the wide-eyed brunette into a blonde *femme fatale*. Pressured by Deneuve's mother to marry, they signed a prenuptial contract and planned a wedding in Tahiti. But then, days before the scheduled ceremony, Stroyberg threatened to fight Vadim for custody of Nathalie if he went ahead and married Deneuve. The marriage was cancelled, but Deneuve nevertheless gave birth out of wedlock to Vadim's son, Christian, in 1962.

Soon afterwards, the relationship, which had always been punctuated by fierce quarrelling, soured for good. Deneuve left, and went on to achieve stardom on her own terms in such films as *The Umbrellas of Cherbourg*, *Belle de Jour* and *Repulsion* (and to conceive another child, this time with actor Marcello Mastroianni).

Vadim's credentials as a connoisseur of the world's most desirable women seemed impeccable. Precisely what they saw in him was less easy to define. In looks, Vadim could hardly be considered competitive with his lovers' co-stars. Tall, bony, and hunched, he had a narrow face, a large nose, a weak chin, and a mouthful of oversized teeth that combined to give him a somewhat equine appearance. Yet he was disarmingly soft-spoken, unfailingly courteous, and, when it came to women, unswervingly attentive. These qualities, coupled with a reputed sexual expertise, apparently made him irresistible to young women in search of a mentor cum father figure cum lover – the basic profile of all his conquests.

Vadim had long had his eye on Jane Fonda. Three years after their initial note-passing encounter at Maxim's, and two years before her return to Paris, Vadim arranged to meet Fonda in the coffee shop of the Beverly Hills Hotel while he was in town for the belated première of *Les Liaisons Dangereuses*. Jane's agent had suggested that she come in her most alluring get-up to impress France's hottest director. Instead, she wore scruffy jeans, a man's shirt, and no make-up.

'My reputation irritated her,' he says. 'However, if she had hoped to shock me by dressing like that, she didn't succeed. On the contrary, it was her natural look that attracted me.'

'I went,' recalled Jane, 'but I was terrified. Like I thought he was going to rape me right there in the Polo Lounge. But he was terribly quiet and polite. I thought, Boy, what a clever act.' Nothing came of that meeting, but in 1963, while Jane was wrapping up *Sunday in New York*, a producer offered her a part in a movie that was to be directed by Vadim. Her agent fired off the following telegram: JANE FONDA IS NOT INTERESTED IN A COSTUME DRAMA. SHE ALSO ASKS ME TO TELL YOU THAT SHE WILL NEVER MAKE A FILM WITH ROGER VADIM.

Jane was midway through shooting *Joy House* and already the toast of France when Vadim was invited by a mutual friend to a small surprise birthday party for Jane. This time, she was surprised to find herself quite attracted to the lanky ladies' man who, she could not fail to notice, behaved with the sort of quiet diffidence that made her father so irresistible to women.

They met again at a New Year's Eve costume party – he dressed as an officer in the Soviet Red Army, she as Charlie Chaplin. Vadim seized the opportunity to give Jane a passionate New Year's Eve kiss. A week passed, and Vadim paid a visit to the Epinay studio where *Joy House* was being shot, ostensibly to have a drink with longtime friend Jean André, the movie's set designer. Jane heard that Vadim was across the car park in the studio's cocktail bar and, when her day's work on the set was done, dashed through the driving rain to meet him. She was still wearing her costume from the last scene – an all but transparent negligée.

That afternoon, back at her hotel, Jane and Vadim tumbled into bed. To his horror, France's Great Seducer could not perform. 'I was blocked, humiliated,' said Vadim, 'and reduced to total impotence.' Vadim later blamed this unfortunate circumstance on Jane's aggressive sexual behaviour. Later, she admitted to Vadim that she had been 'violently attracted' to him, and wanted to 'get rid of her obsession by making love'.

Vadim's impotence had the opposite effect. For three weeks, he repeatedly tried and failed to make love to Jane. 'Any man in his right mind,' said Vadim, 'would have put a bullet through his head or given up exposing himself to such ridicule after a few days.' But to Jane, who had intended to forget Vadim after one torrid night, this famed sexual athlete seemed suddenly sweet and vulnerable. When they finally did consummate the relationship, they stayed in bed for 48 hours straight – 'to make up for lost time'. It was only then that Vadim, at Jane's invitation, moved into her hotel room.

As he had with all his women before her, Vadim set about redesigning Fonda to his specifications. He talked her into doing a remake of *La Ronde*, the sex farce that had made stars of Simone Signoret and Danielle Darrieux a decade earlier. Fonda had clearly forgotten about the telegram in which she had vowed never to work with Vadim.

With the filming of *Joy House* completed and MGM no longer footing Jane's hotel expenses, she and Vadim took an apartment at 12 rue de Séguier, near Place Saint-Michel on the Left Bank. A loft bed big enough to accommodate half a dozen people looked down on the cavernous, beamed living room, the dominant feature of which was an enormous hearth. While he wrestled with preproduction problems on *La Ronde*, she took French lessons, tried to catch up on the classics (having long admitted to being not very well read), and haunted museums.

Fonda went straight from *Joy House* to *La Ronde* (retitled *Circle of Love* for English-speaking audiences). To the cast and crew of *La Ronde*, there was no question but that something more than a director–actor dynamic was at work here. But Vadim, who had spent half his life leaking the juiciest details of his personal life to the press, conducted his latest affair with discretion. Jane was, after all, already famous. And though she had frequently shown a desire to shock, it had always been on her own terms. Vadim did not want to overstep his authority and risk endangering their relationship.

Even after Vadim moved in with Jane at the hotel, she resisted the idea of anything permanent. 'I began making the film,' she says, 'and I fell in love with him. I was terrified. I thought, My God, he's going to roll over me like a bulldozer . . . I'll be destroyed. My heart will be cut out, but I've got to do it. And I discovered a very gentle man. So many men in America are *men*-men, always having to prove their strength and masculinity. Vadim was not afraid to be vulnerable − even feminine, in a way. And I was terrified of being vulnerable.'

As no one knew better than Vadim. According to him, she 'always thought that to be happy you must build walls to protect yourself from unhappiness'. In Jane's case, the walls were 'a fortress! The Great Wall of China!'

Those walls had already begun to crumble when, without warning, Jane announced that she was leaving to meet a producer in Geneva and would be gone for two days. As Vadim tells it, he confronted Jane on her return and she admitted that the 'producer' she had met was another lover. Still dealing with unresolved emotions, Jane had slept with him in Geneva just the night before − one last time to 'see what I really felt'. And what had she decided? She told Vadim that she loved him.

As for Vadim's capacity for fidelity, he made it clear to Jane from the outset that he was incapable of making love to one woman all his life. 'If I have a sex adventure,' he told her, 'I will not lie to you. But one thing I promise you − it will not be important. I could not have a mistress. Also I will not behave in public in such a way as to embarrass you, because it will not be an *elegance* to you.'

At 35, Vadim was viewed by many as a sexual Machiavelli, a shrewd manipulator of women and the media. Although Jane was a decade younger − the age difference he preferred − she was more than a match for him. Vadim's predecessor, Voutsinas, had served Jane's purposes well. By forcing her to confront her demons through her psyche, he had unlocked her potential as an actress. That Henry Fonda all along despised Voutsinas served only as a bonus for Jane, who seemed to revel in ruffling her father's feathers. If she could not have her father's unconditional love, then at least she made sure she had his attention.

After arriving in Paris, she had begun to have serious doubts about Voutsinas and his influence on her acting. By overanalysing everything she thought, said, and did, Jane was suffocating emotionally. Once she had dispensed with him, she turned to Vadim as the perfect antidote. He wanted her to be freer, more spontaneous in her acting − and in her life. Before that could be accomplished, however, he had to overcome her feelings of inadequacy.

It was to be a daunting task. Jane would not easily be convinced of her talent. 'I will be a character actress,' she told Vadim. 'A very good one. But only a character actress.' Vadim would later point out that this seemingly unshakeable lack of self-esteem was 'her greatest weakness'.

She was even more insecure about her looks − a self-consciousness she would never entirely overcome. During the sexually charged bedroom scenes in *Circle of Love*, Vadim tried to coax Jane into appearing nude. She refused. 'I was supposed to be nude in bed, but I wore a bra and panties,' she later said. 'My gosh, there were ninety-five people on the set and I'd have been embarrassed to prance around in the altogether! I have never done and never will do a completely nude scene.'

Ironically, when the film was about to open at New York's DeMille Theater six months later, an eight-storey-high painted hoarding on Times Square showed a tousle-haired Fonda sprawled on rumpled bedsheets, her ten-foot-by-ten-foot pink backside exposed to the world. There was a public outcry, but no one was more outraged than Jane. She promptly filed a $3 million lawsuit against the DeMille Theater's owner, Walter Reade, Jr, and the theatre obliged by draping Jane's posterior with a huge canvas tarpaulin – thus hyping the poster and the film even more. 'It's more ridiculous than ever with that Band-Aid,' Jane responded. Finally Reade, confident of having fully exploited the hoarding, took it down. Jane, whose main objection all along was that the hoarding misleadingly promised nudity that was not in the film, dropped her legal action.

As soon as they finished *Circle of Love*, Jane persuaded Vadim to make a long-delayed pilgrimage to his father's birthplace in Russia. A friend of the USSR's ambassador to France, Vadim pulled strings to get visas for himself and Jane.

After their Aeroflot Ilyushin touched down in Moscow, Jane was surprised to find the Russian people much the same as people anywhere else. 'I couldn't believe it,' she said later. 'All my life I'd been brought up to believe the Russians were some alien, hostile people sitting over there just waiting to swallow up America. Nothing could be further from the truth.' Claiming to have had her 'eyes opened' to American 'propaganda,' she urged that 'every American should go to Russia to see for himself'.

What she had failed to appreciate was the fact that she had been given very special treatment even during that first visit to the Soviet Union, simply because she was the daughter of the great Henry Fonda. John Steinbeck's bleak depictions of America's Depression underclass had helped to make him one of Russia's favourite American authors; in turn, Henry Fonda, who had breathed life into the character of Tom Joad in *The Grapes of Wrath*, was the best-loved American actor in Russia. Henry's daughter had been greeted with open arms wherever she went, at a time when most visitors to the Soviet Union, especially Americans, were confined to bleak government hotels, their movements severely restricted.

Strangely, in blasting US anti-Soviet propaganda, she neglected to mention her first unnerving night in Moscow. Shortly before midnight on the eve of the annual May Day parade, she cowered in bed on the third floor of

Moscow's National Hotel while scores of tanks and intercontinental ballistic missiles on flatbed trucks thundered into position for the next day's festivities.

'It was,' recalled Vadim, 'the first time and the last time I ever saw her so vulnerable.' The next day the couple viewed the procession of Soviet military might from their hotel. Directly opposite them, atop Lenin's Tomb, Nikita Khrushchev reviewed the parade. Within two years, Khrushchev would be ousted and replaced by the man standing at his side, Leonid Brezhnev.

From Moscow, Fonda and Vadim travelled by train to Leningrad, where it had been arranged for them to get a rare glimpse of the imperial jewels stored in the basement of the czars' Winter Palace. Vadim wound up viewing the magnificent collection alone; Jane, after helping Vadim polish off a considerable quantity of vodka, had passed out cold in their hotel room and could not be woken.

Totally apolitical before her visit to Russia, Jane had all but slept through the civil rights movement, the Cuban missile crisis, the assassination of John Kennedy, and America's growing involvement in Vietnam. Whenever her French friends, having seen their country torn by the Indochina and Algerian conflicts, criticised the United States as an imperialist aggressor, Jane would defend America as best she could. She would point out to Vadim that, unlike the French, the Americans were not protecting colonial interests in Vietnam but aiding a country in its fight against a communist invader. Her arguments fell on deaf ears; Vadim's côterie, including many socialists and communists, were not about to cast the United States as anything but the villain on the world stage.

Jane Fonda's real political awakening was still four years away; yet this first trip to Moscow unquestionably helped lay the groundwork for a personal political philosophy based on distrust of the US government. Admittedly unschooled in important areas, she was dismayed to find that the Soviets knew more about American literature and history than she did. Apparently not sophisticated enough to draw a distinction between the professed Soviet system and its realities, she failed to consider the possibility that political oppression might be concealed from an important foreign visitor's officially sanctioned experience. So the seeds of doubt were planted. If our government could lie to us about the Soviet Union, she began to wonder, why should we believe anything else they told us?

The trip did not sit well with her father, already irked by the publicity at home surrounding Jane's very public affair with the profligate Vadim. When a reporter cornered Hank and asked him what he thought of his daughter's antics, he replied, 'Daughter? I don't have a daughter.'

Tiring eventually of Russian austerity, Jane and Vadim became eager to return to the more self-indulgent delights of France. With six-year-old Nathalie and two-year-old Christian in tow, they headed for the Riviera. But while reporters frantically searched for them in glittering St Tropez, Jane and her adopted family stationed themselves in a no-frills hotel at Clauoey, a tiny, out-of-the-way village on the Bay of Arcachon. There were few amenities – no room service, only one bathroom per floor, no phone, and obviously no television. But there were also no prying journalists, and after a day or two of complaining to Vadim about Clauoey's lack of luxury, Jane grew to love their hideaway on the beach.

The stay at Clauoey reminded Jane of how much she missed her childhood at Tigertail and the unfettered ways of country life. When they returned from the seashore in August, she went house-hunting in the provinces and settled on a 130-year-old, three-acre farm 38 miles west of Paris in the picturesque hamlet of St-Ouen-Marchefroid. Featuring tumbledown stone walls and a roof badly in need of retiling, the place dripped with charm. Just as important, the farm's need for renovation presented a sufficiently formidable challenge for Jane. Without a new film to occupy her and having inherited to a substantial degree both her father's Puritan work ethic and her mother's obsession for detail, Jane required a new cause, a challenging project.

The ramshackle French house offered just such a project. Like a general marshalling her forces, Jane enlisted a small army of masons, carpenters, electricians, plumbers, and painters to gut the house, then modernise the interior. 'Try telling ten French workers,' she complained, 'in your French, how to modernise a place and yet keep its original beauty.' Outdoors, she decided she did not like the natural, flat terrain and brought in a bulldozer to give the land 'a more rolling effect. And I had dozens of full-grown trees brought out from Paris and planted. It was wild – every morning you could see these lines of trees advancing up the road like Birnam Wood coming to Dunsinane.' Over the next several years, Jane's fondness for landscaping became an expensive preoccupation, as more and more pine, beech, and birch trees were trucked in and planted right next to the forest trees that grew naturally on the edge of their property.

Landscaping was not Jane's only obsession at St-Ouen-Marchefroid. By the time Jane was finished, the farm boasted a stable, henhouse, greenhouse, guest wing, badminton court, playground, indoor swimming pool – even screening and editing rooms. Vadim's contribution was something surreal: after trying unsuccessfully to get a vintage 1937 Panhard Levasseur limousine to run, he sliced the car in half and welded it around a tree in their garden.

For all the undeniable charm of their little country home, this marked Vadim's first disturbing sight of Jane's capacity for almost robotic efficiency. A compulsive list-maker, she dashed down dozens of tasks to be accomplished each day and – unlike most people – would not retire to bed until she had done them all. With an Italian family of four hired to help take care of Nathalie (Christian remained with his mother) and the household chores, Jane was free to boss the workmen, occasionally whip up a simple meal, and, sitting cross-legged on the floor, play charming hostess to Vadim's bohemian friends. The way she hurled herself into their new domestic life, always with such compulsive zeal, bothered Vadim.

When they returned to Paris from the countryside that October, there was another screenplay waiting for Jane. She viewed the movie Columbia wanted her to do, based on a novel by Roy Chanslor, as a straightforward western. Determined not to do costume pictures, and sure the film would flop at the box office, Jane turned down the part. Vadim gave the script a read and realised that this was not a western at all but an outrageous send-up of the whole cowboy genre. After some prodding, Jane relented. That September, she flew to Hollywood to begin work on *Cat Ballou*.

10

IN THE months following John Kennedy's assassination, it became increasingly evident that America would not soon return to the relative tranquillity that had marked the postwar years. In 1964 the Warren Commission Report concluded that Lee Harvey Oswald had acted alone in killing the president, and a jury in turn convicted Dallas nightclub owner Jack Ruby of murdering Oswald. That was also the year three civil-rights workers – Goodman, Cheney, and Schwerner – were murdered in Philadelphia, Mississippi, to the outrage of the nation.

On 2 August, North Vietnamese torpedo boats allegedly attacked the US destroyers *Maddox* and *Turner Joy*. President Lyndon Johnson, seizing the opportunity to escalate the war effort in Southeast Asia, ordered retaliatory air strikes. The Tonkin Gulf Resolution, passed overwhelmingly by Congress five days later, gave the president authority to take any steps he deemed necessary to 'maintain peace'. Planting trees at her farm in France and charting the course of her career, Jane could not have imagined that her name and the conflict in Vietnam would some day be inextricably entangled in America's collective memory.

When she arrived back in Hollywood that October, she would not recognise the town – and vice versa. Rock music had managed to get what would be a permanent toehold in American culture. California, like the rest of the Western world, was besotted by the mop-topped Beatles and the youth revolution they represented.

There was undeniably, a new emphasis on the young. Jane was excited by the possibilities this trend represented for a 26-year-old woman who had already carved out a reputation for herself as being both defiant and sexy.

The industry, on the other hand, had grown leery of Henry Fonda's prodigal daughter. Members of Hollywood's Old Guard were offended by Jane's cruel pot shots at Dad, and by her frank statements concerning marriage and sex – not to mention her open relationship with France's king of hedonism. The earlier release of *Joy House*, with its overtones of deviant behaviour, only served to confirm suspicions that Jane was under Vadim's sordid spell. This hardly concerned the younger, supposedly more open-minded crowd; to them, Jane was just another movie star's spoiled-rotten daughter. Both camps speculated that Jane had arrived with Vadim in tow because she intended to find him work as a director.

Growing restless after only a few days at the Bel-Air Hotel, Vadim and Jane decided to rent a house in Malibu. There, away from the grandeur and glamour of Beverly Hills, they seemed right at home among the Levi-clad bohemians and self-styled beach bums who made up the arty Malibu Colony. Lining the narrow strip of land between winding, narrow Highway 1 and the Pacific Ocean were 'cottages' that ranged from modest to extravagant, some on stilts and each in its own distinctive architectural style.

Vadim and Fonda soon fell into line behind television actor Larry Hagman, who, waving an American flag and dressed in a gorilla suit or some other outrageous get-up, was given to leading parades down to the beach. Invariably, everybody in the procession ended up in Hagman's enormous hot tub, strategically situated in the centre of his living room.

Cat Ballou was shot on a soundstage in Hollywood and on location in Colorado Springs. While filming at Columbia, Jane would get up before dawn, do stretching exercises, then be driven to the studio by Roberto, their Cuban-born butler-chauffeur. Unlike the Greek Voutsinas, Vadim was careful not to accompany her to the studio. An accomplished director himself, he did not want to appear meddlesome. But when Jane and the rest of the *Cat Ballou* company headed for Colorado, Vadim decided to tag along. 'There we were on location in the hills of Colorado,' a cast member recalls, 'and here was this Frenchman in horn-rimmed glasses reading *Mad* magazine – all by himself, sitting on a chair on the mountainside while Jane was filming.'

As work on *Cat Ballou* progressed, Jane and her colleagues on the picture grew increasingly certain they had a hit on their hands. Jane played the sweet schoolteacher Catherine Ballou, who turns to a life of crime after her father's murder. 'The Cat' soon heads a ragtag gang of amateur outlaws, inadvertently kills her father's murderer, and narrowly escapes the hangman's noose.

Yet *Cat Ballou* belonged to Lee Marvin. After twenty years scowling through television and movie roles, Marvin had been given the chance to play two irresistible parts. As the villainous Jim Strawn, he was dressed head-to-toe in black and sported a silver nose – the real one was 'bit off in a fight'. Marvin's other role was that of Kid Shelleen, a permanently sozzled, way-over-the-hill gunslinger whose horse had a personality as offbeat as his owner's. The film would catapult Marvin from character actor to leading man and earn him an Academy Award as Best Actor in 1965.

Perhaps Marvin was so convincing in the part of Kid Shelleen because of his own hard-drinking ways. One night over dinner with Jane and Vadim,

Marvin launched into a drunken tirade about the French. Then, with a nod to Vadim, he added, 'but I like you because you're half Russian – even though I hate Russians too'.

Actually, Vadim proved to be a huge hit with the Americans who met him. He was warm, friendly, almost self-effacing, and surprisingly devoid of pretence – in short, nothing at all like the heedless satyr they had expected. After six days on the set Vadim, not wishing to overstay his welcome with Elliot Silverstein, the movie's director, returned to Malibu.

It was back at their beach house on Colony Road that Vadim got to know Jane's father and his new love, Shirlee Adams, a stunningly attractive stewardess and part-time model. Shirlee, who had grown up in an orphanage in Aurora, Illinois, and shared many of Henry's Midwestern values, was intelligent and outgoing – and only three years older than Jane.

Predictably, Shirlee was concerned about the younger woman's acceptance. She was all too aware that Jane initially viewed her as a gold digger, even as she tried to convince people that she was genuinely smitten. 'Men much younger and a hundred times richer,' she told a friend, 'have asked me to marry them.'

Jane remained unconvinced. After Susan and Afdera, Jane could not be blamed for shuddering at the thought of yet another Mrs Henry Fonda closer to being a contemporary than a stepmother. At one point, she confronted her father. 'She's too young for you,' she told Hank point-blank. 'She'll drop you.'

'No one,' he said quietly, 'ever drops a Fonda.'

It was an ironic turnabout for Jane, since it was she who worried about what her father's reaction would be to Vadim. She needn't have. Expecting, according to Jane, 'God knows what, an orgy, I suppose,' Henry was delighted to find Vadim fishing off the veranda when they first met. As would be suggested years later in his Academy Award-winning *On Golden Pond* performance, Fonda was a devoted fisherman. Besides, he was so grateful that Jane was no longer under the spell of the cunning Voutsinas, Vadim seemed to shine in comparison.

At first, Peter Fonda was not sure of Vadim as much of an improvement. But neither was he in a position to criticise. He was at a career standstill after a series of flops, and his own recent behaviour had been anything but exemplary. He claimed to have thrown up when he saw himself in *Tammy and the Bachelor*, and the subsequent failure of *The Victors* and *Lilith* did little to settle his stomach. Turned on to marijuana during the making of *The Victors*, Peter had graduated to LSD by the winter of 1964. 'In those days LSD wasn't an illegal drug,' Peter has explained. 'It was pure, non-chromosome-breaking, non-habit-forming, non-dangerous. So I dropped five hundred micrograms and never came back. That's what I liked to say, 'cause then people said, "See, see, I told you, he never came back." I was looking to get my head straight. And it helped.' He found a willing associate in old friend Brooke Hayward's new husband, a wild young actor named Dennis Hopper.

Even more than his father, Peter was prepared to detest the notorious Frenchman. Instead, he too found Vadim to be open, unassuming, and friendly. Most important to Peter, Vadim was neither shocked nor judgemental about the young Fonda's drug use. Indeed, given his and Jane's own 'casual' use of pot, it would have been rather hypocritical for Vadim to object to Peter's penchant for experimentation. Soon Henry Fonda's long-haired, Bob Dylan-quoting son was a frequent guest at the Malibu house, along with Mr and Mrs Hopper.

If Dad found Vadim preferable to his predecessor in Jane's life, he could still voice his disapproval over their highly publicised living arrangements. On this issue, Peter came to his sister's defence. 'The only difference was that he'd send his chick home every night,' Peter said of his father. 'His duplicity blew our minds.'

After *Cat Ballou* finished filming in December, Jane and Vadim packed for the return trip to Paris. 'When I left America,' she recalled, 'I drove to Big Sur and was very startled to see young people from Philadelphia and Chicago and San Francisco — guys with hair down to here and girls with, you know, babies and flutes. What later came to be known as hippies. That was the last thing I saw of America, these people who had fled to this place at Big Sur. The dropouts.' She viewed them at the time as little more than a curiosity.

11

ON HER return to Europe, Jane stopped off in London for the British première of *Circle of Love*. She had by then established what would be a lifelong habit of seeing each movie with an audience, often several times. But this time, in this particular cinema in London, seeing herself on screen was to take on an added significance – 'one of the most extraordinary experiences of my life', she would later say. 'I had seen this movie twice, but I wanted to see it in London. I came in in the middle. I saw the last half and then it began again and suddenly – it was no longer that kind of situation where you're only seeing yourself. I was totally relaxed – sitting there watching myself on screen with people who were watching me on the screen and unaware that I was in the audience. You know how sometimes you say to yourself, I wish I could be someone else and see what I appear like to other people? Because you never see what you look like to other people – certainly not in a mirror.

'Well, I was suddenly seeing myself as someone else. I thought, My God, that's *me*. That's what people see. The me on the screen seemed so much realer than the me in the audience. It was a totally split thing – a shattering moment between reality and unreality. I was watching the real Jane Fonda. I was absolutely panicked and absolutely fascinated.'

During their stop in London that first week in February, Jane managed to shop, in a manner of speaking, for Vadim's 35th birthday present. While Jane sipped coffee in their hotel suite and answered questions posed by a *Daily Express* reporter, a studio press agent telephoned shop after shop in search of the perfect gift. 'He wants a white cashmere sweater,' Jane demanded, 'and it's got to be cashmere because the poor lamb gets kinda itchy with ordinary wool.'

The reporter concluded that the worldly, saturnine Vadim had transformed Jane from a 'gauche American campus girl' with a 'disconcertingly solemn attitude towards her life and art' into a 'dazzling, disquieting, and ethereal beauty'. Where her hair used to look 'riveted in place', the reporter wrote, it was now 'long and wild and filled with splintered sunlight'.

Without hesitating, Jane agreed that Vadim was responsible for her metamorphosis. 'I'm much more relaxed now,' she said. 'I used to work all the time, making three or four films a year. I used to think then that my career was the really important thing in my life. But now, I've questioned myself and I know it is secondary. I could never sacrifice anything for it. And oddly enough, because I'm now more relaxed, I'm a better actress.

'I used to be so nervous before a film I used to come out in boils – pretty, huh? Now, I'm just nervous!'

For the first time, Jane had begun to distance herself from what had been an almost obsessive dependence on psychiatry and analysis. 'Oh, I gave that up,' she replied with a shrug. 'I was travelling so much that I didn't have time. And when I did have time, I found I didn't need it any more. Why? I guess because I'm happy – terribly happy. And I'm happy because I'm in love with Vadim. And whether a woman is happy because she's in love or just happy, she's a better actress, whoever she's working with. It influences everything.'

Declarations of love notwithstanding, Jane still insisted that she had no plans to wed Vadim – though her objections to the idea were noticeably less vehement than in the past. 'In any case it's not really necessary for a family unit to be tight and close,' she mused. 'It can be split up and so long as we all love each other it's all right. I mean, we [the Fondas] are all very close and we never see each other. Just bump into each other at airports.'

To Vadim's delight, *Circle of Love* was far better received in Britain than it had been on the other side of the Atlantic. Before leaving England for France, they once again took the opportunity to plug their next joint venture. 'Oh, what do you think of the title?' Jane coyly asked one Fleet Street reporter. 'We're going to call it *Love*. I think it'll look marvellous: "Jane Fonda in *Love*." "We're going to see Jane Fonda in *Love*." Fonda in *Love*. Fun, huh?'

Awaiting Jane in Paris was the opportunity of a lifetime. David Lean, the celebrated director of *Bridge on the River Kwai* and *Lawrence of Arabia*, had wanted Julie Christie for the lead in his next movie, but when told she was not available he offered the role of Lara in *Dr Zhivago* to Jane. 'He sent me half the script,' Jane said later. 'I said no. Word got back to MGM and they called up and said, "What are you, out of your mind?" But it would have meant spending nine months in the hills of Spain. I wasn't married then, and Vadim is not a camp follower. It's one thing for him to work in Malibu while I'm making a movie, but what would he do in the hills of Spain?'

Although their union might have seemed secure enough, Jane was still realistic enough to know that Vadim would not tolerate an extended separation.

'I wanted to do it,' she said, 'but I was afraid of what it would do to my private life. After all, anything can happen in that long a time.'

As it turned out, Jane played cat-and-mouse with Lean just a little too long. She did finally decide to do *Dr Zhivago*, but by the time she told Lean so it was too late. He had postponed the picture until Christie was free to do it. 'I was quite unhappy about it for a while,' Jane recalled. She was, more accurately, devastated. For reasons she never quite understood, she had manoeuvred herself out of one of the most memorable parts in screen history. Her friends were on the phone instantly to console her. They told her not to worry because 'snow pictures never make money anyway'.

Salvation arrived in the form of another script – this one for *The Chase*, a Sam Spiegel film for which Marlon Brando and movie newcomer Robert Redford had already been cast. *The Chase* dealt with a man falsely accused of murder, his adulterous wife, a small-town sheriff who tries to bring the escapee back alive, and the townspeople-without-pity who would rather see him swinging from the nearest lamppost.

An all-too-obvious indictment of social injustice, *The Chase* hardly seemed like an appropriate vehicle for ingenue-turned-European-sexpot Jane – at least not at this stage in her career. But Jane's agents at Famous Artists were convinced that she was perfect for the role.

Based on a novel and a play by Horton Foote and adapted for the screen by Lillian Hellman (whom Fonda would portray twelve years later in *Julia*), *The Chase* had all the earmarks of a critical and commercial success. After racking up such impressive credits as *The African Queen* (which he produced under the pseudonym S. P. Eagle before reverting to his real name), *On the Waterfront, Bridge on the River Kwai*, and *Lawrence of Arabia*, Spiegel's stock as a producer of quality fare was sky-high. Besides the literary heavyweights who were already part of the project, Spiegel signed Arthur (*The Miracle Worker*) Penn to direct. As far as production values were concerned, Spiegel had already budgeted the film at a then-hefty $7 million. But what ultimately made *The Chase* irresistible to Jane was the chance to star opposite the great Brando. 'I just had to work with him,' she recalls with a shrug.

First, however, Spiegel had to be convinced about Jane. Polish-born Sam Spiegel, one of the new breed of independent producers who sprang up in the wake of the big studios' decline in the 1950s, was considered to be one of Hollywood's master promoters. In true *Gone with the Wind* fashion, he launched a 'nationwide search' for the star of his next movie. After barely a month in France, Jane returned to California to persuade Spiegel personally that she, not some unknown, was ideal for the role opposite Brando.

Once again they set up camp in Malibu, this time renting director William Wyler's rather splendid beach house. While Jane campaigned hard for the female lead in *The Chase*, Vadim busied himself on the script for his next film starring Jane, the jokingly titled *Love*. From the outset Jane had the inside track with Brando himself, since it was Brando's drama-coach mother, Dorothy, who had encouraged Henry Fonda to pursue an acting career back in Omaha. Even before Jane had met Vadim, the French director and Stella Adler's most celebrated graduate had met on the Champs-Elysées and become fast friends. Yet there was nothing Brando could do to improve Jane's chances; Spiegel would brook no interference when it came to casting his pictures.

Hovering on the perimeter of their lives in Malibu were Peter and his wife, Susan, as well as Dennis and Brooke Hopper. Over the course of several days in mid-February, Peter received a number of calls from his old pal Stormy McDonald in Tucson. Each time, says Peter, McDonald was 'very agitated and upset' about the direction his life had taken – or, rather, failed to take. And each time, Peter did his best to help his friend snap out of his depressive state.

One evening, Peter was drinking at a small club with Susan and their friend Mia Farrow when at 11.15 p.m. he inexplicably began crying – some strange reaction, he speculated, to something he had consumed. The next day, after several unsuccessful attempts by Peter to call Stormy, the Tucson sheriff answered Stormy's phone. 'He killed himself, didn't he?' said Peter.

Within hours, Peter was flying to Tucson to identify his best friend's body. McDonald had climbed into a hot tub and slashed his wrists. Then, apparently frustrated that it was taking too long for him to die, he had climbed out of the bath, walked down the hallway to his bedroom, fetched a gun from the wardrobe, and blown his brains out.

Peter's mother, girlfriend, and best friend – all suicides. The chain of tragedies was not lost on Hank, who seemed even more shaken than his son by the obvious pattern that was developing. For the first time in years, the elder Fonda embraced his son. If Peter was impressed by his father's uncharacteristically sympathetic response, the warm feeling did not last. He soon returned to taking pot shots at Dad in the press.

Jane commiserated with her brother, but there was little she could do to comfort him, consumed as she was with winning the prize female role in *The Chase*. While waiting for Spiegel to make up his mind, she arranged with Columbia for him to screen a rough cut of *Cat Ballou*, and the producer was duly impressed. But the deciding factor had absolutely nothing to do with Jane's acting ability. The headline-grabbing brouhaha over that lascivious *Circle of Love* hoarding on Times Square had recently established Jane as a hot number in the mind of the moviegoing public. This was precisely the kind of publicity stunt the crafty old promoter could appreciate, and devoutly hoped would pull them in to see *The Chase*.

Jane rejoiced when Spiegel called late in March to tell her she had the part. She flew with Vadim straight to New York, where her attorneys were still battling Walter Reade over the scandalous hoarding, and sold the apartment near the Museum of Modern Art that she had once shared with the now nearly forgotten Voutsinas. The sale signalled a final break with her former Greek mentor, or at least so she thought.

Returning to her house in Malibu, Jane met Brando. 'When people meet me,' Brando once said, 'they say to themselves, "I hope he isn't going to be rude and uncouth." They remember me from the days I was supposed to be the hot-copy boy who scratched himself and spat in the potted palms.' In 1947, after studying with Adler and Elia Kazan, Brando staggered theatre audiences as the brutish Stanley Kowalski in Tennessee Williams's *A Streetcar Named Desire* – a role that he repeated on film opposite Vivien Leigh four years later. In rapid succession he electrified cinema audiences with *Viva Zapata!*, *The Wild One*, *Julius Caesar*, and *On the Water Front*, for which he won his first Academy Award as Best Actor. In 1957 Brando had received his fifth Oscar nomination – for *Sayonara* – but over the next seven years his career had foundered, reaching its nadir with 1962's *Mutiny on the Bounty*.

The socially conscious theme of *The Chase* made it particularly appealing to Brando, who marched in 1963 with civil-rights workers in Alabama and the following year was arrested near Tacoma on charges of illegal fishing (to dramatise Indian treaty rights). But, more than anything else, Brando needed a hit.

'I was there when he came the first time to discuss the script,' Jane said during the making of the film. 'He will not settle for anything less than the truth. He wants to get at the root of something and not in the way most actors do, in terms of entire script. If he senses something wrong he cannot agree to do it anyway. He just cannot.'

On the issue of Brando's reputation for being moody and temperamental, Jane sprang to the actor's defence. 'People say he is difficult; they also say my father is difficult. My father wants things to be true, honest, real, and important and sometimes that causes problems. I don't think I am courageous enough; that's why I admire Brando.'

Shooting began in May, and it soon became evident that, as Jane had foreseen, Brando had lost interest in the film. Jane, Redford, and co-star James Fox struggled to breathe life into the story, but the linchpin of the operation merely became more and more morose. To alleviate tension on the set, Jane took to imitating Brando's trademark acting style – the seemingly endless brooding silences, the perpetual scowl, and mumbled lines.

For Jane, at least, the frustration was mitigated in the middle of shooting by the release of *Cat Ballou*. Predictably, the most effusive praise went to Marvin for his dual portrayals. And there were a few sour notes sounded, such as the one critic who stated that all the moving parts in the movie outclassed Jane – 'including Lee Marvin's horse'.

But for the most part Jane was praised for her comedic skills. While calling the film 'one of the year's jolliest surprises', *Time*'s critic said of Jane: 'In a performance that nails down her reputation as a girl worth singing about, actress Fonda does every preposterous thing demanded of her with a giddy sincerity that is at once beguiling, poignant, and hilarious. Wearing widow's weeds over her six-guns, she romps through one of the zaniest train robberies ever filmed, a throwback to Pearl White's perilous heyday.' *The New York Times*'s Bosley Crowther called Fonda's Cat a 'big-eyed, big-hearted grown-up child, a veritable Little Mary Sunshine who takes to gunning and robbing a train with the gee-whiz excitement of a youngster confronted with a huge banana split'.

Gratifying as it was to have a bona fide hit on her hands at last, Jane returned to the formidable task of completing *The Chase*. No longer willing even to feign interest in the film, Brando was now sleepwalking through his role. Columbia executives, meanwhile, began leaning on Spiegel and his director to make the film more commercial by adding more sex and violence. Script doctors were called in to make last-minute changes that, Hellman would later charge, diluted and ultimately destroyed the artistic integrity of the story.

Jane gamely slogged away, staying behind in California to finish the picture while Vadim flew to Paris for preproduction work on the movie they had been calling *Love* – actually a screen version of Emile Zola's *La Curée*.

Alone at the house in Malibu, Jane had a chance to light up a joint and, through a cloud of marijuana smoke, reflect on her living arrangements with Vadim. Despite her repeated attacks on the institution of marriage, Jane was beginning to question her own stridency on this question. Her feelings for Vadim were unequivocal; after three years together, she had no doubt that they were both deeply in love and committed to one another.

Contrary to what would later be widely reported, Vadim was not pressuring Jane to marry. Having already cut a noticeable swath through Europe, Vadim had come to the conclusion that it was marginally easier to be the spouse of a famous actress than it was to be her lover and thereby regarded as little more than part of her entourage. Marriage did bestow a certain measure of respectability on the man in these situations and, when she asked, Vadim let Jane know he would not be averse to marriage.

The decision, however, was to be entirely Jane's. 'She has never', reflects Vadim, 'let anyone make the important decisions in her life for her.'

The prospect of motherhood was one factor. At a time when most women were bearing children in their early twenties, 27-year-old Jane began to hear the ticking of her biological clock. Besides, she had enjoyed playing stepmother to Vadim's daughter, Nathalie. Since she was four, Nathalie had regarded Jane as more of a mother than the seldom-seen Annette Stroyberg.

To Jane, who was so accustomed to taking things to the limit, there was also something half-hearted about her current living arrangement. Living together out of wedlock seemed comfortable and natural enough, but increasingly it made her feel like a moral coward. It was time she either moved on to someone else or, if she genuinely loved Vadim, found the courage to make a full legal commitment. Lonely and confused, Jane turned to friends, nearly all of whom voted for marriage.

Ultimately, the deciding factor was, as always, Jane's father – or rather her deep-seated contradictory feelings about him. On the one hand, Henry's marital record seemed to offer mute testimony to the fact that marriage is 'an unnatural state', as Jane was so fond of saying. After four disastrous unions, Hank looked as if he was on the brink of marrying again. Jane was convinced that her father had finally found a worthy soulmate in Shirlee Adams – though it was too soon to tell whether this relationship would last any longer than the others.

Then there was the psychic toll taken by the disintegration of her parents' marriage, leading to her mother's bloody suicide. Although she was no longer slavishly seeing an analyst, Jane had not lost her penchant for introspection. Given her determination to succeed as an actress, she was not about to retreat into her own world the way her mother had. Conversely, she wondered if Vadim would feel eclipsed by her now burning ambition to be an even greater star than her father.

Jane would eventually claim that, after years of appearing to go out of her way to embarrass her father, she owed it to him to marry the man she was living with so openly. When asked why she finally decided to take the plunge, her response was, 'Well, I guess because of my father. I knew I was hurting him.' If that was indeed her reason, she had a strange way of expressing it in the event.

It was a spur-of-the-moment decision, most definitely, and it took Vadim completely by surprise. Two years later, Vadim would insinuate that the decision had been his. 'I got married to Jane because I was lazy,' he sighed. 'People used to ask me, "Why don't you marry Jane?" So as not to have to explain so much, we got married. Now everyone asks, "Why did you marry Jane?"'

In truth, Jane was calling the shots. She was well aware of Vadim's penchant for playing out his private life in the press, and she made it clear that her wedding was under no circumstances to become a media circus. Jane wanted the ceremony to be a top-secret affair, with only a handful of family members and friends in attendance.

Summoned back to Malibu, Vadim brought his mother, the elegant Madame Antoinette Ardiouze, to be matron of honour. (Her earlier prediction to her son that Jane would some day dump him apparently did not dissuade her from participating in the planned nuptials.) On 11 August, three days prior to the event, the couple chartered a private jet and flew the entire wedding party to Las Vegas.

In addition to the bride and groom and Madame Ardiouze, the passenger list included Peter and Susan Brewer Fonda; Vadim's best man, Christian Marquand, and his wife, Tina (the daughter of actor Jean-Pierre Aumont); Dennis and Brooke Hopper; Jane's *Chase* co-star James Fox; Malibu neighbours Robert Walker, Jr and his wife, Ellie; Jane's agent, Dick Clayton; and her cousin George Seymour. There was even a reporter on board: journalist Oriana Fallaci, a friend of Vadim's who would later make a controversial name for herself in the United States.

Everyone checked into the Dunes Hotel on the gaudy Strip, and while Jane hid out in her suite, Vadim made the trip to City Hall for a marriage licence under his real name – Plemiannikov. On the evening of 14 August, everyone (with the exception of Vadim's camera-happy mother, who was so engrossed in snapping photos of Las Vegas that she missed the ceremony altogether) gathered in Jane's six-room suite on the Dunes' twentieth floor in front of Justice of the Peace James Brennan, who only one month before had married Cary Grant and Dyan Cannon. At six foot, six inches, Brennan, an affable Nevadan, towered over everyone, and had to stoop down to squeeze through the doorway. With a nod to her mother's family and her first nickname, the bride signed the register 'Lady Jane Seymour Brokaw Fonda Plemiannikov'. For the next eight years, Plemiannikov was the name she proudly used on all official documents, from contracts to her passport.

Background music was supplied by Peter on the guitar and six lady violinists in skintight blue sequined gowns. Everything moved along smoothly until Justice of the Peace Brennan asked for the bride and groom to produce the all-important rings. When they sheepishly admitted that they had forgotten this detail, Brennan was crestfallen. The Marquands came to the rescue, turning over their rings for the occasion. Tina Marquand's gold band was two sizes too large, and to keep it on Jane had to hold up her ring finger through the ceremony in a gesture that seemed at the very least odd for the occasion. The bride, finger held high, cried copiously. Overcome by emotion? Perhaps, though it was equally likely that Jane was finally realising it was too late to back out. She would later say that she had sleepwalked through the day, repeatedly asking herself, Why am I doing it?

Still, the ceremony went on without any further hitches; in lieu of a reception, the small group headed for a burlesque stage revue – a re-enactment of the French Revolution in which a topless Marie Antoinette is guillotined while similarly unclad 'citizens' cheer. They then proceeded straight to the casino where, elbow-to-elbow with high rollers from New York and grandmas from Glendale, the new Mrs Plemiannikov cheered Mr Plemiannikov on to win $2,000 at baccarat.

Just before dawn, they returned to their room to share a bottle of Dom Perignon and a joint. The next day, everyone flew back to LA on the same chartered plane. While the amiable Vadim chatted with the Marquands, Jane stared out of the window and wondered what she had done.

At his rented Malibu house less than a mile down the beach from Jane's, Henry Fonda picked up the *Los Angeles Times* and learned of his daughter's marriage. The one human being she had supposedly most wanted to please by marrying had been pointedly excluded from the proceedings.

12

JANE RETURNED to the set of *The Chase* for one last week of work. When the film was finished on 4 September 1965, photographers were invited to the end-of-shoot party to snap Fonda, beer bottle in hand, whooping it up with co-stars Fox and Redford. Brando, conspicuous by his absence, had already fled back to Tahiti.

Well aware that *The Chase* would flop, Jane joined Vadim at their farmhouse in France to concentrate on their version of *La Curée*. Having gained whatever mileage they could out of calling the film *Love*, the Plemiannikovs settled on a new (and rather senseless) English-language title for the film: *The Game Is Over*. Obviously *The Chase* was going to do nothing to distance Jane from her reputation as a disarmingly beautiful lightweight, and Vadim yearned to break free from his image as the Henry Higgins of screen sex.

Vadim was banking on the *The Game Is Over* to make their transformation complete. Zola's passionate tale of a young Parisienne who falls in love with her handsome stepson only to have her enraged husband take his revenge, *The Game Is Over* offered both Jane and her director a chance to establish themselves as artists. Vadim chose Royal Shakespeare Company player Peter McEnery for the part of the stepson, and went ahead with plans to shoot two versions – one in English and one in French. By now Jane's French was virtually flawless; McEnery learned his lines phonetically, and a French actor later dubbed in his dialogue. 'It was hard enough to shoot anything once,' she said, 'but doing it twice, I found, seemed perfectly natural.'

While preparing to shoot *The Game Is Over*, Jane received word that in December, after three months of planning, Shirlee Mae Adams had become the fifth Mrs Henry Fonda in a simple double-ring ceremony on Long Island. The only guests present were best man George Peppard, Peppard's wife, Elizabeth Ashley, Fonda's longtime press agent John Springer, and Springer's wife, June. When they returned by limousine to the house on East 74th Street, a mob of reporters waited for them. At first Hank was furious at this intrusion on his privacy, but Shirlee had her own way of handling it: she invited the startled reporters in for a drink. Putting his wedding night aside, Hank then ran to make the curtain for *Generation*, the hit Broadway comedy in which he played (perhaps with special conviction) the long-suffering father of a headstrong girl who marries a ne'er-do-well.

Jane was convinced that in Shirlee her father had at last found a soulmate who could go the distance. It was clear to everyone who knew them that Shirlee, as Jane later put it, would not let him 'tune her out' as he had so many others close to him. 'And she puts up with lots of abuse . . .' said Jane. 'He has an incredible way of striking out cruelly at the people he loves. She has put up with it and I really respect her for it.'

If Jane was determined as she neared her 30th birthday to lay claim to the title of serious actress, she was not about to turn down all lucrative offers on purely artistic grounds. With the success of *Cat Ballou*, Jane's price per picture had become $300,000 – one of the highest salaries paid any star in 1965. When Warner Brothers bypassed Natalie Wood and Audrey Hepburn to offer Jane the lead in *Any Wednesday*, she did not hesitate to accept, even though it meant postponing the completion of *The Game Is Over*.

Muriel Resnick's play about the mistress of a button-down corporate executive who takes a lover of her own when she hits 30, *Any Wednesday* had been a sleeper hit of the 1963 Broadway season with newcomer Sandy Dennis in the starring role. (In true Hollywood fashion, Dennis was not even considered for the movie and would have to wait for her Oscar-winning role in *Who's Afraid of Virginia Woolf?* to prove herself as a credible screen actress.)

In the film version of *Any Wednesday*, Jane is lured away from her married lover (Jason Robards) by a callow-but-caring Dean Jones. Featuring lots of innuendo, hysterical crying and Feydeau-farcical business, *Any Wednesday* was not all that different from *Tall Story, Period of Adjustment*, or *Sunday in New York*: the kind of empty-headed role Jane realised she could sail through effortlessly.

At the time, Robards was battling both a formidable drinking problem and his equally formidable wife, Lauren Bacall. He did not, however, bring his personal problems to work. Although only fifteen years older than Jane, his intense professionalism reminded her of her father; like Hank, Robards had been trained on the stage and was happiest there. Jane instantly recognised Robards as a kindred spirit, and the two would bring their chemistry to the screen again years later in *Julia* and *Comes a Horseman*. Conversely, she had next to nothing in common with romantic interest Jones, who was in the process of changing from king of the Disney lot to devout fundamentalist Christian.

Harmonious as the working conditions on the set of *Any Wednesday* were, Jane missed Vadim. Each afternoon he phoned from Paris, invariably interrupting a scene. While the rest of the cast and crew waited outside her trailer, the Plemiannikovs chatted, often for an hour or two. Still dependent on the direction of others, Jane was relying on her latest mentor to guide her performance long-distance.

Critical response to the film ranged from tepid ('A pleasant enough, somewhat overdrawn film that will dispose of a few hours painlessly') to frigid ('*Any Wednesday* is a good example of the movies taking everything that is crisp and human about the stage and turning it into everything that is loud and vulgar and boring about Hollywood. The story gets all but stomped on with cleated boots by Jane Fonda').

No matter. Light fare such as *Any Wednesday* could pay the bills while Fonda and Vadim worked feverishly to complete their 'serious' work, *The Game Is Over*. During filming in and around Paris, Jane had been drawn into the debate currently raging among French intellectuals concerning America's involvement in Vietnam. While Vadim had been made comparatively cynical by the excesses of both political extremes in postwar Europe, his cinematic colleagues tended to be decidedly left-wing in their outlook. A loose alliance of traditional socialists, hard-line Stalinists, and pacifists, this group had rejoiced in the fall of French colonialism in Indochina and Algeria. In fact, many of then took credit for helping to bring it about by their undermining of French resolve at home. Having long sung the praises of China's Mao and Cuba's Fidel Castro, they now had a new revolutionary hero in Ho Chi Minh, the leader of communist North Vietnam. But what really tied all these disparate leftist groups together was an overriding hatred for the United States, or at least the 'oppressive' American government that they now held responsible for most of the world's ills.

At, first, Jane was resolute in her defence of the United States. She insisted that it was unfair to compare America with the colonial powers of the past, and argued forcefully that American troops were in South Vietnam only to help that country defend itself against communist aggression.

Predictably, this did not sit well with Vadim's left-wing friends, including such leading French film notables as Jean-Luc Godard, Yves Montand, and Montand's wife, Simone Signoret. While Jane played perfect hostess at their country house, ending each meal with strong coffee poured from a Russian samovar, her guests would grill her incessantly concerning what they perceived as America's culpability.

Jane was no match for them. While certainly possessed of a keen natural intelligence, she was ill-read on historical and political matters. In truth, the 'facts' as stated by Vadim's sophisticated friends were nothing more than propaganda from the pages of *Pravda* embraced as gospel by the French 'New Left', as the movement came to be called. In the face of such virulent and seemingly unanimous anti-Americanism, Jane stopped objecting and started listening. After months of this, her will to resist vanished.

While in Los Angeles finishing *Any Wednesday*, Jane had found that Hollywood was also divided on the issue of America's involvement in Vietnam. Draft-card burnings and peace marches were now commonplace; a few American pacifists had even burned themselves to death in sympathy with the self-immolation of Buddhist monks in Saigon.

Woodstock was still nearly four years away, but it was already obvious that a strong counterculture with its roots in the anti-war movement was growing, and rapidly. Those few hippies Jane had noticed at Big Sur several months earlier were now legion. From San Francisco's Haight-Ashbury district to Sunset Boulevard, tie-dyed T-shirts, sandals, beads, and bell-bottom jeans were the uniform of the day. Anti-war troubadours such as Bob Dylan and Joan Baez, as well as such acid rockers as Grace Slick, Janis Joplin, and Jimi Hendrix now shared the airwaves with the Supremes, the Beatles, and the Rolling Stones.

When it came to experimenting with drugs, Peter was in the forefront of the movement. As the vicious cyclist in *The Wild Angels*, he had become the industry's newest leather-jacketed anti-hero. A poster from the film showing an appropriately surly-looking Peter astride a Harley had sold two million copies. Yet the aura of violence that surrounded his screen image had little to do with the real Peter. Most of his trips were not on motorcycles but on speed, LSD, and a host of other supposedly mind-expanding psychedelics. At first it was hard for Jane to see the connection between the freewheeling sex, drugs and rock-and-roll philosophy of America's youth and the turmoil in Vietnam. Added up, it represented a wholesale rebellion against authority. Jane began to think that she had been wrong in defending her homeland against its intellectual critics in Paris. For the first time in her life, she turned to her brother for answers. Perhaps what he and his crowd had to say, unlike Vadim and his in Paris, was more than empty rhetoric. Maybe the United States was wrong in pursuing the war.

To complicate matters further for Jane in the middle of all this intense soul-searching, her father embarked in April on a three-week US-sponsored 'Handshake Tour' to boost the morale of troops stationed in Southeast Asia. At first he'd been reluctant to become involved; but a number of other major stars, notably Jimmy Stewart, Charlton Heston, and, of course, Bob Hope had already paved the way. It all seemed to boil down then to whether American soldiers deserved to see a friendly face from home, and the Mr Roberts in Henry Fonda felt they did.

Armed with a Polaroid camera and suitcases full of film, Hank helicoptered from base to base and had his picture taken with hundreds of soldiers. On the aircraft carriers *Ticonderoga*, *Kitty Hawk* and *Bennington*, he talked to the seamen and pilots. While visiting the *Ticonderoga*, Hank noted with pride that the film they were showing on board was *Cat Ballou*.

The carnage left Fonda shaken. Visiting the wounded in base hospitals throughout South Vietnam, he choked back the tears. 'I had to control my emotions,' he later said. 'Just had to.' On his return in May, Fonda admitted to the press that he had been an 'apathetic' liberal before going to Vietnam. Now he was convinced that the US military presence there was essential. 'Well, my eyes were opened . . . Every time there's a parade or peace rally in this country it will make the war that much longer, because this doesn't escape the attention of Ho Chi Minh.' In the years to come, that refrain would be all too familiar to Jane. For now, however, she put politics on hold to do a film for the dreaded Otto Preminger.

Laurence Olivier once said that his wife, Joan Plowright, could get him to do anything simply by threatening to invite Otto Preminger to stay for the weekend. The notorious 'Mr O', as he was called, seemed to take great pleasure in browbeating and humiliating his actors; Preminger's methods bordered on the sadistic.

Yet this was a side of the man Jane had been spared. She and Vadim had met Preminger on several social occasions in Paris and in Hollywood and had been impressed with his European charm. So she jumped at the opportunity when Preminger offered her a role in *Hurry Sundown* as the spoiled, libidinous wife of a wealthy plantation owner (played by British actor Michael Caine − an incongruous bit of casting much like the choice of Laurence Harvey for *Walk on the Wild Side*). 'I like to be told what to do,' she readily admitted, 'and Otto knows exactly what he wants.'

Based on the best-selling novel by K. B. Gilden, *Hurry Sundown* featured plenty of lust, greed, and violence − all wrapped around the theme of racial injustice in contemporary Georgia. Afraid of possible violence, officials in that state denied Preminger the necessary permits to shoot there. Instead, filming took place in and around Baton Rouge, Louisiana.

For Jane, it was a two-month primer in Deep South racism. Preminger had reserved 120 rooms at Baton Rouge's Bellemont Motel which, despite the fact that it flew the Confederate Stars and Bars rather than the American flag, was accustomed to handling Hollywood folk making films in the area. Nevertheless, those were all-white films. No one seemed prepared to play host to an integrated cast that included Diahann Carroll and Robert Hooks in featured roles.

'We had this swimming pool at the motel,' Jane recalled after the filming, 'and I'll never forget the first day one of the Negro actors jumped into it. There were reverberations all the way to New Orleans. People just stood and stared like they expected the water to turn black! Some day I am going to hitchhike through the South. I want to wake up all the people who are asleep and say, "Hey, it's not necessary, the world is big enough for everybody!"'

People were no more hospitable in St Francisville, the small Louisiana town

Preminger had painstakingly selected to represent the South at its bigoted worst. On the surface, St Francisville reeked of gentility; blue-haired ladies fanned themselves in the parlours of their slightly gone-to-seed pre-Civil War homes, occasionally joined by white-suited gentlemen in Panama hats. What Preminger did not realise was that the sleepy hamlet was to all intents and purposes the state headquarters of the Ku Klux Klan. Outside the St Francisville courthouse where one scene was being filmed, the crew were approached by the sheriff. As Jane later recalled, 'He asked us to finish the scene, get out of town, and never come back.'

Over the two sweltering months they spent in Louisiana making the movie, the cast and crew of *Hurry Sundown* were routinely threatened by mail and by telephone. Tyres were slashed. For the most part, their tormentors remained unseen. 'You could feel their eyes watching you behind lace curtains,' said Hooks. 'Like they could cut your heart out.' Preminger posted round-the-clock armed guards outside the wing housing the cast and crew.

Once again, Jane's lifeline to Vadim was transatlantic. The whole experience was bitter and emotionally draining. Jane had been prepared to hear epithets such as 'nigger' and 'coon' spoken as lines of dialogue, but it genuinely surprised her that life in small-town Louisiana would so closely imitate art.

For all the hatred vented at Jane and her co-workers during the making of *Hurry Sundown*, the critics almost unanimously blasted the film for unfairly depicting white Southerners in a bad light. Writing in *Esquire*, Wilfred Sheed claimed *Hurry Sundown* was one of 'a bunch of movies about the South which are rougher in tone than the latest movies about Nazi Germany . . . Any damn fool can stomp on the South.' Chimed in Rex Reed: 'The white folks are all such mangy, degenerate critters that they are too ignorant to notice anything.'

In truth, the movie deserved to be ridiculed on purely artistic grounds. It was a shameless potboiler, made all the more ludicrous by Preminger's ham-fisted direction. Jane, even though cast as the most open-minded white character in the film, was singled out for special attention. Among the moments that earned the reviewers' derision, she was called upon to slap co-star Diahann Carroll hard across the face for having the audacity to enter a whites-only rest room. In another steamy scene, Jane suggestively plays a saxophone between her husband's legs to try to rouse him out of his alcohol-induced impotence. 'At the screening I attended the audience was hissing, booing, and throwing popcorn boxes at the screen with such nasty vigour,' reported Reed, 'I almost missed the scene where the judge spit into the church communion cup.'

It was during the filming of *Hurry Sundown* that someone brought Jane a copy of the August 1966 issue of *Playboy* magazine. It contained six pages of black-and-white photographs showing her cavorting nude on the set of *The Game Is Over*. During the making of what he hoped would be his masterpiece, Vadim had pleaded with his wife to bare her body for the first time on screen. Apparently she didn't require much persuading. By the time filming was completed, Jane had broken her oft-repeated pledge never to do a completely nude scene, not once but half a dozen times.

The longest and most difficult of these was a swimming sequence in which Jane was to skinny-dip, then towel herself down beside the pool. For this, Jane insisted that the Paris set be closed. The only people allowed to be present were co-star Peter McEnery (remaining clothed for this scene), three camera technicians, and Vadim.

What Jane claimed she did not know at the time was that a French stills photographer was prowling the catwalks overhead, gleefully snapping away as Jane sat naked at the edge of the pool, going over the script with Vadim. Just how did the man get past all the tight security and up into the rafters?

When she learned about the existence of the pictures and of *Playboy*'s intention to use them, Jane was furious. 'It rocked me, it really did,' she proclaimed. 'It's a simple matter of breaking and entering, and invasion of privacy.' She ordered her lawyers to write to *Playboy* publisher Hugh Hefner threatening to sue if his magazine proceeded with its plans to publish the photos.

Now that *Playboy* had gone ahead and used the seven unauthorised shots, Jane intended to make good her threat. From her motel room in Baton Rouge, she conferred by telephone with her lawyers in New York. Within two weeks, she had filed a $19 million lawsuit (or about $2,700,000 per photo) against Hefner and his HMH Publishing Co., claiming invasion of privacy on the grounds that the nudity shown in the movie was her character's, and not her own. By contrast, her lawyers argued, the still photographs taken secretly and without her consent showed not her fictional character, but a very real actress preparing for work. Or as Vadim, casting himself in the part of the outraged husband, put it: in the magazine, 'it is herself which is naked'.

The suit claimed that her professional career and her 'aspirations' were 'incalculably and permanently damaged' by *Playboy*. In addition, 'Miss Fonda will continue to feel emotionally ravaged, has suffered and will continue to suffer intense humiliation and mental anguish, has been immeasurably distressed, and has been and will be subjected to taunts, gibes, and ridicule from her professional community.'

Hefner was unmoved. 'A private life isn't involved here,' he replied. 'This is a professional thing.'

In Paris, where they also filed suit, Vadim won a small victory. Although *Playboy*'s French distributors argued that Vadim had not complained when the offending photos appeared earlier in Swedish newspapers, the French court ordered all copies of the *Playboy* issue to be seized.

'The suit is a matter of principle,' announced Jane. 'I think somebody at some point has to say, '"Now wait a minute, you just can't keep doing that!"'

In one interview, Vadim offered his own explanation justifying the legal action on artistic grounds: 'It is like when you are painting a picture. You start by drawing and then put in some colours – red, white. You know for a while it will be ugly. If at this moment someone is hiding and takes a picture of your painting, it is . . . to *voler*? To steal.'

The suit would drag on in the American courts for nearly a year before Fonda lost. In the meantime, the film reaped a whirlwind of publicity; the 'serious' film they had laboured to create was now all but overshadowed by the film's controversial nudity.

Ironically, when *The Game Is Over* was released later in the year, most critics heaped praise on both the movie and Fonda's performance in it. 'Roger Vadim's films are visual memoirs of his amours,' wrote Kevin Thomas of the *Los Angeles Times*. 'He has made love on camera to former wives Brigitte Bardot and Annette Stroyberg, who glowed on the screen in response. But he has never made it so well as with Jane Fonda, the current Madame Vadim, who is not only as gorgeous as her predecessors but also a gifted actress. Consequently, *The Game Is Over* is his best film since *Les Liaisons Dangereuses* and the finest of Miss Fonda's career.' Brendan Gill of *The New Yorker*, the *New York Post*'s Archer Winsten, and Gene Youngblood of the Los Angeles *Herald-Examiner* all agreed this was Jane's best performance to date. Writing in *Cosmopolitan*, future columnist Liz Smith called the movie 'enthralling . . . one of the most beautiful I've ever seen. Jane has never been so appealing.'

The Game Is Over became a smash hit in Europe, and fared moderately well in the United States. However ecstatic the reviews, moviegoers were for the most part drawn by one thing: the chance to see Jane Fonda in all her naked glory. 'I counted seven full-face bare-breast shots of Fonda,' reported Rex Reed. 'Her father must be purple-faced with embarrassment.' Jane shrugged off such jabs. 'You have to be relaxed, free,' she said. 'Pornography begins when things become self-conscious.'

When it came to embarrassing Dad, Jane was to share honours this time with her brother. At the height of the *Playboy* debacle, Peter went on trial in Los Angeles Superior Court on charges of drug possession. Police in the San Fernando Valley town of Tarzana had raided a house rented by Peter and found nine pounds of pot, as well as some marijuana plants growing in the backyard. Peter, renting the house for two friends who were his co-defendants in the case, insisted he did not know there were drugs on the premises, despite the fact that he was a frequent visitor.

Peter's long-suffering father left the Arizona set of the aptly titled *Welcome to Hard Times* and flew to LA to testify as a character witness on his son's behalf. 'I'm here,' Hank told the press, 'to give moral support and any other support to my son.' Jane, not wanting to make the trial a media event any more than it had to be, did not attend. But she did spring to Peter's defence

111

whenever given the opportunity, whether in LA, New York, or Paris, telling reporters that she staunchly believed in her brother's innocence.

Peter, nevertheless, seemed determined to go to jail. Instead of getting a haircut and donning a conservative dark suit as his lawyer requested, Peter took the stand wearing wire-rimmed sunglasses, scuffed boots, faded Levis, and leather. His hair was nearly shoulder-length. Slouching in the witness chair, he peppered his testimony with wisecracks. The jury was not amused.

At the lunch adjournment, Hank cornered his son and told him to drop the bad-boy act. 'If you want them on your side,' he said, 'don't be a smart ass!' After that, Peter returned to the stand, clearly having taken his father's advice. Hank followed, offering less-than-truthful testimony that he'd 'never had any trouble with the boy'.

Hank would later claim that his son had been acquitted of the charges (though one of his friends was convicted). He would neglect to mention that the jury in Peter's case actually failed to return a verdict. Because a key witness had disappeared, the prosecution decided not to retry Peter, and dropped the charges.

According to Hank, the trial and the very real prospect of going to prison 'shook Peter real good'. His guilt or innocence in this particular possession case notwithstanding, Peter had made no secret of his freewheeling ways, and his father hoped that this was the proverbial 'good scare' that his son needed.

But, as with so many who came of age in the sixties, Peter's 'victory' over the Establishment had quite the opposite effect. He was emboldened to press the limits even further, in ways that would soon have a profound impact on his culture. The important thing now was that all the Fondas had pulled together when one of them was in peril. The clan was united – at least for the moment.

That autumn, exhausted by their seemingly endless legal wrangling with Hefner, Jane and Vadim took a few days off to go boating through the canals of southern France. The couple was shocked to learn at this time that they were not legally married in France, Vadim having forgotten to register their marriage with a French consulate. Plans to 'remarry' before a French magistrate the following spring were quickly announced. But first Paramount made her an offer she couldn't refuse – the lead opposite a fast-rising Robert Redford in the smash-hit Neil Simon comedy *Barefoot in the Park*.

13

WHEN IT was learned that Henry Fonda cold-bloodedly killed a nine-year-old boy in the opening scene of Sergio Leone's *Once Upon a Time in the West*, American audiences were so dismayed that they stayed away from the film in droves. Fonda was the quintessential good guy, and they were not willing to have their fantasy illusions shattered. This phenomenon of screen identity was, of course, not peculiar to Henry Fonda. Nearly all stars have wound up being typecast.

It was a fate Jane Fonda was determined to avoid. On the one hand she could be the brazen sexpot whose flagrant sensuality had made her one of Europe's leading stars. After the *Circle of Love* poster fiasco, the *Playboy* spread, and the release of *The Game Is Over*, it would have been difficult to find someone who had *not* seen Jane Fonda nude. Yet there was another Jane Fonda – the sweetly wholesome, innocently beguiling, and comic Jane Fonda – who still held tremendous appeal for audiences. Unaccountably, the American public could overlook the themes of adultery, rape, racism, and incest that pervaded her dramatic work – just as they could accept her unconventional private life with the hedonistic Vadim – if only to see her in another comedy.

This dichotomy did not escape journalist Gerald Jonas. 'Jane Fonda', he wrote in *The New York Times*, 'has managed to maintain two entirely different public images simultaneously between France and the United States. Over here . . . she sounds and dresses like the pretty roommate of the girl you dated in college, and most people still think of her as Henry Fonda's daughter. Over there she stars in movies like *The Circle of Love* and the just released *The Game Is Over*. She sounds like the girl you eavesdropped on in a Paris café; she undresses like Brigitte Bardot, and everyone knows her as the latest wife of Roger Vadim.'

'I've always sort of played it close to the edge in my personal life,' says Jane, 'but careerwise I don't take risks.' As a means of hedging her bets, Jane knew it was important to remain a bankable star. That meant agreeing to take on a marginally good role so long as the film was assured of being a commercial success.

Barefoot in the Park, one of Neil Simon's earliest Broadway hits, offered Jane the best of both worlds. Although it had many of the elements of her previous comedies, *Barefoot* was far more clever in concept and execution. No sooner does kooky Corie Bratter move into a fifth-floor Manhattan flat with her new husband than she learns he is an insufferable stuffed shirt. Corie spends the rest of the film trying to get him to loosen up and, following a series of urban misadventures, succeeds. After an argument that seems to spell the end of their brief marriage, her faith is renewed when she finds him drunk and – barefoot in the park.

Elizabeth Ashley, who played the role of Corie to perfection opposite Redford on Broadway, was devastated when the film's producer bypassed her in favour of Jane. Jane, a friend and kindred spirit of Redford's since their stint together making *The Chase*, lobbied hard to make sure that Redford would have the opportunity to repeat his role.

The onscreen chemistry of Fonda and Redford was crucial to the success of *Barefoot in the Park*. One veteran leading man who recognised it instantly was Charles Boyer, whose character in the film tries to seduce Jane Fonda's straitlaced mother, played by Mildred Natwick. 'She has an eagerness to learn and do her role as well as she can,' Boyer said of Jane. 'I don't always see that in established actresses. I understand her work for Vadim has been very sensual, but she seems very much at home in comedy, and there is a strong sexual undercurrent between her and Redford. They are almost too attractive a pair.'

Boyer also noticed a certain remote quality in Jane that set her apart from the other actors. 'Jane is a friendly girl,' he added, 'though she does not laugh often and keeps a distance between herself and strangers. But she is compassionate, and she is concerned about more things than her hair and make-up.'

Barefoot in the Park was filmed primarily on a Paramount soundstage in Los Angeles. There were, however, two weeks of location shooting around New York that contributed greatly to the verisimilitude of the movie. 'You can have a fine room on a studio set,' said Jane, 'but it will only have two walls. And I think the audience, without anyone telling it, knows the difference.'

The audience was also soon to learn, if they hadn't already, the difference between the wholesome Jane of *Cat Ballou* and *Any Wednesday*, and the *other* Jane. With *Barefoot in the Park* still being shot, she and Vadim were well committed to a project that for a generation would symbolise Jane Fonda's sex-goddess period.

Barbarella began in a rubbish bin. Or at least that is where Jane's involvement started. Long before the success of such pop fantasies as *Star Wars, E.T.,*

114

Superman, or *Batman*, producer Dino De Laurentiis had been wanting to turn the sexy science-fiction comic strip 'Barbarella' into a full-blown feature film. De Laurentiis first took the idea to Bardot and Sophia Loren. When both declined, he wrote to Jane in Malibu asking if she would be interested in the part. She crumpled up the producer's letter and tossed it away.

When she told Vadim about De Laurentiis's bizarre idea, he fished the proposal out of the rubbish. Vadim had long contemplated the idea of doing a science-fiction film, but worried that the subject matter was beyond his ken. As he envisioned it, *Barbarella* would be another Vadim-orchestrated romp – only this time set in AD 40,000.

Jane resisted at first but was finally won over by her husband's enthusiasm for the project – so much so that she turned down the title role opposite Warren Beatty in *Bonnie and Clyde* (the movie that propelled Faye Dunaway to stardom) and the lead in *Rosemary's Baby*. Director Roman Polanski (who with his wife, Sharon Tate, had become good friends with Jane and Vadim in Malibu) settled on Mia Farrow.

Unaccountably, Jane was persuaded by Vadim's argument that *Barbarella* was a far more important motion picture than anything else she was being offered. It would give her an opportunity to play a type that had never been attempted before, 'a kind of sexual Alice in Wonderland of the future'.

Off-camera, Jane seemed to be living that role in the present. For all his devotion to her, Vadim had stuck by his pledge not to remain entirely faithful. He still considered monogamy an unnatural state, though during their first year of marriage he was at least considerate enough to keep his infidelities to himself.

Still, Vadim seized every opportunity to convert Jane to his hedonist philosophy, and towards that end even enlisted the help of friends. As it turned out, two of these friends would exert a profound influence on Jane sexually *and* politically. Best-selling novelist Roger Vailland and his wife, Elisabeth, had both fought fascism – he with the French Resistance and she with the anti-Mussolini partisans – and emerged from the war devout communists.

What initially intrigued Jane about the Vaillands, however, had nothing to do with politics. The Vaillands both felt that it was Roger's duty to have extramarital affairs – that to deny himself sexual pleasure for the sake of some outmoded puritan ethic would be patently dishonest.

Vadim and Jane had been living together for more than four years now, and he had grown bored with their sexual routine. He had been sleeping with other women for most of that time, and now he began to share the lurid details with Jane. When this failed to satisfy him, Vadim actually began bringing his lovers home to bed. According to Vadim, Jane eagerly complied. 'She seemed to understand,' he said, 'and as always, went all out – all the way.'

Jane does not deny it, though there is considerable question whether she ever really enjoyed these 'games' to the degree Vadim did. Yet clearly, she was willing to follow the course of marital action set by Roger and Elisabeth Vailland – a course that liberated Vadim sexually, but not his wife.

To comply with French law, Vadim and Jane renewed their marriage vows on 18 May in a small civil ceremony at the St Ouen town hall. Vadim actually held to the theory that their marriage had been strengthened by their liberation escapades, keeping either spouse from becoming bored or feeling trapped. Jane would eventually admit to Vadim that she had felt degraded and demeaned by their period of sexual experimentation. She would also reciprocate with adventures of her own. But for now, given the opportunity of *Barbarella*, she was willing to spread Vadim's gospel of eroticism on the screen.

In a sense, *Barbarella* was the first of Fonda's 'message' pictures – a film she chose to make for personal motives, in this case to proselytise the notions of sexual freedom she and Vadim embraced. Perhaps on this account, Jane decided that, rather than try to imbue her character with some otherworldly nature, she would play Barbarella straight. In a typical scene, she unzips her intergalactic wet suit and stands nude before a grandfatherly gentleman. He greets her with a nod. 'Barbarella,' he says. 'Mr President,' she responds. (Vadim had originally offered this role of 'President of Earth', whose first question was 'Will I have to take my clothes off?', to Henry Fonda. This bit of casting was all the more remarkable if, as was the case in this Fonda–Vadim joint venture, the offer was made with Jane's understanding. The role ultimately went to Claude Dauphin.)

Emoting was the least of Jane's problems. The futuristic look and elaborate technical effects of the film turned her performance into a physical nightmare. At various points in *Barbarella*, Jane was gnawed upon by piranha-toothed dolls, swung about by a mechanical arm, hung upside-down over a vat of oil and dry ice (to give the illusion of boiling), and strapped in an 'excessive pleasure' machine that blows up when Jane overloads it. For that, they rigged the machine with smoke bombs and flares.

A visitor to the Rome set one day found Jane covered with Noxzema. During a scene in which she is shot through a gigantic pneumatic tube lined with plastic – the principal mode of transportation on this particular planet – Jane skinned her stomach on the plastic. 'So Roger decided to try it again,' Jane told the visitor, 'only this time they sprinkled the tube with talcum powder. And then it worked so well that I hurtled out of the other end of the tube and practically right out of the studio.' So now they were trying Noxzema. 'She's a brave girl,' sighed Vadim.

Merely getting dressed was an ordeal for Jane, who was alternately trussed in metal-ribbed corsets and crammed into a suffocatingly tight transparent breastplate. She endured all this without complaint until one scene that called for her to be attacked by two thousand killer wrens that pecked at her clothes until they were in tatters. Unfortunately, the birds wouldn't budge. While Jane cowered, guns were fired and giant fans brought in to set the birds fluttering about in a frenzy. Nothing. Birdseed was stuffed in Jane's clothing. Still no interest. By now, the wrens had also made a considerable mess on the studio floor. After days of trying, trained lovebirds would finish the scene. The strain took its toll: Jane checked into a local hospital for three days suffering from nausea and raised blood pressure.

Beyond the demands of the production itself, Jane grew increasingly irritated by the machismo of the Italian men. 'I don't like Rome,' she said to a friend. 'A girl can't walk down the streets alone. The men never stop insulting you.' One indiscreet crew member bragged a little too often about dabbing make-up on to intimate parts of Fonda's anatomy and was nearly shot by his jealous wife. Vadim, approached by the couple's frantic son, intervened to have the make-up man replaced.

Jane remained stoic. 'She was put through hell and didn't complain once,' says one of the film's crew. Jane herself would announce, 'It's extremely relaxing to work with Vadim,' when the film was done. 'How he maintains his calm in a movie like this full of space-age special effects baffles me. If it were me, I'd be in constant tears. Actually, it's not easier to work with Vadim, but I'm much more relaxed because I know that I'm completely protected. So are the others. It isn't only that he's protecting me, his wife, but all the others.'

Much to his chagrin, one of the 'others' Vadim was called upon to protect was none other than Andreas Voutsinas. Down on his luck, Voutsinas had called Jane begging for a job on her new picture. Vadim, who had never met his predecessor in Jane's life, reluctantly agreed to hire him as a dialogue coach – but only if he kept his distance from Jane while she worked.

For all the tortures Jane willingly endured throughout the picture, what viewers remember most are the first moments when a very nude Jane floats weightlessly behind the credits. 'We were supposed to have a costume, but it didn't arrive,' recalls Jane. 'So we sat down, and Vadim said, "Listen, anyone who's ever read the [comic] book expects Barbarella to be naked all the way through. And anyway, we'll do it as a spoof of the sort of pictures people *think* I make."'

Jane grudgingly agreed, so long as Vadim covered up as much of her body as possible with the titles. 'He did the titles once, and I said, "That's not covered enough" – so he did them again.'

Vadim knew that she still felt self-conscious disrobing for the camera. To control her weight, she still engaged in a dangerous binge-purge ritual. But as far as the rest of the world was concerned, she had few qualms about displaying her body in public. One nude photograph of a windswept Jane sitting on a beach quickly became the prevailing public image of Henry's liberated and not-so-little girl. 'It's practically old-fashioned today', she maintained, 'to think of nudity in any other terms than normal.' Normal or not, on 13 November, while she was still filming, *Newsweek* ran a bare-from-behind shot of Jane on the cover with the headline 'ANYTHING GOES: THE PERMISSIVE SOCIETY'.

At about the same time, an ex-*Newsweek* writer named David Slavitt published a leering novel called *The Exhibitionist* under the pseudonym Henry Sutton. The book, concerning the lives of a sex-crazed movie star and his nymphomaniacal movie-star daughter, contained all the ingredients for success – incest, lesbianism, orgies. This was no accident. Slavitt had produced the book on a bet with his publisher that he could write a first-rate piece of trash on demand. He won the bet handsomely: *The Exhibitionist* quickly became a best-seller.

Random House publisher Bennett Cerf, who had read the book in manuscript form, warned Henry of its transparent allusion to the Fondas. Father and daughter decided to take the high road. Was she an exhibitionist, reporters wanted to know. 'No, I don't think I'm an exhibitionist.' Had she read *the book*? 'No, I don't read trash,' she sniffed. 'Is that the book that everyone says is about me? I understand from my friends that one of the women the girl's father marries is a lesbian. Now the last kind of woman my father would marry is a lesbian.'

As the work on *Barbarella* progressed, while the rest of the world might be debating the relative merits of public nudity, Jane was merely trying to hold body and soul together. Each day after filming on the prop-filled sound stage in central Rome, the Plemiannikovs retreated to an ancient villa on Rome's Via Appia Antica. They shared the house with John Phillip Law, the winged 'Blind Angel' who makes love to Barbarella. One morning Law brought along a friend whose life, along with Jane's would soon take a dramatic turn: folksinger Joan Baez.

Barbarella was dismissed by the critics, but once again few found fault with Fonda. '*Barbarella* is a barely tolerable entertainment,' wrote John Simon in *The New York Times*. 'Granted, almost any film that starts with Jane Fonda in the nude is doomed to going downhill from there. But at least Miss Fonda, even if approximately clothed, remains omnipresent, lending grace, suavity, and a jocund toothsomeness to a foolish comic strip that emerges, in the movie version, a foolish comic strip.' *The New Yorker*'s Pauline Kael likened Jane to a Henry James heroine (and Vadim to a wickedly sophisticated European villain). 'And Jane Fonda having sex on the wilted feathers and rough, scroungy furs of *Barbarella* is more charming and fresh and bouncy than ever.' 'You could subtitle the film *2002: A Space Idiocy*,' sniped Charles Champlin in the *Los Angeles Times*.

Predictably, much of the public was shocked and outraged by *Barbarella*, sparking a controversy that ensured the film's blockbuster success at the box office. Jane was again being compared with those other tousle-haired blonde bombshells, Monroe and Bardot. She chafed at the comparison. Where only months earlier she had said she thought it was 'nice' to be thought of as a sex symbol, now she protested that it was 'silly. I'm no sex siren. I think the whole obsession with sex, and with the size of a girl's breasts, is a perversion – and it's sad comment on the state of manhood in America. The real homosexuals are the big tough guys who think they're so manly. All they're doing is hiding behind their fears. They all want to go back to their mother's breasts, that's all. If you ask me, the whole business about sex is sickness because it's dishonest.'

Criticised by some for wasting her talent on a movie viewed as being at best in questionable taste, Jane sprang to the defence of *Barbarella* and its director: 'Why *not* go out on a limb and do something like *Barbarella*? I would never have done *Barbarella* with anyone but Vadim. He convinced me that it was right for me, and I'm very glad he did.' *Barbarella* and all it represented would return to haunt her in her later incarnations as serious actress and social activist; she would even be moved to condemn publicly her once beloved Vadim as an exploiter of women. But again, that dramatic change of heart was still years in the future.

As soon as they had completed the last shot in *Barbarella*, director and star flew to Brittany to begin work on a new film, *Spirits of the Dead*. The movie was actually three separate tales by Edgar Allan Poe, each interpreted by a different director – Federico Fellini, Louis Malle, and Vadim.

Again, it became clear that Vadim and Fonda were out to shock audiences. The Vadim-directed sequence, a gothic story of preternatural lust called 'Mezergenstein,' involved a woman obsessed with a stallion that might or might not be the reincarnation of her dead lover. To compound matters, the lover also happened to be her cousin in the film, and he was played by none other than Peter Fonda.

'Mezergenstein' served up a variety of perversions, including orgies, lesbianism, and a hint of bestiality, all of which paled in comparison with the fact that real-life brother and sister were playing incestuous lovers, one of whom is dead and takes the form of a horse, no less.

'It was not our intention to titillate this way,' Jane insisted, seemingly mystified that anyone could draw such a conclusion. 'And in Europe, at least, no one took it like that. Not that I'm against incest,' she added, 'but our style is more direct. When the time comes for incest we will do it head on and leave the titillating for others. Give us credit, at least, for honesty.'

Peter never doubted that the movie would raise eyebrows, but for some time that had been his *raison d'être*. And by now Peter was not only immersed in the drug culture, he was intent on enhancing its image – to do on screen for pot and LSD what Jane was doing for sex. Between takes, he worked with writer Terry Southern (*Candy, Dr Strangelove*) on the script for a low-budget movie about two hippie dealers who hop on their choppers for a harrowing trip across the United States. The perennially out-of-control Dennis Hopper was to be Peter's co-producer and co-star on the film.

Meantime, Peter strummed on his guitar, tuned out, and filled his sister in on growing unrest at home over the war. Jane's brother was not so much anti-war as he was anti-Establishment, flouting society's rules and holding to the Timothy Leary line that hallucinogenic drugs had the power to expand the mind and change society for the good. 'He used to tell me eating a carrot was the same thing as being a racist,' recalled Jane. 'He felt that to hurt a single living thing, even a vegetable, was like abusing a human being. He couldn't even walk across the lawn without a guilt complex about squashing all that grass. No pun intended.'

At the time, Jane was impressed by her brother's newfound zeal but also somewhat irritated by it. 'I think proselytisers become as square as the people they're proselytising against,' she said. 'Why all this proselytising by takers of LSD? An alcoholic drinks, but an alcoholic doesn't say, "Come on, you have to be an alcoholic, too." Sure, I've taken pot. I prefer a good drink.'

Watching all this family sparring from the sidelines was Voutsinas, who had tagged along to play the role of a traitor in *Spirits of the Dead*. He was very convincing in the part, and Vadim would later discover why.

As she neared her 30th birthday, the ticking of Jane's biological clock drowned out other noises in her life. For the past five years, Nathalie had been a constant presence, and Jane had come to marvel at the ease with which she had assumed the role of mother in Stroyberg's absence. While Christian, Vadim's son by Deneuve, lived with his mother, Jane felt just as much at ease with the boy when he visited them in France or Malibu. 'I've watched the way you behave with your children,' she told Vadim one evening. 'I'm not frightened any more, I think, of having a baby.'

Work on *Spirits of the Dead* ended in mid-December, and the Plemiannikovs headed for a skiing holiday in the French Alps. It was there, according to Vadim, that their only child was conceived in the last days of 1967.

14

FROM THE vantage point of the Plemiannikov farmhouse in the French countryside, America seemed like a distant planet. While the United States was being torn apart by war and domestic racial unrest, Jane concentrated on nest building as she awaited the arrival of her firstborn. In late January 1968, she contracted a bothersome case of mumps, but it subsided quickly and she thought nothing more of it.

The prospect of motherhood was having a profound and complex effect on Jane. Her maternal role models – a mentally ill mother who killed herself, followed by a succession of stepmothers not much older than Jane – left her understandably confused and frightened. Hyped by Hollywood as a sex goddess, she also suffered, to a far lesser degree, from the self-loathing – having always to face herself as an *object* – that eventually destroyed Marilyn Monroe. On one level she deeply resented that role – somehow it made her feel ashamed of her sex. But then pregnancy, as Jane later told Vadim, transformed her – 'my fears, my hang-ups . . . they just vanished!'

Unencumbered by career distractions – having turned down two films to prepare for the real-life role of mother – Jane fell under the influence of constant house guests Roger and Elisabeth Vailland. Though they had severed ties with party leaders who still toed the Moscow line, the Vaillands remained dedicated communists. They felt it was their mission to open Jane's eyes to the 'evils' being visited on the world by her homeland. Jane no longer felt compelled to defend US foreign policy against the criticism of snobbish foreigners; obviously there were plenty of Americans who agreed with them. 'I began by being defensive,' she says, 'but then I saw Americans at home protesting the war by the hundreds of thousands, and soldiers deserting. I began to study and read.'

For the first time in her adult life, Jane took an active interest in world events. The anti-war movement had grown from a ragtag bunch of wild-eyed Marxists and spaced-out hippies to a cross section of the general population. President Lyndon Johnson's dramatic decision not to seek re-election seemed to lend legitimacy to the anti-war movement. Anti-war senators Eugene McCarthy and Robert F. Kennedy sat poised to snatch the Democratic nomination away from Johnson's anointed successor, Vice President Hubert Humphrey.

That March, the assassination of Martin Luther King triggered bloody riots in several American cities. Jane tried to make sense of it all. The Vaillands, all too happy to oblige, introduced her to their rhetoric-spouting friends. 'In Paris,' Jane recalled, 'I also met American deserters and Vietnamese of the National Liberation Front, who knew facts that I had not been aware of. Then I saw a movie on the Washington march, boys with long hair and radicals putting flowers into the guns of the guards standing in front of the Pentagon.'

Another influence on Jane during this formative period in her political awakening was Vanessa Redgrave. The two film stars, who met in Paris, shared the distinction of coming from famous acting families: Vanessa's father was Sir Michael Redgrave; her sister, Lynn Redgrave. Vanessa had actually paved the way for nudity in films when she crawled around on the floor nude with David Hemmings in *Blow-Up*. In 1967 she had divorced British director Tony Richardson after his affair with Jeanne Moreau, and she was about to become pregnant by her *Camelot* co-star Franco Nero (and cause a major stir by refusing to marry him).

Redgrave was a second-generation radical. Sir Michael had once been banned by the BBC for supporting the leftist People's Convention in the 1930s, and his eldest daughter followed her father's political lead. Evolving into a vehemently anti-American Trotskyite whose causes ranged from pacifism to support of Fidel Castro's regime, Vanessa Redgrave would later stand twice for parliament as a Workers Revolutionary Party candidate and be thoroughly trounced. As their friendship grew, Redgrave became a willing catalyst in Jane's political conversion.

In the absence of any opposing influence, Jane came to accept the premise that the United States was pursuing the same ruinous policies that the French had in Indochina, that Washington was lying to the American people about the horrors being carried out in their name, and that hundreds of thousands of innocent Vietnamese civilians were being slaughtered by indiscriminate bombing.

When philosopher Bertrand Russell and writer Jean-Paul Sartre convened an 'International War Crimes Tribunal' in Stockholm, Jane followed the proceedings carefully. She accepted unreservedly the tribunal's assertion that by 1967 the US military had dropped more explosives on Vietnam than it had dropped in the Pacific during all of World War II. Moreover, the tribunal concluded that 'in the South, the US forces and their docile Saigon allies have herded eight million people, peasants and their families, into barbed wire encampments under the surveillance of the political police'. More than half a million Vietnamese men, women and children, the report charged, 'have perished under this onslaught'. No mention, of course, was made of North Vietnamese or Vietcong atrocities against the local civilian population.

Jane's impending motherhood heightened her newfound sense of social consciousness. 'I began to love people,' she recalled, 'to understand that we don't give life to a human being only to have it killed by B-52 bombs, or to have it jailed by fascists, or to have it destroyed by social injustice.'

In the third month of her pregnancy, Jane's political transformation was interrupted by a personal crisis. She and Vadim were stunned to learn that mumps contracted in the early months of pregnancy could lead to birth defects. There was a chance that their child would be born with Down's syndrome. The doctors recommended an abortion, but Jane made the agonising decision to go ahead with her pregnancy.

Although her intellectual curiosity had been aroused, until now Jane had been able to view the tumultuous events across the ocean with some detachment. That all changed in May when the revolution came to her doorstep. A student revolt at the University of Suresnes had mushroomed into a violent national strike backed by France's trade unions and left-of-centre parties. Paris began to look like a battleground; windows were smashed, cars overturned and set on fire. The police stormed the protesters' barricades, lobbing tear-gas grenades and swinging truncheons.

With the powers-that-be off balance, Vadim was asked by his fellow directors to take over as president of France's important technicians' union. He was reluctant at first, but at Jane's urging he accepted. Then, within a matter of weeks, the French mini-revolution collapsed and things returned to normal. Vadim, who had intended all along merely to be a transitional leader of the union, stepped down.

Jane, more fired up than ever about the world political scene, turned her attention back to the United States. None of the news was good. After winning the California primary, Robert Kennedy was gunned down in Los Angeles's Ambassador Hotel. Richard Nixon was nominated by the Republicans while race riots erupted outside Miami's convention hall.

Events seemed to reach their zenith on the night of the Democratic Party Convention. At the invitation of Vadim's friend (and Kennedy in-law) Sargent Shriver, then ambassador to France, Vadim and his wife watched the nomination process on television at the US Embassy. Inside the convention hall, delegates were busy choosing Humphrey over McCarthy. Outside, television cameras covered the bloody clash between anti-war demonstrators and Mayor Richard Daley's police. In the front ranks of the protesters was a young man whose face, contorted with rage, caught Jane's attention – Tom Hayden.

'In '68,' she recalls, 'you had to deal with it. If you were in Paris, Paris was up in arms. Most everyone I knew was in the streets. Everything was changing overnight. I didn't have any political understanding of what was going on, except that people were moving. And people were moving in Chicago.' The other specific event she remembers watching on television from that time was the march of half a million people on the Pentagon.

Jane spent the last three months of her pregnancy relaxing with Vadim at a rented villa in St Tropez. The couple made no effort to hide from reporters who prowled the famous seaside resort in search of celebrities. Dining at a café with several friends, Vadim jokingly stuck his hand up the blouse of his eight-months-pregnant wife and squeezed her breast. The incident, duly reported in the French press, hardly altered the couple's lusty image.

To confound Fonda watchers further, the other women in Vadim's life took a keen interest in Jane's welfare. Catherine Deneuve generously offered prenatal advice and words of comfort. Year-round St Tropez resident Bardot dropped in routinely to check on Jane's progress. The only one of Vadim's women not to have given him a child, Bardot coyly predicted that it would be born on her birthday, 28 September. And though the parents firmly believed Jane was carrying a boy, Brigitte announced confidently that Jane would give birth to a girl. Whatever anxieties Jane had had about the mumps were replaced by bizarre nightmares of the child being born a miniature version of Bardot.

Vadim and Jane returned to the farmhouse in late September. Susan Blanchard, Jane's favourite stepmother, was staying in Paris when she got the call from Vadim shortly before midnight. Jane was experiencing labour pains, and he was going to rush her to the hospital an hour away. Blanchard rushed to meet them. After a difficult delivery, Jane gave birth to a baby girl on 28 September, just as Bardot had predicted. They named her Vanessa, after Jane's friend Vanessa Redgrave. 'When she was born – my baby – it was as if the sun had opened up for me,' Jane remembers. 'I felt whole. I became free.'

Free, it would turn out, to experiment in ways that would end her marriage, threaten her career, and make her simultaneously one of the most admired and hated women of her time.

PART TWO
Citizen Jane

When I get an idea, I usually plunge in. I plunged.

All I can say is that through the people I've met, the experiences I've had, the reading I've done, I realise the American system must be changed . . . through socialism. Of course I am a socialist.

Because of the success of my films, I have more power — and I intend to use it.

Contrary to belief, I am not Wonder Woman. I lack confidence. I am vulnerable. But I am also resilient.

15

PARENTHOOD SUITED Jane. More than that, it transformed her. 'I can't get over the miracle of giving birth,' she marvelled. 'I feel fulfilled . . . I want more children. I miss being pregnant. I've never been so elated. The pleasure and the pain were so extraordinary that I try to hang on to every memory of them.'

Like millions of other mothers, Jane quickly came to rely on Dr Benjamin Spock's *Baby and Child Care* as her bible. She breast-fed Vanessa, and learned from Vadim, a battle-hardened veteran of the baby wars, the finer points of nappy changing. Domestic bliss of this sort was something she had longed for, but strangely, she began to grow more restless. Instead of wanting to recover from the ordeal of birth, she felt infused with tremendous energy.

Vadim warily took notice of this increasing restlessness. The events unfolding in America still troubled Jane. As Sargent Shriver had predicted on the night they watched the Chicago Convention from the comfort of the ambassador's residence, by nominating Humphrey the Democrats had put Richard Nixon in the White House – though by a much smaller margin than expected. The American electorate now waited for the new president to implement his 'secret plan' to end the war. All this, says Jane, 'had a profound effect on me, because I suddenly realised to what degree the country had changed since I'd been away. I watched women leading marches. I watched women getting beaten up. I watched women walking up to bayonets . . . and they were not afraid. It was the soldiers who were afraid. I will never forget that experience. It completely changed me . . . it began my searching for what was behind it all.'

Jane's search started with a simple question. 'The words, "What am I doing in France?" were brewing around inside me,' Jane said of that time. 'With every visit I made to America I felt more and more that is where I belonged.'

When she did return to America, however, it would not be to whip up another celluloid confection like *Any Wednesday* or *Barefoot in the Park*. Hailed by the likes of Sartre, André Malraux, and Albert Camus as a modern masterpiece, Horace McCoy's stark 1935 novel *The Shoot Horses, Don't They?* focused on the desperate souls who participate in a gruelling Depression-era dance marathon. There had been numerous attempts to bring the book to the screen. All had failed, until screenwriter James Poe persuaded producers Irwin Winkler and Robert Chartoff to produce his adaptation with him as director.

To everyone's dismay, Poe suggested Jane to play the chronically depressed Gloria in *They Shoot Horses*. It was a bold and wholly unexpected choice. *Barbarella* had just been released in the United States, securing Jane's naughty-girl image. She was even on the cover of *Life* magazine in full Barbarella gear, caressing a phallic ray-gun. But Poe saw in Jane's eyes the same 'hunted animal' quality that had so impressed Lee Strasberg. He overcame resistance to the idea from almost every other party to the film, and in November the script was sent to Jane in Paris.

Beyond the film's obvious power as a dramatic work – 'the first existential novel to come out of America,' according to none other than existentialist Albert Camus – Jane was drawn to *They Shoot Horses* on political grounds. In its graphic depiction of poverty and hopelessness, the book showed the dark, callously exploitative side of the capitalist dream. Without having to resort to polemics, she could accomplish as much as any placard-waving protester to stir the American conscience. (In order to land her as their star, the producers acquiesced to her demand that she be given final script approval.)

Jane would have to return to California in December 1968 to start work on the picture – the first, in her words, 'explicitly social thing' she would do. But first, there were loose ends to tie up. Eleven-year-old Nathalie, despite obvious feelings of insecurity stemming from the arrival of a sibling, was shipped off to a Swiss boarding school at Jane's insistence. Then an English nanny was hired to care for Vanessa.

Vadim and Jane arrived in California in early January, renting a house in Malibu that was even larger and more luxurious than the one they had leased from William Wyler. There was a bar in the living room, a huge wraparound veranda, and a master suite with a bed the size of a small soccer field.

Jane's reputation preceded her. A widow in the house two doors down sat silhouetted in a window all day, shouting insults at Jane and Vadim as they strolled along the beach. 'She's decided we're living in sin,' Jane told a friend. ' "You'll be punished, you're living in sin," she'll scream. Suddenly the other day, I shouted back, "We're *not!* We're *married*." And then I thought, What am I angry about? We *did* live together for years.'

While Vadim angled to direct *Myra Breckinridge*, the movie version of his friend Gore Vidal's outrageous sex-change best-seller, Jane got down to work on *They Shoot Horses* with a ferocity that Vadim found both admirable and frightening. She had quickly become, as so many of her friends would later describe the 'real Jane Fonda' to me, 'all business'.

When Jane lopped off her hair for the lead role of Gloria, Vadim was stunned. Those luxurious blonde tresses had become one of her trademark features . . . and one of her physical attributes that most appealed to her husband. ('Vadim likes his women blonde,' Jane was prone to say, pointing to the rather obvious examples of Bardot, Stroyberg, and Deneuve.) Fonda could easily have worn a short wig for *Horses*, as she had in several of her previous films, and the fact that she refused the suggestion led Vadim to believe that cutting off her long hair was an act of symbolic defiance aimed squarely at him. Jane's avowed view was more circumspect. 'When it got around that I was doing *Horses*, and that I wanted to cut my hair for it, you know what people said? "Jane, *dahling*, you're out of your mind, don't you cut your hair!" I thought, Oh wow, so that's what I've become − a lotta goddamn blonde hair.'

Three weeks before shooting, James Poe, who seemed to be starting off well with Jane, was abruptly fired as director and replaced by Sydney Pollack. Poe had been a major reason, perhaps *the* reason, the movie was being made at all. Yet Jane approved of his dismissal. 'I couldn't understand that attitude coming from a woman who was so sensitive to social injustice, to the corrupting power of money, and to the lack of humanity in Hollywood's moguls,' Vadim wrote in *Bardot, Deneuve, Fonda*. 'This incident revealed to me another side of my wife's character: her ability to forget compassion when it was a question of better results. Efficiency came before all else.'

Her hair shorn and marcel-waved, Jane started doing her homework. Gloria, at the start of the script, has just been discharged from hospital after trying to kill herself over a broken love affair. She decides to seek stardom in the Hollywood she reads about in movie magazines but is crushed when confronted with the seedy reality. Gloria and a would-be director named Robert (played by Michael Sarrazin) decide to enter a dance marathon for the cash prize, but it turns out to be a gruelling, dehumanising experience. Utterly defeated emotionally, Gloria asks Robert to put her out of her misery − and he complies with a bullet to her head.

While Jane was to shoulder most of the acting burden, there were several choice character parts. Red Buttons would play an old sailor who dies of a heart attack on the dance floor (in the film Jane just keeps on dancing with his corpse), while Gig Young was to earn an Oscar as best supporting actor for his performance as Rocky, the coldhearted and corrupt promoter – MC of the marathon, who keeps the dancers moving by shouting 'Yowza, Yowza, Yowza' through a megaphone.

To nail down the era, Jane pored over scores of publications on the 1930s in general and on dance marathons in particular. During rehearsals, she and Red Buttons danced around the darkened ballroom alone for fourteen hours straight to work out the various positions marathoners could actually fall asleep in while still legitimately 'dancing'.

It was difficult enough to sustain the level of melancholia the part required, but one aspect of Gloria's character Jane found almost impossible to accept was her dislike of children. As a new mother, this seemed all but inconceivable. 'One day, I heard on the radio that a seventeen-year-old woman who had just had a baby left the child in the middle of a busy intersection in downtown Los Angeles,' Jane would recall. 'I got information on the woman and read about her background.'

Instead of returning home every night to her family in Malibu, Jane moved into Mae West's old dressing room on the Warner Brothers set. She kept her make-up on and stayed in costume, convinced it was the only way she could sustain her character's deepening cynicism. To stay on the edge of despair, she periodically leafed through a grisly California Highway Patrol training manual she kept in her trailer. It was filled with gory photographs of gunshot wounds, decapitated bodies, and mangled car-accident victims. Vadim brought Vanessa with him to visit Mommy occasionally, but for the most part they stayed away. 'Gloria was such a desperate, negative, depressed person,' Jane tried to explain. 'Gradually, I let myself become that way too. How could I go home like that? I'd walk in the door and . . . *aarrgh*! So I stayed away . . . It took me months to get over it.'

In Sydney Pollack, Jane had met her match as a perfectionist. So that his actors would appear suitably exhausted, Pollack shot the movie in sequence – much of it in an exact replica of the famed Aragon Ballroom that had stood on a pier south of Santa Monica. It was at the Aragon that many of the biggest and most widely publicised dance marathons of the era had taken place. As filming progressed, Jane lost more and more weight; to give herself the appropriate gaunt, hollow-eyed look, she was again turning to bulimia.

Jane also saw the filming as an opportunity to put her dance training to work. Foreshadowing the Workout, Jane showed up on the soundstage each morning at around 6.30 to do her warm-up exercises with the extras, and was soon offering them tips on how to get the maximum benefit out of their exercise routines. Although open with other cast members at the beginning, she gradually withdrew into her character's impenetrable shell – all part of her Actors Studio training.

Jane had, for all intents and purposes, *become* Gloria – or at least, in the words of one cast member, they were becoming 'harder and harder to tell apart' off the set. Jane now walked and talked like the despondent Gloria, and Vadim worried that this transformation might have a lasting effect on his wife's psyche. It certainly was having a lasting effect on the way she viewed Vadim. When he brought Vanessa to visit, Mommy, who had stopped breast-feeding after three months, was openly very affectionate with the child, while doing her best to ignore Vadim. Supporting actress Jacquelyn Hyde noticed 'a kind of distance between them. There wasn't a lot of touching.'

'She was completely involved and totally professional,' Pollack said of Jane. 'She carried a copy of the book around with her, and because she had strong opinions about it, she was slow to be persuaded if she disagreed with somebody else's interpretation of a point or a scene. It was so much more exciting than working with a puppet.'

With the exception of two shouting matches with Pollack over the shooting of a particularly intense scene, Jane refrained from playing the prima donna. But she did keep a regal distance between herself and other cast members. Several of her co-workers on the film interpreted Jane's frostiness as arrogance. 'She had this way of looking right through you once a scene was over,' said one. 'I mean, it was a very tough movie and we all were nervous and tired and felt under the gun. So it was even more important to break the tension. But Jane was pretty distant. She wasn't in the mood to chat. She just gave off those vibes.'

'She had a kind of remote quality,' admitted Pollack. 'There was no social-ising at the end of the day, no need to send her flowers or give her the "Good morning, dear," treatment. She wanted none of that.' The results, he added, proved that her approach to the role was the right one. 'This was her chance really to make an indelible mark as a character that was fully done, fully executed – and she held nothing back. There was no vanity in the performance, no self-preservation. There was no hiding in it. She went all the way.'

Jane would later give Vadim credit for sticking by her during this time. 'I became so unhealthily immersed in the role of Gloria I couldn't tell reality from illusion,' she confessed. 'Big black wells of loneliness and depression fell over me. I became a manic-depressive. My speech pattern changed. I even started *talking* like Gloria. And I was so uncertain about the part. It was like having a dead baby inside me and I went around wondering why I couldn't give birth. By the last days of shooting, I had delivered Gloria. The symptoms of her character were gone. I was rid of her. Now a lot of speed freaks have told me they liked me so much they thought I was on speed.'

Once filming was completed in May, Pollack was delighted with the result. Jane was not. After viewing the edited movie for the first time, she complained about the series of flash-forwards that supposedly prepared the audience for the movie's gruesome climax. 'I felt it was a very straightforward film that didn't need gimmicks,' she said. When Pollack had the flash-forwards cut out, the preview audiences, according to Jane, 'acted like they were at a football game. When Red Buttons dropped dead, they laughed their heads off. So we put them back in.'

There had also been cuts of segments that Jane felt were crucial to explaining her character's motivation. 'The script I agreed to do was so different from the movie we shot, it was like night and day,' she said. 'One whole hour ended up on the cutting-room floor — whole pages and scenes about who I was and where I came from were taken out.' Another last-minute 'gimmick' that Jane objected to was the addition of a dreamy prologue showing horses galloping through a field. 'Too arty,' said Jane. Perhaps, but preview audiences clearly responded to Pollack's 'arty' touches. His version of the film, not Jane's, prevailed.

Now that *They Shoot Horses* was behind her, Jane tried to crawl out from under Gloria's skin. Again, she started with her hair. 'I felt like I was a victim of that hair,' she said, 'so I went to Vadim's barber.' In a curious echo of her mother's prenatal hopes and her own earliest upbringing, she said of her new bob, 'I always had a deep-rooted psychological need to be a boy. Now I am one. You have to learn how to get down off the screen and be a real person again. If you start believing the screen, one day you wake up and you are nothing inside, just another pretty face that isn't so pretty any more.'

Through the sad eyes of Gloria, a woman who had been repeatedly exploited by men, Jane had begun to reassess her life with Vadim. She had grown embarrassed by her larger-than-life Barbarella-doll image. While acknowledging herself as an accomplice in its cultivation, Jane placed much of the blame squarely on Vadim. He viewed the world with a certain hedonistic detachment she felt she could no longer afford. In the same vein, she saw parallels between the grim reality depicted in *They Shoot Horses* and the situation confronting America in 1969: 'The war we're going through now — out country has never gone through such a long, agonising experience, except before the Depression. The Depression is the closest America ever came before to national disaster. Perhaps audiences — especially kids — will be able to come away from seeing *They Shoot Horses* with the feeling that if we could pull out of the Depression, we can pull out of the mess we're in now.'

'I wasted the first thirty-two years of my life,' Jane would grow fond of saying.

She would spend the rest of her life trying to make up for those 'wasted' years — with a vengeance.

Jane fell asleep along with most of the audience when she saw the original four-hour version of her brother's low-budget biker film. Reluctantly, Peter and his partner on the project, Dennis Hopper, whittled it down to a manageable length. After its release in May 1969, *Easy Rider* quickly became not only an instant blockbuster at the box office but a phenomenon of global proportions. As Wyatt and Billy, the free-spirited, cycle-straddling dope peddlers, Fonda and Hopper captured the imagination of moviegoers the way Clift, Brando, and Dean had done a generation before. Overnight, Peter was

– for a time at least – the most famous Fonda of all – and, with 22 per cent of the film's profits, the wealthiest. More significantly, *Easy Rider* also gave Henry Fonda's troublesome son tremendous clout in the industry. He had made, as *Time* put it, the little movie that killed the big picture. Studio heads stood in line for a shot at distributing his next 'little' movie.

In truth, *Easy Rider* today hardly seems a very good, much less a great, film. Blatantly self-indulgent, virtually plotless, often unintentionally funny, it has not stood the test of time. But as the tumultuous sixties drew to a close, it served as a cinematic reflection of an era of violence and drugs. If *Easy Rider* did not go so far as to celebrate the drug culture, it validated it, lending a certain legitimacy to what had hitherto been regarded as deviant behaviour.

Peter was lionised as prophet of the new nihilism, a bona fide teen idol. Pinned over the fireplace of his Bel Air mansion was a newspaper cartoon showing two pubescent girls waiting for a thunderstorm to pass. 'Do you think,' one of the girls asks, 'that it rains on Peter Fonda too?'

Henry, who had recently moved with Shirlee to an estate not far from Peter's in the platinum hills of Bel Air, was clearly uncomfortable with the fact that his son was so closely identified with the drug culture. He viewed wild-card Dennis Hopper as nothing more than a 'whacked-out idiot'. Yet, Hollywood pro that he was, he found it difficult to argue with financial success.

Jane was stunned by the magnitude of *Easy Rider*'s success, but hardly scandalised by the subject matter. After all, she and Vadim had been witness to the wild New York pop scene presided over by Andy Warhol and the group of gays, bisexuals, cross-dressers, sadomasochists, drug addicts, freaked-out *artistes*, and uptown dilettantes who flowed in and out of Andy's famous Factory. They sampled nude theatre long before *Oh, Calcutta!* and *Hair* shocked the nation, and partied with a crowd so fast it made even the jaded Vadim feel like a starched-collared Puritan.

Until 1968-9, Jane had always taken a backseat to her husband in sexual matters. That apparently ended when, on one sojourn in New York, Jane met a good-looking young blond man whose face, said Vadim, had 'the sublime purity of an archangel. He was, however, a completely amoral person.' The young man, identified only as 'E', marked Jane's final liberation from the double standard. Whenever they breezed through town, usually on their way to California, 'E' would be an active participant in their nocturnal prowls.

In California, the Plemiannikovs were running with an even wilder crowd. Vadim's successor as European *enfant terrible* was Roman Polanski, the cocky young Pole who, ironically, had scored his first major success directing Catherine Deneuve in the unsettling thriller *Repulsion*. Jane decided to make good her earlier promise to star with Peter in a straightforward incest film, and Polanski owned the rights to the story she wanted – a charming tale of brotherly/sisterly love entitled *Blue Guitar*. Polanski, who had earlier offered Jane *Rosemary's Baby*, did not hold a grudge against her for having turned him down. During the negotiations for *Blue Guitar*, a friendship developed between Vadim and Jane and the Polanskis – Roman and his beautiful actress wife, Sharon Tate.

By the time Jane got to know Tate, she had already made a sizeable splash in the camp *Valley of the Dolls* playing Jennifer, the sex bomb who takes an overdose rather than undergo a mastectomy. The movie and the huge Jacqueline Susann best-seller on which it was based depicted a Hollywood awash in 'dolls' – amphetamines and barbiturates popularly known as 'uppers' and 'downers'. But the Hollywood described by book and movie was a Norman Rockwell painting compared with the drug scene that actually enveloped the film community in the late 1960s. Added to the usual pharmacist's list of uppers and downers were LSD, STP, mescaline, peyote, methamphetamine, and cocaine. Marijuana and hashish were by then hardly considered drugs at all. (Heroin was practically the only thing left that frightened even dedicated thrill-seekers.)

A steady diet of mood-altering substances did little to promote mental health within the moviemaking community and the legions of hangers-on. Their perception of reality seriously distorted by one too many trips on LSD or from nibbling on magic mushrooms once too often, many users became obsessed with the dark sciences – witchcraft, satanism, the occult. Jane did not fall into this category. Ouija boards, seances, and voodoo were of absolutely no interest to her. While marijuana had become something of a staple in her life (she would carry a supply of joints with her in a tiny silver snuffbox and often light up in public), it is doubtful whether Jane ever dabbled to any extent in the mind-bending hallucinations extolled by her brother. But Jane did continue to expand her sexual horizons.

After years of catering to Vadim's need for sexual variety, Jane began to demand the same open-mindedness of Vadim. At one of the Polanskis' wild, drug-fuelled bashes at 10050 Cielo Drive in up-market Brentwood, the housekeeper could not get into the bathroom and began pounding on the locked door. Eventually, the door opened and out came Jane, hair in disarray and clothing askew, with another (male) guest. She made no apologies to the stunned Vadim. In fact, as Vadim relates in *Bardot, Deneuve, Fonda*, she complained to him about being interrupted. 'I hate it,' she said, 'when something's half finished.' A guest recalled that the mysterious 'other man' may have been handsome millionaire hairstylist Jay Sebring, who had been Sharon Tate's lover before she met Polanski.

It was a milestone in the relationship between Jane and Vadim. Having essentially declared herself to be a free agent, she went on to test Vadim's commitment to sexual equality. This included bringing servicemen – some reportedly fresh from tours of duty in Vietnam – home.

The emotional aftereffects of *They Shoot Horses* had not yet worn off, as Jane still harboured a fragment of the tormented Gloria inside her. Then, too, there was this restlessness Vadim had come to notice in France, after the first joys of motherhood had apparently worn thin. And finally, Jane seemed to be finding it more and more difficult to reconcile her comfortable life with Vadim with her expanding awareness of the world around her.

Jane was changing. Vadim was not. Or, rather, he could not. Growing up in occupied France during World War II, he had witnessed firsthand the shifting loyalties, the compromised principles and outright hypocrisy of governments and their leaders. He was, like many Europeans, cynical about politics. He was not, however, cynical about life. Vadim might be perceived as an unrepentant orgiast, but he was in fact almost childlike in his appreciation of beauty, pleasure, and comfort – a quality Jane had once found irresistible. Now, in her heightened awareness, she found it frivolous.

Exhausted, confused, and restless, Jane needed to go somewhere to sort out her feelings. Peter had used some of the early proceeds from *Easy Rider* to buy a home in Hawaii, and he invited Jane to join him there. She took him up on the offer early in June, leaving Vadim and Vanessa behind in Malibu. During her first two weeks in Hawaii, Jane took guitar lessons and listened to her brother drone on about corporate polluters and the wonderful benefits of drugs. Peter had also fallen under the spell of Krishnamurti, and Jane, desperate for a new mentor, read all she could about the Indian philosopher. Like any earnest student, each night she retired to her room, Magic Marker in hand, to underline the important passages in Krishnamurti's work. Strung out with nervous energy, she was also now chain-smoking her way through three packets of cigarettes a day.

Jane returned to Malibu as confused as ever about the world and her future in it. Vadim, Vanessa, and Vanessa's nanny flew to New York during the last week in June. There the couple again immersed themselves in Andy Warhol's surreal world before boarding the *France* for Le Havre. Warhol came aboard the luxurious ocean liner to see them off but was soon distracted by the old-fashioned green Coke bottles aboard ship. 'Coca-Cola hasn't been making embossed bottles for four years now,' Andy said as he stuffed a large bag with the empties. 'You just can't find them in the United States any more. They'll soon be worth a fortune.' One of the recent history's shrewdest pack rats was eventually proved right.

Once back at their farm in France, Jane hurled herself into a number of domestic projects. Once again, she was making copious lists and completing each and every assigned task. More trees and shrubs were trucked in and planted, missing stones in the patio were replaced, furniture was delivered for Vanessa's nursery. The major undertaking of the season, however, was the conversion of a barn into an indoor swimming pool – all personally supervised by Jane.

Twice a week, she drove in to Paris for her dancing lessons, and for a speed-reading course she hoped would make it easier for her to plough through the heavy books she now felt compelled to read. Jane had become, according to Vadim, a most efficient machine – precisely the quality that would make her such a phenomenal success at almost every enterprise she would undertake.

On 20 July, while they watched live television coverage of Neil Armstrong's historic walk on the moon, Vanessa decided it was an appropriate time to take her first steps. Vadim was in no mood to celebrate. For some time he had been feeling Jane slip away. 'The erosion of love,' he wrote in *Memoirs of the Devil*, 'is a sordid, shabby, absurd thing. A shameful and useless sickness. It is not even a lost battle, it is a cancer that eats away body, soul, and mind. No one ever completely recovers from it.'

Word concerning the Plemiannikovs' marital troubles had by now drifted across the Atlantic. True to form, Voutsinas re-entered the picture. On a visit to the farm, he whispered into Jane's ear that it was time she left her husband. While she was not about to return to her psychoanalytical Greek, she still valued his opinion. Yet before taking any drastic action, Jane was determined to chart a new course for herself.

To do some redubbing on *They Shoot Horses*, Jane flew back to California with Vadim. As their brief stay wound to a close, they were again fêted by Sharon Tate at the Polanskis' charming Benedict Canyon home. With Polanski himself in London working on a film, Tate, eight months pregnant with their child, had asked several friends to stay with her. By now, Vadim and Jane were well acquainted with the Polanskis' friends – Wociech Frykowski, a drug-dealing Polish émigré specialising in the sale of 'meth'; Frykowski's coffee-heiress girlfriend, Abigail Folger; and Frykowski's best customer, Jay Sebring.

Two weeks after her return to Paris, friends called Jane with horrifying news: everyone in the Polanski house on the night of 8 August – Tate, Sebring, Frykowski, and Folger – had been slaughtered, along with a young man who had the sad misfortune of stumbling upon the scene.

The following evening, wealthy businessman Leno La Bianca and his wife, Rosemary, were also bludgeoned to death in their luxurious home in Los Angeles's Los Feliz district. The nation may have been stunned and upset by the brutal crimes, but the entertainment industry was thrown into an absolute state of collective panic. Stars had old security systems beefed up or new, state-of-the-art systems installed. They hired bodyguards, bought attack dogs, even began carrying their own handguns.

The cloud of fear hanging over Hollywood only grew blacker as the gruesome details of the killings were leaked to the press. The word 'PIG' had been written in Sharon Tate's blood on the front door. Inside, blood from all the victims had spattered the walls, the floors, the ceiling. Jay Sebring had been sexually mutilated; a rope was tied around his neck and thrown over a beam in the living room. On the other end was Sharon Tate, one of her breasts hacked off, and an X carved into her swollen belly with a fork. Frykowski and Folger had been stabbed hundreds of times.

Speculation as to the murderers and their possible motives ran rampant. But of one thing Hollywood's radical community was certain: the killers had scrawled 'PIG' at the scene to throw investigators off the track. There was no way this could have been the handiwork of members of the peace-and-love generation.

Less than two weeks after the killings, the long-anticipated Woodstock Festival took place on schedule, those in attendance firmly believing that none of their spiritual brethren had been involved in one of the bloodiest crimes of the century.

Five months later, the counter-culture generation gathered once again – this time at Altamont, a racetrack in the hills of Northern California some forty miles east of San Francisco. About 300,000 people swarmed over the hills to hear the Rolling Stones, the Jefferson Airplane, Santana, and a number of other supergroups of the era perform over a two-day period. But there the similarity with Woodstock ended. A makeshift clinic treated hundreds of people who had overdosed on LSD, speed, or heroin. While the Stones' lead singer, Mick Jagger, dressed in red-and-black court jester's garb, pranced on stage singing 'Jumping Jack Flash', 'Brown Sugar', 'Under My Thumb' and 'Satisfaction', the notorious Hell's Angels ringed the stage as the Stones' official 'bodyguards'. Randomly the Angels beat anyone who came within swinging distance, and wound up fatally stabbing a black man. By the time the Altamont festival was over, three others had died: a freaked-out teenage boy who jumped into a nearby irrigation canal and drowned, and two others who were run over in their sleeping bags.

That same week, Charles Manson and his followers were indicted for the Tate–La Bianca murders. Operating from the Spahn Ranch on the outskirts of LA, Manson had instructed his LSD-drugged 'family' of misfits, psychotics, and runaways to go on their bloody rampage. The prosecution argued that the house on Cielo Drive was leased to the Polanskis by Doris Day's record-producer son, Terry Melcher, and that Manson wanted to take revenge on Melcher for refusing to help Manson with his musical career. Sharon Tate and the rest, said the authorities, just happened to be in the wrong place at the wrong time. (Manson is currently serving a life sentence, as are his co-defendants Susan Atkins, Patricia Krenwinkel, and Leslie Van Houten, in a maximum-security cell at San Quentin.)

Radical diehards persisted in their belief that it was all a right-wing plot to persecute an innocent hippie. A number of underground publications followed that line, as did Chicago Seven co-defendant Jerry Rubin, who visited Manson in jail. 'In my frame of mind,' Rubin told Tom Hayden decades later, 'I was so into romanticising outlaw behaviour that I looked for any possible explanation to find something good in the outlaw. And that attitude was part of the madness of the times.'

It would be months before the truth of the Manson murders became publicly known, yet the dark underbelly of Hollywood's 'liberated' new breed had been exposed. At the crime scene, police had found a considerable quantity of drugs, not to mention a cache of videotapes graphically depicting all sorts of kinky goings-on among the Polanskis and their crowd – including satanic rituals, sadomasochistic beatings and whippings, orgies, and bestiality.

The horrible news of her friends' murder and the grotesque circumstances surrounding it only compounded Jane's confusion. She had to face the obvious parallels between Sharon Tate and herself: both were self-styled screen sex sirens. Both had husbands who were not only foreign-born directors but notorious hedonists. Jane was a new mother, Sharon was about to become one. And both had dabbled in a world that was obviously more dangerous than either could have dreamed.

More than anything, Jane felt grateful. Grateful that she was not partying with Sharon and the others at the house that fateful night. Grateful that she was geographically removed from a Hollywood community now enveloped in fear. Most important, she was grateful that she had been given another chance to focus on what she truly wanted to accomplish in life.

Vadim was having his own problems. The job of directing *Myra Breckinridge* had gone not to him but to British director Michael Sarne (another close friend of the Polanskis). With nothing else to occupy his time, Vadim concentrated on lining up *The Blue Guitar* for Jane and Peter. Jane had long admired the work of Irish novelist Edna O'Brien, and it was suggested that O'Brien be approached to write the screenplay.

The Plemiannikovs spent the last two weeks of September ensconced in a luxury hotel on the beach at St Tropez. The highlight of the holiday was a party to celebrate Vanessa's first birthday. While the birthday girl smeared herself with chocolate cake, Jane gleefully recorded the event with a home movie camera.

Still, she grew increasingly restless, and was plagued by self-doubt and indecision. Jane had read all the books about Krishnamurti that Peter had given her and was wondering if Indian philosophy held the answers to her dilemma. Starting with George Harrison, the first of the Beatles to embrace the teachings of the Maharishi Mahesh Yogi, many celebrities had already made highly publicised trips to India searching for the key to inner peace. Mia Farrow, who, as the daughter of director John Farrow and Maureen O'Sullivan was a member of Jane's informal Hollywood brat pack, came back a true believer; she told Jane that her trip to India had helped her overcome the pain caused by her messy divorce from Frank Sinatra.

When another friend passed through Paris on her way to Bombay, Jane did not hesitate to accept her invitation to come along. During her month-long stay in India, Jane was impressed more by the grim realities that confronted her than by the gurus and transcendental meditation. She was sickened by the bodies that littered the streets of Calcutta, by rampant disease and poverty on so colossal a scale as to be unimaginable to most Westerners. After a few days on the subcontinent, she was sufficiently moved by the plight of small children begging in the streets to sit down in her hotel suite and pen a letter to Vadim. In it, she professed her undying devotion to her husband and to Vanessa, and her eagerness to return home. Vadim found the letter disconcerting. 'It was touching, and so full of good intentions,' recalled Vadim, 'that it sent a shiver down my spine.' She was, it seemed to him, trying desperately to convince herself that the marriage could be saved. Had she really wanted to strengthen their union, he reasoned, she would have asked Vadim to 'get on the next plane and join her'. But she didn't.

In truth, the letter was probably most reflective of Jane's maternal feelings; the sight of so many starving children reminded her that she was responsible for the welfare of another tiny human being who waited for her thousands of miles away.

On her travels through India and Nepal, Jane met a number of memorable characters, including a Buddhist monk whose contact with visiting Westerners had resulted in his becoming a heroin addict. She also came upon long-haired American youths who seemed to have no problem at all with the appalling conditions they encountered.

When she visited the tiny Himalayan kingdom of Sikkim, Jane became even more incensed at the disparity between rich and poor. Her hostess, the queen of Sikkim, was actually New York socialite Hope Cooke, who had married Sikkim's crown prince and become queen when he ascended the throne. Jane stayed as guest of the royal couple in their spectacular mountaintop palace. (The king was imprisoned and Cooke fled Sikkim after it was annexed by India in 1975. She later divorced the king and, in 1980, settled in New York City, where she found employment as a social worker.)

Far from having found the path to inner peace, Jane returned from her Indian odyssey convinced that the solution was to turn outward, not inward. 'I could easily have gone on that kind of trip – kind of a dropout, metaphysical, hippie-type trip,' she recalls, 'but I suddenly understood the incredible responsibility of it. And then I suddenly thought, what am I doing over here?'

That November, after her return to France and following two weeks in London to discuss *The Blue Guitar* with Edna O'Brien, Jane flew to California for the first press screening of *They Shoot Horses, Don't They?* As she got off the plane in Los Angeles, she spotted a copy of *Ramparts* on the newsstands. The magazine's cover story was about the Indian activists who had seized

Alcatraz. 'Indians were on my mind,' she recalls. 'On the magazine's cover was an American Indian woman looking angry and the words "Red Power". I thought, What is this? It blew my mind. I hadn't known anything. I couldn't believe what we had done to the Indians.'

Still 'traumatised' by her experience on the Asian subcontinent, Jane was whisked in a limousine to her pink-and-gold suite in the Beverly Wilshire Hotel (Vanessa and her nanny were dispatched to the guest house of Grandpa Henry's Bel Air estate). As usual, crystal vases full of expensive cut flowers, fruit baskets, and a supply of Dom Perignon awaited Jane's arrival – with the compliments of the hotel management.

Soon Jane was joined by her husband. 'I got up in the morning and I said to Vadim, "Something has happened. There has been a plague. Only the brave survivors are out. It's so empty." Then I realised it had always been that way. I had just never noticed what a clean, orderly, rich life we live . . . I saw those houses of Beverly Hills, those immaculate gardens, those neat, silent streets where the rich drive their big cars and send their children to the psychoanalyst and employ exploited Mexican gardeners and black servants.'

Jane's exposure to the 'urine, noise, colour, misery, disease, and teeming masses' of India had prompted her to 'see our culture in a different light. We've come so far and we have done so many things that could be working for us, and they all seem to be working against us. Instead of helping us to enjoy, they are not. Something is really wrong.'

Her first priority, however, was the picture. So that it would qualify for Academy Award consideration, *They Shoot Horses* was released on 12 December. The film, nearly everyone agreed, was a cinematic event. 'Sharp-tongued Gloria, the hard, defiantly masochistic girl who expects nothing and gets it, the girl who thinks the worst of everybody and makes everybody act it out, the girl who can't ask for anything except death, is the strongest role an American actress has had on the screen this year,' wrote *The New Yorker*'s hard-nosed Pauline Kael. 'Jane Fonda goes all the way with it, as screen actresses rarely do once they become stars.' Concurred John Simon in *The New York Times*: 'Jane Fonda, that fine little actress, graduates into a fine big actress.'

The actress herself, more politicised than ever, was viewing *They Shoot Horses* not simply as *cinéma vérité* (albeit expertly crafted *cinéma vérité*) but as an indictment of American values. 'I think,' she said, 'that it's a very forceful condemnation of the capitalist system.'

So what role would Jane tackle next? Certainly not the one offered by a man regarded at the time as the hottest director in the business. 'Mike Nichols had just offered me the part of a girl with forty-inch boobs! I turned it down. I'd give anything to work with Mike, but can you imagine *me* with forty-inch boobs?' The part of Jack Nicholson's wife in *Carnal Knowledge* went instead to Ann-Margret, who received an Academy Award nomination for her efforts.

At a party in Los Angeles, Jane was introduced for the first time to director-producer Alan J. Pakula. As Pakula recalls, 'We talked for several hours about a lot of things – about women in our society, about sexuality in our society. It was just a wonderful, freewheeling discussion. I came out of it thinking, I'd love to work with that woman.' Two weeks later, Pakula received a script from the screenwriting brothers Andy K. and Dave Lewis dealing with a New York prostitute being stalked by a murderer. As soon as he'd read the screenplay for *Klute*, Pakula sent it to Jane.

The movie's central character, Bree Daniel, shared some of the toughness and cynicism that made Gloria so unforgettable in *They Shoot Horses*. But Bree Daniel was also a high-class call girl, and Jane was reluctant to take on another sexually explicit role so soon after shedding her Barbarella image.

When Pakula approached her in late December for an answer, Jane was still vacillating. 'I don't know how I feel about it,' she told him. Recalls Pakula: 'We talked for a half hour; she had an interviewer waiting and she had to get rid of me. She said, "Look, do you really want me to do it?" I said yes. She said, "Okay, I'll do it." Out of such little statements things get made.'

On New Year's Eve, 1969, Jane stepped off a plane at Kennedy Airport and was told that she had just won the New York Film Critics Award for *They Shoot Horses* as best actress of the year – an honour that made her odds-on favourite to pick up her first Academy Award.

She had agreed to be interviewed by Rex Reed for *The New York Times*, and a little before 10 p.m. that evening actress and journalist sat down in the living room of Henry Fonda's 74th Street town house for a chat. It would turn out to be Jane's most memorable encounter with the press to date.

Dressed in a leather miniskirt and purple sweater, Jane sat curled up on the couch. Reed watched as her 'fire-ice fingernails' slowly removed the tobacco from a Winston, then opened her snuffbox and replaced the tobacco with 'fine grey pot she had just brought back from where? India? Morocco? She couldn't remember; all she knew was it wasn't that tacky stuff they mix with hay in Tijuana, this was the real thing.' Then, without batting an eyelid: 'You don't mind if I turn on, do you?'

'Then', Reed recalled, 'she lay back on the sofa, inhaled a lung full of dreams, and continued.' Jane wondered aloud if the 1970s would bring as much change as the 1960s had. 'We were the sloth generation,' she said of her contemporaries who came of age in the 1950s. 'Now the kids are active . . . Take a simple thing like turning on. Doctors, lawyers, politicians – I don't know anyone who doesn't turn on. Except maybe in the South. I guess the South is still fifty years behind.'

For the next two hours she talked nonstop about the speed-reading courses she was taking, the autohypnosis classes that she hoped would help her kick her three-packets-a-day habit, and all she had learned from being a mother. 'The course of my daughter's day is a constant source of discovery . . . From the beginning I watched her – listening, learning, perceiving – and I thought, why her and not me? Why is it that in growing old we lose the ability to see, smell, touch, and feel?'

Jane's doting comments about Vanessa belied the fact that she was spending little time with the child. During most of her daughter's first year of life Jane had been working on *They Shoot Horses* and searching for herself in Europe and India. As her political activity increased, she would spend even less time with Vanessa, though frequently making a point of posing with her daughter for the press.

Jane let loose on the critics: 'I don't know one critic from another . . . except that there is a woman named Judith Crist who hates me.' On the Academy Awards: 'If you win an Oscar, what happens to your career is not to be believed – your price goes up, you get offered all kinds of things.' And on her father: 'I don't understand him, but I love him. You must admit my father, with the kind of image he had, produced peculiar offshoots. He's always been the all-American liberal democratic good solid citizen – look at all the presidents and senators he's played – and here his son is, a pot-smoking hippie, whatever that means, and his daughter – I don't know *what* she is!'

Midnight. As New Year's Eve fireworks exploded over Central Park two blocks away, Hank and Shirlee Fonda arrived home from a party and began heading up the stairs. Then, as Reed recalled, 'Jane leaped up and waved her arms to blow the pot smoke out of the room.'

The family toasted in 1970 with Dom Perignon, then Jane placed a 'Happy Decade' call to Peter in California. 'Boy,' said Jane after she hung up, 'was he *stoned*.' The Fondas then traded stories about Peter's spaced-out friend Dennis Hopper – for Christmas he had given his daughter a cardboard box filled with his dirty, matted hair – and shook their heads.

When the Rex Reed interview appeared on 25 January, it created a much bigger stir than her 'marriage is obsolete' comments to Hedda Hopper a decade earlier. Readers were outraged that a movie star would openly smoke dope, and that a supposedly responsible newspaper such as *The New York Times* would appear to condone such illegal activity.

Reed himself came in for plenty of criticism from both those who thought Jane's behaviour disgraceful and those who felt he had betrayed her by including the pot-smoking incident in his story. 'So Jane Fonda smokes pot. Big deal,' replied Reed. 'So does just about everyone else I know . . . It has never been my purpose as a writer to conceal the realities of an interview, and I do not intend to start now.' As for Miss Fonda, 'I don't think she needs any defence from me . . . I think she can take care of herself.'

Amidst the furore over Jane's grass smoking, many readers failed to take notice of her comments concerning Vadim. 'We are very friendly with all his former wives and mistresses,' she had said, and went on to praise him for being *alive*, with all the imperfections that entails. 'He's taught me how to live, and if anything ever happens to our marriage, he'll always be my friend. Forever,' she concluded with a sigh, 'is a very difficult word.'

Two weeks later, Jane was spilling all to the press again – this time joined by the other Fondas. Along with Peter and their father, she had agreed to be interviewed *en famille* for the cover of *Time*. Lined up on a sofa in the handsome library of Hank's Bel Air home, the 'Flying Fondas', as they would be billed on the cover, thrusted and parried with three *Time* reporters between swigs of Red Eric beer.

Jane admitted that the session was 'really one of the first times in as long as I can remember that the three of us have been together and talked about acting'. Peter seized the opportunity to blast his interviewers for their intentions. 'Well, I think it's bloody bullshit for somebody from a magazine to come in and sit down – a young cat – and say, "I identify with you, kid. Come on, let's get it on." And I say, OK . . . and when it comes out in *Time*, it's a whole different gig.' Peter's tirade ended when Dad, who had been simmering in silence, erupted. While Hank, that purple vein throbbing in his forehead, scolded his son for his bad manners, Jane 'felt like I was three years old all over again'.

There was no hint in the interview of Jane's smouldering political consciousness. The part of social rebel was left for Peter, who played it to the hilt. Jane talked instead of the great Italian actress Eleonora Duse, of her own recent ten-pound weight loss ('I like to feel close to the bone'), of her decision to replace her designer wardrobe with secondhand threads, and of her growing conservatism in sexual matters. 'You have to keep some of the mystery,' she said. 'If you bring a plastic penis into the classroom as they do in Sweden, that removes all the mystery. If you go to bed with *Human Sexual Response* under your arm, things can get very boring.'

On Valentine's Day, Jane dropped her bombshell. She told Vadim that she was leaving him. And what of Vanessa, Vadim asked. They would, she informed him coolly, work out a custody arrangement at a later date.

Henry's words – 'No one ever drops a Fonda' – reverberated inside Vadim's skull.

16

DAVID HOROWITZ and Peter Collier, two self-described sixties revolutionaries, had been at the helm of *Ramparts* for only a few months when Collier got a call from Steve Jaffe, Fonda's press agent. Jane, having split with her husband after her soul-searching pilgrimage to India, and having read Collier's cover piece on the American Indian takeover of Alcatraz, had decided that she wanted to 'get involved' with important political issues at home. The press agent wondered if Collier might be willing to introduce her to leaders of the New Left. 'Naturally,' he recalls, 'I said yes.' Not long after, Fonda called personally and asked if Collier would take her to Alcatraz. 'Delighted,' replied Collier, who recalls that it was at this moment he realised the New Left had become chic.

Collier's article had indeed contained some disturbing statistics: 'The American Indian today has a life expectancy of approximately 44 years, more than 25 years below the national average . . . the highest infant mortality rate in the country . . . suffers from epidemics of disease which were supposed to have disappeared from America long ago . . . has an income per family of just $1,500 – the lowest of any group in the country . . . and his supposed guardian is in effect his "keeper", the Bureau of Indian Affairs.'

A band of Native Americans had taken over Alcatraz the previous November with the intention of transforming the one-time island prison into an Indian cultural affairs centre and research facility. Since 'the rock' had long since been abandoned and was serving no function, authorities were not eager to force a confrontation. As a result of the government's passive and understanding approach, press interest waned.

Jane Fonda's arrival put the Alcatraz squatters on the front page again. Sporting the new short shag haircut she would wear as Bree Daniel in *Klute*, Jane explained her newfound civic-mindedness to Collier as they stood on a fog-shrouded San Francisco pier waiting for a boat to carry them to Alcatraz. She likened her 'numb, apathetic, cynical' existence in Paris to 'a kind of limbo'. She wanted to be 'home in America, where it's "happening"'. When

Collier cracked that maybe she was too late, he recalls that 'a look of horror came over her face, and she said, "Oh, I hope not."'

Collier was impressed with Jane's instinctive political skills. 'As we landed on the rock, she moved among the Indians with charming self-abasement. She was an incredibly quick student, understanding intuitively what the power arrangements were on the island.' The Sioux were the most militant of the tribes, and they sought control of the island. 'By the time I left,' said Collier, 'she was over in the Sioux corner of the old prison exercise yard, smoking dope with them.'

Alcatraz marked Jane's induction into the ranks of radicals, and she attacked the role of activist with the same fervour she would any acting part. 'I learned about the genocide that had taken place,' she says of that encounter with the Indians, 'that is still taking place, the infamies we had done to the Indians in the name of efficiency, in the interest of white farmers. And I learned that the senators who are supposed to defend the Indians haven't done a thing.' It was quite a lot to learn in three hours.

At a Beverly Hills party for acclaimed Italian director Michelangelo Antonioni, Jane was introduced to Fred Gardner, a young part-time screenwriter who had been hired to work on Antonioni's *Zabriskie Point*. The two men shared the same political philosophy: Antonioni was an active member of the Italian Communist Party, Gardner an outspoken Marxist.

Already famous in anti-war circles, Gardner had hit on the idea of radicalising the Army by appealing to disgruntled enlisted men, particularly draftees. To accomplish this, he opened the first GI 'coffeehouse' where servicemen could get a dose of anti-war propaganda along with free coffee and rock music. Soon dozens of GI coffeehouses were springing up outside military bases across the country, and Gardner was a hero of the movement.

Jane fell under Gardner's spell and, before long, into his bed. Men who stimulated her intellectually always seemed to do so physically as well.

One of the protesters Jane had spoken to on Alcatraz was Sid Mills, a young Yakima who had served in Vietnam and was now fighting to preserve his tribe's fishing rights in the state of Washington. Jane had promised Mills she would visit the Seattle–Tacoma area. Now Gardner was telling her that Mark Lane, the radical lawyer best known for popularising the idea of a Kennedy assassination conspiracy with his book *Rush to Judgment*, was planning a major Indian rights protest in Seattle.

Before meeting Lane, Jane – in typically efficient Fonda fashion – first squeezed in a visit to northwest Washington's McNeil Island prison for a chat with the inmates. From there, she went to Fort Lawson, a practically deserted Army base inside the Seattle city limits that was in the process of deactivation. The plans were to turn Fort Lawson into a city park, but Lane and a group of Indian leaders intended to claim part of it under the Federal

Lands Act. As in the case of the Alcatraz takeover, the protesters meant to turn the facility into a Native American cultural affairs centre.

Jane's formal entry into the world of militant protest took place on 8 March 1970. Arm in arm with Mark Lane, she joined 150 Indians, some clad in buckskin, beads, and feathers, in their march on Fort Lawson. Jane was the obvious choice to read a declaration informing the 'Great White Father' – then-president Richard Nixon – of the Indians' intention to reclaim their property.

A phalanx of grim-faced military police tried to hold the line at the main gate, but a number of younger Indians managed to charge past them and on to the base. In the mêlée, Lane, along with 96 other demonstrators, was arrested. Jane was not taken into custody, but she was manhandled during the scuffle.

Hours later, Lane and Fonda were standing before television cameras decrying the 'provoked brutality' of the military police. To take full advantage of the day's press coverage, Lane and Fonda then headed for Fort Lewis, just a few minutes away. There, they led a caravan of protesters straight through the main gates.

This time Jane was taken into custody for trespassing – the first time Jane Fonda had ever been arrested. When police did not allow her to call a lawyer immediately, she lay down on the provost marshal's floor and declared, 'I will not move until you let me call a lawyer. And if you don't let me call a lawyer, you're going to be in such trouble . . .'

The next morning, Jane shared centre stage with Lane at a press conference in Seattle. Significantly, she did not confine her comments to the Indian-rights movement. 'The last two days have been very educational for me,' she said. 'I went to McNeil Island Prison and a black prisoner told me, "If I'm in prison, you're in prison." What is urgently needed is a halfway house to prepare these men for life on the outside.' As for her experience at Fort Lewis: 'I was detained for three hours illegally,' she said angrily, 'and given an order of expulsion, which means that if I return I am subject to a $500 fine and six months in prison. I fully intend to return to Fort Lewis and my main concern is that nothing happen to the GIs who accompanied me.' Jane then announced that she and Lane had filed a lawsuit against the United States Army for being 'unlawfully' barred from Fort Lawson and Fort Lewis. The suit demanded that they be permitted free access not only to those bases, but to all US military installations.

There was a practical reason for wanting access to all US bases. Jane had now committed herself to Fred Gardner's GI coffeehouses, as well as to the Indian cause. She was also drawn to the Black Panthers, the feminist movement, welfare mothers, farm workers. The best way to tackle all these issues and at the same time reacquaint herself with the country she had abandoned years before, Jane decided, was by way of a cross-country tour.

It was beginning to dawn on the Left that Jane could be a powerful public relations weapon. *Ramparts* editor Peter Collier, Gardner, and Steve Jaffe wasted no time arranging Jane's whirlwind tour of reservations, bases, and campuses.

For political inspiration, she invited her old friend Elisabeth Vailland, the French Marxist, to tag along. On her arrival in New York, Vailland was proud to show that she knew only enough English to say, 'All power to the people', 'Right on', 'jail', 'strike', and 'peace'.

FBI director J. Edgar Hoover had also taken notice of Jane and her new set of decidedly left-of-centre friends. Beginning with the Fort Lewis incident, he ordered that a thorough dossier be kept on Miss Fonda. It was labelled simply: 'Jane Fonda: Anarchist.' From this point on, Jane would be under intense scrutiny from the government.

With Mark Lane and an Indian activist named La Nada Means, Jane made her first political television appearance on ABC's highly rated 'Dick Cavett Show'. From the moment she stepped on the set, sat down, and gave the raised clenched-fist salute of the Black Panthers, millions of Americans were awakened to the fact that they had a new Jane Fonda on their hands.

From the standpoint of Jane's credibility, the 'Dick Cavett' appearance was an unmitigated disaster. It was bad enough that she appeared arrogant and shrill; Jane's comments were riddled with gross factual errors, and betrayed an ignorance of history that was almost comical. The imperialist American aggressors were only pursuing the Vietnam war because they wanted the region's 'tung and tinsten' (*sic*). As she left the studio, someone from the audience walked up to Fonda and spat in her face.

'I was acting out of instinct and emotion,' she conceded much later. 'I had no structural, ideological framework in which to put what I was thinking and feeling and doing. I thought I was better equipped to handle questions that I really was. And what happens when somebody is in that kind of position? You're very defensive. And all too often I would strike back – because everyone wanted to back me into a corner and that was so easy to do.'

Al Capp, the creator of *Li'l Abner* and a syndicated columnist a good deal to the right of centre (after years as a liberal democrat), found Jane an easy target. 'Jane Fonda has revealed a new side of herself, which is the last thing the world expected from a girl who has revealed every side of herself in a movie career in which she has mainly played nymphomaniacs in their working clothes,' wrote Capp in his column.

Taking aim at Jane's 'attack' on Fort Lawson, Capp went on to suggest that, instead of demanding that the Army turn over bases, 'there's a simpler way to get her Indians their cultural centres. It may occur to Jane (and if it hasn't already, I'm glad to suggest it) that the Fonda town house in Manhattan sits on land that rightfully belongs to the Manhattan tribe. And that her brother Peter's ranch rightfully belongs to some California tribe. And that they are both much nicer and handier locations for cultural centres than a bleak old fort way off in the State of Washington.' Capp went on to caution Indians to 'beware of those who seek to use their suffering, trust, and aspirations to trick them into acting as nonpaid extras in a two-bit western'.

As it turned out, the Indians themselves were already voicing displeasure with Jane's 'take-charge' approach to their movement. Jane had certainly not expected Native Americans to be among her harshest critics, but many were seeing in Jane nothing more than an ill-informed, publicity-craving dilettante. They also worried that Jane's obvious sympathies for the Black Panthers and the anti-war movement might damage their own cause in the public eye.

At a taping of the 'Virginia Graham Show', another popular national TV talk programme of the time, Jane was going on about the plight of the Native American when one militant Indian leader got up in the audience and shouted, 'Who the hell are you to butt into Indian affairs?'

That sentiment was shared by Kahn-Tineta Horn, a Mohawk activist who also was a successful model and actress. 'The sooner she never mentions Indians again the better,' said Horn. 'She led the Indians into Fort Lawton, and when the television and newspaper people came around and started interviewing her, she was protesting Vietnam. She forgot which crusade she was on. She's done *so* much harm to Indians. She makes us look ridiculous. Do we need a white woman to lead us? She's just exploiting us. If she really wants to help, why doesn't she give money for legal aid and stay in the background, as a lot of sincere white people do? Not her. She has to be in the forefront. She degrades Indians and makes white people lose respect for us. What makes it even worse is that she's a leftist. No good can come of Indians associating with any leftist or socialist or communist.'

Singer Buffy St Marie joined in the chorus, though with somewhat more finesse. 'Jane's greatest help to us is telling other people what is going on,' she said. 'But she has unintentionally blown a couple of our most important issues by not understanding the problems.'

Indian leaders were so concerned about the damage being done that they held an emergency meeting at which they pleaded with Jane to remain in the background. Jane grudgingly agreed, having turned her attention by then to another cause. At the urging of two of her Malibu neighbours – actor Donald Sutherland and his wife, Shirley – Jane had become increasingly interested in the Black Panthers.

In their trademark black leather uniforms, stormtrooper boots, dark glasses, and black berets, the Panthers cultivated a swaggering, menacing image that, according to one former member, appealed to the 'strong masochistic streak' in the New Left. The party had been formed out of an Oakland, California, street gang in 1967 by Huey Newton and Bobby Seale. Panthers, many of whom had done prison time for serious crimes, brandished weapons and patrolled the streets in armed cadres, focusing on cases of police brutality that they said proliferated in the ghetto.

Although it was Stokely Carmichael who coined the slogan 'Black Power' and booted whites out of the Student Nonviolent Coordinating Committee (SNCC), the Panthers were the first blatantly to reject the notion of nonviolence. They also differed from other reform-minded groups such as the Congress of Racial Equality (CORE), Martin Luther King's Southern Christian Leadership Conference, and the Urban League in that theirs was an openly Marxist organisation with a forthright revolutionary agenda.

The Panthers remained a local Bay Area phenomenon until October 1967, when a single bloody incident thrust them to centre stage. Newton, the party's founder and 'minister of defence,' was leaving a party celebrating the end of his probation for a knifing incident when he was stopped by Oakland policeman John Frey. There was a struggle, and within minutes Frey was dead – the victim of five gunshot wounds, including two in the back from close range. A backup officer was wounded, as was Newton.

With the help of such fellow Panther ideologues as Bobby Seale (who would later gain national fame along with Tom Hayden as one of the Chicago Seven, the group that led the disruptions at the Democratic National Convention) and convicted-rapist-turned-*Soul on Ice*-author Eldridge Cleaver, the Newton trial became a *cause célèbre*. On college campuses everywhere, posters went up on dormitory walls showing Newton sitting on a rattan throne, a rifle in one hand and a spear in the other.

Defence lawyers in the Newton case argued that there was a distinct possibility that the backup officer, not their client, had accidentally shot his partner in the scuffle. In what would soon become a standard radical tactic, they concluded that it was not Newton who was on trial but the *system*.

Newton was found guilty of manslaughter, but the conviction was overturned on a technicality. When Newton was released, he went to live in a luxurious penthouse overlooking Oakland's Lake Merritt. The glass-walled apartment was always filled with fresh-cut flowers at a reputed cost (in 1970 dollars) of nearly $750 a month – about the same as the rent on the apartment. Another interesting feature was a telescope through which he gazed at his old cell in the Alameda County jailhouse.

Surrounded by sullen guards and sympathisers – including several Hollywood directors, screenwriters, and actors – Newton would swagger around his apartment shirtless, guzzling vodka and expounding endlessly on the coming revolution. It was, in the words of a former friend, 'like attending a performance that played well enough at the time but left the viewer with doubts that couldn't be answered'.

Those disturbing doubts were justified. The Black Panthers, who had in fact been dealing in drugs and taking protection money, would be involved in numerous shootouts with police across the country. As for Newton, he turned out to be a chronic alcoholic and abuser of hard drugs. In 1974, he would flee to Cuba after being accused of fatally shooting a seventeen-year-old prostitute in the face because she failed to recognise him and of pistol-whipping a tailor for affectionately calling him 'baby'. Three years later, Newton returned to face the charges, which were dropped after both trials ended in hung juries. Later he served time for a parole violation and for misappropriating funds raised by the Panthers for one of their Oakland community projects.

In 1984, Newton received a Ph.D. from the University of California at Santa Cruz, but only after allegedly threatening to kill his professor if he didn't receive pass marks. And there would be continuing skirmishes with the law until August 1989, when Newton was shot and killed after being locked out of an Oakland crack house. Newton had apparently stolen fourteen rocks of cocaine and $160 from his drug-dealing assailant.

In 1970, however, the Black Panthers were the new darlings of the Left. In his best-selling book *Radical Chic*, Tom Wolfe described a cocktail party held in the Panthers' honour at the Manhattan apartment of conductor Leonard Bernstein. One of the Panthers' most outspoken admirers was a man Jane had yet to meet – Tom Hayden, who praised the Panthers as nothing less than 'America's Vietcong'.

Jane read about the pitched battles between the Panthers and the police and instantly sided against authority. 'I immediately contacted the Panthers,' she recalls. 'People were saying, "You can't do that! It's going to ruin your career, you're going to get killed." And I was frightened. But I wanted to find out, so I talked to Panther leaders in Los Angeles. I was very impressed, extremely moved, and it was the first time I met black people who were going to the fundamental problem, the root problem of the system, and they were saying that black capitalism isn't going to change anything. It's simply going to create a black elite, it's going to end up exploiting black people.'

Jane was particularly taken by the handsome, charismatic Newton. 'He's the only man I've ever met,' she said in total seriousness, 'who approaches sainthood.' She also quickly allied herself with Angela Davis, who had just been fired from her position as a professor at the University of California at Los Angeles for being an outspoken communist. Joining the Panther supporters was the celebrated homosexual French playwright Jean Genet, who was so smitten with the Panthers that he spent considerable time in the United States speaking – through an interpreter – on their behalf.

Davis told Jane that the first item on their agenda should be to raise bail for Black Panthers accused of various crimes – most notably the Panthers involved in a spectacular shootout with Los Angeles police. Jane visited Newton and other imprisoned Panthers and, impressed with their rhetoric, decided to put up the bail money herself.

In the weeks prior to her cross-country tour, Jane's life became a blur of marches, meetings, and speeches on behalf of a bewildering array of causes. 'Wherever there was a rally,' recalls one observer, 'there was Jane.' Since she did not own a car – she had always been ferried around by limousine – Jane did take time out to go shopping for the car that would take her on her journey. She settled on a practical Mercury estate car.

'I didn't have time,' she says, 'to sit down with books and get a historical analysis and put it all into perspective. It was an emotional, gut kind of thing.' So Jane took a crash course in world history and Marxist theory from Vailland, Huey Newton, and Angela Davis.

Vadim looked on helplessly. While they had not yet formally announced their separation, both had hinted broadly of trouble in paradise. On the topic of marriage, Jane harked back to her earlier headline-making observations on the obsolescence of monogamy. 'Forever', she kept saying, 'is a very difficult word.' Vadim was more specific about his arrangements with Jane. 'I do much more giving,' he said flatly. 'In a way, in our relationship she is the man and I am the woman.' He went on to say, 'I prefer being married to someone soft and vulnerable than to an American Joan of Arc.'

Jane was not amused. 'When you saw me,' she says of that time, 'everything was churning away inside. Finally, I couldn't stand that façade any longer. I had to let go. I thought if I left my husband I would fall apart.'

The 'strange and intense physical rapport' Vadim claims they shared in the weeks immediately following their separation had by now evaporated. Vadim was crushed. 'If there had been the slightest suicidal tendency in my make-up,' he revealed, he would have taken his own life.

Jane knew her husband was suffering. 'Vadim is an intelligent man,' she said shortly after the breakup, 'but he wasn't prepared for what happened. He would better understand a woman who leaves him for another man than a woman who leaves him for herself.' Vadim was inextricably linked to Jane's sex-kitten persona, and if she was to be free of that past, he had to go too. Not that she blamed him for that stage of her career. 'I was so used to being considered a sex symbol that I began to like it,' she admitted. 'I didn't expect people to treat me as a person who thinks. But when I went to the Indians and I came in contact with the Panthers, the GIs, my new friends, I realised that they were treating me as a person. This was so beautiful that I began to feel uncomfortable with people who still considered me a doll. And it completed my own personal revolution, and Vadim was the first victim of it.'

As with everything she undertook, Jane became obsessed with her new causes. The raising of their daughter was basically left to her husband, and even when she was ostensibly spending time with their daughter, the media were never far away. While Jane gave press conferences, Vanessa often sat alone, watching her mother's performance from a few yards away.

Vadim moved out of Henry Fonda's guest house with Vanessa and into another rented house in Malibu. Jane remained behind with Hank and Shirlee. Before leaving on her cross-country tour, she dashed off a note in a hurried scrawl to *Ramparts* editor Peter Collier pledging herself to 'the struggle'. The note ended with 'Power to the People!' But instead of a dot beneath the exclamation point, Collier recalls, 'there was a little circle. My wife looked at it later on and said, "I'm surprised she didn't make it into a little smiley face."'

On the evening of 25 March, Jane sped off behind the wheel of her Mercury estate car with Elisabeth Vailland at her side. For the next two and a half months, they would snake across the nation, dropping in on reservations, Army bases, GI coffeehouses, and campuses – anywhere they could commune with their ideological brethren or convert nonbelievers.

'I took off on that trip a liberal', says Jane, 'and I ended up a radical. What that means is this: I ended up understanding that there are many forms of starvation and that the struggle is my struggle. The same system in this wealthy, vast, rich country that makes it so that there are people starving and people illiterate and people who can't get medical care and people who are being framed and shot and put into prison for political reasons is the same system that has messed me over as an upper-class white person.'

This apotheosis did not occur overnight. Stopping off at reservations in Nevada and Idaho, Jane and Vailland were stunned at the apathy of the tribal leaders they encountered. Body-conscious Jane also found their appearance disconcerting: nearly all the Indians they encountered were bloated by alcohol.

After two weeks on the road, Jane flew back to California for the Academy Awards. As winner of the New York Film Critics Award for *They Shoot Horses*, Jane was conceded to have the inside track among her fellow Best Actress nominees. Yet there remained the nagging question of Jane's newfound radicalism. In a town still dominated by the conservative likes of John Wayne and Bob Hope, would her politics cost Jane her industry's highest accolade? Or would she win and then deliver a wild-eyed acceptance speech on national television? Hollywood held its breath.

Came the night, and even before the ceremonies began she provided cause for concern. As she climbed out of her limousine, a dark ranch mink draped over her Chanel dress, Jane acknowledged the crowd by raising her hand in the Black Panthers' clenched-fist salute.

The Oscar went to English actress Maggie Smith for *The Prime of Miss Jean Brodie*. While Jane's admirers cried foul, the choice was highly defensible. Smith's performance had been universally praised. Nor could Academy members be accused of skirting a sensitive issue. Also set in the 1930s, *The Prime of*

Miss Jean Brodie deals with a flamboyant, frustrated Scottish schoolteacher who romanticises the Fascists so convincingly that one of her female students runs off to fight in the Spanish Civil War and gets killed. The message of Smith's film – an artful plea against blind fanaticism of any kind – was in fact more overtly political than anything in *They Shoot Horses*.

The next day, bitterly disappointed by her defeat, Jane turned down an invitation from Elizabeth Taylor and Richard Burton to attend a losers' party at the Beverly Hills Hotel. Instead she went ahead with plans to hold a Black Panther rally. Jane was eventually persuaded to do both, and went to the Taylor–Burton party with Donald Sutherland as her escort. They stayed just long enough to chat with their hosts, and when they left at 7 p.m., it was not empty-handed. Sutherland had persuaded Burton to write out a sizeable cheque to the Black Panthers, while Jane had cajoled Taylor (who disapproved of the Panthers) to make a substantial donation to her Indian cause.

Within days, Jane was back on the road. In Denver, she lent support to Duane Bird Bear, a Colorado Indian who had led a sit-in at the Bureau of Indian Affairs in the Colorado town of Littleton. After that came a 'fast for peace' in downtown Denver. 'We're fighting for what America is supposed to stand for. I think we are the most American of all,' she shouted to the crowd. 'Every individual can find a way in his own life that he can use to protest the war. I can't believe all these people aren't willing to stand up and sacrifice for what they know is wrong; why don't they join in the protest?' Among those who did join the protest were Dr Benjamin Spock and several Black Panthers.

Following her 36-hour fast, Jane paid an unwelcome call on Fort Carson, an Army base near Colorado Springs. She was allowed to visit the glasshouse, where she jumped to the conclusion that several of the black prisoners were being held because they were Panther sympathisers. 'They're in there', she told the crowd of television reporters, 'because they are lining up in front of the dispensary giving the peace sign and saying they are sick of war.'

After conferring with Fred Gardner, she returned to Fort Carson – this time with the plan to maximise press coverage. Barred from entering the base itself, she gave a speech to about forty GIs at the nearby Home Front coffeehouse. The United States, she told them, had $160 million in holdings in Vietnam, and the military was there to protect those holdings. 'The mass of [the Vietnamese] population are fighting us,' she said. 'Why? For the same reason we fought the English, for the same reason the French underground fought the Nazis.'

Whenever she spoke at one of Fred Gardner's GI coffeehouses, Jane was speaking to the converted – mostly disillusioned draftees, some on the verge of desertion. Never more than a few thousand spread out across the entire country, they represented a tiny fraction of the nation's fighting force of more than three million.

The coffeehouse regulars, however, were vocal in their support of Jane. One of the men present at Home Front the day of Jane's visit claimed that a number of soldiers had been put on restriction. 'Apparently,' he reasoned, 'the word got around that you were going to be here.' Another yelled out that he was under investigation because he owned a picture of Lenin.

Jane had no doubt all this was true. 'I'm sure there is a fink here right now,' she said, 'who is going to go back and distort every word we say.' That would hardly have seemed necessary. Jane continued to draw parallels, however inappropriate, between the American Revolution and Vietnam. 'Suppose the English had come over here and dropped chemicals on us and sprayed us with poisons, destroyed our cities and put up concentration camps. The majority of the rural population of Vietnam are in concentration camps, and we put them there. They are tortured and killed.'

The next day, she managed to sneak into Fort Carson, driven past the guardhouse by a sympathetic private in his Volkswagen minibus. Once inside, she went straight to Inscape, a religious gathering place on the base. Unannounced, she strode into the dimly lit meeting hall and mounted the small stage. Her small entourage of anti-war activists trailed behind, carrying boxes filled with anti-war books and leaflets. Within minutes, the servicemen realised just who was in their midst. Word spread, and the curious flocked to Inscape for their first close-up look at a genuine movie star.

Not everyone was an admirer. When Jane charged that American soldiers were nothing more than controlled 'slaves' of the rich, an Army chaplain in the crowd pointed out that she was by any standards quite wealthy – and therefore, by her own reckoning, part of the problem. 'Yes, I could be lying out in the sun in Beverly Hills,' she replied. 'It is very beautiful in Beverly Hills right now. But when I get up in the morning, I can't look at myself in the mirror knowing all the things that are going on right now that are wrong.'

When the military police arrived at the coffeehouse and took positions near the doors, Jane was not at all worried. 'They won't arrest me here,' she complained, adding that every time she was arrested it helped the cause 'because I can sue the Army again'. By the time she attempted to leave the camp the way she had come in, Jane was in fact stopped at the gate by MPs and taken into custody. The base commander did not take the bait; rather than press charges, he ordered Jane released. Profoundly disappointed, Jane spent the next few days dropping in on more Indian reservations, this time in the Southwest.

In Santa Fe, Jane rendezvoused with Peter, who had come to New Mexico to film *The Hired Hand*. She checked into her hotel just in time to watch

Richard Nixon announce in a special television address to the nation that he was sending US troops into Cambodia.

By stepping up military pressure on Hanoi, the Republican administration was convinced it could force the North Vietnamese to the bargaining table. While polls showed that the American people approved of the incursion 2–1, anti-war forces saw the invasion of Cambodia as nothing less than a betrayal. They had been convinced that they had so undermined American resolve vis-à-vis Vietnam that no president would dare escalate the war.

As usual, Jane took it personally – as if the president were speaking directly to her. Watching the broadcast, she wept with rage. Hastily she called a press conference of her own for the next day, barely able to contain her anger as she denounced the president as a 'warmonger'. Nixon responded by calling anti-war demonstrators 'just a bunch of bums'.

On 4 May 1970, the day four Kent State students were shot and killed by the National Guard, Jane spoke at the University of New Mexico – it was the first time she had faced a crowd numbering in the thousands. 'You suddenly open up the floodgates and you have no words to express what it is you're feeling,' she recalled later, 'so you grasp. I mean there were a lot of words that I just was beginning to understand what they meant. I borrowed a lot of rhetoric from a lot of people to try to give train-rails to what it was that I was feeling.'

What she felt was 'rage – rage that people feel when they've been lied to and suddenly realise it. Rage of someone who was, to a certain degree, despite the cynicism, very idealistic about my country and was very angry about the deception. Just so angry. It comes from inexperience, it comes from not being part of an organisation, it comes from being famous and easily backed into a corner. It comes from being a woman . . .'

If her activism stemmed from being riddled by self-doubt, as she often stated later, Jane gave no sign of it at the time. At a rally across from the White House on 9 May, Jane launched into her speech with a rousing 'Welcome, fellow bums!' After blasting America's 'immoral' foreign policy, she ended by raising her hand in the now-familiar clenched-fist salute and shouting 'Power to the people!' The throng responded with a chorus of 'Right on!'

Following the invasion of Cambodia and the Kent State killings, outrage turned to frenzy. A new wave of protest swept the nation, and Jane rode its crest as the movement's most visible and controversial spokesperson.

Once again behind the wheel of her estate car, Jane embarked on the second half of her cross-country trip. At the University of New Mexico, she led a march on the president's office, demanding that the school be shut down to protest about Kent State. At Fort Hood in Texas, she was arrested for illegally distributing anti-war leaflets. 'Bob Hope was greeted differently by the local branch of the military industrial complex,' she told reporters. 'But then, I

155

did not come here to glamorise war or to urge young men to fight.' After leading a march of two thousand to Fort Bragg in Fayetteville, North Carolina, she was again arrested by military police for handing out literature on the base.

At the University of Maryland, about two thousand students sprawled lazily on the lawn waiting for the famous actress to appear. On the periphery of the crowd, bearded, barefoot young men tossed Frisbees back and forth. At first no one noticed when she arrived fifteen minutes late with Mark Lane. That all changed when they heard the piercing, unmistakable sound of the Fonda voice.

'Who's getting rich off this war?' she called. 'When World War II ended, the Defense Department had $160 billion worth of property – it's doubled since then.' The figures sounded impressive, but they bore no resemblance to reality.

'The Army builds a tolerance for violence,' she continued. 'I find that intolerable. They say it's normal to throw prisoners out of helicopters because "it's the only way you can make 'em talk". I find that tragic.'

Gazing over the crowd at the shirtless students still tossing Frisbees back and forth, Jane pointed out that 'some people are just here to get a suntan and have some fun and this weekend they will go to the beach and lap up beer'.

As she threaded her way through the crowd after her speech, Jane was trailed by a number of male students who pelted her with questions. Why was she still part of the acting 'establishment', a drama student wanted to know, though he quickly added, 'but I'm not questioning your motives, of course'.

Jane was indignant. 'Well, you are. That's just what you're doing!'

Another man asked if she was 'in it' for the publicity. When she professed not to understand him, the man said, 'Well, you must be getting something out of this.'

She stopped in her tracks. 'You think this is *fun*?' she snapped. 'Standing in this heat talking to a bunch of lethargic students? I could be lying by a pool in Beverly Hills getting a suntan. You think this is for kicks?'

Jane did not mention that, although her fee (around $2,000 per appearance) was among the highest paid to campus speakers at the time, that money went to support Jane's various anti-capitalist causes – a practice she would employ in the coming years with spectacular results.

An hour after the University of Maryland speech, Jane was under arrest by military police again – this time for bringing her petitions and pamphlets into nearby Fort Meade. The caravan of newsmen who had been following Jane, Lane, Vailland, and the others waited outside the office of the provost marshal, guarded by three stolid MPs. From an upper window came Fonda's angry voice. 'We are being searched now,' she yelled down to the reporters, flashing the V peace sign. 'We are going to get them on a charge of brutality . . .'

Brutality was something that George Jackson knew quite a lot about. On 16 January 1970, Jackson and two of his fellow inmates at California's Soledad Prison, John Cluchette and Fleeta Drumgo, were charged with beating a guard and then hurling him off a prison wall to his death. Radical lawyer Fay Stender, whose deft manipulation of the media had made Huey Newton a household name, did the same for Jackson.

By the summer of 1970, Stender had engineered the publication of *Soledad Brother: The Prison Letters of George Jackson*, with a foreword by French playwright Jean Genet. In the so-called Soledad Brothers, the New Left had a new trio of heroes – three victims, Angela Davis and others would argue, of a racist society.

Blindly springing to the defence of the Soledad Brothers, Jane gave an impassioned address on their behalf in Los Angeles on 19 June. 'If you strip away the face and the false sense of freedom and social justice and comfort that lulls the white middle class into thinking they're safe, you can see the system for what it is – racist, oppressive, totalitarian, and monstrous . . . Rigged criminal trials for the purpose of wiping out anybody that the authorities don't want around, for the purpose of repressing political ideas and organisations, by exterminating the leaders . . . is nothing new in this country . . .'

Building momentum, Jane shouted, 'This is not Los Angeles in 1970, it is Berlin in 1936, and we are all Jews . . . Kent State and the Chicago trial showed us all, I think, that we are niggers to this system.'

As for Soledad Brother George Jackson, Jane eagerly spread the Fay Stender version of the facts. 'George Jackson is twenty-nine years old,' Jane would tell college audiences, 'and he has spent the last ten years in prison for a robbery which he committed when he was eighteen in which seventy dollars was stolen. No one was killed, no one was hurt. His accomplice was armed but George was not. And yet his accomplice has been free for years while George Jackson received a one-year-to-life sentence and has been denied parole every year since the first. George Jackson is the kind of man they want incarcerated because he is proud and because he is militant. If you read his book, you will sense the mind and hear the voice that the California adult authority wants to silence.'

Had she researched the Jackson case the way she did all her acting roles, Jane would have learned that her new black-militant hero was actually sentenced for his third serious offence. Jackson had been up for parole several times, but was turned down for his less-than-exemplary behaviour behind bars. Inside prison, he formed a bloody gang called the Wolf Pack, controlled all drugs and gambling among inmates, and, by his own account, had murdered a dozen fellow prisoners. He bragged of his plot to poison Chicago's water supply once he got out.

As in the case of Henry Newton, these facts were available to anyone who cared to listen. Jane obviously did not.

As if to thumb her nose at the critics of her sudden and drastic shift to the radical left, she returned to her farmhouse in St Ouen and granted a lengthy interview to *L'Humanité*, the daily organ of the French Communist Party.

Hiding behind dark sunglasses in the back of a bar, Fonda told the reporter, 'My father is a rather liberal Democrat. I too was "liberal". But I used to live out of all these things because I had a privileged social position. I sympathised very much with emancipation movements. However, I could not identify myself with these problems. I was barely conscious of the problems . . .'

As she continued, Fonda began to wind up. 'I have seen people who were literally dying of hunger in a country which is so rich,' she said. 'That is unacceptable. I am still asking myself how I did not notice it before.'

Henry Fonda might have wondered the same thing – and asked why she was being so *loud* about it now. Jane wanted passionately to convert her father. She routinely dragged fellow activists to Henry's New York town house or to the estate in Bel Air to try and sway Dad. Veterans from the coffeehouses told of GI atrocities – prisoners pushed to their deaths from helicopters, genitals cut off Vietcong for trophies, civilians tortured and killed. She also brought home Angela Davis to meet her father; surely the senior Fonda did not have an inkling that this particular guest would soon be one of America's most wanted fugitives.

Hank would not be easily swayed. More sophisticated than his daughter, he argued forcefully and intelligently against the half-truths Jane had accepted as gospel. 'Dad and I would fight,' she recalls. 'And he was worried. Obviously, he thought, What foreign agent is manipulating my daughter? . . .'

That was, in fact, precisely his concern. When unsmiling FBI agents in dark suits began showing up at both of his residences to question Jane, he decided it was time to confront her. Standing on the terrace outside the study of the East 74th Street house, Hank and his daughter were watching the sunset when suddenly he turned to her and blurted out what he had long wondered. 'Jane, if I ever discover for a fact that you're a communist or a true communist sympathiser, I, your father, will be the first to turn you in . . .' and, Henry recalled, 'tears trickled down her cheeks. She shook her head, "No".'

Jane does not recall the incident.

During this period, Henry let his parental dissatisfaction show only on rare occasions. When Guy Flatley showed up at the Fonda house to interview Jane's dad for *The New York Times*, Hank kept him waiting. 'Sorry I'm late. But I was on a long-distance call to Washington,' Hank tried to explain. 'I was talking with my – how should I say it? – with my erstwhile, with my alleged daughter.' Jane had asked, Fonda went on, if she could bring her entourage to stay at the New York town house for an entire week. He did not object to the numbers: 'It's not how many. It's how unattractive they all are.'

Back in Los Angeles, Henry Fonda's son-in-law, not exactly a political conservative himself, had become an expert practitioner of the shrug and the sigh. Vadim was now occupied on the MGM back lot filming a Rock Hudson movie called *Pretty Maids All in a Row*, but it seemed to him even more time was spent fending off inquiries about his wife. 'I feel', he told one reporter wearily, 'as if I were baby-sitting for Lenin.'

17

ON THE surface, *Klute* was a straightforward, fast-paced murder mystery about a highly strung New York call girl, Bree Daniel, stalked by a crazed killer. But from the start, Jane sought to make a 'significant social statement with the film. These women', she noted, 'are a product of a society in which the emphasis is on money.'

Once again, Jane burrowed under the skin of her character. She spent three nights sleeping on the set, in Bree's drab 'apartment'. Over a period of weeks she toured Manhattan's sleaziest pick-up bars and sought out advice from 'the hierarchy of the prostitute world, from streetwalkers to call girls, madams and pimps'. She was, by all accounts, an enthusiastic participant in the research for her role as a hooker.

'I noticed in all of these women a terrible hardness,' said Jane. 'Many of them are sleeping with senators, executives of major corporations, of TV networks. They told me names, and they told me unbelievable stories about sadomasochism. You can imagine the view that it gives them of the rules of this country.'

No matter how immersed she might become in the character of Bree, she was determined not to lose herself the way she had in *They Shoot Horses, Don't They?* She was no longer first and foremost an actress. 'Being a movie star', she explained, 'is not a purpose.'

Sitting in a New York hotel room discussing the script, she abruptly turned to Alan Pakula. 'Don't I look different?' she asked the director.

Pakula looked up, nonplussed. 'What?'

'Don't I look different?' she demanded. 'I've changed.'

'The change in just those few months had been so enormous to her', Pakula recalls, 'that she felt it showed all over her face.'

Pakula also had to deal with tensions in the studio resulting from his star's newfound notoriety. 'There was flak from outside,' recalls Pakula. 'You'd say to somebody, "I'm working with Jane Fonda" and eyes would roll.' One day Jane arrived on the set to find it decorated with American flags – the crew's silent response to Fonda's militancy. (According to Pakula, by the end of filming, she had won over the crew because 'above all else, she is quintessentially an American'.)

Co-star Donald Sutherland had no misgivings about his opionated leading lady. After all, during the time they lived down the beach from her in Malibu, the Sutherlands introduced Jane to the Black Panthers, and politically Donald's wife, Shirley, was more radical than Jane.

In the title role of *Klute*, Sutherland plays a small-town private detective searching for a missing friend. The trail leads to New York and to the sad, cynical Bree. At first she is suspicious of him, but as the murderer closes in, she comes to rely on – and eventually fall in love with – Klute.

Yet Jane's attention was now clearly divided between acting and her myriad causes. 'A year ago, for me to pick up the phone and call practically anyone except the people I was really intimate with was a trauma,' said Jane at the time. 'I hated the telephone. I never answered the phone; Vadim always answered. Now, I must make forty calls a day to people I don't even know . . . asking them for favours, for money. I sometimes think, What am I doing? It's impossible that someone has changed this much!' (Indeed, she was now picking up the phone so often between takes that she became known on the set of *Klute* as 'the Mad Caller'.)

Pakula fretted that she might not be able to focus on the job at hand. 'I was concerned that her mind was not going to be on the film. But she had this extraordinary kind of concentration. She can make endless phone calls and seem to be totally uninterested in the film. But when you say, "We're ready for you, Jane," she says, "All right, give me a few minutes." She stands quietly for three minutes and concentrates, and then she's totally and completely in the film, and nothing else exists.'

Much of *Klute*'s power comes from moments improvised by Jane. For example, there is a scene in her psychiatrist's office when Bree visibly shudders at the realisation that she has deep feelings for Klute, something she had thought impossible for her with any man. At the film's climax, the killer forces her to listen to a tape recording of a friend's murder. Rather than rehearse the scene, Pakula decided to roll the cameras while Jane, as Bree, heard the chilling tape for the first time. Fonda's uncontrollable sobs were so gut-wrenchingly authentic that Pakula went with this first take, providing *Klute* with what may be its most compelling moment.

While Jane was dealing with pathological violence on the screen, a horrifying true-life scenario was being acted out in a San Francisco suburb three thousand miles away. One August morning, George Jackson's brother Jonathan walked into the Marin County courthouse with weapons purchased by Jane's friend Angela Davis. Demanding that his brother be freed, Jonathan Jackson taped a shotgun to the judge's neck, then with the help of two prisoners took the judge, an assistant district attorney, and several jurors hostage. The authorities refused to release George Jackson, and the San Francisco Bay Area held its breath for tense minutes until the drama reached its bloody climax. In the inevitable shootout, the judge's head was blown off by a shotgun blast, Jonathan Jackson and the two prisoners were killed, and the young assistant DA was left paralysed from the waist down.

Angela Davis had vanished after the mêlée and promptly soared to the top of the FBI's Most Wanted list. A nationwide manhunt was launched. Only weeks after Jane had brought Davis along to meet her husband, two FBI agents paid a call on Vadim, on the MGM set of *Pretty Maids All in a Row*. Did he know where Angela Davis was? Did Jane? What did he know about Jane's friendship with the Panthers, the Soledad Brothers, the anti-war movement? Vadim was blissfully ignorant of Jane's activities, though he contends that he would not have told the FBI anything that might have proved damaging to her in any way.

Henry Fonda had begun worrying about his daughter months earlier, when Jane brought Davis to meet him. After the FBI came to question him in New York, he instructed Jane to leave. She quickly leased a cavernous, opulently decorated penthouse just a few blocks away. When the FBI visited her there, Jane insisted repeatedly that she had no idea where Davis was hiding out. When Davis was finally tracked down two months later, it was at a Howard Johnson's just a few minutes from Jane's apartment in midtown Manhattan. News of her arrest was big enough to land Davis on the cover of the then-weekly *Life* magazine under the heading, 'The Making of a Fugitive'.

If anything, the violent turn of events seemed only to intensify Jane's radical commitment. The trial of Black Panther founder Bobby Seale was to begin in New Haven, and Huey Newton, newly released from San Quentin on $50,000 bail, flew east to whip up support. He was greeted at JFK by Mark Lane, Donald Sutherland, and Jane, who raised her fist in a Black Power salute as Newton got off the plane. Later, Jane staged a press conference at her penthouse. There, beneath crystal chandeliers, Newton railed against fascist 'Amerika' and called for full-scale revolution.

To the chagrin of police officers who felt she was merely putting violent street criminals into circulation, Jane put up bail for Zayd Malik Shakur, 'deputy minister of education' for the Panthers, Shakur, whose brother and sister-in-law were accused of a New York bombing plot, was charged with felonious possession of three sawn-off shotguns and a revolver. Shakur was also a defence witness in the New Haven trial of Lonnie McLucas, one of eight Panthers charged with the torture and murder of a fellow Panther who presumably had informed police of the New York bombing conspiracy.

Jane explained at the time, 'I'm a friend of Mr Shakur, and I know he'll show up for his trial.' She continued to put up bail for the Panthers – until one skipped town, leaving her $50,000 poorer.

As America's *pasionaria*, Jane had by now mastered the lingo of the left, sprinkling her conversation liberally with words such as 'genocide', 'racist', 'imperialist', and 'oppression'. But at times it still appeared that her grasp of history was not as firm as it could have been. Unfortunatley, Jane chose to commit some of her biggest gaffes very publicly. During yet another appearance on the 'Dick Cavett Show', Jane was asked why she felt the South Vietnamese government didn't have the right to ask for outside help in its war with the North. During the American Revolution, didn't we colonists ask for help in fighting the British?

'Not that I know of,' Jane shot back haughtily. When she was reminded that the success of the American Revolution owed a great deal to the Marquis de Lafayette and French support, Jane tried to shrug it off. 'Of course,' she now recalls, wincing, 'everybody jumped on me.'

J. Edgar Hoover took little solace from Jane's blunders. To him, and therefore to the agency, she posed a clear and present danger to the nation. Unbeknown to Jane, an FBI plot had already been hatched to discredit her. On 11 June 1970, Wesley G. Grapp, then head of the FBI's Los Angeles office, noticed a two-line item in Army Archerd's *Variety* column noting that Fonda was scheduled to appear at a Black Panther fund-raiser. Six days later, Grapp wrote a top-secret letter to Hoover asking permission to fake the following letter to Archerd:

Dear Army,

I saw your article about Jane Fonda in *Daily Variety* last Thursday and happened to be present for Vadim's *Joan of Arc*'s performance for the Black Panthers Saturday night. I hadn't been confronted with this Panther phenomena before but we were searched upon entering Embassy Auditorium, encouraged in revival-like fashion to contribute to defend jailed Panther leaders and buy guns for 'the coming revolution', and led by Jane and one of the Panther chaps in 'We will kill Richard Nixon, and any other M_____ F_____ who stands in our way' refrain (which was shocking to say the least!). I think Jane has gotten in over her head as the whole atmosphere had the 1930s Munich beer-hall aura.

I also think my curiosity about the Panthers has been satisfied.

Regards
Morris

The reply was:

TO: Los Angeles
FROM: Director, FBI

    COUNTERINTELLIGENCE PROGRAM.
    BLACK NATIONALIST-HATE GROUPS.
    RACIAL INTELLIGENCE.
    BLACK PANTHER PARTY (BPP)

You are authorised to prepare a letter as set forth and mail to Army Archerd, the Hollywood 'gossip' columnist. Ensure that mailing cannot be traced to the Bureau.

In a postscript, Hoover went on to predict that 'Fonda's involvement with the BPP cause could detract from her status with the general public if reported in a Hollywood "gossip" column.'

For whatever reason, the letter was apparently never sent. If it had been, said Archerd when he learned of its existence years later, he would not have printed it anyway. Since public opinion polls showed Jane was rapidly becoming one of the most hated people in America, Hoover's attempt to undermine her credibility seemed both laughable and unncessary.

18

BY THE time she had finished work on *Klute* in October 1970, Jane was ready to devote her full energies to what she repeatedly referred to as 'The Revolution'. She now freely admitted that she was out to 'change the American system through socialism. Of course I am a socialist.' When a coalition of anti-war groups decided to hold a hearing in Detroit at which Vietnam veterans would describe American atrocities they had presumably witnessed, Jane eagerly volunteered her services. The media event was to be called the Winter Soldier Investigation – a reference to Thomas Paine's distinction between 'sunshine patriots' and the truly committed. Of course, Jane and the anti-war activists cast themselves as the true patriots, the winter soldiers.

To raise funds for the Winter Soldier Investigation, Jane hit the lecture circuit once again. First stop Canada, where Jane could speak to students at Ontario's Fanshaw College and, at the same time, recruit deserters to 'testify'.

Returning to the United States on the way to her next speaking engagement, Jane stopped over in Cleveland. The plane landed at Cleveland's Hopkins Airport shortly after midnight on 3 November and Jane, alone and exhausted, looked forward to catching up on her sleep at an airport motel.

Clad in soiled jeans and a T-shirt beneath a cloth overcoat that brushed the floor, Jane lined up with the other passengers to have her passport stamped by the lone US Immigration officer on duty that night. They then proceeded to the customs area, where Jane and the others placed their bags on the counter and waited in line. By now, the authorities present had recognised the celebrity in their midst. 'The customs man said, "You, go over there," and singled me out,' Jane recalls. 'He hadn't opened my bags, he hadn't seen anything. He just singled me out.'

Jane sat quietly for about twenty minutes before demanding to know why she had been ordered out of line. 'I told him, "Your job is to look into my bags." So he opened the bag and he took out my address book, which he then began to read aloud to everyone in line.' The book, which was the size of a small telephone directory and organised state by state, was confiscated on the spot. 'When I got it back from the FBI under protest two days later, Canada was in Florida, and Colorado was in Texas. Everything was completely mixed up and backward. They obviously had taken it and Xeroxed every page.'

Next, the customs officer pulled a bag out of Fonda's suitcase containing 102 plastic vials. On the top of each vial, scrawled in red nail varnish, was one of three letters: B, L, or D. The customs officer held them up and smiled broadly. He was not about to buy Jane's explanation that these were merely organic vitamins, and that the letters merely stood for Breakfast, Lunch, and Dinner. The vitamins were to help her keep up her energy level during her hectic month and a half on the road.

By the time Special Agent Edward Matuszack showed up at the customs counter, Jane was at a pay phone calling Mark Lane in Boston. Matuszack instructed her to hang up immediately, and then led her into an office where, according to Jane, 'two husky FBI agents kept shoving me down into a chair telling me to shut up. All I could do is sing, which I did a lot of – good revolutionary French songs, which sent them off.' Although they denied it later, Jane claimed the FBI agents admitted together that, in her words, 'orders were coming from Washington and that I was on the list of the people to be watched coming in and out of the country'.

'At the end of three hours,' Jane recalled, 'not having superhuman powers over my body, I had to go to the bathroom.' Since she was experiencing her monthly period and hadn't been to the toilet on the plane, her situation was, as she put it, 'desperate'. When Matuszak, afraid she might try to flush something down the toilet, told her she'd have to wait until two prison matrons arrived to strip-search her for 'additional drugs', Jane got up and walked straight towards the lavatory. 'What do you want me to do, pee all over your floor?' she yelled, trying to get around him. 'You'd better let me by or I'll have to go right here!' Furious, she took a swing at Matuszak and missed. 'His face literally lit up, and he looked at his fellow officers and said, "Did you see that?" And then he clamped handcuffs on me and said, "You're under arrest for assaulting a police officer." He was just waiting, waiting for a chance to arrest me.'

When Cleveland Patrolman Robert S. Pieper joined the fracas, Jane shouted, 'Get the fuck out of here, you pig!' and kicked him in the upper left thigh.

It was another hour before the two policewomen arrived, and she was finally supplied with a sanitary towel. Then she was strip-searched twice. Inside Jane's bag, they found amphetamines, as well as the tranquilliser Valium – 'all prescribed medicines,' says Jane, 'which I carried around for a number of years in and out of this country, and which no one ever hassled me about'. While Jane, who had indeed obtained the prescription drugs in Los Angeles, was not required by law to declare them on her return, she was nonetheless hit with an additional charge: smuggling drugs into the country illegally.

Patrolman Pieper drove Jane to the Cuyahoga County Jail, where she was photographed and fingerprinted before being led to the women's holding cell. All the while, Jane screamed paint-peeling obscenities at the 'pigs' who had arrested her.

The ten hours she spent behind bars were not totally wasted, at least not from a revolutionary point of view. Among Jane's dozen cellmates was an eighteen-year-old who claimed she'd been beaten after her arrest for attacking a Cleveland policeman during an anti-war protest. Jane promised to spread the word about conditions at the jail and alleged police brutality.

The next morning, Mark Lane, fresh off the plane from Boston, held an impromptu press conference at the jail. He decried conditions inside the jail, and denounced his client's arrest as 'an act of terror, an act of violence. This is the Nixon–Agnew terror!'

Even before she was led in handcuffs before US Commissioner Clifford Bruce early the next afternoon, papers across the country trumpeted the news of Jane's arrest. JANE FONDA ACCUSED OF SMUGGLING DRUGS, KICKING OFFICER, screamed one headline. Another blared: JANE FONDA IN SCRAP WITH LAW: ARRESTED FOR SMUGGLING PILLS AND ASSAULTING POLICEMAN. The Associated Press carried photographs of Jane, wearing shackles and an expression of barely contained rage, being led from jail by police.

While reporters swarmed in the corridors of the federal building, Jane, wearing sunglasses and a suede trousersuit, was arraigned on the federal drug charges. The maximum penalty: $10,000 or five years in prison, or both. She pleaded innocent and was promptly released on $5000 personal bond.

Jane went through the motions of being rearrested, this time on the assault charge. Her road show then moved on to Municipal Court – better known locally as 'Drunk Court' – for arraignment. Flanked by Mark Lane and Cleveland lawyer Irwin Barnett, Jane pushed her way through a crowd of onlookers and newsmen. She sat in the front row waiting for Judge Edward F. Feighan to dispose of five cases of public drunkenness before her case was called. After entering her not guilty plea, she was released on a $500 surety bond.

With scores of reporters in tow, Fonda and her lawyers then marched to the county courthouse to file a formal complaint with Prosecutor John T. Corrigan charging that Barbara Kahn, the protester who had been her overnight cellmate, had been 'systematically beaten' by guards. As she left, a deputy sheriff wearing a Spiro Agnew wristwatch raised his fist in the air and shouted, not doubt sarcastically, 'Right on, doll!'

One of Jane's surprise defenders was none other than her husband. Vadim broke his long-held silence concerning his wife's political activities to tell Hollywood columnist Joyce Haber that he was outraged by reports of Jane's treatment in Cleveland.

'My position, not being an American, has always been not to get involved in politics,' said Vadim. 'With Jane doing it, I have accepted that. But there's a difference between politics and police harassment. I know about police harassment because I went through three years of the Nazi occupation of France . . . When a woman gets ill as a woman can get ill and has to go to the bathroom and the police won't let her I think those methods must be called fascism.'

Not about to let the Cleveland incident interfere with her Winter Soldier tour, Jane headed for her next speaking date at Central Michigan University. Back at Cleveland Hopkins Airport, however, she was served with a summons informing her that Officer Pieper had filed a $100,000 personal injury lawsuit against Jane claiming that she had 'unlawfully and maliciously' kicked him. The assault, claimed Pieper, had left him 'weak, sore, and partially disabled'. Jane was nonplussed. 'He wasn't on crutches or in a wheelchair or anything like that,' she responded. 'I don't know what's happening to the manhood of the FBI.'

Within months, all the charges against Jane would be dropped. The federal government was not about to admit in the course of a trial that it did indeed have a list of citizens who were to be carefully watched as they left and entered the country. As for Pieper, as a local law enforcement officer he had no jurisdictional right to detain her at the customs area at the airport, since this was technically federal property.

The dismissals, when they were granted, received little publicity. What persisted in the collective memory of the American public was the image of an unrepentant Jane Fonda being taken in handcuffs to face drug smuggling charges.

Jane's skirmish with the authorities in Cleveland did nothing to discourage her. In fact, her single day in jail so infused her with righteous indignation that she returned to the lecture circuit with a fire-breathing zeal. The arrest also enhanced her standing among radicals, serving to dispel any lingering doubts they might have had about her motives.

Now Jane counted herself among the 'political prisoners' she had often cited as martyrs to the cause. 'I became aware of two very important things during the time I was in jail,' she said later. 'Up until then, my support of political prisoners had been rather theoretical. I realised that . . . if they can be isolated and shut off from the community they are lost. The other thing I realised, of course, is that *everyone* in jail is a political prisoner. The murderers, the junkies, the thieves, all victims of this oppressive, dehumanising, threatening society that we live in . . . Some of the best people in America today are behind bars – Angela Davis, Bobby Seale, Reverend Daniel Berrigan and, of course, Christ, the greatest revolutionary of them all!'

Jane's rhetoric heated up from November into the new year. She dismissed the US electoral process as meaningless. 'I do not vote . . . I've become cynical. The answer is revolution.' No longer concealing the fact that she was advocating state socialism, Jane now cited Fidel Castro's Cuba as an example of a near-utopian society. To an audience of several thousand Michigan State University students, she proclaimed: 'I would think that if you knew what communism was, you would hope, you would pray on your knees that we would someday become communist.'

'Revolution' was now perhaps the most frequently used word in Jane's public vocabulary. Yes, she believed there would be a revolution, and 'I'm afraid it will be a bloody one.'

Jane went on to praise 'the new kind of soldier' in Vietnam. 'They're not John Wayne freaks over there. No order goes unchallenged. When they're sent out on patrol, they just go out a little ways, lie down on a little knoll, and blow grass and stargaze.' (Fonda, incidentally, did take the position that heroin and speed were dangerous drugs. The future health-and-fitness queen, however, also went on record as not opposing the recreational use of 'grass, mescaline, and acid'.)

'They're good soldiers,' Jane went on to say about US servicemen – or at least her kind of US servicemen. 'We should be proud of them. They're not only doing what they're not supposed to do, but they're not even performing the basic functions of soldiers.'

A few moment later, without any hint of irony, Jane allowed that 'the hardest thing for me is to take the subway instead of taxis. It's very hard for someone who has all the luxuries to understand people who are less fortunate.' She also worried about Vanessa's nanny: 'The fact that I have a governess means I can't relate to people who don't.'

As for Vadim: 'I am no longer a wife,' declared Jane, adding that she had no intention of filing for divorce. 'It's only a piece of paper. My husband and I are very close friends, which is more than I can say for most married people I know.'

On the eve of the Winter Soldier Investigation, Jane shared the stage with one of the more familiar faces on the anti-Establishment scene: Tom Hayden. Jane had admired him ever since 1968, when, while still living in France, she tried to make sense of the political turmoil back home. 'In the midst of chaos,' she would recall, 'this fellow Tom Hayden was always the voice of reason and direction. I would clip his articles and quote from them.'

Now, on a stage in Ann Arbor, it was Hayden's turn to admire. 'She was skinny and taut,' he wrote of that first meeting in his autobiography, *Reunion*, 'her long fingers playing nervously with the purple shirt that was pulled over her jeans.' The next day in Detroit, they met for breakfast in the coffee shop at the Howard Johnson's where Jane was staying. 'It wasn't love at first sight,' wrote Hayden. 'All in all . . . it was a casual conversation. Nothing clicked.'

Although she does not remember what they talked about at the coffee shop that day, Jane does recall being intimidated by Hayden. When she did not understand what he was saying – this was the case much of the time – she simply nodded in agreement.

While he was being dropped off at the airport the following day, Hayden impulsively put his cap on Jane's head. 'She turned, and our eyes locked,' he recalled. 'We found ourselves laughing absurdly in the middle of a war crimes discussion.'

Fonda and Hayden would not see each other again for over a year. Hayden was involved with a fellow Berkeley activist, and Jane was in the throes of an affair with Klute himself, Donald Sutherland.

A native of New Brunswick, the lanky, bellows-voiced Sutherland had studied engineering at the University of Toronto, then acted in theatre workshops before the role of Trapper John in Robert Altman's hit film *M*A*S*H* propelled him to stardom in 1969. Although the Sutherlands lived in an exclusive Malibu enclave near Jane's old house and had made millions in the United States, Canadians Donald and Shirley were not at all shy about publicly railing against their host country at every opportunity.

The Sutherlands, known to split a large bottle of Scotch a day, were on the verge of divorce when Donald and Jane began their affair on the set of *Klute*. 'Jane and I never lived together continuously,' he says. 'It was one big bowl of soup and it was terrific, wonderful. You couldn't ask for a more generous, exciting, funny, sensuous woman than Jane. I loved her with all my heart.'

After the Cleveland incident, however, they both became convinced that the FBI was bugging her phone. To get around that, explains Sutherland, he and Jane communicated in code and 'gobbledygook. We'd have a super-secret rendezvous . . . I'd leave the house at night, drive around the block, and drive back to the garage, which had a door that led directly to the bedroom, and then we'd go to sleep.'

If, in fact, Fonda ever had time to sleep. Hayden had been among those urging Jane not to abandon her acting career, but to put it to political use. But how? A 'liberated' singer named Barbara Dane approached Jane with the idea of staging an anti-war revue to compete with the morale-building Bob Hope tours to which servicemen had become accustomed.

Jane announced the birth of FTA – standing for 'Fuck the Army' – on 16 February 1971, at yet another press conference, this time in New York. 'It is disturbing that Bob Hope, Martha Raye, and company seem to have a corner on the market in speaking to soldiers in the country and Vietnam,' she complained. 'The time has come for entertainers who take a different view on the war to reach the soldiers.' They would present shows, Jane added, 'soldiers really want to see'.

Written by playwright Herb Gardner (*A Thousand Clowns*) and cartoonist-satirist Jules Feiffer, FTA was a collection of skits, songs, and dance numbers that Jane described as 'political vaudeville – basically a series of Beetle Bailey blackouts and longer skits'. At various times, the FTA cast included actors Sutherland and Peter Boyle, comic Dick Gregory, and singer-songwriters Holly Near and Len Chandler.

The show had its debut at the GI coffeehouse outside Fort Bragg. In the days before, Jane, among other things, led two thousand marchers down the Las Vegas strip and into casinos to protest against Nevada state welfare cuts; visited Angela Davis in her Marin County jail ('Angela sends revolutionary greetings,' Jane announced: 'She talked about the importance of a united front, and how important it is for us to forget our political differences and join together if we are to win the struggle!'); and addressed a San Francisco rally in support of activists charged with conspiring to kidnap Henry Kissinger. Dressed in jeans and an Army field jacket, she raised her fist in the familiar salute. 'I'm not a do-gooder,' she declared. 'I'm a revolutionary, a revolutionary woman.'

Finally, before flying off to her FTA rehearsals in New York, Jane called for a spring 'peace offensive' of 'massive civil disobedience' in the nation's capital and other major cities. 'What we need,' she cried, 'is laying our lives, our bodies on the line in massive protests.' Plans included hunger strikes, veterans' marches, work stoppages and 'a mule train down Wall Street'.

For Jane, 1971 would continue to be a blur of speeches and marches and slogans and protests. But her top priority, at least for a time, was FTA. Not unexpectedly, the military barred Jane and her travelling band of radicals from performing on bases or, as they requested at one point, aboard a US carrier. 'They allowed racists and all kinds of other discriminatory groups,' said Jane, 'but not us.' Once again they preached largely to the converted, performing at coffeehouses and in high school gyms.

Jane saw the FTA material as 'good fun. The skits are funny. We don't pretend to be bringing in a polished theatrical event. We're just having a good time.' Chimed in Sutherland: 'The show is not trying to lay some heavy political line on somebody.'

By any objective standard, it was heavy-handed. Childishly so, as these examples show:

'Mr President?'
'What is it, Pat?'
'Mr President, there's a terrible demonstration going on outside.'
'Oh, there's always a demonstration going on outside, Pat.'
'Yeah, but Richard, this one is completely out of control.'
'Well, we have people to take care of that. They'll do their job, you do your job, and I'll do my job.'

'But Richard, you don't understand, they're storming the White House.'

'Oh, in that case I'd better call out the Third Marines.'

'You can't, Richard.'

'Why not?'

'It *is* the Third Marines!'

'Ohhh . . .'

Or:

Nothing could be finer
Than to be in Indochina
Making money.

Hating is a hobby
When you're in the
China Lobby –
Life is sunny.

The soldiers are expendable
Who cares if they die?!

Nothing could be finer
Than an overflight to
China, ain't that funny?
You'll hear me singing,
Bomb another city
Today . . . oh, yeah,
Bomb another city today!

From a performing standpoint, FTA did give Jane the opportunity to sing, dance, and ham it up before generally appreciative audiences. And the show did not slow down her manic pace; between performances at the GI coffeehouse outside Fort Bragg, for instance, she found herself with a free moment, so she used it to picket a Fayetteville supermarket for selling non-union lettuce.

Above all else, Jane insisted, FTA was supposed to be funny – politically 'correct', but funny nonetheless. Yet her own sense of humour during this period was apparent only on the stage. 'She is desperately full of caring,' wrote John Frook, interviewing her for *Life*, 'and she walks around with a solemn Red Guard face. I doubt if I ever saw her laugh. It is as if she thought a show of cheerfulness might betray her.'

Frook went on to speculate that 'Jane Fonda really wants to be Vanessa

172

Redgrave . . . She would like to go Vanessa one better, and be burned at the stake . . . You cannot help but be impressed by how college students regard her with something approaching reverence. Standing there dealing out radical verities and political catchphrases, many of them as naïve as they are sincere, she has students hanging on every word. If Jane Fonda only had a sense of humour, a sense of history, and a power base,' concluded the article, 'she could cause a real commotion.'

Vadim also mourned the fun-loving Jane of the past. 'Because she can't do anything halfway, she wanted to take on the sins of her country in becoming one of the most active militants in the peace-in-Vietnam movement,' he reflected. 'And so she is happy, very happy! She uses 99 per cent of the energy from a Marxist of 1905. She's a romantic pre-Leninist. Unfortunately, she has lost her sense of humour. One day I called her Joan of Arc. She didn't laugh at all.'

Though there was little she could do about regaining a sense of humour, Jane did take steps to establish a power base for herself by joining Sutherland, Barbra Streisand, Burt Lancaster, and other stars to form Entertainment Industry for Peace and Justice (EIPJ).

'She may well be', observed one reporter, 'the only revolutionary with a public relations man.'

With FTA launched, Jane hopped on a plane on 14 March for a five-day blitz of Europe. With her were the omnipresent Mark Lane and Michael Hunter, a former Army sergeant and Vietnam veteran. In France, she privately met North Vietnam's intractable negotiator at the Paris Peace Talks, Madame Binh. After assuring Madame Binh that the American people were against the war and pledging her support, Jane emerged from the meeting to tell the French press that the US government, the Pentagon, and the CIA were reponsible for the My Lai massacre. 'In fact,' she said, 'these organisations are the real war criminals in Vietnam.'

From Paris, the trio moved to London, where Jane repeated allegations of US atrocities: 'applying electrodes to prisoners' genitals, mass rapes, slicing off of body parts, scalping, skinning alive, and leaving "heat tablets" around which burned the insides of children who ate them'. American soldiers, she also told British reporters, were 'indoctrinated with racist thinking: "The only good gook is a dead gook," and "The Vietnamese people don't feel pain."'

Jane returned from Europe fired up with the idea of taking her FTA follies direct to the Far East — Okinawa, Japan, the Philippines and, in the unlikely event the State Department would allow it, South Vietnam.

The release of *Klute* that summer reminded the world that Jane was first and foremost an actress; despite public outrage over her most recent call for 'a Vietcong victory', her cinematic performance met with almost universal praise. Pauline Kael pinpointed Jane's formula for success both on and off screen. 'As an actress,' wrote Kael in *The New Yorker*, 'she has a special kind of smartness that takes the form of speed. She's always a little ahead of everybody, and this quicker beat – this quicker responsiveness – makes her more exciting to watch. She has somehow got to a plane of acting at which even the closest close-up never reveals a false thought, and, seen on the movie street a block away, she's Bree, not Jane Fonda, walking toward us. There isn't another dramatic actress in American films who can touch her.'

Jane bridled at the notion still being raised by others, that she was merely playing her complex, cynical self. 'I'm not a loser. I don't get frightened. I am not somebody who needs to rely on men for my identity anymore, if I ever was.'

Even as the accolades for *Klute* rolled in, Jane chose to play another prostitute in her next film, *Steelyard Blues*. A clumsily crafted tale about several misfits who decide to fix up an old plane and simply fly away from their troubles, *Steelyard Blues* marked the directorial debut of Jane's FTA pal Alan Myerson. Indeed, the entire project, starring FTA's Sutherland and Peter Boyle, was very much a family affair.

Much of *Steelyard Blues* was shot in Berkeley. Jane, who had spent little time with daughter Vanessa, decided to bring her along. When they arrived, Fonda turned her two-year-old daughter over to the Blue Fairyland, a nursery school 'collective' run by a number of Berkeley-based radicals, most notably Tom Hayden. Its director was Bruce Gilbert, a young Beverly Hills High School graduate turned revolutionary. Through caring for Vanessa, Gilbert would ultimately realise his true ambition – to become a rich and powerful Hollywood producer.

While Jane made *Steelyard Blues* in Berkeley, a bloody drama was unfolding across the bay at San Quentin. On the morning of 21 August, Black Panther 'field marshal' and *Soledad Brother* author George Jackson led a prison revolt. Waving a 9mm automatic pistol, Jackson shouted, 'The Black Dragon has come to free you!' to his fellow inmates as he forced guards to open the cellblocks. Using razor blades hidden in toothbrushes, prisoners slashed the throats of three guards and two white convicts before Jackson, firing as he dashed through the prison yard, was finally gunned down by rooftop marksmen. Jackson's lawyer, Stephen Bingham, who was suspected of smuggling the handgun to Jackson, vanished.

Jane joined her fellow revolutionaries in condemning 'the system' for Jackson's death, and speculating that the bloodbath in San Quentin had actually been orchestrated by the government as part of a plot to decimate the ranks of the Panthers. George Jackson was hailed as a martyr to the movement. Significantly, neither Jane nor her colleagues expressed the slightest sympathy for the five men slaughtered in the uprising.

The Panthers and Vietnam had been Jane's top priorities, but during the filming of *Steelyard Blues* she began to feel strong feminist stirrings. 'I was playing a bit part,' she explained in *The New York Times*, 'which meant that since I wasn't the star, they didn't have to treat me the way they probably didn't *want* to treat me, but normally had to. I was becoming sensitised at that particular time to the way men treat women, things I never noticed before – a lack of respect, a glossing over. Like when a woman starts telling a story, the men interrupt and finish it because they assume that no one will really understand or find amusing or interesting the way the woman tells it. And so the man has to take over and tell it his own way.'

The result: 'I really prefer to talk to women. I prefer to spend time with women . . . I do not want to work with men.' And what of her romance with Sutherland? 'We are friends,' she said. 'We think the same things. When we're together it's delightful. When we are apart we remain friends. He is not indispensable to me. I am not indispensable to him. Our attraction involved learning and respect, and we don't expect our relationship to continue forever.'

To be sure, *Steelyard Blues* ended their affair. It also led to a purge within FTA ranks. Up to this point, Jane was content with her status as first among equals – respected for bringing her star power to the movement, but required to share decision making as part of a 'collective leadership'.

That changed when some of the female FTA members began complaining that the show was still dominated by men. Jane heeded these charges of sexism, and by the spring a number of her former allies – including GI movement founder Fred Gardner and rock star Country Joe McDonald – departed in disgust. Jane, they contended, had become dictatorial, rigid, and irrational – sentiments they now shared, though for entirely different reasons, with her critics on the Right.

'Overnight,' recalls a friend from FTA days, 'Jane turned into one of those shrieking feminist militant man-haters. It had a lot to do with a few of the women at FTA who obviously had some major hang-ups in this area. All of a sudden the sisterhood was more important than ending the war.'

Jane's passionate embrace of feminism was rooted in her own sense of guilt. She had, after all, probably done more than anyone since Marilyn Monroe to sustain the image of women as little more than objects of sexual gratification. 'Being a sex symbol', she has conceded, 'is something I battle constantly.'

To make amends, Jane agreed to act in *Fascinating Woman*, a segment of PBS's 'Great American Dream Machine' series, in which she portrayed everything from a Playboy bunny to a housewife.

At the same time, she published a lengthy *New York Times* article straightforwardly entitled 'I Want to Work with Women'. Once again, she was swept away in a sea of rhetoric: 'We women think that we are in control of our lives, that we are defining ourselves when, in fact, none of us are. Our lives are defined by men, directly by men – the men we live with, or

175

the men we love, or the men we're married to, or the men we work for . . .'

Jane's personal solution was to 'stop being liberal about it. I began to say, "Hey, wait a minute, guys . . ." I'm not going to take it any more. Of course, I'm hated. Right? Hated . . . First they'll accuse you of losing your temper, then they'll say that the only reason you're doing it is that you're frustrated, because you haven't had a good time with a man lately . . . Well, bull.'

In defining the FTA's purpose, she now emphasised the show's sensitivity to women. 'We're not going to be that kind of chauvinist show with topless dancers and tits flying around. If that's the only kind of entertainment soldiers can get, that's what they'll watch. But that's also why American men and soldiers feel women are to be used as sex objects. The violence against Vietnamese women is terrible, and those shows contribute to it.'

Those FTA performers who found the new Jane 'bossy and undemocratic' resigned before the Far East tour, but not before firing a few parting shots. Blasting both Fonda and Sutherland as publicity-hungry dilettantes, a bitter Country Joe McDonald told reporters that he was 'not going to be part of their ego trip'.

Steelyard Blues would turn out to be a dismal flop, as would a film version of FTA released the following year. At a Los Angeles screening of FTA (now formally defined as '*Free* the Army' to get past censors), Fonda and Sutherland walked by an angry protester holding up the popular 1967 poster showing a nude, wind-blown Fonda on the beach. Across it he had scrawled, 'Naked Came the Traitor'.

19

THEY WERE to become known, in due course, as the 'Mork and Mindy of the New Left'. Indeed, apart from a shared disdain for capitalism and traditional American values, they seemed to have little in common. Born on 12 December 1940, in the Detroit suburb of Royal Oak, Tom Hayden was raised by his school-librarian mother after his father, a Chrysler accountant, left the family. The Haydens were devout Irish Catholics. As a boy, Hayden attended his parish school, run by Father Charles E. Coughlin, the controversial anti-FDR 'radio priest' of the Depression.

Rebelling against the 'tyranny of the nuns', Hayden was a self-described 'hell raiser' by the time he hit high school. From there, he enrolled in the University of Michigan at Ann Arbor, and after graduating in 1961 headed south to join the civil-rights struggle in Georgia and Mississippi.

Hayden joined 35 other young activists in December 1961 to form Students for a Democratic Society (SDS). Six months later he wrote the first draft of the 'Port Huron Statement', which quickly became the Magna Carta of the New Left. From Michigan, Hayden went to Newark, organising strikes and demonstrations that preceded that city's 1967 riots.

By then, Hayden had already travelled to Hanoi with Communist Party theoretician Herbert Aptheker and returned to call for the defeat of 'Pig Amerika'. In 1967, Hayden was among American radicals who met North Vietnamese leaders at a conference in Bratislava, Czechoslovakia. As a gesture of 'solidarity' with American activists, the Vietcong agreed to release an unspecified number of US prisoners of war to Hayden.

One of the three POWs who accompanied Hayden back to the United States was Dan Pitzer, who had been in captivity for five years. 'I asked him if he was some kind of communist,' says Pitzer. 'He was very chummy with those VC bastards, and I didn't trust him. Still don't.' As for Hayden's role in freeing him: 'He just played right into the North Vietnamese hands. Besides, Hayden's visa and passport had been yanked by the US. The only way the

State Department would let him back in the States without a hassle was with us. *We* were his ticket home – not the other way around.'

As he approached the age of fifty, Hayden would turn nostalgic about his role as founder and head of SDS. 'Our values were decent ones, even if we could not always live up to them,' he states. 'We of the sixties accomplished more than most generations in American history.'

In painting himself as an ingenuous idealist, Hayden neglects to mention that he sought to incite what Peter Collier calls 'paramilitary insurrections' in a number of cities. 'Perhaps the only forms of action appropriate to the angry people are violent,' Hayden wrote as early as 1966. 'Perhaps a small minority, by setting ablaze New York and Washington, could damage this country forever in the court of world opinion.'

Two years later, Hayden – who had privately excoriated Robert Kennedy as 'a little fascist' only days before RFK's assassination – showed up to serve as a pallbearer at Kennedy's funeral. He then returned to his Red Family commune in Berkeley to take up rifle practice.

Hayden acknowledges that 'the lure of violence and martyrdom were powerful subterranean forces in my make-up'. According to his SDS cohort Todd Gitlin, Hayden concluded that a violent 'showdown' at the Democratic Convention in Chicago was necessary.

Such a confrontation, of course, did occur. In its aftermath Hayden became one of the famous Chicago Eight (the other defendants were Jerry Rubin, Abbie Hoffman, Rennie Davis, Bobby Seale, Lee Weiner, John Froines, and David Dellinger) tried on conspiracy charges. Hayden, one of four found guilty of inciting to riot and contempt of court, was sentenced to five years in prison. (The conspiracy conviction was overturned on appeal, and Hayden was never sentenced on the contempt charges.)

From that time on, Hayden revelled in his status as a fully-fledged hero of the movement. Yet even his fellow activists viewed him as a self-aggrandising careerist. 'Tom gives opportunism a bad name,' cracked one Hayden sidekick. To Abbie Hoffman, Hayden was nothing less than 'our Nixon'. Eventually, Hayden's Red Family collective, which was rife with sexual politics, would expel him for 'oppressive male chauvinism' and 'manipulating people'.

Since confrontation had paid off so handsomely in Chicago, Hayden called for an escalation against the establishment, specifically for the creation of 'liberated zones' in American cities. The first of these was to be Berkeley. While Hayden worked behind the scenes writing his 'Berkeley Liberation Program', rioters seized a plot of land owned by the University of California and claimed it as 'People's Park'. What ensued was a pitched battle in which one protester was killed by a shotgun blast, another blinded by buckshot, and hundreds of others injured by flying bricks, bottles, and chunks of concrete.

'Power to the People': Fonda at a 1970 Washington anti-war rally.
PICTORIAL PARADE

4 November 1970: arrested in Cleveland for assaulting a police officer. UPI/BETTMANN NEWSPHOTO

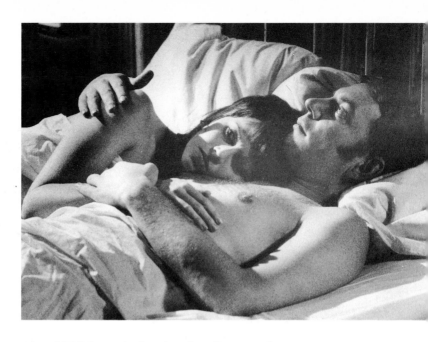

Klute (1971) brought Jane her first Oscar, and
an affair with Donald Sutherland. MOVIE STAR NEWS

Jane as Bree Daniel.
MOVIE STAR NEWS

Receiving her Academy Award for *Klute*, with
Gene Hackman, who won for *The French
Connection*. UPI/BETTMANN NEWSPHOTO

During her 1972 trip to Hanoi, Jane
applauds North Vietnamese soldiers manning
an anti-aircraft gun used to shoot down US
pilots, then looks through the sights herself.
GAMMA

Jane's FTA show took aim at the US
military. UPI/BETTMANN NEWSPHOTO

Jane and Tom Hayden back from Paris,
where they had met North Vietnamese
negotiators. UPI/BETTMANN NEWSPHOTO

Fun with Dick and Jane— Jane's comeback comedy of 1975. MOVIE STAR NEWS

Jane and co-star Vanessa Redgrave in *Julia* (1977). With husband Tom Hayden's career under way, Jane chose to distance her politics from those of her radical longtime friend. MOVIE STAR NEWS

Both Jane and Jon Voight won Oscars for their performances in her IPC production *Coming Home.* MOVIE STAR NEWS

Three Mile Island showed that *The China Syndrome*—which also starred Jack Lemmon and Michael Douglas—wasn't so far-fetched.
MOVIE STAR NEWS

Lily Tomlin, Dolly Parton and Fonda strike a blow for secretaries in the 1980 blockbuster *Nine to Five*.
MOVIE STAR NEWS

On the *Nine to Five* set, Jane horses around with her IPC partner Bruce Gilbert. They met when he cared for Jane's daughter in a Berkeley commune.
MOVIE STAR NEWS

Peter and Jane were
on hand to help their father
celebrate his 75th birthday
in 1980.
UPI/BETTMANN NEWSPHOTO

On Golden Pond. MOVIE STAR NEWS

Early publicity photo
for Jane Fonda's *Workout*.
MOVIE STAR NEWS

By 1985, Jane boasted
three *Workout* videos in
the Top Ten. UPI/BETTMANN
NEWSPHOTO

The family (*clockwise from left*): Amy,
Peter's daughter Bridget, Jane, Tom, Vanessa and
Troy at the 1982 Academy Awards with Henry's
Oscar for *On Golden Pond*.

Less than an hour later, Jane hands the
award to her dying father. UPI/BETTMANN
NEWSPHOTO

Shortly after Henry's death, Jane, Amy,
Shirlee and Peter talked to reporters outside the
Fondas' Bel Air home. MOVIE STAR NEWS

Vanessa Vadim after her arrest in 1989.
UPI/BETTMANN NEWSPHOTO

With Gregory Peck
on the set of *Old Gringo*
in Mexico.
MOVIE STAR NEWS

On location in Waterbury, Connecticut,
with Robert De Niro, for the filming of
Stanley and Iris. Demonstrators were kept
out of camera range. MOVIE STAR NEWS

Jane emerging from an emotional secret
meeting with Vietnam vets. JOHN HARVEY,
THE WATERBURY *REPUBLICAN*

Order was restored only when then-governor Ronald Reagan called in the National Guard.

In the aftermath of the People's Park insurrection, Hayden contemplated an escalation of the violence. According to Peter Collier, an ally from those days, Hayden felt 'the only ones who could bring off "armed resistance" were the Panthers, whom Hayden called "our" NLF . . . I heard that he went to David Hilliard, the Panthers' interim leader, to talk about the possibility of trying to shoot down an Alameda sheriff's helicopter. Hilliard is said to have looked at Hayden in disgust and responded: "Just like you, Tom. Get a nigger to pull the trigger."'

On one occasions, Collier and David Horowitz visited Hayden at his Red Family collective. 'Well,' Hayden said matter-of-factly, 'there will be civil war soon.' Recalls Collier: 'On his advice, I bought a gun.'

Jane, too, was becoming increasingly militant. In January 1972, she departed for Paris to begin work with acclaimed New Wave director Jean-Luc Godard, a Maoist whose pedantic films included *La Chinoise* and *The Assassination of Trotsky*. In *Tout Va Bien* ('Everything's OK'), Jane played the nameless 'She' opposite Yves Montand as 'He' – two members of the bourgeoisie who become radicalised after being trapped overnight during a strike in a Paris sausage factory.

Jane, who was sharing a seedy Left Bank apartment with five other women during shooting, looked forward to working with Godard. But she walked away disillusioned by his tyrannical behaviour on the set. 'Godard really hates people. Especially women. He never told me what was going on, and when I realised, I wanted to leave, but he threatened to rough me up if I did. It was a terrible experience. A true revolutionary', she concluded, 'has to care about people.'

Tout Va Bien turned out to be another unmitigated catastrophe, convincing Jane once and for all that overt propaganda was ineffectual. But her Paris stint was not entirely in vain; Jane attended the Hanoi-sponsored International Assembly for Peace and Independence in Indochina at Versailles, at which she condemned the American delegation at the Paris Peace Talks for misrepresenting the North's seven-point peace proposal.

More significantly, she also used her time off-camera clandestinely to meet Vietcong and North Vietnamese operatives. These meetings would pave the way for a voyage that would forever change Jane's life – not to mention alter her place in America's collective consciousness.

By early spring, with corruption in the Saigon government of General Thieu growing ever more flagrant and the American people becoming increasingly impatient, there was a break in the Paris Peace Talks. In response,

Hanoi launched a major drive across the DMZ (demilitarised zone) to bring the enemy back to the negotiating table. Nixon then ordered stepped-up bombing of the North and the mining of Haiphong harbour. Nixon himself was, Jane felt, the personification of evil. She returned to Los Angeles full of righteous indignation, and determined to share that outrage with the public.

At LA's Embassy Theater, she showed slides provided by her communist friends in Paris — Vietcong troops launching heroic attacks against the Yankee invaders, the results of US bombing raids, and so forth. Among those in the audience was a long-haired, bearded Hayden. Afterwards, he climbed on to the stage and reintroduced himself. She would date the start of the romance to the moment when he casually put his hand on her knee. 'I came home to my roommate [Jane was sharing her small rented house on and off with several women] and I said, "I'm going to marry him." I just *knew* it. He was stronger than I was, he was one of the only men that I'd ever met that I knew I would never be bored with — and I knew he wouldn't be intimidated by me.'

Hayden was also intrigued, though it took him an extra day to figure out what Jane already knew. 'I went to Jane's Laurel Canyon house to show her my Indochina materials,' Hayden wrote in *Reunion*. 'We sat on her living-room floor in front of the fireplace, and I flashed slide after slide on the opposite wall . . . of Saigon, the impoverished refugees, the brothels and bars full of teenage prostitutes. Jane was starting to cry. I kept flipping through slides of grotesque young Saigon women, talking about the breast and eye operations performed to turn them into round-eyed, round-bodied Westernised women . . . Suddenly I understood why she was weeping: I was talking about the image of superficial sexiness she once promoted and was now trying to shake. I looked at her in a new way. Maybe I could love someone like this.'

At the moment, however, Jane was 'seeing' *Ramparts* editor Bob Scheer, whose ex-wife Anne had in fact been Hayden's long-standing lover. 'Complicated relationships', said Hayden, 'would not go away.'

Nevertheless, their shared passion for politics quickly turned to romance. The first night Hayden and Jane made love, Vanessa stumbled out of her bedroom. 'Instead of ignoring her or saying I should take her back to bed,' recalls Jane, 'Tom turned on the lights, introduced himself, and took her in his arms. I thought — at last, a human being.'

Says Hayden: 'It was important that Jane was a woman who could not be eclipsed or diminished in my shadow, and I was a man who was not threatened by her greater fame and power.'

Practically speaking, Hayden validated Jane in the eyes of sceptics within the movement who still viewed her as a dilettante. Conversely, she offered him the power, fame, and money that he felt could be harnessed for the movement.

'To understand Tom and Jane,' says a former colleague, 'all you have to know is that they are both very, very ambitious people. Tom was a big hero to the people who mattered most to Jane. She still had lingering doubts about herself, and he could dispel them. I mean, this great intellectual was taking her seriously, so she figured everyone else would have to, too.' And Hayden? 'Jane was still a pretty glamorous creature, and Tom was a fan, let's face it. When they got together, he was broke and she was worth millions. Jane was also a powerful force − she was a hundred times more famous than he was − and he had been out of the spotlight for a while. He wanted the access to Middle America she gave him.'

Overriding all else in Jane's mind was one paramount consideration. Sisterhood aside, she needed another mentor, another substitute for her father. Hayden filled the bill nicely.

As Oscar night approached, Hollywood waited to see just what Jane would do if, as expected, she won the award for *Klute*. She had already been given the 'Sour Apple' Award by the Hollywood Women's Press Club for presenting the worst image of the film capital to the world. At the Golden Globes in February, a scruffy-looking Vietnam veteran she dispatched to accept the award for her pelted the audience with anti-war rhetoric before being hooted off the stage.

Her first inclination was to refuse the Academy Award outright in protest against the war. A friend changed her mind. 'You're a frigging elite individual,' she told Jane. 'It's really typical of the bourgeois middle-class family girl to want to refuse the Oscar.' By accepting, Jane would have a unique opportunity to show 'the masses' that she wasn't a 'freak' or 'some kind of monster'.

Still, there was heavy pressure from allies within the movement to seize the moment for a political speech. On this, she sought her father's advice. Henry Fonda 'implored' his daughter not to take advantage of the Oscar ceremony to deliver a shrill diatribe. It would only damage her cause, he argued. Besides, it was simply bad manners.

When her name was finally called out that night at Los Angeles's Dorothy Chandler Pavilion, Jane, dressed in a black knitted trousersuit, walked briskly to the stage, smiled gently into the camera, and milked the tentative applause for dramatic effect. What, dear God, was she going to say?

'There's a lot I could say tonight,' she said softly. 'But this isn't the time or the place. So I'll just say "Thank you."'

Hank Fonda was right. By leaving the obvious unsaid, she had regained a measure of respect − at least for the moment − from those who had been turned against her. One wonders, however, if Jane would have taken her father's advice had she known, as he admitted to me, that he had not voted for his own daughter.

In the wake of her gracious Oscar speech, the American public began to reassess its opinion of Jane. But her truce did not last long. In mid-July, travelling under the name Jane Seymour Plemiannikov, Fonda boarded an Aeroflot flight in Paris. Her eventual destination: Hanoi.

20

CLAD IN black pyjamas and a white tunic, Jane stepped off her Aeroflot jet on 8 July 1972, and into a maelstrom of controversy. She arrived, she told her uniformed, helmeted hosts, with 'greetings' from revolutionary 'comrades' in America. Over the next two weeks Jane, several cameras slung around her neck, was led on a tour of bombed-out hospitals, schools, factories, villages, and dykes. The devastation left her shaken, but not so shaken that she was unable to do some front-line morale-boosting for the enemy.

It was then that Jane, surrounded by applauding soldiers, took her notorious joy ride aboard a North Vietnamese anti-aircraft gun whose sights were normally trained on American planes. The image of a euphoric Jane aboard the gun, captured as it was on film, would be the hardest for Jane to shake; in this sense she was undone by the very medium she had mastered.

Still, had she stopped there and returned home with 'revolutionary greetings' from Hanoi, Jane's trip might soon have been forgotten. Instead, she volunteered to make ten propaganda broadcasts over Radio Hanoi squarely aimed at demoralising American servicemen in combat. The broadcasts, aired between 14 and 22 July, were delivered in the same warm, almost seductive tone of voice used by enemy propagandists Tokyo Rose and Axis Sally during World War II. The comparison would be made often. Here are excerpts from those broadcasts – italics mark the words Jane emphasised.

This is Jane Fonda speaking in Hanoi, and I'm speaking privately to US servicemen who are stationed in the Gulf of Tonkin . . . Seventh Fleet in the Anglico Corps [Marine spotters for naval gunfire] in the south of Vietnam . . .

You are very far away, perhaps, and removed from the country you're being ordered to shoot shells at and bomb, and the use of these bombs, or the condoning of the use of these bombs, makes one *a war criminal*.

The men who are ordering you to use these weapons are *war criminals* according to international law, and in the past in Germany and Japan, men who were guilty of these kinds of crimes were *tried and executed*.

In a broadcast to US pilots on 21 July:

Nixon is continuing to risk your lives and the lives of the American prisoners of war under the bombs in a last desperate gamble to keep his office come November.

How does it feel to be used as pawns? You may be shot down, you may perhaps even be killed, but for what, and for whom?

The people back home are crying for you. We are afraid of what, what must be happening to you as human beings. For it isn't possible to destroy, to receive salary for pushing buttons and pulling levers that are dropping illegal bombs on innocent people, without having that damage your own soul.

Tonight when you are alone, ask yourselves: What are you doing? Accept no ready answers fed to you by rote from basic training on up; but as men, as human beings, can you justify what you are doing? Do you know why you are flying these missions, collecting extra combat pay on Sunday?

The next day, Jane hit the airwaves again:

This is Jane Fonda in Hanoi. I'm speaking to the men in the cockpits of the Phantoms, in the B-52s, in the F-4s; those of you who are still here fighting the war, in the air, on the ground: the guys in the Anglico Corps, on the Seventh Fleet, the Constellation, the Coral Sea, the Hancock, Ticonderoga, the Kitty Hawk, the Enterprise . . .

All of you, in your heart of hearts, know the lies – cheating on body counts, falsified battle reports, the numbers of planes that are shot down, what your targets really are. Knowing who was doing the lying . . . should you allow these same liars to decide for you who your enemy is? Should we examine the reasons given to justify the *murder you are being paid to commit?*

If they told you the truth, you wouldn't fight, you wouldn't kill. You were not born and brought up by your mothers to be killers. So . . . you have been told lies so that it would be possible for you to kill.

To American servicemen with Jane Fonda pin-ups taped to their lockers, it was as if Betty Grable had begun making Nazi broadcasts from Berlin. Yet their anguish could not compare with that of POWs in Hanoi. Inside the famed 'Hanoi Hilton' POW camp, Fonda's words were broadcast over loudspeakers day and night until, in the words of one prisoner, 'we almost went fucking crazy'.

'It's difficult to put into words how terrible it is to hear that siren song that is so absolutely rotten and wrong,' says Colonel George Day, who was senior officer at the Hanoi Hilton. 'It was worse than being manipulated and used. She got into it with all her heart. She wanted the North Vietnamese to win. She caused the deaths of unknown numbers of Americans by buoying up the enemy's spirits and keeping them in the fight. That's not what you'd expect from Henry Fonda's daughter.'

Adding insult to injury, the North Vietnamese then rounded up POWs to hold a press conference with Jane and former US Attorney General Ramsey Clark, another outspoken anti-war activist. Those prisoners who refused to appear with Fonda – and many did – were tortured. Day, who had already spent 37 months in solitary confinement, was flogged with a fan belt until his buttocks were 'hamburger'.

Civilian Michael Benge, an official of the Agency for International Development, had been captured in Cambodia in 1968. 'I had to laugh,' he recalls. 'The Political Commissar of the camp told me that Fonda and the others were being paid by the CIA to come over', and that he should co-operate.

Benge, a survivor of 28 months in solitary (a year of that in a tiny, airless hole he called the 'Black Box') did not co-operate. For his refusal to meet Fonda, Benge was forced to kneel on the cold cement floor of his cell holding a steel rod in front of him for two days. Every time the rod dipped to the floor he was brutally beaten. When he finally returned home with the other POWs years later, he was missing part of his right foot.

Eventually, eight POWs did meet Jane and Ramsey Clark at a meticulously orchestrated news conference. Lieutenant Commander David Hoffman, a Navy pilot, was one of them – though at first he refused. His captors broke his arm, then yanked on it until he agreed. 'I was hung by that broken arm several times,' he recalls, 'and allowed to drop at the end of a rope from a table which was kicked out from under me. If Miss Fonda feels for a minute that any of the people she saw were able to speak freely, and were not fully aware that any deviation from what we were told to say or could say would bring instant punishment the minute she departed, then she's got another think coming. I reject everything I said during those press conferences with Jane Fonda.'

Another POW, a captured pilot held in solitary, whose identity has never been established, was rumoured to have been executed for refusing to meet Jane.

In their carefully scripted remarks, the POWs forced to go on display with their movie-star visitor claimed they were being treated humanely, that they were not being tortured, and that they were eager to see the United States pull out of Vietnam. From the strain on their faces and the robotic delivery of their lines, it was obvious that they were not speaking freely. Jane chose not to notice. Nor did she wonder why she was not permitted to visit the Hanoi Hilton and inspect conditions there for herself.

On her last day in Hanoi, Jane met North Vietnam's vice premier Nguyen Duy Trinh. She told him that she was deeply impressed by the Vietnamese people's determination to emerge victorious. She also told the vice premier that his people would 'certainly triumph' over the Americans.

The communists could not have been more pleased. 'That visit and the support it showed had great impact on the Vietnamese people,' said North Vietnam's Colonel Bui Tin. ''We realised there were two Americas – one who dropped bombs on us, and the other who had sympathy.'

Boarding the Aeroflot jet in Hanoi for the flight to Paris, Jane carried with her 240 letters from POWs to their families. She hugged her Vietnamese hosts. As a pledge of their solidarity, they gave her a ring made out of the wreckage of a downed US plane. The memento was not unlike the one given Tom Hayden when he visited Hanoi: a comb made from the fuselage of an F-105 and fashioned in the shape of that plane. The comb bears an inscription: 'The American Pirates 1700th plane shot down in North Vietnam.'

The trip to Hanoi moved Jane up several notches on Nixon's 'Enemies List'. Yet one high-level member of the administration felt that, if the complexities of the situation were explained to her, Jane might tone down her rhetoric. At one point, Henry Kissinger invited Jane to meet him secretly to discuss US policy. She declined; unless she could call a press conference afterwards to talk about what was discussed at the meeting, Jane was not interested. To Kissinger, Jane seemed intent on publicising the North Vietnamese cause. 'She knew precisely what she was doing – she wanted Hanoi to win,' says Kissinger. 'What she did was totally immoral.'

Several congressmen agreed, called Fonda a traitor for making her broadcasts on Radio Hanoi. 'What is a traitor?' she asked reporters upon her arrival in Paris. 'I cried every day I was in Vietnam. The bombs are falling on Vietnam, but it is an American tragedy . . . I believe the people in this country who are speaking out are the real patriots.'

Was she being entirely fair and looking at both sides of the issue? 'There *are* no both sides in this question,' snapped Jane. She went on to assert that North Vietnam was blameless, that Nixon was a 'cynic, liar, and murderer. Nixon has gone further than any human being, in my opinion, in history in terms of slaughter.'

At a Paris press conference, Jane delivered the narration for a 25-minute silent film she had shot in and around Hanoi. Most of the film showed her talking to villagers, examining the ruins of buildings and dykes. One segment showed the POWs, dressed in purple-and-red-striped uniforms, having dinner with Fonda. The expressions on their faces varied from strained to dazed.

Jane, who on film was shown laughing and talking with the POWs, insisted that they were being well cared for by their North Vietnamese captors. 'They [the POWs] assured me they were in good health,' she said. 'When I asked them if they were brainwashed, they all laughed. Without exception, they expressed shame at what they had done.'

Jane then launched into an attack on American prisoner-of-war camps, where, she charged, North Vietnamese POWs were systematically tortured.

As for the forthcoming presidential elections, Jane said that the POWs were urging the ousting of Nixon and the election of anti-war Democrat George McGovern. 'They fear', she said, 'that if Nixon stays in office they will be prisoners forever.' In truth, these lines had been fed to the POWs directly by their captors.

Pat Nixon did not take kindly to Jane's remarks. At one of her rare press conferences in the Yellow Oval Room of the White House family quarters, the first lady responded sharply to a question about Jane's Hanoi broadcasts. 'I think she should have been in Hanoi asking them to stop their aggression,' she said. 'Then there wouldn't be any conflict. I'd have her go there and beg on bended knees.'

Henry Fonda, an erstwhile dove, confessed nonetheless to being 'appalled' by his daughter's actions. Still, he was just as angry at those who expected him to disown his daughter. 'She's a good woman who had good instincts,' he said after her return from Hanoi. 'But I don't think it's necessary to overthrow the government to achieve some of the things she's after.' He left no doubt that, in his mind, that was her goal.

Demonstrators who had waited for Jane's plane to touch down at New York's Kennedy Airport shouted, 'Hanoi Rose! Red pinko!' as she rushed by wearing black Vietcong pyjamas and a coolie hat. The next day, she held yet another press conference in Park Avenue's Drake Hotel. There she angrily defended herself against charges of treason.

Had she merely been a propaganda tool for the North Vietnamese?

'Do you think they blow up their own buildings?' she exploded. 'Are they bombing their own dykes? Are their women and children being mutilated in order to move Americans?'

Jane then dismissed as 'absurd' charges that she had urged airmen to defect over the radio. 'I would no more tell the soldiers to defect and fight on the side of North Vietnam . . . The North Vietnamese don't need American soldiers to fight for them. They're doing just fine!'

Actually, Jane's career on Hanoi radio was not over. The day after her New

York press conference, messages she had recorded during her visit were broadcast to South Vietnamese troops. In them, she called upon the American allies to desert, telling them they were being used as 'cannon fodder for US imperialism'. The US presence in Southeast Asia, she added, constituted 'racist aggression' being vented in a 'white man's war'.

She went on to say US bombings – 'wantonly, accidentally, perhaps' – of South Vietnamese troops showed a 'lack of concern for your lives by the white American officers, both in Vietnam and in the Pentagon and in the White House'.

South Vietnamese soldiers also heard Jane offer what amounted to an invitation to desert: 'We read with interest about the growing number of you who are understanding the truth and joining with your fellow countrymen to fight for freedom and independence and democracy. We note with interest, for example, that, as in the case of the 56th Regiment of the Third Division of the Saigon Army, Army of the Republic soldiers are taken into the ranks of the National Liberation Front [the Vietcong], including officers, who may retain their rank.'

Jane concluded with yet another condemnation of America: 'We know what US imperialism has done to our country in the United States . . . and so we know what lies in store for any Third World country that could have the misfortune of falling into the hands of . . . the United States and becoming a colony.'

Incensed by Jane's actions, congressmen again urged that she be indicted. Meanwhile, resolutions censuring Jane were promptly introduced in the Colorado and Maryland legislatures. An editorial in the right-wing Manchester (New Hampshire) *Union Leader* called for her to be tried for sedition and, if convicted, shot.

Justice Department officials, fearing that they might create a martyr, declined to move against Jane. That decision did not sit well with her critics. 'Declared war or undeclared war,' said Georgia Republican Fletcher Thompson, 'this is treason.'

Hayden professed to being nonplussed at the reaction to Jane's Hanoi broadcasts. 'Was it because she was a woman?' he asked in *Reunion*. 'A sex symbol turned into an accuser of macho men? A successful American rejecting the system that rewarded her? Why the hate? I wondered.'

Shortly after Jane returned from Hanoi, Hayden said, 'she felt a lot more solidly about me, and I felt the same way, and it will probably take years for us to understand that. It doesn't mean that our relationship is based entirely on Vietnam, but I think that just as Vietnam brings out the genocidal characteristics of some people, it also brings out the better qualities of people as well. And it magnifies feelings.'

Hayden continued to explain the beginnings of his romance with Jane, with an air of cold, calculated detachment. 'The degree to which Jane had changed and the mutual strategic outlook was right,' he said. 'It sounds mechanical, but it was a recognition of the important meaning of Vietnam.'

Jane's reaction was less analytical. 'I don't know how to describe this without feeling overly romantic, but Vietnam had a very important effect on me . . . I have never . . . been in a country in which the life force was so strong. . .'

The experience stirred other feelings in Jane. In their elegant (and very expensive) New York hotel suite, she told Hayden she wanted to have a child. Naked, she stood behind him and whispered, 'I want to have a child with you.' 'With a tearful smile,' recalled Hayden, 'I said yes.'

In November, allegedly 'in the upper berth of a van between speeches in Upstate New York', a child was conceived. 'We had stopped thinking the world was a bad place to bring up a child,' says Hayden, 'to feeling optimistic about life, even in the midst of war.'

Jane's pregnancy forced her to confront a personal demon. For twenty-three years she had been caught in the binge–purge cycle of bulimia, stuffing herself with food and then forcing herself to vomit fifteen to twenty times a day. 'I would literally empty a refrigerator,' she admits. 'I spent most of every day either thinking about food, shopping for it, or bingeing and purging. It's an addiction like drugs or alcohol. And it is tremendously debilitating.'

Now, Jane was determined to kick the habit not only because she was concerned about her foetus's health, but because 'I had lost control of my life. The choice was between being a good mother and wife and being a bulimic.'

Even with this courageous decision, she could hardly yet be considered a health fanatic, or even a prudent mother-to-be: Jane still chain-smoked, and continued using diuretics to rid her body of excess water – another dangerous habit she acquired when she was nineteen.

The prospect of parenthood certainly did not interfere with Tom and Jane's political lives. If anything, they hurled themselves into the movement with renewed zeal. They pieced together a national organisation called the Indochina Peace Campaign (IPC) and hit the road again – a 90-city speaking tour designed to muster support for Democratic presidential candidate George McGovern against incumbent Richard Nixon.

Campus audiences seemed largely sympathetic, though there were the inevitable catcalls and a few threats. On more than one occasion, Jane was hanged in effigy. Hayden worried that she might be martyred like 'other mass figures of my lifetime – Martin Luther King, the Kennedys, Malcolm X. It's the sort of thing . . . from which killings have typically come.'

A sexual component, Hayden theorised, heightened public feelings about Jane. 'There is a lot of sexual feeling involved in it. All these people expected

189

her to be a certain kind of person . . . and when your fantasy life is threatened, and Barbarella becomes revolutionary, it's very upsetting.'

In believing that most Americans shared their hatred for Richard Nixon, Tom and Jane were indulging in a fantasy life of their own. Despite the public's impatience with the war, troops were at their lowest levels in seven years – down to 180,000 from a maximum of nearly 550,000. Confidence in Nixon and his chief foreign policy adviser, Henry Kissinger, was relatively high. Nixon was re-elected over George McGovern by what was then the largest margin in US electoral history.

Disillusioned, Jane took time to assess the damage she was doing to her career. Fewer and fewer scripts were coming her way. 'I keep asking,' she told Tom, 'and my agents say as long as producers can make money off me, they will.' So, was she now 'unbankable'? There was no official 'blacklist' like the one that ended so many brilliant careers during the McCarthy era of the 1950s; but studios were not courting controversy, and when given a choice they were not offering her the plum roles. Jane was, in the new vernacular, being 'greylisted'.

One who understood Jane's predicament was director Joseph Losey, an expatriate American who had fled the United States after the Army–McCarthy hearings and settled in London. He invited her to essay the role of Nora in Ibsen's feminist classic *A Doll's House*, and she agreed – but only after demanding first-class round-trip air tickets (even at the movement's height, Jane insisted on first class) to the film's location in Norway for herself and an assistant. Also tagging along was little Vanessa, who now had the opportunity to spend some unexpected time with her mother, and Vanessa's ever-present nurse.

For Losey, the dream of making a first-rate film adaptation with a first-rate cast (it included Trevor Howard, David Warner, and French actress Delphine Seyrig) quickly dissolved into a nightmare.

Seyrig, Fonda, and the women members of the cast promptly formed a cabal hostile to Losey and his concept of the film. All the men working on the film stayed in one hotel, the women in another. 'Jane Fonda seemed totally unaware of my existence, the existence of the crew, or the male members of the cast,' said Losey in an interview shortly after the débâcle. 'The first week, the women spent their time in their houses, sending in pages of notes on what should be done to change the film.'

Eventually, after Losey threatened to cancel the project, they reached a tense understanding. 'Jane had encased herself from being hurt by men,' he observed. 'In a love scene on the set, she would kiss her leading men energetically, but once the scene was over, she would walk off the set and never speak to any of them. The problem, I think, is her family, her uptight background, and her marriage to Roger Vadim.'

Jane did confide in Losey to the extent that Henry Fonda did not understand what his daughter stood for 'and since she loved him she could not understand his lack of understanding. "But if Daddy did understand,"' she went on, '"it would be the negation of his whole life."'

And again, Jane was roasted for not having a sense of humour. When the British crew put a sign in front of the camera reading 'Cleopatra needed liberation like a hole in the head,' Jane was furious. 'She knew right then how the company felt about her hostility towards them,' said Losey, 'but she made no attempt to break the ice.

'I have directed the most temperamental stars of all time,' he concluded, 'but I have never encountered the likes of Jane Fonda. Compared with her, the Burtons were angels.'

Jane fired back in a *Village Voice* interview that it was Losey who was unprofessional. 'We were being called dykes, a gaggle of bitches,' she said. 'Actually, most of the men were drunk all the time. They painted it as a conspiracy of dykes ganging up on us poor men! I was a well-disciplined actress who had some ideas about the play that he couldn't handle. And this from a man who calls himself a progressive, a Marxist.'

For all the *Sturm und Drang*, *A Doll's House* could not find a distributor willing to gamble on a film starring 'Hanoi Jane'. So instead, it was purchased by ABC and broadcast as a TV special. Ratings, given the subject matter, were small. Although the production was panned, Jane once again emerged unscathed. While calling the film 'ferociously flawed', *The New York Times*'s Nora Sayre wrote that Fonda 'again proves herself to be one of our finest actresses'.

While shooting was still proceeding in Norway, Hayden visited the set. Tom (the only man, according to Losey, allowed to touch Jane off-camera) told Jane that his Catholic mother was mortified at the thought of a grandchild born out of wedlock. 'Do we', he asked Jane, 'want to fight the war, fight Nixon, and fight marriage?'

After Hayden had left, Jane's quandary was compounded when Vadim dropped by to see his daughter. Jane refused to let him stay with her. Instead, she insisted he check into the hotel where the rest of the men were staying. She then informed Vadim point-blank that she was pregnant with Hayden's child and wanted to marry him.

There was only one small problem: Vadim and Jane had never got around to obtaining a divorce. Under the circumstances, Vadim was happy to oblige.

A Doll's House behind her, Jane left Norway to spend Christmas with Tom in Paris. It was there, while watching Marlon Brando find imaginative new uses for butter in *Last Tango in Paris*, that they overheard other cinemagoers talking about Nixon's Christmas bombing of the north. To bring the North

Vietnamese back to the bargaining table, the newly re-elected president had again ordered the saturation bombing of Hanoi and Haiphong.

Jane and Tom left the cinema and headed directly for the North Vietnamese mission. There they expressed their outrage to North Vietnamese diplomat Nguyen Minh Vy, Vietcong negotiator Madame Nguyen Thi Binh, and other communist negotiators, and asked what they could do to help.

Within days, at a rally in Stockholm, Jane took to the stage to denounce Nixon before a crowd of over six thousand people. A woman tossed a can of red paint at her, but Jane, wiping the paint from her hair and face, went right ahead blasting Nixon. 'His concept of peace is to escalate the killing. The US election did not give Nixon a mandate to carry on the war.'

Tom and Jane's next move was to start planning a massive protest to disrupt the forthcoming presidential inauguration in Washington. But first they returned to California to make good their promise to Tom's mother that they would indeed get married.

The minor obstacle of Jane's marriage to Vadim was handled by Richard Rosenthal, who had served as Henry Fonda's attorney and now worked for his daughter. Recalling the divorce, Rosenthal says, 'I remember sitting on the floor of their darkened room in the Beverly Wilshire Hotel, working on custody arrangements for Vanessa. There were no problems, everything was very friendly, very cordial. But sitting there in the dark, you couldn't help but feel a sadness in the room.'

Virtually overnight, Jane received a Dominican Republic divorce that freed her to wed Hayden. Still, there was one last niggling problem: when Tom was asked to sign a prenuptial agreement, he refused. 'It offended his sensibilities,' says a friend. Jane did not press the matter – much to her eventual regret.

On 19 January, about one hundred guests – including Henry, Shirlee, Peter Fonda, and FTA trouper Holly Near, as well as several Vietnamese students – jammed into Jane's small Laurel Canyon house for her marriage to Tom Hayden. Vanessa, now four, sat by the fireplace on Grandpa Henry's lap. The bride wore a work shirt and slacks, the groom, corduroy trousers and a pullover.

Henry's presence, after he had not even been invited to Jane's first wedding, marked a significant turn in their relationship. He was mellowing with age, certainly, but there were other reasons for the thaw between father and daughter. Tom Hayden was easier for Hank to accept than either Voutsinas or Vadim. Fonda had always been suspicious of those smooth European men Jane seemed to attract, whereas Hayden, despite his radicalism, came across as a down-to-earth, middle-class American.

Jane's political escapades also seemed to upset Henry far less than her sexual ones. Given his basically Puritanical perspective, this was understandable; however upsetting it was to have Jane denounced as a Red, it was harder for him to stomach his daughter being exploited as an international sex symbol.

Perhaps the most important factor leading to Henry's change of heart was his newfound professional respect for Jane. Having broken away from Vadim's influence, she had proved herself a formidable peer with her performances in *They Shoot Horses* and *Klute*. Seeing her taken seriously by his cherished film industry, he had reassessed his daughter with, for the first time, a large degree of paternal pride.

There in Jane's Laurel Canyon house, he happily listened to his son, Peter, and Holly Near sing, and to several Vietnamese students read poetry. Then Richard York, an iconoclastic Episcopal minister from Berkeley's Free Church, stood before the couple for the 'free-form' ceremony. 'Will you, Jane,' asked York, 'marry Tom, and will you try in this marriage to grow together, to be honest, to share responsibility for your children, and to maintain a sense of humour?'

'Yes, I will,' replied Jane.

After Tom made the same vow, the guests, led by Henry, burst into applause. The rest of the evening was spent singing Vietnamese folk songs and dancing Irish jigs.

Jane told the well-wishers that, romanticism aside, she was four months pregnant and had decided to marry 'rather than hassle with criticism that would drain our energies from our real work'.

Reverend York was later reprimanded for conducting the ceremony. In a 'letter of Godly Admonition' from the Episcopal bishop of California, the priest was suspended for having remarried a divorced person without obtaining permission from a bishop.

Before the Haydens could launch their global drive to stop the war, a peace agreement was signed in Paris by Henry Kissinger, North Vietnam's Le Duc Tho, and the Vietcong's Madame Binh. The United States agreed to withdraw all its remaining troops, though it reserved the right to continue to supply the Saigon government with economic and military aid.

Both Kissinger and Le Duc Tho were awarded the Nobel Peace Prize for their efforts, though Le Duc Tho turned it down. Two weeks after her wedding, Jane led a crowd of 250 protesters to the State Department to present Kissinger with an 'Ignoble Peace Prize' – a 20mm cannon shell mounted on a plywood plaque.

On the same trip to Washington, Tom and Jane were banned from a scheduled appearance on the then-popular TV talk programme 'Panorama'. The Haydens had refused to share the show with other guests – including former presidential candidate Eugene McCarthy – and demanded that host Maury Povich should not 'challenge' them. 'I couldn't even consider letting them on the air with those demands,' the show's producer, Jane Henry Caper, said. 'Nobody uses my show for a private forum, and nobody tyrannises the format.'

By early spring, the American prisoners of war – some of whom had been held for up to nine years – returned to a hero's welcome; millions watched on television as they stepped off aeroplanes into the arms of wives and children. More than any other single event, this return of the POWs constituted an emotional catharsis for the nation, symbolising the end of America's involvement in Vietnam.

No sooner did they get off the planes than, one-by-one, POWs began describing in detail the torture they had endured at the hands of the North Vietnamese. Michael Benge, Lieutenant Commander David Hoffman, Colonel George Day (who would be awarded a Medal of Honor): each spoke of the agonies they and others were subjected to directly as a result of Jane's visit to Hanoi.

Jane wasted no time retaliating. 'I think that one of the only ways that we are going to redeem ourselves as a country for what we have done there,' she said, 'is not to hail the POWs as heroes, because they are *hypocrites and liars*. History will judge them severely.'

Jane shrugged off the notion that the eight POWs she had met in Hanoi might have been coerced as 'laughable. These were not men who had been tortured. These were not men who had been starved. These were not men who've [sic] been brainwashed.'

What of those POWs who insisted they were tortured? 'They are exaggerating,' said Jane, 'probably for their own self-interest.'

Years later Jane would tell Barbara Walters on '20/20' that these remarks were 'popped off'. In fact, she continued her public attacks on the POWs for months. 'We should recognise that there is considerable room for doubting these charges of torture, at the very least,' she told an audience of three thousand at the University of California at Los Angeles. 'We should remain sceptical. We have no reason to believe that US Air Force officers tell the truth. They are professional killers . . .' She went on to joke about the stories of mistreatment, and asked why the POWs looked so healthy. 'Never in the history of the United States have POWs come home looking like football players. These war criminals are being made heroes. These football players are no more heroes than Custer was. They're military careerists and professional killers.'

Was it possible that there were atrocities committed on both sides, asked a student? 'No!' she shouted emphatically. 'It is not possible.' In a lengthy letter to the *Los Angeles Times*, Jane again defended Hanoi: 'It is a lie, an orchestrated lie, to give the impression that the general policy of the Vietnamese was torture.'

Eventually, she grudgingly conceded that there was probably torture of POWs. 'Guys who misbehaved and treated their guards in a racist fashion or tried to escape were tortured. Some pilots were beaten to death by the people they had bombed when they parachuted from their planes. But to say that torture was systematic and a policy of the North Vietnamese government is a lie. And the guys are hypocrites. They're trying to make themselves look self-righteous, but they are war criminals according to law.'

This time Jane seemed to have gone too far. For daring to cast aspersions on the character of POWs, Jane was pilloried by the press. 'Jane Fonda found herself very much alone in her charge that former US POWs were "hypocrites and liars,"' editorialised the *Wall Street Journal*. The *Journal* went on to brand her statements 'outlandish, shrill, repugnant'.

While repeating her allegations at the University of Southern California, Jane was heckled and, outside the hall, burned in effigy on a ten-foot scaffold. In Washington, Connecticut Congressman Robert H. Steele 'nominated' her for an award: 'the rottenest, most miserable performance by any one individual American in the history of our country'. The Indiana State Senate, meanwhile, adopted a resolution censuring her for her statements.

A similar bill in the California Senate called for her censure as 'one of a small group of well-fed, secure, pampered, and privileged persons' who 'spread the lies of our enemies'. Justifiably worried that such attacks could end her film career, Jane sought help from her friend Jerry Brown, then California's secretary of state.

Brown, who was about to make his own successful bid to succeed Ronald Reagan as governor, worked tirelessly behind the scenes to defeat the California bill. Before the censure motion could get to the Senate floor, where there was a good chance it would be passed, Brown managed to get it killed in the Rules Committee. This would be the beginning of an enduring alliance between Brown and Jane, who would emerge as his chief fundraiser in his eventual drive for the presidency.

Not that Jane herself was shy about speaking up in her own defence. Testifying before the Los Angeles City Council as it considered its own censure motion, she presented an 'Indochina Peace Campaign' (IPC) report challenging POW claims. The council declined to censure Jane – not on the basis of her testimony but on the grounds that such action would be 'beyond the scope of city business'.

Not satisfied with the terms of the Paris Peace Agreement, Jane and Tom launched a nationwide campaign through the IPC to force a total cut-off in US funds to Saigon. A scandal was gently simmering that would eventually topple the Nixon administration, and IPC leaders devised a strategy to exploit the crisis. They called it 'the Watergate Opportunity'.

Spurred on by the public outcry over Jane's statements, the Haydens brought their act to San Clemente. There they stood outside the walls of Nixon's 'Western White House' and serenaded visiting South Vietnamese President Thieu with Vietcong revolutionary songs. Not long after, when Nixon and Kissinger attended ceremonies honouring director John Ford with the American Film Institute's Life Achievement Award, Tom and Jane led marchers outside the Beverly Hills Hotel in a chorus of 'Five, four, three, two! Down with Nixon, down with Thieu!'

The Haydens were hoping their child would arrive on 4 July, but it was three days later when Jane gave birth to a boy. They named him Troi (later Americanised to Troy) O'Donovan Garrity. The first name was chosen in honour of a Vietcong hero, the second to honour an Irish revolutionary, and the third was Tom's mother's maiden name. As had been the case with Vanessa, Jane promptly turned Troi over to a nanny, this time to throw her energies behind the IPC.

That autumn,, Washington columnist Jack Anderson handed Jane a new weapon to use against the Nixon White House: the FBI's secret dossier on her. The file, several thousand pages in length, confirmed what Jane had long known — that she had been tailed and spied upon, her phones bugged, her mail opened, and her bank records checked. Not only was she being spied on by the FBI, but dossiers were also kept on her by the Secret Service, the State Department, the CIA, and the White House. In fact, a White House request for an IRS audit had also been made, but was turned down.

None of this surprised Jane. 'You know,' she said, 'to tell you the truth, at the time we were so sure that it was going on that it was something that was almost laughable. Now it is front-page news . . . but we knew it was going on. We were quite convinced that the phones were tapped, mail was being opened, people were being followed.'

Yet there was a surprise buried in the dossier — the fake letter to *Variety* concocted by FBI editors in which Fonda purportedly led Black Panthers in an obscenity-laden 'Kill Nixon' cheer. The phoney letter was never sent, but the fact that J. Edgar Hoover initially approved such a scheme was indeed shocking.

Jane responded with a $2.8 million suit against the government charging that her First, Fourth, Fifth, and Ninth Amendment rights had been violated. The documents, she charged, were 'part of an organised systematic attempt to discredit me . . . to make those of us who opposed the Nixon administration appear irresponsible, dangerous, and foul-mouthed'.

The suit would drag on for eight years before Jane dropped it, having received in exchange no money but rather a pledge that such government surveillance and harassment of its citizens would stop. It was, she said, a 'moral victory'.

More than any single factor, Watergate made possible Jane Fonda's redemption in the public mind. As Nixon's stock plummeted, his most outspoken foes gradually looked less menacing. Whether or not the administration's misdeeds justified Jane's conduct was immaterial to many. 'Watergate has given us legitimacy,' Tom boasted. 'The people who wanted to put us in jail are going to jail themselves.' At the age of 36, through no effort of her own, Jane was back in the mainstream.

21

HANK FONDA was two months away from his 69th birthday, but he still had to be aged for the part. First he donned a foam-rubber paunch, then a special hairpiece with an unruly, grey forelock. By the time he strolled on stage an hour later, he had transformed himself into the stooped, braces-tugging hero of David W. Rintels's hit one-character play, *Darrow*.

'I'm lucky,' Fonda said. 'Guys my age, like Freddie March and Jim Stewart, don't work much any more. Coming when it did, in what should have been the waning portion of a fifty-year career, *Darrow* is the most rewarding thing that ever happened to me.'

Jane flew to New York for her father's opening, and on to Paris where Peter was working on a film. In Paris, she and Tom stayed with Vadim and his new wife, Catherine Schneider. One evening when then-president Valéry Giscard d'Estaing dropped in for tea, Hayden was sitting on the floor devouring a chicken leg *à la* Henry VIII. As chicken fat splattered the expensive carpet, the aristocratic French president matter-of-factly asked Catherine Schneider who Jane was talking to in the next room. 'A terrorist, a Maoist, and the president of the Trotskyist movement,' the new Mrs Roger Vadim answered. One lump or two?

Jane returned home in time to give a speech at the Los Angeles Press Club on 14 March 1974. With Tom at her side, she held up a telegram from Cambodian Prince Norodom Sihanouk as evidence of continued American involvement in the region. In addition to a halt in funds to the Saigon government, the Haydens were now demanding that the United States halt all arms shipments to Cambodia. 'The planes and the bombs and the bullets are still ours,' she said, 'and if the American people knew, they wouldn't stand for their tax dollars being spent like that.'

That spring, they launched yet another offensive – this time directly on Washington. For six weeks, Jane lobbied Congress to end military funding, occasionally ducking into conference rooms or hallways to breast-feed Troy. California Congressman Ronald Dellums even set them up in an office in the Longworth Building on Capitol Hill.

When cornered about Jane's continuing anti-government agitation, Henry Fonda bristled: 'I've not said much about Jane before and I resent people who expect me to denounce her. Hers is not my way of life and hers is not too often my exact way of thinking. But I love her, I respect her right to say what she says, and she and her husband are obviously deeply in love. That's the way I feel about my daughter.'

Midway through their lobbying blitz, Jane had to break off her efforts and fly to New York. Henry had been rushed to Lenox Hill Hospital with a heart attack. Peter, filming in France, also flew in to their father's bedside. A pacemaker was installed, and Hank picked up where he left off, dazzling Broadway audiences in *Darrow*.

After her six-week Washington stint, Jane returned to a new home, but hardly a new house. To blunt the charges of hypocrisy in her life-style, she and Tom had bought a decidedly ramshackle $45,000 two-family wood frame house in a run-down part of Santa Monica. Hank Fonda called it 'The Shack'. He was being kind. Behind a row of corroded mailboxes and a rickety picket fence, Jane, often loaded down with groceries from her latest trip to the local Food King supermarket, climbed two flights to the Haydens' upstairs apartment. Inside, the Haydens occupied four cramped rooms, each brightly painted a different shade – iridescent orange, lime green, fire-engine red, canary yellow. If the colour scheme was sixties psychedelic, the decor was distinctly junk shop. In the bedroom, with its leak-stained ceiling and mildewing walls, a dirty mattress covered the otherwise bare bedroom floor. The only reminder of Jane's celebrity – her Oscar for *Klute* – was tucked away on a shelf, serving a practical purpose as a bookend. The couple's only car was a dented estate used by Jane to ferry Vanessa to and from her 'experimental kindergarten'.

Many viewed Jane's self-enforced poverty with a jaundiced eye. While she had indeed sold off her mother's jewellery, it was not – as many assumed – because she was broke. During her adult life, Jane's assets have never dipped below six figures, and seldom below seven.

In her new real-life role as working-class homebody, Jane was likened to Marie Antoinette playing milkmaid. She was straightforward about her motives. 'There's a contradiction between being involved in a movement for social change,' she said at the time, 'and also being a movie actress in Hollywood. I am trying to reduce that contradiction as much as possible.'

As for going without, Jane professed that she 'couldn't care less'. Of her new spartan life-style, she said, 'I've had my taste of wealth and all the material things. They don't mean a thing. There's a psychiatrist that goes with every swimming pool out here, not to mention divorces and children who hate their parents. It's easy for me to say that I don't want anything, because I have had it all.'

What she had not had in three years, however, was a decent film role. Convinced by now that she had alienated too many powerful producers, Jane decided that the best way to get around that obstacle was to form her own production company – one that would make socially 'relevant' films. Jane and old Berkeley pal Bruce Gilbert formed IPC (Indochina Peace Campaign) Films, with the intention of using their profits to bankroll their political causes. In two short years Gilbert, without any experience in moviemaking, had gone from caring for Vanessa at the Red Family collective's Blue Fairyland nursery school to major Hollywood producer.

For IPC Films' first effort, Jane returned to Vietnam – this time with Tom and infant Troy in tow – to investigate conditions following the withdrawal of US forces from the region. The result was a 60-minute documentary, *Introduction to the Enemy*, made with cinematographer Haskell Wexler. This time adhering to her father's less-is-more advice, Jane remained in the background, allowing the Vietnamese to talk about the war's impact on their lives and efforts at reconstruction – without editorial embellishment. Yet only a few critics even bothered to review it, and it quickly sank from sight.

With her first production effort a failure, and given the auspices of the project, Jane didn't hesitate to accept George Cukor's invitation to Russia to play the role of Night in *The Bluebird*. Based on the fairy tale by Maurice Maeterlinck, *The Bluebird* was being hailed as something of a breakthrough in US–Soviet relations – the first time a major feature had been shot in Russia with American actors and a Soviet crew. Although Elizabeth Taylor was Cukor's star, Jane would be in company with a cast of supporting players that included Ava Gardner, Cicely Tyson, Will Geer, and Robert Morley.

Jane spent much of January and February 1975 filming in Leningrad, where she took the opportunity to express her thanks 'for the assistance which the Soviet people are sending to Vietnam', and, rather churlishly under the circumstances, slamming the American movie community. 'In Hollywood it is difficult to make films which convey something important,' she said, taking the opportunity to praise Cuba as 'the country where very interesting films are being made'. One thing she failed to note was that *Klute* had never been shown in Moscow, nor had most of her other pictures; Soviet censors had banned them for being too explicit.

Like most things in the Soviet Union, the top-heavy government-controlled moviemaking apparatus proved clumsy and inefficient. The film took an entire year to complete, and the budget ballooned accordingly.

Ultimately, most of Jane's performance wound up on the cutting-room floor. 'I could have phoned in my part from Santa Monica!' she complained. Just as well. *The Bluebird* rivalled another Elizabeth Taylor epic, 1964's

Cleopatra, as one of the most expensive flops ever. According to the *Daily Express*, the film was 'a mixture of Soviet ineptitude and the American belief that the grotesque expenditure of dollars can set anything right'.

While Jane was in Russia making *The Bluebird*, Tom was in Washington conferring with a handful of supporters on 'how to keep the underlying issues of Vietnam alive after the war'. One suggestion, from McGovern aide John Holum, was that Hayden try to wrest the Democratic nomination from incumbent US Senator John Tunney.

Tunney, son of the famous boxing champion and Harvard roommate of Edward Kennedy, was an Old School liberal. It was unlikely that he could be beaten in the primary, but Jerry Brown's election to succeed Ronald Reagan as governor in 1974 had proved that anything was possible in Californian politics.

With Jane's blessing, Hayden entered the race. He went out and cut his greying hair executive-length, bought his first new suit since high school, and held his first strategy session at an International House of Pancakes in Santa Monica. There it was decided to attack Tunney on his corporate connections. Blasting Tunney as a 'tool' of such forces as the Gallo Brothers (of wine-making fame) and Northrop Aviation, Hayden earnestly promised not to accept contributions from any business larger than the neighbourhood pizzeria.

He didn't have to. Jane was his not-so-secret resource, asking some of her Hollywood friends for contributions and persuading others to speak or perform at 'Hayden for Senate' fundraisers. Henry Fonda was the first to join up, and was quickly followed by the disparate likes of Linda Ronstadt (who also happened to be Governor Brown's girlfriend at the time), Red Buttons, Arlo Guthrie, and Groucho Marx.

Out of her own pocket, Jane financed her husband's 1976 primary campaign to the tune of at least $500,000 (the equivalent of $4 million in 1990 dollars). Her largesse almost got them in trouble with the law. There was a major complaint from the Tunney camp that the $500,000 Jane put into Tom's campaign actually violated federal election laws limiting individual contributions to $1,000. Says Jane's former attorney, Richard Rosenthal, 'We worked together to get the feds off Tom and Jane's back.' They argued (rather ironically, given Jane's views on women and the institution of marriage) that California's community-property laws gave Tom dominion over all her funds. 'There is no law restricting how much of your own money you use,' says Rosenthal, 'and our strategy worked. Jane went on to pay for practically all of Tom's races.'

Meanwhile, Jane was waging a campaign of her own – a campaign to salvage her career from oblivion after the catastrophe of *The Bluebird*. She had her own strategy session with her agents, and decided to star in *Fun with*

Dick and Jane, a good-natured romp that might have been called *Barefoot in the Park Meets Cat Ballou*.

Fun with Dick and Jane is the story of an affluent suburban couple living well beyond their ample means. When the husband loses his job in the aerospace industry, they take to armed robbery, with hilarious results. Jane wanted the role badly enough to accept second billing to George Segal and a salary of only $100,000.

Between takes, Jane solicited funds by phone for Tom's senate run – a bit of moonlighting that did not sit well with the politically unsympathetic crew. The producers of the film were also barred from certain locations because of Jane's reputation. 'A supermarket let us shoot outside,' said producer Peter Bart during shooting, 'but not inside, as if Jane might contaminate the produce.' For a scene in an auditorium, Jane lugged around a bagful of coins so she could make her fund-raising appeals from a phone box on the street; the manager of the building had prohibited her from using his phone.

Jane viewed *Fun with Dick and Jane* as an indictment of consumerism run amok, a trenchant comment on the 'false American dream'; but mostly she wanted to prove to the filmgoing public that she 'could still be pretty and still have a sense of humour. This part is not a great part. I didn't take it for that. But I have a feeling it's going to come out all right because there's a lot of creative juices flowing.'

Her first day inside the suburban house that was supposed to be Dick and Jane's home, she began finding fault. The house did not look lived in. She wanted children's drawings hung on the refrigerator door; the young boy playing her son in the film was promptly given paper and crayon and told to go to work. And where was the avocado plant? Every suburban family has an avocado plant growing in a glass of water on a windowsill.

The film may have been a comedy, but Jane was deadly serious. To the make-up woman arranging her angora sweater for a scene: 'Hide my falsies! I dont want the press to know.' And later: 'I'm going to need perfume.' (A nice touch, but one that would hardly be picked up by the camera.)

Jane's no-nonsense approach to comedy paid off. *Fun with Dick and Jane* turned out more than just 'all right' when it was released the following year. Reviewers hailed Jane's return to comedy in what proved to be her first unqualified hit in seven years. Even so, she could not bring herself to succumb altogether to middle-class acceptance; reserving her right to shock every audience at least once, she was taken to task for one unnecessary bathroom scene in which she held a conversation while using the toilet.

'People had been saying, "Oh, have you seen Jane Fonda lately? Boy, she's really lost her looks – and her sense of humour,"' recalls Jane. 'Suddenly all the headlines were JANE FONDA MAKES A COMEBACK, and offers started pouring in.' Just as important, the success of *Dick and Jane* showed that it was possible to make commercially viable 'message' movies, as long as they were done with subtlety and finesse.

With *Dick and Jane* in the can, Tom and Jane forged ahead on the primary trail. Polls showed Tunney with a comfortable 5–1 lead until the spring of 1976, when Hayden's quixotic campaign began gaining momentum. In the closing weeks leading up to the June primary election date, Tunney launched a counterstrike. In radio and television spots crafted by media consultant David Garth, he reminded the electorate of Hayden's radical past.

When the dust cleared, Tunney had won. But Hayden had received a very respectable 37 per cent of the vote. (As it turned out, a conservative gadfly would win the US Senate seat in the general election that November: Republican S. I. Hayakawa, the tough former president of San Francisco State University. Ironically, perhaps appropriately, Hayakawa had built his political reputation opposing Hayden's SDS and other radical elements that sought to take control of college campuses in the 1960s.)

From that first defeat for elective office, Tom and Jane learned one hard capitalistic lesson: money fuelled the democratic process. With enough cash, they might have been able to counter Tom's adverse image. A consummate organiser, Hayden immediately set up the Campaign for Economic Democracy (CED) to serve as a launch pad for his next Senate bid in 1982. 'Sure, Tom lost his bid for the nomination,' said Jane. 'But don't forget that neither of the Kennedys won the first time around, either. [Actually, John, Robert *and* Edward Kennedy were elected in their first try for the Senate.] The movement will continue because we're putting together a coalition as broad as any in forty years.'

Over the next several years, Hayden's CED would embrace a galaxy of causes, from solar power to the rights of secretaries (foreshadowing Jane's 1980 film *Nine to Five*), to the plight of Cesar Chavez's farm workers. To house the CED staff, a 120-acre ranch north of Santa Barbara was purchased with $700,000 of Jane's money. Before the Haydens could move in to begin work on their priority issue – rent control and affordable housing – they first had to evict a dozen tenants from the property.

The Haydens' political machinery was in place, but the question remained: Who was going to pay for it? 'Jane was distraught that she'd have to keep using her own money,' recalls Richard Rosenthal. 'She needed a business that would pay for itself – to fund the political arm of their organisation.'

IPC Films seemed to be the only answer. While Jane's IPC partner Bruce Gilbert worked on several projects, Jane mulled over a number of offers that had come her way in the wake of *Fun with Dick and Jane*.

The one film that she most wanted to make was one she never would:

a movie about the American Revolution in which all three famous Fondas – father, brother, sister – would star. Jane's motive went beyond reuniting her family. 'What did the soldiers freezing together at Valley Forge *really* think of George Washington?' she typically wanted to know. 'And what property interests did he represent?'

22

'EVERYTHING SHE writes is a lie,' Mary McCarthy once said of her archrival Lillian Hellman, 'and that includes the words "a" and "the".' That famous quote led to a defamation lawsuit that ended only with Hellman's death in 1984. One of the supposedly autobiographical accounts that Hellman was accused of inventing was the story that was made into the film *Julia*.

It hardly mattered whether *Julia*, actually a single chapter in Hellman's best-selling memoir *Pentimento*, was truth or fiction. The heartbreaking story of an aspiring playwright and the childhood friend who rebels against her wealthy family to become a martyr in the anti-Nazi underground, it offered the two strongest film roles for women in recent Hollywood memory.

Accordingly, as one observer put it, 'every actress who was ambulatory went after the roles'. Jane, newly 'bankable' after the resounding success of *Fun with Dick and Jane*, had no trouble landing the part of Lillian. For the role of Julia, she persuaded producer Richard Roth to hire Vanessa Redgrave. 'Why not?' says Roth. 'It was perfect symmetry. The two most famous left-wing women of the seventies playing two left-wing women of the thirties. I liked it. Of course, the fact that Jane and Vanessa were both terrific actresses didn't hurt, either. Not to mention that they both agreed to work cheap.' For Jane, that was $250,000 – a fraction of her normal salary.

Before filming began, Jane visited the Pulitzer Prize-winning playwright at her summer cottage in Edgartown on Martha's Vineyard. The real Lillian Hellman and the actress who would portray her discussed the script while battening down for a hurricane. The storm passed by Martha's Vineyard, but not before Jane had time to observe the chain-smoking, basset-faced Hellman in action. 'Lillian is a homely woman,' Jane observed, 'and yet she moves as if she were Marilyn Monroe. She sits with her legs apart, with her satin underwear partly showing – she's a very sexual, sensual woman. Well, that's fine for Lillian, but it wouldn't look right if I did it. So I played her more ascetic than she really is.

'There's a lot about Lillian Hellman I don't understand. I don't really identify with her, but I came to care about her very much. She is a woman of many facets. I hadn't expected her bad temper and irritability. There is a lot of that in the script. I'm not that way at all.'

In August, Jane left to start filming in Paris and London. Planning to be on location for nearly four months, Jane left Troy behind with Tom in California. She then deposited Vanessa with Vadim in Paris, and moved into a high-rise apartment building in another part of the city. Freed of distracting family obligations, she threw herself into the role.

Jane was still very much in awe of Vanessa's acting ability, regarding Sir Michael Redgrave's daughter as the greatest film actress of her generation. 'In the goodbye scene,' Jane recalls, 'we'd stand there and before the shooting began she'd say things to me like "Lilly, I want you to be brave, I don't want you to give up on your writing . . ." I looked at her hands and I started to cry because she's got these huge hands that are very moving to me.'

'With Vanessa,' says director Fred Zinnemann, 'you don't feel there's any work, any effort. Her acting just flows. With Jane, there's a lot of painstaking detail and work. Fonda has one quality she shares with Porfirio Diaz, the old Mexican dictator, and Louis B. Mayer, the old MGM dictator – she can cry at will and be totally convincing.'

Their mutual admiration notwithstanding, it was no longer prudent for Jane to share Redgrave's ideology. Now calling herself a 'progressive Democrat', Jane claimed to disagree with her co-star's Trotskyite beliefs. The two women came to terms with Jane's position by not discussing politics.

Publicly, Jane went one step further in distancing herself from the volatile Redgrave. She told a *Newsweek* reporter that, contrary to what she had said earlier, she did not name her daughter after her longstanding idol.

Still, at a time when Redford and Newman loomed large as Hollywood's hottest male tandem, *Julia* was being hailed as the first female 'buddy' film. 'Oh,' gushed Jane, 'to be able to play scenes with another woman! People will see a movie about women who think and who care for each other . . . In every other movie I've every done and most movies I see where there's a woman, she's either falling in or out of love or worried that she's going to lose a man. She's always defined in relationship to a man.'

Indeed, the relationship has a strong sexual undercurrent. When the mood is intensely romantic, Lillian turns to her friend and says, 'I love you, Julia.' That line uttered by one woman to another set tongues wagging. Did Hellman, who wrote about lesbianism in *The Children's Hour*, have an affair with her friend? Were Redgrave and Fonda endorsing homosexuality? In short order, Fonda's critics had unfairly retitled the film *Reds in Bed*.

'It's *not* neurotic or sexually aberrant,' countered Jane. 'It's just about two friends who care about each other tremendously, who are interested in each other's growth. There isn't any gossip or jealousy.'

Audiences in general accepted *Julia* for what it was — a landmark attempt to portray a serious relationship between adult women. With a superlative supporting cast that included Jason Robards (as Hellman's longterm lover and mentor Dashiell Hammett), Maximilian Schell, and Hal Holbrook, *Julia* was both a commercial hit and a *succès d'estime*. '*Julia*', wrote Jack Kroll in *Newsweek*, 'is moving in its glowing commitment to the power of friendship . . . Fonda and Redgrave are close to perfection.'

Hollywood agreed. After picking up a Golden Globe, Jane was nominated for a Best Acress Oscar. *Julia* lost out to Woody Allen's *Annie Hall* that year, as did Jane to *Annie Hall* star Diane Keaton, but Robards and Redgrave were selected Best Supporting Actor and Actress.

Not since *Klute* had there been so much anxiety over what the winner might say. A staunch backer of Yasser Arafat and the Palestine Liberation Organisation, Redgrave showed up to thank the Academy and blast the 'Zionist hoodlums' that picketed her presence at the ceremonies. Redgrave was practically booed off the stage for her remarks, and for the next seven years acted only sporadically. (Her talent for provoking controversy was as great as her acting talent. Being cast as a Holocaust survivor in television's *Playing for Time* sparked off furious debate. When the Boston Symphony cancelled an appearance with Redgrave, presumably because her anti-Israel sentiments had resulted in threats of violence, she sued for damages, and won.)

Jane's reputation, however, was on the road to recovery even before the filming of *Julia*. When the break-up of the Burton–Taylor marriage prompted Taylor to bow out of her agreement to co-host the Tenth Annual Tony Awards, producer Alexander Cohen asked Jane to replace Liz at the podium. She agreed, and Cohen pronounced it to the audience as 'the casting coup of the decade'. Echoing the sentiments of many in the theatre, Cohen gushed, 'Jane rarely appears on TV except in her movies. She's a superstar, and I admire her theatrically, socially, and politically. Every single word that Jane Fonda said about the government and the CIA turned out to be true. She was the first to call the shots on the CIA.'

Cohen's somewhat revisionist view of Fonda was gaining popularity. Once *Julia* hit the cinemas, her reinstatement was all but assured. In March 1977 Jane, previously shunned by Hollywood's Old Guard, was invited to host the nationally televised American Film Institute Tribute to Bette Davis. Wearing an elegant satin dress and a chic swept-up hairdo, Jane bore not the slightest resemblance to the bra-less hell-raiser of only three years before. Tanned and smiling, she looked healthier than she had done in years. And she was. While shooting *Julia* in London, she had been persuaded by a holistic doctor to kick her dependence on diuretics.

In presenting the AFI award to Davis (the first woman to win it), Jane recalled the story of her own birth and how it complicated Davis's life during the making of *Jezebel*. 'My connection with Bette Davis is a little oblique,' she explained. 'During the filming of *Jezebel*, my father's contract guaranteed that he would be through with his job and back in New York in time for my birth.' Fonda's abrupt departure had meant, of course, that Davis had to deliver some of her most impassioned lines to empty space. 'Bette Davis won her second Academy Award,' Jane smiled, 'in spite of what I unintentionally put her through.'

Davis offered one word to describe Jane's performance as mistress of ceremonies that night: 'smashing'.

'I never thought I'd be respectable again,' Jane marvelled afterwards. 'I don't give a damn about respectability, but I do care about the ideas I represent being taken seriously. And though there were times when I was nervous about me, I never became frustrated.'

Jane's fortieth year would turn out to be her most productive. In rapid succession, she notched up three starring roles in three major films – *Coming Home*, *California Suite* and *Comes a Horseman*. The most important of these, by far, was *Coming Home*.

Five years earlier, Jane had met paraplegic Vietnam veteran Ron Kovic at an anti-war rally. The charismatic Kovic, who had re-enlisted twice for Vietnam duty before being wounded, turned against the war after he experienced at first hand the way wounded veterans were being treated at military hospitals and rehabilitation centres.

Kovic, who went on to write *Born on the Fourth of July*, was a magnetic speaker. Before going up to the microphone that day at the rally, he had turned to Jane and said, 'I may have lost my body, but I have gained my mind.'

Jane had already decided to do a Vietnam film, and Kovic's remark stirred her to action. In 1972 she hired Nancy Dowd, an old friend from her days in the feminist movement, to write a script about the consequences of the war as seen through the eyes of a military wife. The project dragged on for six years, until Gilbert and producer Jerome Hellman – who got the job after promising Fonda he would be careful to have women and minorities represented on the crew – saw a 'window of opportunity' open in Jane's schedule.

After she finished *Julia*, Jane was committed to do the western *Comes a Horseman* for Alan Pakula, her director on *They Shoot Horses*. Between the two there would be just enough time to squeeze in IPC's first feature.

In 1969, before he taught little Vanessa at the Blue Fairyland day-care centre, psychology student Bruce Gilbert had dropped out of Berkeley. 'After the campus was teargassed by helicopter and people were shot,' he says, 'I found it untenable to go back to classes as though nothing had happened.'

After the noble failure of *Introduction to the Enemy*, Gilbert and Jane had set out to make socially relevant films that could also be *commercial*. Originally,

Dowd's story, tentatively titled *Buffalo Ghosts*, resembled *Julia* in that it focused on two women – in this case volunteers at a veterans' hospital who must come to grips with the emotional toll the war takes on its casualties and their families.

Jane felt that the story would be more effective as a love story, and Gilbert concurred. Scenarists Waldo Salt and Robert C. Jones were called in to rework Dowd's script. The result was *Coming Home*, in which Jane plays Sally Hyde, the decidedly unliberated wife of a macho career officer. While her husband is fighting in Vietnam, Sally volunteers to work with disabled veterans and falls in love with one of them.

Jon Voight, a steadfast Hayden–Fonda supporter, was approached to play the supporting role of Sally's uptight blood-and-guts husband. But after Jack Nicholson, Al Pacino, and Sylvester Stallone had turned down the central part of Sally's paraplegic lover, Voight grabbed it instead. Bruce Dern donned Captain Hyde's uniform. At the film's climax, Hyde takes his own life, Norman Main-style, by strolling into the surf.

For obvious reasons, *Coming Home* was a major gamble for Jane. Just as people were starting to forget 'Hanoi Jane,' she risked rekindling old hatreds. 'All we wanted to do in the movie is to show this woman moving from point A to point B. That's all,' explained Jane. 'It would have been phoney to have her undergo some great liberal conversion.' No, she did not want to do anything that might ring false. 'Remember,' she added, 'there are still a lot of people out there who would like to see me dead.' As might have been expected, all requests to film on location at Veterans Administration hospitals and on military installations were turned down.

In this, their first major IPC collaboration, Jane and Gilbert settled into a pattern of working that would stand them in good stead on future projects. 'We go about developing movies backwards,' she said. 'Usually you start with a character, but we start with what we want to say. Then we figure out a story, because no matter how right or justified you feel, unless you interest people it's not getting across.'

Jane was not entirely happy with the result. As with *They Shoot Horses*, she quarrelled with director Hal Ashby about the ending. Although she had not liked the original climax, in which Dern kills Voight and himself, Jane thought it unlikely that the Dern character would commit suicide by walking into the sea. She voted for having him turn his gun on himself. Jane felt this would 'acknowledge the violence built up in him'.

By and large, however, Jane would admit that *Comning Home* 'came out pretty much the way we wanted. It meant a great deal to a lot of guys who had been in Vietnam, and to handicapped people, too.' This time around, the 'shocker' was a graphic scene in which Fonda and the wheelchair-bound Voight, both nude, use a variety of imaginative techniques during a steamy lovemaking session. 'Ron Kovic', she later quipped, 'said it improved his sex life immeasurably.'

Jane coasted through her next two films. With a face as weather-beaten as her father's in *The Grapes of Wrath*, Jane played an embattled Montana rancher fighting off land barons and oil tycoons in *Comes a Horseman*.

The old calico-and-sunbonnet image of the frontier woman went out of the window for this production; Jane's character, Ella, was as rawhide-tough as any hired hand. 'The idea of dealing with a heroine of the West, very much a woman yet willing to fight with the same passion as a man, was a great attraction,' says Pakula. 'I thought there was no one better than Jane Fonda to represent that kind of strong yet vulnerable American woman.'

Jane's co-star James Caan, a frustrated cowboy and longtime rodeo fanatic, insisted on doing his own stunts. Jane, comfortable astride a horse ever since her tomboy days back at Tigertail, had a stuntwoman teach her how to rope a steer and herd cattle.

The appeal of *Comes a Horseman* for Jane was obvious. Not only did it take a swipe at powerful special interests in general and the energy industry in particular, but it also struck a strong feminist blow. Still, Jane's first cowgirl picture since *Cat Ballou* got a mixed reception. It seemed that, when it came to western women, the public was still partial to calico.

Jane veered to the other extreme in Neil Simon's *California Suite*, playing Hannah Warren, a cynical, hard-bitten chain-smoking New Yorker. In one of four vignettes that make up the film, Jane as Hannah comes to California to 'rescue' her daughter from her ex-husband and his laid-back LA life-style. Hannah's ex-spouse is played by Alan Alda, who instantly endeared himself to Fonda by claiming to be a passionate feminist. After the movie he would prove it by marching with Fonda on behalf of the Equal Rights Amendment.

Jane took the role partly because it did not require her to be away on some far-off location for an extended period. It also gave her a chance to work with Simon for the first time since *Barefoot in the Park*. 'The dialogue is fast and sophisticated,' she said. 'It's the kind of quick repartee that harks back to the bright, brittle screen comedies of the good old days. But . . . it has depth. I wouldn't have done it if this were just a string of gags or slapstick.'

California Suite also gave Jane the chance to show off her sensational 40-year-old body in a skimpy bikini. Suddenly, after years of getting only tough political questions to field, she was being quizzed by curious reporters on her diet and exercise regimen. She had kept up her ballet routines for twenty years, she replied, and tried to spend an hour at them every day. 'The result', she said, 'is that I have a smaller waist now than when I was around twenty.'

There were more signs that all was forgiven. The same Hollywood Women's Press Club that had awarded her its Sour Apple in 1972 for doing the most to tarnish the image of Tinseltown proudly presented her with its Golden Apple Award for co-operating with the press.

Over the next few years, the profession's highest honours would alternate between father and daughter. In February 1978, Jane and Peter would be on hand in Los Angeles to see Henry follow right behind Bette Davis in receiving the American Film Institute's Life Achievement Award.

A year later, she coaxed him to the Shubert Theater on the pretext of co-presenting an award to Joshua Logan. Henry stood offstage as Jane stepped up to the rostrum and announced that her dad was being awarded a special Tony for his lifetime contribution to the American theatre. He admitted that he was impressed that she could 'carry off a stunt like that', and before the cameras Hank looked every inch the proud paterfamilias. While Jane and Peter seemed to bask in the glow of familial warmth, nothing had really changed. Emotionally, Dad remained a cold, aloof figure.

Jane's turn in the spotlight came that April, when both she and Jon Voight picked up Academy Awards for their performances in *Coming Home*. In stark contrast to the tension that pervaded the Dorothy Chandler Pavilion when she accepted the Oscar for *Klute*, the mood this time was festive. Wearing a sequined, off-the-shoulder dress, flaming red lipstick, and what she called her 'blonde Farrah Fawcett wig', a beaming Fonda bounded up the stairs and gleefully grabbed the statuette.

Never one to waste a prime opportunity to make a relevant social statement, she began delivering her acceptance speech in sign language. 'I'm signing part of what I'm saying tonight because while we were making the movie, we all became more aware of the problems of the handicapped,' she said. 'Over fourteen million people are deaf.' She expressed her gratitude to her colleagues on the film, and then thanked Vanessa and Troy 'for being understanding and forgiving me my absences – and again, my husband. He helped me believe that besides being entertaining, movies can inspire and teach and even be healing. Thank you all very much.'

Movies about Vietnam swept the top awards that year. *The Deer Hunter*, a film focusing on the lives of a group of young Pennsylvanians before and after the war, was named Best Picture and earned Michael Cimino an Oscar for direction. *The Deer Hunter*'s Christopher Walken was named Best Supporting Actor (ironically, Best Supporting Actress went to Jane's old Oscar nemesis Maggie Smith for her role in *California Suite*).

At 1 a.m. the morning after the awards, Jane called Michael Reese Hospital in Chicago, where her father was undergoing tests on his left hip. He had watched the ceremonies on television and told Jane he was thrilled for her. What she did not know at the time – what Henry did not tell her – was that on the day Jane received her Oscar he had been diagnosed as suffering from prostate cancer, and that the cancer had spread to his hip. Nor did Henry tell Jane that he was returning to Los Angeles the next day to be operated on. It would actually be another full week before she learned of her father's condition. But for now, Jane's victory seemed sweet, and complete.

Jane's comeback had been nothing less than phenomenal. In one decade, she had gone from sixties sex toy to wild-eyed feminist radical, to aspiring grande dame of the American cinema. Now she stood on the brink of a decade that, more than any other star of her generation, she would come to dominate.

23

'IT'S TIME to look at crime in the suites,' Jane was saying in early 1979, 'not just in the streets.' This time her target was no longer the Pentagon, it was Big Business – or, rather, 'unbridled corporate power' in America. Jane thought this a popular cause, and in tackling it, she was confident she could do no wrong.

An early target was J. P. Stevens, the non-union textile giant that had been embroiled in a labour dispute for years. Smuggled into a J. P. Stevens plant in Roanoke, Virginia, Jane got an inside look at the conditions under which employees were forced to work.

'I couldn't believe my own eyes and ears,' she said. 'What I saw was absolutely horrendous. The sound . . . was deafening. I screamed to see if I could hear, and I couldn't hear my own voice. There was dust flying through the air, clinging to everyone and everything. It looked like a snowstorm.' Citing inadequate health and safety standards in the plant, Jane called for a boycott of all J. P. Stevens products.

Tom Hayden was also seeking to mine a popular vein. Through his growing Campaign for Economic Democracy, he helped elect a majority to the Santa Monica City Council and more than fifty other local candidates throughout California. They continued to press for rent control, low-income housing, solar energy, and sanctions against South Africa.

Business interests did not take Jane's attacks lying down. After Central Michigan University paid Jane $3,500 for a campus speech in which she skewered Dow Chemical and other corporations, Dow moved swiftly to cut off direct financial aid to the university.

In a more personal way, both Haydens sought to touch young lives by turning part of Laurel Springs, their magnificent 160-acre mountaintop ranch in Santa Barbara, into a children's summer camp (a house on the property was reserved for their private use). Ostensibly, the children's camp stressed 'environmental education' and taught children to express themselves through the performing arts. Political critics charged that the camp was designed to brainwash the next generation of voters. Fonda calmly denied this, saying it 'teaches them how to be responsible citizens and effective representatives of their people'.

Most of the CED's firepower was directed at the nuclear energy industry. Preaching Armageddon, Tom and Jane fought so hard to stop the nuclear industry in its tracks that when he suffered a heart attack, 'Father of the H-Bomb' Dr Edward Teller blamed Fonda personally for causing it.

Once again, Jane would make her strongest statement on film, this time in another IPC production, *The China Syndrome*.

At various times entitled *Eyewitness* and *Power*, the project was actually conceived by documentary film-maker Michael Gray after he heard a physicist talk about the 'China Syndrome': if there were a meltdown in a nuclear reactor, the core would theoretically melt through the centre of the earth – all the way to China.

Gray was not the only person with his eye on making a movie about the hazards of nuclear power. Jane had unsuccessfully tried to persuade a major studio to make a film based on the life of Karen Silkwood, the nuclear power plant employee who died in a mysterious car crash on 13 November 1974. Such a movie would be made, but not by Jane. *Silkwood*, starring Meryl Streep, Kurt Russell, and Cher, was released by Fox in 1983.

Gray, meanwhile, had sold his story for *The China Syndrome* to actor-producer Michael Douglas, who cast himself and Richard Dreyfuss in the lead roles. After Dreyfuss pulled out in a salary dispute, Jane entered the picture. Over dinner in a Mexican restaurant on LA's trendy Melrose Avenue, she bought the idea – on the condition that she play the role originally intended for Dreyfuss. And she wanted James Bridges as director, not Gray. The fact that it had been his baby for six years meant nothing; Jane had become coolly pragmatic – some would say ruthless – when it came to getting things done.

In *The China Syndrome*, TV reporter Kimberly Wells (Fonda) and her cameraman (Michael Douglas) are doing a feature story on the operation of the fictional 'Ventana Nuclear Power Plant' when they inadvertently witness a near-catastrophic accident. Unbeknown to Wells, her cameraman has surreptitiously recorded the whole event on tape. Jack Lemmon, as the manager of the facility, is so shaken by the mishap that he begins to question whether the plant is as safe as he believed. Realising that his superiors have been involved in a massive cover-up, he agrees to provide Kimberly with evidence that will expose the plant as a threat to the public.

A technician delivering incriminating evidence to Wells is run off the road (harking back to the case of Karen Silkwood). Ultimately, Lemmon seizes the plant, and is eventually gunned down by a police team. Wells then goes on the air and, choking back tears, reveals the whole story.

As always, Jane did her homework, tagging along on various hard-news assignments with Los Angeles-based TV reporters Connie Chung, Kelly Lange, and Heidi Shulman. Sporting a red wig ('My Brenda Starr fantasy'), she portrayed the standard Fonda – Gilbert character – a guileless Everywoman who hasn't a clue but gradually wises up as events unfold.

'You can't propagandise,' insisted the new Jane, who in addition to her $1 million salary stood to share in any profits from the IPC film. 'It has to be a good, well-told story. If you don't have that, people won't go.' But as soon as it was released on 16 March, several critics did dismiss *The China Syndrome* as precisely that – propaganda, and a fantasy to boot.

The movie's acceptance was hardly helped by an interview the Haydens had agreed to do with Barbara Walters. 'She had a terrific opportunity,' Jane said of the show, 'but I'm real disappointed. Wow! Barbara Walters has a way of asking questions that makes it sound like what she's asking is important, but it was just institutionalised meaninglessness. What was left was gossip.'

Walters did coax a Freudian slip out of Hayden. What's it like for the family of a famous actress, Walters wanted to know. 'It turns the house and the kids and me into props,' he said wanly.

Then, on 28 March, less than two weeks after *The China Syndrome*'s release, an accident at the Three Mile Island nuclear power plant near Harrisburg, Pennsylvania, triggered mass evacuations and widespread panic that suggested core meltdown as a real and chilling possibility.

Overnight, Fonda and her film were transformed into nuclear prophets – and *The China Syndrome* easily vaulted to the number-one box-office position. Until *On Golden Pond*'s release two years later, it would be IPC's biggest-grossing release by far.

'*China Syndrome* was just this incredible phenomenon of timing,' admits Jane, who seized the opportunity to flog the picture on an exhaustive nationwide press tour (co-star Jack Lemmon, not wanting to appear to be exploiting the Three Mile Island disaster, cancelled his). 'People were actually going to the movie to understand what was going on at Three Mile Island.' *The China Syndrome* brought Jane her fifth Oscar nomination (in another twist, she would ultimately lose to Sally Field for Field's portrayal of the defiant factory worker in *Norma Rae*).

Basking in the glow of her new public acceptance, Jane was relaxed enough to make her singing debut on a Helen Reddy television special. Trying her hand at a comedy sketch, she did a credible job playing an actress who accepts an award, then trashes her enemies until she is dragged kicking and screaming from the podium.

Jane was also encouraged by her father's quick recovery from cancer surgery. The two even gave a rare interview to Tom Brokaw on NBC's 'Today Show'. When asked if he would ever have been happily married to 'a woman like Jane', Dad cautiously replied, 'Think so.'

'I don't know about living happily,' Jane chimed in impulsively, 'but we could have had a good affair.'

In mid-1979, millions of dollars generated by Jane's IPC Films continued to flow into the Campaign for Economic Democracy. But when it came down to how and where those funds were to be spent, Hayden was boss. 'Jane was treated like a functionary by Tom,' says Richard Rosenthal, Jane's long-standing friend and lawyer. 'Tom was the theoretician. He called the shots. He told her what to do, and she did it.'

It did not take much persuading to get Jane to go along with Tom's plan to back Governor Jerry Brown's presidential aspirations. It was Brown, after all, who back in 1973 worked so effectively behind the scenes to kill the motion in the State Senate that would have censured Jane for 'spreading enemy lies'.

The son of Reagan's predecessor in the State House, ex-governor Edmund G. 'Pat' Brown, young Jerry had first rebelled against his father's political plans for him by entering the Jesuit Sacred Heart novitiate. But after three and a half years he dropped out and earned a degree in Latin and Greek at Berkeley before attending Yale Law School. An anti-war activist and strong campaigner for Democratic candidate Eugene McCarthy in 1968, Jerry Brown decided to run for the modest office of California Secretary of State and won. When Ronald Reagan decided against seeking a third term in 1974, Jerry Brown was elected governor by a slim margin.

From the outset, Brown showed the same conspicuous penury that remained to a large degree the hallmark of the Haydens' life-style. He cancelled his own inaugural ball, refused to move into the new $1.3 million governor's mansion built by Reagan contributors (he rented a $250-a-month bachelor pad instead), sold the governor's limousine, and began to espouse Zen and transcendental meditation.

In 1976, enjoying an unprecedented degree of popularity in his home state, Brown presented his approach to the rest of the country in a last-minute attempt to wrest the Democratic Presidential nomination from Jimmy Carter. That try failed, but Brown was re-elected governor by a wide margin in 1978.

Poised to make another try for the White House in 1980, Brown carefully cultivated his Hollywood contacts. That included dating Natalie Wood, Candice Bergen, Liv Ullmann and, most notably, Linda Ronstadt.

Yet none of these contacts could match the Haydens' influence with the governor. 'Jane and Tom say jump,' said one wag, 'and Jerry says, "How high?"' The reason for this was quite simple: Brown needed a minimum of $12 million for his presidential war chest, and Jane offered to raise $3 million of that sum.

In return Brown appointed several CED members to prominent positions in his administration. He also took a strong anti-nuclear stand and named

216

Tom his energy adviser. Yet much of the Haydens' influence was unseen. Brown attended CED meetings closed to the press, and with Ronstadt tagging along spent weekends at the Haydens' Santa Monica home or at the Laurel Springs ranch. There they conferred on all important issues facing the state and the nation – from solar power and disarmament to Mexican farm workers and secretaries' rights. They talked about what Brown would do if elected president, and who he would appoint to the cabinet. Jane, Brown agreed, would make an excellent secretary of state. Apart from a position in a Brown administration, Jane was seriously weighing the possibility of running for office herself.

When Brown appointed her to the California Arts Council in March 1979, Jane viewed it as one more sign that she had been totally reassimilated into the body politic. Her popularity was indeed phenomenal: *The China Syndrome* had made Jane – for the first time in her long career – the world's number-one female box-office star, with the accident at Three Mile Island contributing to her growing reputation in some quarters as a kind of environmental visionary.

But as Jane settled into her new post on the Arts Council, the spectre of Vietnam again reared into view. Following the US withdrawal in 1975, the North Vietnamese – far from liberating the South – indulged in a genocidal orgy. Tens of thousands of Vietnamese were summarily executed. Millions more vanished into labour camps. And at least half of the estimated one million 'boat people' who risked their lives trying to flee to the West perished in the attempt.

The North Vietnamese bloodbath engulfed Laos and Cambodia, where the Hanoi-backed Khmer Rouge slaughtered an estimated two million peasants.

These horrifying events stunned many of Jane's former colleagues in the anti-war movement, causing them to reassess their unqualified support of the communist regime. An outraged Joan Baez issued an 'Appeal to the Conscience of Vietnam', calling on her former colleagues to join in condemning Hanoi's brutal policies. Eighty former anti-war activists signed Baez's appeal. Jane not only refused to sign, she fired off a fiercely worded eight-page letter condemning Baez and all who did sign for criticising Hanoi.

Even in the 1980s, Jane continued to make excuses for the North Vietnamese government's genocidal policies. 'People *want* to think what they want to think about the Vietnamese because they won and we can't stand that,' she said. 'It's a country that was totally devastated by war, and I'm sure that harsh measures have been taken to try to rally people around the cause of rebuilding, and that means taking intellectuals and urban people and saying you've got to go into the country and work in the fields, and they don't want to and they're forced to. Well, from our perspective, that's rotten, but I don't know enough about what's going on there to criticise.'

Baez was both shocked and saddened by Jane's expressions of solidarity with the repressive government in Hanoi. 'I'm opposed to all forms of oppression,' said the folk singer, 'no matter whose flag it's under.'

Confident that she could do no wrong in the eyes of the wider American public, Jane then persuaded Brown to appoint one of the POWs who met her in Hanoi, Colonel Edison Miller, to a prestigious post on the Board of Supervisors of conservative Orange County.

Miller, a career officer, had been discharged from the Marines in 1972 and censured for collaborating with the enemy when he joined with Fonda in making anti-war statements during her Hanoi stay. On their return, his fellow POWs said they had been tortured for refusing to follow Miller's example.

Miller's appointment and Jane's hand in it further fanned flames of indignation. Nancy Reagan, just one year away from becoming first lady, called Brown's choice of Miller 'an insult to every former POW. My heart breaks for them and their families at watching this man, who took the easier, dishonourable route of collaboration, take the oath of office.'

Jane was held accountable, and reaction was swift. By a vote of 28 to 5, the Democrat-controlled California Senate rejected her appointment to the Arts Council, describing her pro-Hanoi actions as 'traitorous'. Jane was at the hairdresser's when the call came through with the news. She burst into tears.

A few days later in Sacramento, Jerry Brown fired back. 'If these senators were as tough and big as they like to think,' asked the governor, 'why didn't they invite Jane Fonda to be heard and call her to her face the names they called her like a bunch of little kids?'

Jane, who had done more to politicise art than any actor in memory, told reporters that it was 'shocking' that the Senate voted 'to inject politics into what should have been a discussion of my merits as an artist to represent the arts community in California'. Accusing the senators of 'McCarthyism' and 'red-baiting', she charged that they had 'forgotten the meaning of the word *democracy*'.

Jane's friends in the entertainment industry rallied to her side. The Screen Actors Guild voted to censure the 28 senators who voted against Fonda, and in a full-page newspaper ad more than three hundred celebrities lined up behind the actress. Among the signatories were Alan Alda, Jack Nicholson, Cher, Woody Allen, Joanne Woodward, Robin Williams, Burt Reynolds, Gregory Peck, Mel Brooks, Norman Lear, and George Cukor.

Nevertheless, legislators were swamped with mail praising their action. Jane was out, and she was powerless to do anything about it.

'Jane was scared to death,' recalls Rosenthal. 'The intensity of hatred she and Tom were subjected to was awesome, and she became hysterical. It's like the Israelis – growing up in the shadow of a machine gun gives you a different perspective.

'It was at that point that Jane changed. She became absolutely, totally obsessed with money. Money was power. Without money and without power, Jane feared she and Tom would be destroyed. "We'll beat them at their own game," she said. In the process,' contends Rosenthal, 'I watched this high-minded person I had known turn into the sort of money-mad monster she had always fought against.'

24

THE COOLING towers of Three Mile Island looming behind them like Don Quixote's windmills, Tom and Jane kicked off a nonstop 32-day, 52-city campaign against 'unbridled corporate power'. At an anti-nuclear rally that brought two hundred thousand banner-waving demonstrators to New York City's Battery Park, Jane told the throng: 'We have to think of ourselves as Paul and Pauline Revere, going through our country town by town, city by city, warning people about the dangers.'

'Jane Fonda's Road Show', as it soon came to be known, criss-crossed the nation serving up the Haydens' familiar issues – energy, the environment, food, housing and health care, the elderly, welfare, etc. But the real motive was, as Jane had said so succinctly, to 'get the CED off my fucking back' by making it economically more self-sufficient. At the outset of their membership drive, the grass-roots organisation had a membership of 7500, each paying annual dues of $50. Hayden's goal was to boost dues-paying membership to 50,000 – enough to ease the pressure on Jane. The $100,000 tab for their trip would be covered by Jane's $5000-per-appearance lecture fees.

There were plenty of bumps along the road. During their appearance on NBC's 'Meet the Press' – the first ever by an actress – Jane was asked about her trip to Hanoi. 'I did', she said, 'what I had to do.' At most stops there were pickets as well as admirers. Yet the huge crowds that showed up seemed to accept the Hayden – Fonda anti-nuclear message without question – prompting the Edison Electric Institute to send along an energy 'truth squad' of two engineers to counter with the case for nuclear power. Tom and Jane brushed aside their request to debate the issue. 'We're not', declared Hayden, 'going to debate anyone who is not in a policy-making position.'

Halfway through their tour, Jane found herself nursing a broken toe, fighting a heavy cold, and reciting statistics in her sleep. Tom, exhausted, his eyes bloodshot, was beginning to feel threatened by the crowds. It was hardly worth the effort. Despite the turn-outs there was no groundswell of support, and with the dust beginning to settle Jane and Tom had attracted only 2500 new members to the CED.

On film, her efforts against the corporate establishment gained far greater results. In director Sydney Pollack's *The Electric Horseman* Jane teamed up with the number-one box-office actor, Robert Redford. The Electric Horseman is Sonny Steele, a washed-up rodeo legend turned cereal huckster. Steele learns during a personal appearance at a Las Vegas casino that the magnificent racehorse purchased to serve as the company symbol is being drugged by its handlers. Sonny kidnaps the horse and heads for the canyons to set it loose. Hot on his trail is Jane, again playing a television newswoman. She catches up with Sonny, and before long becomes his willing accomplice.

Sharing a deep-seated distrust of corporations and a concern for the ecology, Fonda and Redford were able to make statements about both in the film. They were not exactly equal partners, however. *The Electric Horseman* was actually a co-production of Redford's Wildwood Films and Ray Stark, and Redford's $3.5 million salary was three times that of Jane. So that he could get a break on state taxes, much of the movie was shot near his home in Utah. Storms caused repeated delays, but there was no such excuse for the kissing scene that required 48 takes. 'It would have been cheaper', said one accountant who reviewed the $280,000 bill for the famous kiss, 'if Redford had kissed the horse.'

For all the shooting difficulties in Utah, Jane found it preferable to filming in Las Vegas. 'It's a place built on greed,' she said, 'representing the absolute worst in our culture. The ethic that built this city is horrendous.'

The Electric Horseman was the top-grossing film of the autumn 1979 movie season. 'Miss Fonda,' wrote Vincent Canby in *The New York Times*, 'in addition to being a fine dramatic actress, is a first-rate comedienne, whether she's stumbling over a Utah mountain in her chic, spike-heeled patent-leather boots or suddenly becoming shy after a night well spent in the cowboy's sleeping bag.'

Still, other reviewers were beginning to echo Samuel Goldwyn's philosophy about movies and messages: if you want to send a message, use Western Union. 'Since these stars are celebrated mavericks, supposedly resistant to movie-biz stereotyping,' wrote Jack Kroll in *Newsweek*, 'it's interesting that they seem to see themselves as behavioural models, icons of righteousness pointing the way towards proper conduct in a corrupting world . . . In *The Electric Horseman* they're at their most golden, ethical, and sexy . . . In their love scenes they actually make you believe that pure virtue is the strongest of aphrodisiacs.'

Jane's next film was *Nine to Five*, the first IPC film since *The China Syndrome*. *Nine to Five* began with Jane's own brief experience as a secretary at the *Paris*

Review ('I was fired when I wouldn't sleep with the boss,' she told audiences), and grew as she interviewed office workers around the country. During a meeting in Cleveland with 30 women office workers, recalls Jane, 'I couldn't believe what I heard. They told about sexual harassment, about being on the job fifteen years and seeing men they trained promoted right by them to being their superiors, and about clerical workers at some of the wealthiest banks who are paid so little they are eligible for food stamps.'

Jane had actually become more 'sensitised' to the unfair treatment of office workers, she confessed, when she saw the way women were treated at her own studio and during the organisation of Tom's own CED activities. 'They are often treated as non-people. Office workers are usually the first to arrive at the office and the last to leave. They often work fifteen-hour days but are paid for forty hours of work a week. And sometimes they have to do things like fill petrol tanks, or get racing forms, or buy their boss's lunch.'

Jane and Bruce Gilbert hired Patricia Resnick to work undercover as a clerical worker at an employment agency and a major insurance firm, gathering material for the final screenplay Resnick co-scripted with director Colin *(Silver Streak, Foul Play)* Higgins. They came up with the story of three secretaries who conspire to murder their insufferably chauvinistic boss.

Nine to Five was conceived at the outset as a joint vehicle for Fonda, Lily Tomlin, and Dolly Parton. As Violet Newstead, head of the secretarial pool, Lily Tomlin clearly is more capable than most of the executives around but is continually passed over for promotion. Dolly Parton's Doralee Rhodes is fed up with being drooled over.

In preparation for her part as Judy Bernly, a newly divorced housewife taking her first job ever outside the home, Jane 'went about seeking women who had entered the job market late in life because they were recently widowed or divorced. These were women who had been defined by their husbands all their lives. You know, all the decisions were made for them. What they wore, what they did on their vacations, what they did on weekends . . . now they were in their forties and on their own.

'One thing that they all told me was how they arrived overdressed on the first day. How they felt out of place. So I asked our costume designer, Ann Roth, to overdress me. Give me a hat, an uptight suit. Make me look out of place.' Jane also chose a fifties hairdo, oversized glasses and a 'prim but frilly' blouse.

In the film, Judy soon learns that she is more than up to the job, and that leads to friction with the boss (Dabney Coleman). The secretaries wind up kidnapping Coleman, and taking over the office. In his absence, they send out all the memos under his name, adopt a new dress code, transform a storage room into a crèche, and promote typists to executive levels.

Buoyed up by the stellar cast and Parton's hit title song, *Nine to Five* (IPC's fourth effort) struck a nerve with white-collar workers of both sexes. And while it definitely sent a message – Fonda would go on into the 1980s urging office workers to organise – *Nine to Five* worked best as a zany, slapstick-filled romp through the pinstripe jungle. (Fonda had wanted the secretaries to end up murdering the boss, but, she says, 'Fox wouldn't allow it.')

Nine to Five was to be IPC's biggest money-maker by far, ringing up receipts in excess of $105 million. With the film's release, Jane could add yet another honour to her lengthening list: in addition to being a hit at the box office, Jane was listed in a 1980 Gallup poll among the world's ten most admired women.

There was more to come. By the end of the decade, in addition to her fame as an actress and an activist, Jane would be lionised in yet another incarnation: fitness queen.

25

ACCORDING TO Richard Rosenthal, Jane and Tom were not averse to invoking 'a high-minded purpose to make themselves rich. Overnight, money became the driving impulse. Power was the objective.' To her friends, Fonda made no effort to conceal this fact. 'Now I have more power,' she admitted, 'and I intend to use it.'

With virtually no income of his own, Tom continued to press his wife to make more money. At one point, a Fonda insider recalls, Tom turned to Jane and said, 'You have wrinkles around your eyes. You'll just be another worn-out actress if you don't find something else to do.'

The Campaign for Economic Democracy was still a major drain on Jane's bank account. Rosenthal remembers a meeting with Tom and Jane at Laurel Springs to solve the problem: 'We sat on the ground at the ranch in Santa Barbara trying to figure out what kind of business Jane should go into.' Out of that brainstorming session, Jane's Workout empire was born.

First, Jane remembers, they considered starting a restaurant chain, 'or maybe a car repair place that didn't rip people off'. But when a friend advised Jane and Tom, 'Never go into a business you don't understand,' their options narrowed. 'That was a problem,' says Jane, 'since there wasn't much about business I did understand.' Then, she recalls, 'it came to me like a bolt of lightning, the way my best ideas usually do, that the one thing I really do know about is being healthy, being fit. I knew I had credibility in that area, so it made sense to make it my business.'

It was already the business of Gilda Marx, who had her own national chain of exercise studios — Body Design By Gilda. In 1978, Jane signed on as a pupil at Marx's Los Angeles studio. So many of the curious joined just to sweat with Fonda and other celebrities that Jane soon recognised this as a market she could exploit. 'I'm enough like other women,' Jane says, 'to be able to give them what they — and I — want. For twenty-five years I went to dance classes. I saw so many women like me who took the rigorous training not because they wanted to become professional dancers but because they wanted to reshape their bodies.'

So Jane decided to open her own exercise studio in Beverly Hills, though she was hesitant to put her name on it. 'She was reluctant to call it "Jane Fonda's Workout,"' recalls Richard Rosenthal, because 'she thought that had an elitist connotation. And she didn't want her signature in neon. It was a strange situation. She was the owner, but she didn't want to *be* the owner. She wanted the Campaign for Economic Democracy to be the owner, since the enterprise had, in fact, been invented for the purpose of financing the CED.' But then, at Tom's urging, Jane agreed to affix her name – in neon – to the logo. She opened the first Jane Fonda Workout Studio in 1979 at 369 Robertson Boulevard, around the corner from Beverly Hills' glitzy Rodeo Drive. Soon there would be branches in nearby Encino and in San Francisco.

None of the exercises was new, but Jane claimed, 'The particular combinations are our own. We take each muscle group and work through it systematically. We include aerobics, too . . . it's a total approach.'

The Workout also offered no frills: 'We have no jacuzzis. No saunas. We cater to women who are busy, who travel, who have irregular schedules. This is not a social gathering place.' Paying $6 an hour (the rate was $8.50 by 1990), thousands of women flocked to the Workout – most to get a glimpse of the famous Jane, who taught many of the classes herself. When she wasn't there, other stars such as Ali MacGraw, Jill Clayburgh, and Kate Jackson were. Within six months, Workout was in the black.

Jane's success did not sit well with Gilda Marx, who soon charged her former pupil with stealing her basic concept and then distorting it. 'Jane is an actress,' said Marx. 'Her profession is to copy what someone else has done.' More significantly, Marx called the high-impact Workout regimen 'violent', and said that it might pose a physical risk to some people.

A decade later, Jane would concede that she had overdone the strenuousness of her regimen, but in the beginning she merely shrugged off criticism. 'I shed no tears for the Beverly Hills matron who cries and drinks and takes drugs. You have the ability to get off your butt and find out what life is about. If you don't, that's your problem, not someone else's.'

Her exercise business successfully launched, Jane focused on a film project that would profoundly alter her life – *On Golden Pond*. Written as a play by Ernest Thompson and produced in the autumn of 1978 off Broadway at the Hudson Guild Theatre, *On Golden Pond* told the story of a couple married for fifty years and returning to their summer cottage on the shores of Golden Pond in Maine. Norman Thayer, a somewhat cantankerous retired professor, is confronting heart disease, the first terrifying signs of senility, and his own mortality. Norman's wife, Ethel, is devoted to him despite his stubbornness. When on the eve of Norman's eightieth birthday their divorced daughter Chelsea arrives with her boyfriend and his bratty teenage son, the love between father and daughter is put to the test.

Screen legend Greer Garson was so enthralled with the play that she teamed up with Arthur Cantor to produce it for Broadway. But first there were try-outs in Wilmington, Delaware, and in Washington, DC. Among those in the audience at the Kennedy Center – three times – was Katharine Hepburn. She wanted to portray Ethel Thayer on the screen – but who was possibly up to the role of Norman?

Cantor sent a copy of the script for *On Golden Pond* to Henry in New York. Fonda read it and 'got all fired up', but questions remained about his health. He had been carrying around a pacemaker in his chest for five years and had just recovered from cancer surgery. Studios wouldn't exactly be eager to risk a $7 million budget on him or, for that matter, on Hepburn, then 73, whose head-shaking palsy had got markedly worse in recent years.

Henry sent a copy of the script to Jane. Her first reaction: 'I could hear my father saying those words.' She called Hank as soon as she put the script down. 'It's wonderful,' she told him. 'I want to play the daughter.' At first he balked – the part was too small for her, he pointed out. But Jane was excited about this golden opportunity – to bridge the emotional gap that had always separated them. She would play the supporting role, and IPC would co-produce the film.

On Golden Pond marked not only the first time Katharine Hepburn and Henry Fonda ever worked together – it was also the first time the two screen giants had ever met. At their first pre-production meeting in a conference room at Twentieth Century-Fox in Los Angeles, she walked straight up to Henry, stuck out her hand, and said, 'Well, it's about time.'

The occasion was also to mark Kate's first meeting with Henry's daughter, but much to Kate's consternation, Jane was not there: she was travelling through the South instead, doing research with Dolly Parton for her TV role in *The Dollmaker*. 'I'm a big believer in delegating,' Jane says. 'I didn't think my presence was necessary. I knew everything was going to be fine, even though in some respects it was a historic occasion.'

When Jane finally did meet Hepburn at Kate's New York town house a month later, she was 'absolutely terrified. I walked in, totally in awe of her, and Kate greeted me with a pointed finger saying, "I don't like you." Well, it's like God condemning you. We had a rocky few hours there, but then I realised she was testing the waters.'

It became clear to Jane that Hepburn first saw her as 'some arrogant, upstart whippersnapper who expected to get top billing. I had not spoken to her about billing, because quite honestly there was no question in my mind that she and my father would get top billing, and that I would have billing below them. I never really cared about billing – whether that comes from stupidity or confidence, I don't know.' (Katharine Hepburn had also once expressed her concern for billing to her longtime love Spencer Tracy. When she suggested that he take second billing to her, a female star, on a 'ladies first' premise, Tracy replied: 'This is a movie, not a lifeboat.')

'I think Katharine has a healthy dose of competition, and I do too,' says Jane. Kate, she soon discovered, was 'always testing'. In April 1980, three months before shooting was scheduled to begin, Kate dislocated her shoulder playing tennis. She called Jane and ran down a list of other actresses she thought Jane should hire to replace her. 'It was ludicrous,' says Jane. 'Why in the hell would we settle for somebody else when we could get *her*? When she seemed satisfied that it was Katharine Hepburn we really wanted, she started grilling me about my role in the movie.'

Since they would be spending the rest of the summer on location at New Hampshire's Squam Lake, Jane agreed to fly up ahead and scout out available house rentals while Hepburn drove north. 'We rendezvoused in some parking lot, and she asked me which place I wanted. I said, "Miss Hepburn, you choose where you want to stay and I'll go from there."

'"Now you're talking," she said, and then opened up the boot of her car, where she'd packed the most gorgeous picnic with china, silver, and linens, and we had lunch.'

All was harmony between Henry and Kate. The first day on the set, she presented him with Spencer Tracy's favourite hat. (Touched, Henry reciprocated by painting a still life of three crumpled hats – Tracy's, and two of Fonda's favourite fishing and rain hats.)

The film's director, Mark Rydell, was worried, however, that there would be friction between Jane and Hepburn. 'After all,' he said, 'Jane is the big star of the eighties and Katharine *was* the big star. You had the sense in the first few days of two lionesses prowling the same ground.'

Jane's memories of her childhood fantasies resurfaced during filming. 'I remembered how I fantasised what it would have been like if Dad and Kate had had an affair and she was my mother.' Actually, Jane recalls the prospect of working with her father and Hepburn as a 'terrifying experience. I was very nervous. I tended to overact in the beginning and I threw up a lot.'

Dad, conversely, was unflappable. 'That's what is so scary about him – nothing seems to faze him. He arrives on time and knows his lines. He sits and waits like an empty vessel and when they need him he fills up, does his thing, and sits down.' Jane calmed down when she finally realised that, beneath it all, her father and Hepburn were 'just as nervous as I was'.

Still, Kate kept testing Jane. In one scene, Chelsea, Jane's character in the film, does a back flip off a jetty. Did Jane intend to do the flip herself? Kate wanted to know. 'I thought, Holy cow! I'm afraid of diving, especially backwards, and I really had no intention of doing it. But I remembered reading about Hepburn as a young athlete, and I thought, Oh my God, I'm going to have to do it, I'm going to have to learn to do the back flip to prove myself to her. So I said, "Of course I'm going to do it myself!"'

Each day on the set, Jane spent hours out on a raft in the middle of the lake, practising her back flip. 'I could see Katherine watching from the shore,' she recalls. 'Finally, one day I did about six back flips in a row, and I climbed out of the water all covered with bruises. She wrapped me up in a towel and said, "How do you feel?" When I told her I felt great, she smiled and said, "Of course you do. Nothing is more important than overcoming fear."'

Ultimately, Jane was charmed by Hepburn's candour. 'What I love about Katharine is that she wears her emotions on her sleeve. If she is angry or hurt or worried or concerned, it's right there out front where you can deal with it.'

Looking back on the filming of *On Golden Pond*, Jane says she 'learned more from Katharine than from anyone I've ever met. At this stage in her life, she has cast herself as a teacher. She has these incredible gifts, this wealth of knowledge that she wants to pass on. I felt chosen to be her friend.'

When Jane brought singer Michael Jackson, whom she had met in Los Angeles, on to the set of *On Golden Pond*, Kate 'didn't know who he was, or quite what to make of him', recalls Jane. Each day Jackson would come to watch the filming, armed with a tape recorder, and at the end of every take Hepburn would take him aside. 'They sat on a rock and he listened to her stories. At the core of every anecdote she told was a lesson – the most wonderful, valuable, deep lessons for a young talent. She told him never to settle in, never to lose his hunger, his edge.' After that, Kate and Michael Jackson became fast if decidedly unlikely pals, chatting over the telephone.

Yet all was not harmonious on the set. As Hepburn herself saw, there was a tension, an awkwardness between father and daughter. Of course there were striking parallels between the characters of Norman and Chelsea and the actors who portrayed them on screen. 'The grouchiness is real,' Jane would say of Henry. 'The difficulty is seeing that one causes suffering for someone else – that's true of my dad. He doesn't always know when he's hurt somebody.'

Jane recalls one scene in which Ethel, Norman, and Chelsea's fiancé, Bill (Dabney Coleman), play Parcheesi while Chelsea sulks. 'Chelsea doesn't like to play,' Norman observes, 'because she's afraid of losing.' Chelsea shoots back, 'Why does he like to beat people so much?' Jane remembers the exchange as a moment of 'real hostility, and I felt I really had to look him in the eye'.

When the time came for close-ups, she asked her father if he could see her. 'I don't need to see you,' he snapped. 'I'm not one of those damned Method actors.' Jane was stunned. 'It hurt me deeply,' she admits. 'I was mortified and furious – I felt like crying. Here I was forty-four years old, I have my life and my family, and still he can reduce me to feeling abject helplessness.'

Kate turned out to be Jane's comforter off-camera as well as on. 'She put her arm on me and said: "Don't be upset. Spence [Spencer Tracy] used to do that to me all the time."'

For the most intense scene between Norman and Chelsea, when she tells him she wants to be his friend, Hepburn stood on the sidelines and watched. 'I knew that for it to work we had to be naked, as it were, prepared to reveal ourselves,' says Jane. 'That is never easy. We would read scenes at the dining-room table at the house. The moment I opened my mouth the tears came . . . so much emotion I could hardly control it. He cried, too – it was very hard for him.'

But when the moment came for Jane's big close-up, her crying before the camera, she 'dried up – it was not there'. Jane took Hepburn aside and quietly asked for help. 'She knew exactly what I meant. So she stood in the bushes behind me off camera, and I turned and looked into her eyes . . . and it was Katharine Hepburn to Jane Fonda saying, "I know what this means to you and by God you *tell* him." She *fed* me. I could feel it coming from her right into me. It was wonderful. At the end, I said [the line] "I want to be your friend," and I'll never forget it, because my dad was never very emotional – he didn't cry on camera or on stage. I touched him. I waited until his last close-up and he didn't expect it, and I touched him and I could see the tears well up in his eyes . . . '

That evening over dinner, Jane remembers, 'We never talked about the meaning of the whole experience, but we knew it had been profound both professionally and personally.'

That time in New Hampshire also gave Henry and his wife, Shirlee, a chance to get to know Jane's family in a way that had been impossible in the frenzied worlds of New York, Paris, and Los Angeles. Vanessa, now thirteen, and eight-year-old Troy stayed with Tom and Jane in a cabin just down the road from Henry's house. Henry joined Troy and Tom, an accomplished bass angler, on fishing expeditions. 'Fishing is a great way to get to know Henry Fonda,' said Hayden (echoing Vadim's earlier experience). 'Henry is not a big talker and fishing doesn't require it. We enjoy each other. He knows his daughter's marriage hasn't been short-lived or disastrous. And he's got a grandson out of it.'

Shirlee and Jane were left to console each other. 'I got to know Shirlee better than I ever had,' says Jane, 'and to love her a lot.'

While acting on Broadway in *Darrow* years earlier, Henry had said, referring to Jane and Peter, 'People are always asking me when we had our reconciliation.

What reconciliation? They told me years ago they were sorry for the things they said.' But in truth, an emotional chasm still separated Henry from his children. Even the summer on Golden Pond did not entirely bridge that gap for Jane. 'Dad is not a communicative person, he just isn't,' she said. 'In the last act of life one doesn't change. I won't. And one is wrong to expect it of a person.'

For a time after the movie's completion, it looked as though Henry Fonda might not survive to see On Golden Pond on the screen. While getting ready to do final dubbing on the film, director Mark Rydell received an urgent phone call from Jane asking him to set up a special screening for her father. Rydell assured Jane it would be ready in a couple of weeks, but she was adamant. 'No, Mark,' she explained, 'you have to show On Golden Pond to my father now – he may not live to see it.'

Fonda arrived for the special screening that night, and, using two canes, slowly made his way to his seat in the auditorium. Rydell, heartbroken at the degree to which Henry's health had deteriorated since filming, waited outside. Once the screening was over, Rydell went back inside. Fonda struggled towards Rydell, then stumbled and fell, 'so that I had to catch him in my arms', remembered the director. 'He began to shudder, so that I thought he might be dying in my arms. But he regained his strength and whispered to me: "Thank you for the most important film of my life. Thank you!"'

Henry rallied over the following months. Still, when On Golden Pond was released in November 1981, his physical condition remained precarious. Now, for audiences watching Henry play a man dying of a heart condition, it was hard to tell actor and character apart. Fonda's portrayal of Norman Thayer was hailed as his crowning achievement, and speculation ran high that this performance would at last win Fonda the Academy Award he had long been denied.

'If it is to be his last performance,' wrote Richard Schickel, 'then its perfect setting is On Golden Pond. If it is to be his only Oscar, however belated, then it could not be for anything that more appropriately, or more movingly, summarises a career that has endured almost half a century.'

Fonda himself knew all too well how much he owed to On Golden Pond, and to his daughter for making it possible. 'I'm not a religious man,' he said, 'but I thank God every morning that I lived long enough to play that role.'

Peter may have seemed odd man out through the experience of On Golden Pond, but he was still fiercely loyal to the clan. En route from his home in Aspen, Colorado, to his ranch in Livingstone, Montana, Peter had a brief stopover in Denver. At the airport terminal, he came across a sign taped to a phone booth. Posted by the pro-nuclear Fusion Energy Foundation, it read,

'FEED JANE FONDA TO THE WHALES'. Jane's brother whipped out his pocket knife, tore the sign to shreds – and was promptly arrested for destroying private property.

'She's my sister, and in my neck of the woods', Peter declared, 'you don't get away with saying anything bad about someone's sister, mother, or grandmother.' When two witnesses failed to appear in court, the charges were dropped.

Far from Squam Lake, Jane began shooting IPC's fifth production, *Rollover*, in New York. Once again she was working with Alan J. Pakula, and once again she was squaring up to Big Business – this time, big bankers and high-flying international financiers. A radical departure from the rustic doings in New Hampshire, *Rollover* featured Jane as the glamorous Lee Winters, an ex-film star and petrochemical heiress who tries to win control of her husband's empire after he is murdered. She enlists the help of a hotshot bank troubleshooter (Kris Kristofferson) to secure a loan from the Saudis, and as the plot unfolds she is caught up in a web of deception that ultimately leads to a global economic collapse.

Rollover constituted a major departure in style and substance for both its stars. The satin-sheathed, sable-wrapped, emerald-dripping Winters was antithetical to the Everywoman roles that had brought Jane acclaim, while the rugged, whisky-voiced Kristofferson was woefully miscast, and knew it from the moment he was told to shave off his trademark salt-and-pepper beard. 'I used it as a protective mask. I felt naked without it,' he confessed, 'terribly exposed. The fact is, I wasn't right for the film, but Jane wanted me and I wanted to work with her and Alan [Pakula]. So I did it.'

Most of Winters's life in the film is spent 'making business deals and attending parties'. In the Ocean Life Room of New York's American Museum of Natural History, Jane, draped in shimmering blue sequins, shot one party scene with 300 extras. It was originally described in the screenplay as a 'Save the Whales' benefit, but now producer Bruce Gilbert decided to make the party 'a wealthy society-type benefit, because a woman in Lee Winters's position wouldn't be interested in things like whales'.

Nothing, of course, could be less true of Jane. The longer she played a gilt-edged member of the moneyed elite, the more anxious she became to jump back into the political fray. Could you move a little to the left, a cameraman asked? 'Always,' she replied. Cast and crew laughed. Jane did not.

Further complicating matters was the widely circulated rumour that Jane and Kristofferson had become romantically involved. When the tabloids published photographs of the couple out together, both Fonda and Kristofferson professed to be mortified. 'The worst thing about the rumours', said

Kristofferson, 'was that it changed the atmosphere a little for me. It wasn't as much fun, and we kind of lost an innocence.'

Jane was outraged. 'It took me by surprise, and it was embarrassing. Fortunately, Tom is who he is and we could just talk about it. It was hard to figure out what to do. You can't sue, because that just calls attention to it, so we just decided to forget about it.'

A Christmas-season release that landed in cinemas immediately after *On Golden Pond*, *Rollover* was an unmitigated disaster. Most of the reviewers criticised its muddled plot and wooden, curiously lifeless characters. '*Rollover* works as neither a love story nor a satire,' wrote Janet Maslin in *The New York Times*, 'and it isn't even the thriller it sets out to be.' The *Wall Street Journal* claimed that the only thing startling about *Rollover* was 'its total ineptitude'.

Grossing a scant $6 million at the box office, *Rollover* marked Jane's first flop as a producer. (By contrast, *On Golden Pond* earned more than $100 million, making it the highest-grossing film of 1981.) *Rollover's* failure hit Jane so hard that she spent the next three and a half years 'trying to sort things out. When I pour my heart into something and it fails, it hurts. I kept asking myself, Where did I go wrong? What happened, and why?'

While taking stock of herself as an actress, Jane joined the rest of Hollywood in honouring her father at the Academy Awards in 1982. The previous year, Robert Redford had presented Henry Fonda with a special Oscar in 'recognition of his brilliant accomplishments and enduring contribution to the art of motion pictures'.

But this time Henry, now too ill to attend, stayed at home in Bel Air with Shirlee and watched the ceremonies. When Jane, having just lost in the Best Supporting Actress category for *On Golden Pond*, stepped on to the stage to accept the Best Actor Oscar for him, Henry started to cry.

Jane looked into the camera and held up the Oscar. 'Oh, Dad, I'm so happy and proud for you,' she said, beaming as she blinked back her own tears. Then she turned to the audience: 'My father didn't really believe that this was going to happen – but he told me a while back that if it did, he wanted his wife, Shirlee, to accept the award for him. But Shirlee wanted to be with him tonight, as is her way, and so I'm here . . . I know that he's very, very honoured and very happy and surprised – and I bet he said, "Hey, ain't I lucky," as though luck had anything to do with it. I know,' she continued, 'that he feels that he never would have won this if it hadn't been for Katharine Hepburn, and I know that lastly – but really first – he is thanking Shirlee Fonda, who he calls his "Rock of Gibraltar". I think she's his Ethel Thayer. Dad, me and all the grandchildren are coming over with this right away!'

The family – Jane, Tom, Vanessa, Troy, and Peter's daughter, Bridget – posed briefly backstage, then piled into the family estate car. An hour later, when Jane handed her father his prize, he admitted that he really hadn't been taken by surprise. 'It was in the wind,' whispered Henry, wrapped up to his grey-white beard in sweaters and blankets.

'It was very, very touching,' recalls Tom. 'He was so overwhelmed when Jane handed the Oscar to him, he couldn't say a word. He was just sitting there in a state of bemused shock with the Oscar resting in his lap.'

Veteran photographer John Bryson, a longtime friend of Hepburn, Tracy, John Huston, and a number of Hollywood luminaries, was on hand to record the moment. As Bryson snapped photos of father, daughter, and Oscar, Hank admitted that he was not nonchalant about the honour. 'There's no question about it,' said Fonda, 'this has to be one of the high points of my life. I'm really happy and I'm proud, and I'm particularly happy that Katharine won, and Ernest [Thompson], too.'

Yet no one, not even Henry Fonda, seemed as thrilled as Jane: 'It was, I think, the happiest night of my life.'

Four months later, on 11 August 1982, Henry Fonda died at the age of 77. At Cedars-Sinai hospital, Shirlee had kept a vigil at her husband's bedside. While there were still tensions between Hank and his children – particularly Peter, who at one point had argued with his father for snubbing his children in favour of Jane's – Jane was also a near-constant presence in Henry's hospital room. As it happened, however, she was at home when Shirlee called to tell her her father had died. She sped to the hospital and leapt out of her car in such a panic that she forgot to put the automatic transmission in park. The car almost rolled into the street before a passer-by jumped in and applied the brake.

Later that day, Henry's widow and children stood outside the gates of the Fondas' Bel Air estate and talked to the press. Shirlee – flanked by Peter, Amy, and Jane, who draped a comforting arm around her – described her husband's death: 'He woke up this morning, sat up in bed, and just stopped breathing.' Then the family closed the wrought-iron gates and walked, arm in arm, back to Henry's house. Henry's death altered the dynamics of the family. 'It handed down to me,' says Jane, 'the role of elder.'

26

WHEN IT came to making bodies more beautiful, Jane Fonda proved to be her own best advertisement. With her Workout studio going strong and a book on its way, the sight of a taut, tanned, bikini-clad Jane Fonda in *On Golden Pond* was enough to make the fitness-conscious not yet recruited into her ranks sit up and take notice.

In the spring of 1982, *Jane Fonda's Workout Book* was published by Simon & Schuster and shot to the top of the *New York Times* best-seller list. The 254-page manual urged readers to 'go for the burn' – in other words, flat out – through daily routines (27 minutes for beginners, and 40 minutes for the more advanced) of muscle-toning stretches, lunges and leg lifts. Fonda's book also prescribed a salt-free diet featuring nuts, wheat-germ seeds, unprocessed bran, yogurt, fruits and vegetables, and six to eight glasses of water daily. (When Simon & Schuster threw a party for Jane in the publisher's office to celebrate the millionth copy of *Workout*, only the second million-copy hardback best-seller in the history of the house, Jane showed up an hour late, stayed only a few minutes, and offered no words of thanks to her editors or anyone else who contributed to the book's success. It was a performance that would become typical of Fonda in her new role as steel-hard businesswoman.)

At about the same time, a young waterbed salesman turned video entrepreneur, Stuart Karl, persuaded Jane to do a video version of her book. 'To his surprise and everyone else's, it became a blockbuster and made the company,' says Tim Baskerville of *Video Marketing Newsletter*. 'You can say he was lucky, or you can say he was brilliant.'

Prior to Jane Fonda's *Workout* video, every videocassette hit had been a movie; feature film rentals constituted 80 per cent of any video shop's revenues. But Fonda's videos were purchased rather than rented.

Jane then released a Workout record and audio tape using previously recorded music, shrewdly persuading the artists to forgo their royalties. Much to their surprise, the records and tapes sold millions of copies – for which the performers received nothing. One of the singers stated publicly that he had been tricked but never moved to substantiate his claim against Fonda.

Within a year, *Jane Fonda's Workout Book* would sell 1.8 million copies (an enormous sale for a hardback book). Her follow-up *Workout Book for Pregnancy, Birth, and Recovery*, written by exercise expert Femmy DeLyser, sold 250,000 copies. Fees and royalties poured in. By the end of 1982, the Fonda fitness empire had easily earned an astonishing $20 million. And it was only the beginning.

With all the profits being funnelled into the Campaign for Economic Democracy, Hayden's war chest was full to overflowing, and his political career in full stride. With Jane at his side, Tom ran for the California State Assembly in the heavily Democratic 44th District. Encompassing Santa Monica, West Los Angeles, and Malibu, the district, Tom quipped, 'has the greatest variation of income in the US — mine and my wife's'.

Behind closed doors, say insiders, Tom was nothing if not direct about the clout derived from Jane's prodigious income. Recalls one colleague: 'Tom always bragged about his "rich wife". With her millions, he felt nothing could stop him.'

As for her role in his campaign, Jane told the press, 'I'm there to see that he's happy.' She was being overly modest. As Hayden's campaign manager, Michael Dieden, put it, 'There's not a political decision this campaign or Tom personally makes that Jane does not play a role in.'

Others inside the campaign claim that both Tom and Jane saw this race as only the first step on a longer road — to 1600 Pennsylvania Avenue. 'It really irked Jane that, of all the people in Hollywood, the Reagans would end up in the White House,' says a friend, 'and Nancy Reagan really got on her nerves — this look of rage came over Jane's face any time somebody mentioned her name. Jane really believed that Tom was a great man, a man of destiny, and that he would wind up in the White House by 1992. "Tom", she said, "is going to be president."'

During the campaign, Jane trudged from door to door, five or six hours a day, six days a week. Her delivery this time was low-key, in sharp contrast to her campaigning in the Hayden–Tunney contest. 'I was frequently shrill,' she confessed in retrospect. 'People view us, and me in particular, as angry and humourless. I'm just happy I'm able to correct that impression.'

As it turned out, it would be a struggle simply to edge out Tom's competition in the Democratic Primary. Hayden's Jewish opponent, an aide to Los Angeles's popular mayor Tom Bradley, implied that Hayden was pro-PLO — a particularly damaging charge in a district that was one-quarter Jewish.

To counter this, Jane joined Tom on a highly publicised visit to Israel arranged by the Israeli Association for the Welfare of Soldiers.

'We have come to Israel and Lebanon during this time of war and suffering,' they said in a joint release, 'for humanitarian reasons, and to find out for ourselves the prospects of peace.' Jane was quick to correct any misleading questions from the past − 'I don't know why people confuse my views with Vanessa Redgrave's' − and was soon photographed bringing flowers to wounded Israeli soldiers in Tel Aviv. Two days later she marched with her husband to the front lines. There they watched from the courtyard of St Anthony's School on the outskirts of Beirut as Israeli gunners fired shells into the residential neighbourhoods of West Beirut while a radio blared the Beatles' *Eight Days a Week*.

'By its repeated calls for the annihilation of the Zionist state and by its use of terrorism', concluded Hayden, the PLO had made the Israeli actions 'inevitable'. The Haydens rushed home to report their findings to the electorate.

They also hired top-notch outside media consultants to reshape Hayden's left-of-centre image. Their main weapon was a TV advertisement that showed a nattily dressed, clean-cut Hayden and Troy kissing Jane goodbye and driving downtown. There, an ugly crowd menaces Hayden and his son with shouts of 'Traitor' − a staged scene that succeeded in portraying Hayden as misunderstood victim. Later in the ad, as he strolls through his neighbourhood, Tom says 'I'm not the same angry young man I used to be, but I still believe in change, in improving my community.' Then Troy and his schoolmates 'surprised' Dad by spelling out HAYDEN FOR ASSEMBLY with placards − the final Y turned upside down.

By way of further polishing their new 'Father Knows Best' image, Jane claimed that she would come down hard on either Troy or Vanessa if she caught either 'messing around' with drugs or alcohol. 'I'll take them right down to the hospital, to the floor where all the burnt-out kids are,' she promised. On the issue of sex, Jane would be less strict. 'Both children know the physical part of it,' she said. 'But lately I've tried to tell Vanessa how beautiful sex can be if you love the person you're with.'

There were times when Vanessa rebelled at being used as a campaign prop. When photographers showed up at a rally to snap Hayden delivering a major speech, Vanessa mugged for the cameras in whiteface. Now a teenager, Vanessa remained close to her natural father, and friction with Hayden was increasing. 'They get mad sometimes,' said Jane, finding herself caught between husband and daughter, 'but she likes Tom, I think.'

As the campaign progressed, Jane became increasingly concerned that some new controversy might irreparably damage Tom's chances. When she learned that a new unauthorised biography of her was about to be published by Doubleday, she ordered her lawyers into action. Although the book was adoring and contained nothing remotely controversial, Jane's attorney Barry L. Hirsch wrote a letter telling Doubleday it was 'hereby ordered to desist' from selling the book.

The action, coinciding as it did with Jane's reading the First Amendment on a nationally televised *I Love Liberty* special, backfired. 'Having stirred the nation with her rendition of the First Amendment,' wrote journalist Nat Hentoff, 'Jane Fonda (!) was trying to kill a book.' Jane dropped her action.

After a narrow victory in the primary, Hayden went on to beat his Republican opponent by a modest nine points. The campaign had cost a staggering $1.3 million. Of that, Jane had contributed $615,000 – not counting the hundreds of thousands of dollars in Workout profits channelled into the campaign via the CED. (From the outset, Workout, Inc. paid business taxes, but its dividends to Hayden's nonprofit CED were tax-exempt. By 1989, those dividends topped $10 million, many times the amount the CED collected from grass-roots donations.)

As Tom was sworn in by Governor Jerry Brown, all eyes were on Jane in the visitors' gallery. 'With all the ruckus over his wife,' recalls a spectator, 'he sort of crept to the back row and took his seat like a sad schoolboy. It was sort of pathetic. Nobody noticed him.' His salary: $42,000.

Getting elected proved to be only half the battle. Gil Ferguson, a Republican assemblyman from Newport Beach, demanded Hayden be expelled on the grounds that the California State Constitution prohibited anyone who had once 'given comfort to the enemies of the United States' from holding statewide office. Ferguson and his allies backed up their crusade with a $3 million mail campaign. 'Every inflammatory remark I ever made, usually distorted for heightened effect, was mailed out to the voters,' recalls Hayden. One such quote – 'Abolish private property' – was emblazoned on hoardings in West Los Angeles.

Hayden called it Red-baiting and anti-democratic, but it took the intervention of Democratic Assembly speaker Willie Brown to get the motion ruled out of order. Then there was a move to override Brown, which was defeated by only a narrow margin of 41 – 36.

In the future, Tom would be careful not to rock the legislative boat. Working inside party ranks, he managed to get fifteen bills signed into law, among them a state-funded Agent Orange counselling programme for Vietnam veterans, a tax credit for solar energy, and a bill requiring greater supervision of nuclear weapons work done on University of California campuses. Before long he was chairman of two key committees – Higher Education, and Labor and Employment – and was writing speeches for Brown and presidential aspirant Gary Hart; Jane was a particularly avid admirer of Hart.

During the 1988 presidential race between Massachusetts governor Michael Dukakis and Vice President George Bush, Hayden and Fonda contributed

$100,000 – again, not counting whatever was routed from the Workout through the CED, now called Campaign California.

From Tom's election onwards, the Fonda – Hayden union would become less and less a marriage and more and more a political and business partnership. Tom took a pied-à-terre near the capitol in Sacramento, and commuted at weekends to the Haydens' new, larger, solar-heated Santa Monica house. Jane, still timid about acting after the *Rollover* débâcle, continued to build her fitness empire.

Occasionally she stumbled, ironically on issues of sex discrimination and equal wages. In April 1983, three women who once worked at Jane's San Francisco Workout studio (which had closed the previous year because it failed to make a profit) filed a sex-discrimination suit against Fonda claiming they were paid only $6 an hour to train customers on Nautilus equipment while two men doing the same job were getting as much as $8.50 for the same work.

'We're really upset,' said Mary Conn, who with the other disgruntled women had tried to work out a private settlement but had got nowhere. 'Jane has always stood for high ideals – like women's rights. But she hasn't come through when it comes to her own business. I think she's a hypocrite.'

Jane's attorney on the case, Larry Stein, countered that the men were paid more because they were 'more productive at running people through the Nautilus. More people asked for them.' After the suit was filed, the three women received a cheque for a grand total of $2,500 to be divided among them – $1 extra for each hour they had worked. The women rejected the offer, and over a year later settled for slightly more.

In 1983, the British *Daily Mail* published a rumour that Jane had suffered a heart attack. The story was picked up by *USA Today* and quickly spread worldwide; soon Jane began getting phone calls from concerned friends as far away as Australia and Japan.

Fonda went on national television to refute the story. 'I've never been better,' she protested. 'I've never even had a cold this year.' As for the source of the gossip: 'I'm not particularly paranoid, but the fact it keeps happening indicates that somebody or other would like to make me look unhealthy.' To reassure the public that she was as fit as ever, Jane conducted a gruelling 90-minute workout before reporters at the Beverly Hills Workout studio.

At the moment, she was more concerned with the health of her business. Convinced by the failure of her San Francisco operation that she should not franchise her studios, Jane found herself more and more concerned with profits and losses. 'Changed? Oh, yes. This has changed me. I am much more sensitive to the bottom line, and I must live with the tensions and contradictions that that brings . . . I want to pay my teachers fairly. Then I sit and look at the books, and I realise that my wanting to do well by the workers really hurts the bottom line.'

Her newfound business acumen aside, Jane still could not shake her radical past. When she was invited to the launching of the *Challenger* space shuttle, the White House protested. A few months later, NASA public affairs officer Robert Duff left the agency largely because of the incident.

Jane's successful marketing of the Workout books, tapes and records had all been immune to any criticism stemming from her activist past. So when she went ahead with an ambitious plan to launch a line of Jane Fonda Workout and ActiveWear clothes, no one had any reason to suspect there would be trouble.

But there was. When Jane went on a personal appearance tour to promote the line in department stores around the country, several cancelled after protests and, in at least one case, a bomb threat. After a year, sales seemed to have fizzled, falling far short of the anticipated $35 million. The manufacturer was forced into bankruptcy. Jane blamed it on the fact that she was not in direct control of the operation. 'When I do something myself, like my book or tapes or movies, I do all right,' she said, 'but with the clothing, I didn't realise until too late that the management was making mistakes.'

Another project fared far better – Jane's first foray as a producer into television. Her acting inactivity and doubt over the three years since *Rollover* came to an end with *The Dollmaker*. For twelve years Jane had been wanting to bring the 1954 novel by Harriette Arnow to the big screen, but accepting the failure of her efforts she agreed – against her agent's advice – to film it for ABC. (Actually, she first called and pitched the story to the network the day after picking up her Academy Award for *Coming Home*. 'What were they going to say? I had just won my second Oscar. They said yes.')

The dollmaker is Gertie Nevels, a rawboned Kentucky farm woman who must relocate to a city housing settlement when her husband gets a job in a Detroit factory immediately after World War II. Gertie is unschooled yet fights for her five young children to learn to read and write. Overcoming hardship, tragedy, and soul-crushing grief, she manages to hold her family together through sheer grit – and to pay the bills by carving wooden dolls.

Jane, who said she felt her father's voice coming out of her mouth in the film, owed much to Dolly Parton for helping her research the role. 'Dolly', said Jane, 'was the first hillbilly I ever met.' From Parton, who took her through the hill country, Jane 'learned to milk a cow and churn butter and bake biscuits and learn the rhythm of the mountains'.

Once filming was completed, director Daniel Petrie recalls, Jane 'reached out and put her arm around me. And she sobbed for ten minutes. Her whole body was shaking. I think it was because the character was dead, and she was in mourning.'

This was Jane's *Grapes of Wrath*, and both critics and audiences responded enthusiastically. Ratings were high. 'Miss Fonda may not, at first glance, be most people's idea of a plain and gritty mountain woman,' wrote John J. O'Connor in *The New York Times*. 'But Miss Fonda is indeed an actress and, as has been demonstrated in films ranging from *Klute* to *On Golden Pond*, a good one. She has clearly prepared strenuously for the role of Gertie, and the result is a performance that is nearly always spellbinding.'

'You don't know how happy this makes me,' Jane said when she accepted her first Emmy ever for *The Dollmaker*, 'because this project was very, very important to me.'

By the middle of the decade Jane was at the peak of her power and popularity. If there was to be a Woman of the Eighties, she seemed to have the title sewn up. The 1984 *World Almanac* listed her as the country's third most influential woman – 'Yeah, right behind Nancy Reagan,' she noted – and Gallup moved her from tenth all the way up to fourth on its roster of 'America's Most Admired Women'.

Jane's third volume, *Women Coming of Age*, went into the bookshops in early 1985. In the preface to the book, co-authored with Mignon McCarthy, Jane talked about her own mother, who felt her life was all but over at 40. Now 47, Jane sought to prove her mother wrong.

Women Coming of Age covered the physical and psychological aspects of ageing from 40 on, with chapters on exercise, nutrition, menopause, beauty, even plastic surgery. Another instant best-seller, it underscored Jane's concern for her fellow middle-aged women – 'healthy survivors in a culture that rejects us and that does not want our full participation'.

She was also starting to take her own ageing personally, particularly since hers was openly an age-obsessed profession. 'What I really hate is watching Robert Redford get younger and younger leading ladies,' Jane complained. 'We're living in a society that makes it more difficult for women to get older than men. There is a definite double standard. Men,' she added, 'get lines of distinction. Women get crow's-feet.'

This was especially true of Hollywood. 'For men and women, sex is such a huge component of stardom. A man can usually hang on to that much longer, but traditionally the big women stars hit forty or forty-five and vanish – just disappear. Then, years later, they resurface as big character stars and have a whole new career.'

Jane still hopes to forgo that midlife vanishing act and remain on top in leading-lady roles. 'Sure I wish I was forty again,' she says, 'but I'm not, so why waste time moaning about it? Besides, I don't think I'm going to have a normal career. Don't forget – I am the number-one major late starter – living proof that it's never too late. I'm going to be growing and experiencing into my nineties.'

For her return to feature films, Jane began work in Canada on the 1985 screen version of the hit Broadway play *Agnes of God*. As psychiatrist Martha

Livingstone, a chain-smoking workaholic, Fonda is dispatched to a convent where a young nun (Meg Tilly) has killed her baby. Dr Livingstone struggles to get to the bottom of the tragedy, but must contend with an obstructive Mother Superior (Anne Bancroft) who is covering up the incident to protect the Order and the girl. While Fonda's hard-boiled psychiatrist searches for a rational explanation, she is instead drawn into the young nun's world of angels, stigmata, and epiphanies.

Before taking the role, Jane checked to see if the Roman Catholic Church had taken a position on John Pielmeier's Tony Award-winning play. 'If they had,' she conceded, 'I wouldn't have done the movie. I did not want to become embroiled in any Catholic controversy.'

In the end Jane was so moved by the film, shot on location at an abbey in Quebec, that she 'returned to a sense of the importance of a Greater Power in my own life. When I was young, I used to pray. I loved to go and sit in the quiet of churches. I loved the peace and the calm and the chance to think about important things like . . . oh, the Meaning of Life.'

Now that she was back to believing in a 'benevolent, loving God', Jane pointed out that she was passing her newfound faith on to Troy. When Katharine Hepburn won her Oscar for *On Golden Pond*, Troy told his mother, 'Mommy! I prayed and she won!' The experience, smiles Fonda, 'made him a believer'.

Agnes of God received mixed reviews, and given its unorthodox subject matter could be called only a modest commercial success. Although Jane was overlooked by the Academy, *Agnes* did bring Bancroft a nomination as Best Actress, and one for Tilly in the supporting category.

Meanwhile, Jane had her hands full on the home front trying to persuade her publisher, Simon & Schuster, to edit some of the more embarrassing details out of Roger Vadim's forthcoming Simon & Schuster book, *Bardot, Deneuve, Fonda*.

Unlike Bardot and Deneuve, who both threatened legal actions over the tell-all book, Jane preferred to work behind the scenes. As the author of *Workout*, by then Simon & Schuster's biggest-selling non-fiction title ever, Jane was assured a fair hearing. Ultimately, Vadim reportedly toned down a few of the racier scenes in the book, but what remained still upset Fonda. 'I had a very long talk with my daughter about the book,' said Jane. 'I think it was difficult for her in the sense that she knew her father had done something that was upsetting to people she cared about, including her mother. And that I think was hard, because she loves her father and feels very protective of him. We talked about what was said, about how I felt about it. I didn't want to pretend it hadn't happened.'

During a stay in Montreal for the première of *Agnes of God*, Jane was already doing research for her next role – that of fading, alcoholic movie star Alex Sternbergen in Sidney Lumet's thriller *The Morning After*. In the script, Alex blacks out after a night of heavy drinking and wakes up with a dead body next to her. The rest of the film – which has its amusing moments as well – is devoted to Alex's attempts to find out how the body got there.

After the customary round of television talk-show interviews in Montreal, Jane returned to her penthouse suite in the Château Champlain, ordered up a bottle of vodka, and drank it in a single sitting. 'I'm a moderate drinker,' she says, 'but I wanted to find out what it was like to be totally drunk, and if blackouts are really possible. Well, it is possible all right. I blacked out that night – totally. Of course, the major drawback in doing research this way is that you can't remember any of it!'

Screenwriter James Hicks had been inspired to write the screenplay by reading about the lives of two alcoholic actresses: Frances Farmer and Gail Russell. 'His empathy for those women really touched me,' said Fonda, who herself screened all their films 'trying to trace the progress of the disease from one movie to the next'. She also looked at all the films about alcoholism ('Two are really great: James Mason in *A Star Is Born* and Susan Hayward in *I'll Cry Tomorrow*'), attended meetings of Alcoholics Anonymous, and talked to former heavy drinkers.

In the end, Jane had to overcome her own fears. 'I was so scared about playing a drunk. An actor wants to have some control over a performance, and being drunk is about losing control.' Had it not been for the feistiness of her character, Jane would not have taken the risk: 'Alex is a wreck, a loser, almost down and out. But she also has a lot of spunk and humour. I like to play women who have potential and don't realise it.'

Although it did not break any box-office records, *The Morning After* was a success. The film was praised as a stylish comedy-mystery, and to her surprise Jane received her seventh Academy Award nomination.

Her success in the role of a woman older than any other she had played did point up, however, the undeniable fact that even sleek, sexy Jane was being overlooked for certain parts that would have gone to her only two or three years earlier. 'Most women's roles,' she said at the time, 'are written for thirty-two to forty-two. So things don't just come to me – although I think I can still play thirty-five.'

Many of her contemporaries in Hollywood – women battling booze or drugs and the ravages of time – might have easily identified with Alex Sternbergen in *The Morning After*. Not Jane. She was managing her life like one of her finely tuned businesses. 'The decision was made for vertical rather than lateral development,' she says. 'Instead of spreading myself thinly over a lot of projects and areas, I wanted to concentrate with more depth on the things that were going to be the mainstays of my life. That meant my family, my film work, and the Workout. Those three areas.' As for politics: 'Oh, my politics haven't changed at all. Not really.'

Despite continuing rumours of Tom's infidelity and gossip about a supposed romance between Jane and her *Morning After* co-star Jeff Bridges, the Fonda – Hayden partnership continued to flourish – or at least that is the way it appeared. 'My husband', Jane kept saying, 'is an anchor for me.' Tom, for his part, was now flying home from Sacramento practically every night, and in Los Angeles they maintained a high public profile. Yet there were times when Tom seemed to be chafing at the situation. 'If Jane and I have one evening at home alone,' he remarked on one occasion, 'it is a scheduling mistake by the staff.'

Jane, too – with Vanessa across the country at Rhode Island's Brown University and Troy attending public high school in Santa Monica – was showing signs of restlessness. Those longstanding rumours that Hayden was not being completely faithful began to bother her (she would admit later). Shortly before their fifteenth anniversary, someone asked for her secret to staying married. 'I don't know,' Jane answered hesitantly. 'It's hard. I think we're understanding of each other. We respect each other's work . . . We try to take good vacations. Tom and I go out to dinner, just the two of us.' She paused for a moment. 'I drive around and see these very old couples walking along holding hands,' Jane said wistfully. 'I keep thinking we'll be like that when we're old. Then I think, Will we?'

27

SHE WAS more fit than she had ever been, but at 48 all the signs of ageing were there – crow's-feet, liver spots, grey hair, even a touch of arthritis. Undaunted, Jane kept spreading her upbeat *Women Coming of Age* message. 'I'm actually looking forward', she asserted, 'to my first hot flush.'

With more exercise videos, records and tapes on the market, Jane railed against cosmetic surgery. 'I'm really appalled by what I see going on in plastic surgery in this country,' Jane said. 'We've got to make friends with those wrinkles and sags and grey hairs. We've got to understand they represent our lifetime experience. We see these women who have been nipped and tucked and injected and peeled to within an inch of their shiny, taut lives. Are they beautiful? No! Where is the personality, the life experience? It's gone. Besides, you can spot an inflated breast a mile away.'

One year after issuing that stinging indictment of plastic surgery, Jane reportedly had the fat around her upper and lower eyelids removed by noted Beverly Hills plastic surgeon Dr Frank Kamer. According to published reports, six months later, in February 1987, she secretly went to Dr Norman Leaf to have her breasts enlarged with implants – the smallest available, designed to give her a small C-cup bra size.

Both operations were conducted on an out-patient basis in the doctors' surgeries. Jane, hiding behind sunglasses, furtively entered and left through side doors leading straight into private examining rooms. In both cases, Jane paid for the surgery with cheques made out for cash so they could not be traced to either doctor – $2500 for the eye surgery, $5000 for the breast implant surgery.

The breast surgery turned out to be considerably more uncomfortable than Jane had anticipated. Told she would not be able to exercise for a month following the surgery, Jane got up early on the morning of the operation and did a particularly strenuous workout.

Jane was given general anaesthesia, and after two hours in surgery, spent another three in the recovery room. During one of the house calls he made to keep an eye on her recovery, Dr Leaf apparently discovered several cysts that had developed in her breasts. They had to be drained twice.

Jane made her first public appearance following the operation at the March 1987 Oscar ceremonies. Although it was not noticeable, her left breast was slightly higher than the other – a common development – and she returned to Dr Leaf in July to have it corrected.

While Jane was reportedly being resculpted by her plastic surgeon, Tom was doing research for his autobiography with his first wife, Casey. To relive some of the moments they shared during the civil-rights movement in the early 1960s, the former spouses travelled together throughout Mississippi. 'I know her,' Jane said of Casey, 'so I felt okay about it – although you know when he calls me and he says they've checked into a motel together and says they asked for separate rooms, part of me is saying, "Yeah, sure."'

It was during work on his book, *Reunion*, in fact, that Tom shared his feelings of foreboding with Jane. 'He became convinced that no sooner would he write the book,' said Jane, 'than our family would fall apart – that by going out on a limb and ending the book on a happy note it couldn't stay that way. Everything was going to fall apart. He talked about that *a lot*, but it's *not* going to happen.'

Jane got her first chance to show off her new bustline on the big screen in her next film, *Old Gringo*. Jane and Bruce Gilbert had decided to dissolve their partnership in 1986, and *Old Gringo* was the first film produced by Jane's new company Fonda Films.

Like her IPC projects, this one had taken years to get off the ground. It began, Jane recalls, 'when I went to Mexico for the very first time in 1980 and was struck by this common border shared by the richest country in the world – well, it was then – and one of the poorest countries. I was only there for ten days, but I was very, very moved by the history we shared.'

By chance, when she returned to the ranch in Santa Barbara, her husband was playing host to Mexican novelist Carlos Fuentes. 'I told him I wanted very much to do a movie about our two countries, and he told me about this book he was writing called *Frontiers*.' She asked Fuentes to send her the manuscript when it was finished.

Jane was still making *On Golden Pond* in New Hampshire when the manuscript, now called *El Gringo Viejo (The Old Gringo)* arrived. It was about an American schoolteacher who finds herself caught up in the Mexican Revolution and the lives of two men – famed American journalist Ambrose Bierce and a fictional character, a young firebrand in Pancho Villa's army. 'It was very complicated – you know, what is dream and what is reality? It was not linear, but I wanted to do it.'

One of the stumbling blocks was coming up with a decent script. After several tries by other writers, she turned to husband–wife novelists John

Gregory Dunne and Joan Didion. Jane, made bottom-line-conscious by her Workout experience, asked the writers to take a pay cut. 'You know,' Jane told them, 'on this kind of movie, everybody will have to take a cut in price.' They refused. 'Whenever they talk that way about everybody taking a cut in price,' said Dunne, 'they mean that the writers will have to take a cut in price. If the movie gets made, nobody else takes a cut. So we said we would do it for free – for the Writers Guild scale – with a huge payoff later if the picture got made.'

The next major hurdle was casting. For the role of Tomas Arroyo, the headstrong young general, Jane, her partner Lois Bonfiglio, and director Luis Puenzo spent months auditioning young actors until they decided on Jimmy Smits, who had just emerged as a major new television star during the first season of 'LA Law' on NBC.

Then came the role of the Old Gringo himself. The aspect of the story that most appealed to Jane was the father – daughter-like relationship between her character and Bierce. 'All you have to do,' says Jane, 'is say the word "dad" and I start to cry. As you can imagine, it's always been an emotionally charged subject for me.'

Fonda first cast Burt Lancaster as Bierce. But just before filming was to begin in early 1988, Lancaster, who had successfully undergone open-heart surgery, was terminated. He was reportedly deemed a poor risk by the studio's insurance company, which worried that the high altitude of the Mexican location (7000 feet above sea level) might prove too hazardous for him.

Lancaster's replacement was Gregory Peck. At the time Peck's career had spanned fifty years and more than fifty films, including *Spellbound*, *The Yearling*, *Gentlemen's Agreement*, *Twelve O'Clock High*, *Moby Dick*, *To Kill a Mockingbird* (for which he won an Oscar), *The Omen* and *The Boys from Brazil*. But it had been seven years since his last film, and Peck, now seventy-two, was grateful to Fonda for the chance to work in a major production. 'I'd look around at all the hundreds of people on the set in Mexico,' he recalls, 'and then look at Jane and think to myself, God, this girl is the reason we are all here. It all rests on her slender shoulders.'

Peck was in awe of Jane's perfectionism; she had spent days working over their one screen kiss. It may have been the same fanaticism that had marked her other endeavours, but, says Peck, it was a 'benevolent fanaticism'.

'Both were real gentlemen,' Fonda says of her co-stars in *Old Gringo*. 'I mean *gentle* men – professional, generous, kind, funny. No ego hang-ups.' Although she admits that Peck's acting 'looks seamless, almost effortless' on the screen, the legendary star was as 'hungry, driven, and passionate as any young actor' during filming.

As for Smits, Fonda admits to being 'absolutely blown away. Jimmy is awesome. It was clear from the first scene that this guy has got it. Stardom has a lot to do with sexuality, and, barring some career mistakes, he is going to be a very big star. He is very, very sexy.'

Rumours began to circulate that Fonda's interest in Smits was more than professional – they were quickly linked in the tabloids as a duo off the set. When Tom heard the stories, he flew down to Mexico unannounced. Jane, according to witnesses, was furious. At this time, Jane was in the midst of her crisis over the screen kiss with Gregory Peck. 'We were supposed to finish the scene on Saturday, and we didn't,' she says. 'There was something wrong, and we didn't know what. So we held over until Monday – and I had my nervous breakdown on the weekend. My husband was there, and it's so hard when husbands come . . . I cried all night . . . ' In retrospect, Jane's 'nervous breakdown' on the set of Old Gringo had more to do with her slowly disintegrating marriage.

While Jane faced the challenge of playing a spinster in Old Gringo ('A thirty-five-year-old virgin – how's that for a stretch?') and pondered the state of her personal life, the tempest over her film with Robert De Niro was brewing in New England.

By April, attention focused on the strongest anti-Fonda protests, centred in Waterbury. After her carefully worded and limited prime-time apology to Vietnam veterans and their families during the Barbara Walters interview on ABC's '20/20', a secret meeting with the veterans, and a local appearance at a fund-raiser for the handicapped children of victims of Agent Orange, the path seemed clear for Jane to begin filming in the summer.

Clad in an olive jumpsuit and shouting orders through a megaphone, Stanley and Iris director Martin Ritt had already rehearsed 70 extras by the time Jane arrived in Waterbury, Connecticut, to film her first scene on 26 July 1988. The set was the old Waterbury Companies brass factory at South Main and Washington streets, which had been transformed into the fictitious Nevins & Davis Bakery, 'established in 1923' and 'Home of the Johnny Joy Trademark'.

That first day of shooting, more than a thousand people pressed against police lines and barricades to catch a glimpse of Fonda and Robert De Niro doing take after retake in the baking midsummer heat. Lost in the large crowd that first day were thirty or so hard-core demonstrators, including Guy Russo, who had not agreed to drop their protest in exchange for Fonda's agreement to stage a benefit for victims of Agent Orange. But as the crowds of the curious dwindled and eventually vanished, these were the people who remained to taunt Fonda throughout the filming. One afternoon, a black stretch limousine pulled up at the edge of the set, and out climbed Cher and her then-boyfriend, bagel maker Rob Camilletti, coming to pay a visit to Fonda. They were careful not to react to the demonstrators across the street chanting 'Traitor', or to the placards proclaiming HANOI JANE and YOUR FATHER WAS ASHAMED OF YOU AND SO ARE WE.

It was a different scene one sweltering Saturday night at nearby Quassy Amusement Park, when a crowd of 2500 gathered for Fonda's promised 'Evening of Stars' Agent Orange benefit, organised by a group called Veterans Who Care. Fans waited for over an hour and paid $15 to have their picture taken with both Fonda and De Niro. 'Many veterans are suffering from Agent Orange-related illnesses,' Jane told the crowd. 'This event is a little bit like a dream come true. From the bottom of my heart I want to thank Veterans Who Care.' By the evening's end, the event had raised more than $10,000.

Stanley and Iris finished filming in late August, and Fonda boarded the first flight out of Hartford's Bradley International Airport for Los Angeles. She would clandestinely return to Waterbury several months later, staying just a few hours to film a brief exterior scene. For the time being at least, Fonda could look upon her days in Connecticut as a personal triumph. The spectre of wartime disloyalty had loomed more prominently than since the mid-1970s, and she had still managed to win over many of her critics. In the process, Jane devoutly hoped, she had put the matter to rest once and for all – without ever having to say that her visit to Hanoi was wrong, or that she should not have made those radio broadcasts.

But then, on 26 August, 13,400 delegates, representing more than two million veterans, attended the 89th annual Veterans of Foreign Wars convention in Chicago, and by a unanimous voice vote passed three separate resolutions condemning *Stanley and Iris*, urging an investigation into Fonda's 'many treasonable actions' during the Vietnam War, and calling on Congress to try her for treason.

For Jane Fonda, as for the veterans who still hated her, the war was not yet over.

The political fallout from the 'Hanoi Jane' protests came at a bad time for Tom Hayden. With his hands full promoting *Reunion*, running for re-election to a fifth term in the Assembly, and campaigning for Democratic presidential hopeful Michael Dukakis, he was now also constantly being put in the position of defending actions he and Jane had taken fifteen years earlier. In one instance, an angry Hayden confronted South Vietnamese protesters outside his home with a baseball bat. Most of the time, however, he and Jane merely shrugged off the protests and pickets that inevitably materialised at any pre-announced public function.

Before the start of filming on *Stanley and Iris*, Jane had been honoured at a Jewish temple for getting 'refusenik' Ida Nudel out of the Soviet Union.

Hayden, in the midst of his re-election campaign and determined to maintain his close ties with Los Angeles's Jewish Community, was on hand to share the spotlight. It was Hayden's political director, Havi Scheindlin, who had engineered Jane's involvement in the refusenik case. 'It's been an extraordinary experience for me,' Jane said in her acceptance speech, 'and when I got involved, I was told what to do and I did it . . . Havi said, "Go to the Soviet consul and say if you don't let her out *I'm* going [to Moscow]" . . . and I didn't want to go. But I had to go.' After claiming that she did not deserve the award, Jane pledged, 'I'm yours forever.' An elaborate tape shown at the ceremonies, featuring tributes from co-stars, political admirers, and famous friends, was then copied for distribution to the press.

Given the continuing controversy about her Hanoi time, Jane maintained a surprisingly high political profile. She and Tom continued to be the chief backers of Network, the Hollywood political action group whose members included such Brat Packers as Ally Sheedy, Judd Nelson, and Demi Moore. Jane was particularly taken with Rob Lowe. 'He's a phenomenon,' she said, 'much like a young Frank Sinatra in the way he works the women in the audience.' (Hayden and Lowe conferred at the Democratic National Convention in Atlanta at about the same time Lowe was making videotapes of himself having sex with minors.)

Vanessa had also become active, in a way that was scarcely designed to win her mother new admirers. At the height of the Waterbury imbroglio, Vanessa travelled to Nicaragua, where she spent her summer working as a volunteer hauling plywood at a construction project – all with her mother's blessing. 'I expected a lot of military protocol,' said Vanessa, 'but the leader, Daniel Ortega, drives his own Jeep. Could you imagine President Reagan driving his own car around Washington?

'I never felt threatened at all,' she continued. 'The people who live there, however, live in constant fear of being invaded by Americans.' Vanessa stressed that her trip did not necessarily imply that she supported Ortega's Marxist Sandinista government, but comparisons to her mother's Hanoi journey were inevitable.

The Waterbury movie was completed on schedule – though that small band of picketers was on hand to protest on every day of shooting. 'People need scapegoats to focus their hatred and their venom on because they are angry,' says Jane. 'The fact that I'm a lightning rod saddens me, but I understand it. How can *they* be expected to put the war to rest when I can't?'

For Fonda, *Stanley and Iris* was also memorable because it gave her the chance to work opposite two-time Academy Award-winner Robert De Niro. 'Bobby was one of my father's favourite actors, and after working with him I understood why,' she says. 'They both have the same quiet integrity on the screen. It's very, very pure.'

Director Martin Ritt, Jane's friend, had first approached her with the story of a factory worker who teaches an illiterate man how to read. 'I wanted to work with Marty, and I loved the chance to play a working-class woman,' she says. 'It's a romantic story. He's a grown man – very intelligent, very good-looking – and he can't read. I have to get him' – puckering her lips seductively – 'to wrap his mouth around words like "bird" and "woman". To me there's something very sexy about that.'

Stanley and Iris – in the tradition of Fonda films such as *Coming Home*, *The China Syndrome* and *Nine to Five* – also presents a pressing issue in a commercial way. 'This story', she says, 'deals with an enormous social problem and it does it without being preachy. It can't be a polemic, or people won't come.'

As Jane was putting the finishing touches to both *Old Gringo* and *Stanley and Iris*, Tom hitched his wagon to the political star of Massachusetts governor Michael Dukakis. During the campaign, he was linked in the tabloids with actresses Morgan Fairchild and Margot Kidder – both Dukakis supporters and longstanding Hayden friends. More credible was the story that Hayden had fallen for Vicky Rideout, a Harvard-educated Dukakis speechwriter twenty years Jane's junior.

News of the Rideout liaison hit Jane particularly hard; after a bitter confrontation, the Haydens separated in December 1988, after seventeen years together. They managed to keep it out of the papers for three months. 'I don't believe either one of them was completely faithful,' observes a longtime associate, 'but the break-up of the political partnership surprised me.' Says another: 'They were the king and queen with their royal court; they both played to that. They'd both just been famous for so long.'

Jealousy was only one of several factors leading to the Fonda–Hayden split. In 1988, Jane had effectively taken Campaign California off the Workout dole, resuming all control of the millions generated by her fitness empire. The grass-roots operation would, for the first time, be forced to survive with grass-roots support.

Meanwhile Hayden, his eye now on the newly created office of California state insurance commissioner, was weighing a secret poll that showed negative feelings about Jane were hurting Tom's popularity with voters. This, needless to say, did not sit well with Jane. The weekend following the announcement of their separation, she chartered a private jet to fly her, Troy, and a high-school friend to Sun Valley, Idaho. There, between occasional forays to the slopes, she holed up in the Pervis House, a three-bedroom, $300-per-night lodge where only weeks earlier Barbra Streisand had stayed while getting over her romance with actor Don Johnson.

In April 1989, Jane and Tom met secretly in Los Angeles to try to hammer out a divorce settlement. Earning just $40,816 a year, Hayden's holdings were not at issue. Under California's community property laws, however, he stood to walk away with half of Jane's fortune. In 1988, according to *Forbes* magazine, Jane made an estimated $20 million. As for her assets, they included Fonda Films (worth around $40 million in 1989), the couple's Santa Monica house ($2.5 million), a prize Arab stallion, the Laurel Springs ranch and spa at Santa Barbara (another $8 million, not counting income from a spa operating on the property and charging clients $2500 per week), and the fitness empire that netted $35 million annually from videos, books, audiotapes, and records.

Jane's initial offer to Tom – $1 million in cash and $1000 a month alimony – was rejected out of hand. When Jane argued that she had poured at least $10 million into her husband's lack-lustre political career over the years, his lawyers countered that that had been merely a gift between spouses and did not figure in a joint property settlement under California law.

The tabloids then reported that Hayden threatened to expose Jane's less-than-generous management style. She had, for example, been reluctant to offer raises to employees at the Workout studios. She also paid performers in her exercise videos the minimum wage, arguing that they should be happy to get the exposure. Her multimillion-dollar stock portfolio, if made public, might also have proved embarrassing to the anti-corporate crusader; she reportedly has large holdings in such companies as Du Pont and IBM. To determine the exact size of her fortune, Hayden hired an outside investigator.

In return, Jane reportedly promised to expose details of Hayden's past marijuana use and extramarital carousing – behaviour that could deal a blow to any further political aspirations. The session ended in a shouting match, with Jane storming out.

Attorney Richard Rosenthal was not surprised that it should all come down to money. Rosenthal filed a lawsuit against Jane claiming that she had cheated him out of $2 million. He claimed that they'd agreed he would receive 10 per cent of any projects begun while he served as her attorney, including *On Golden Pond*. He later charged that falsified documents were produced to discredit his claim, but eventually lost the case.

'The obvious mendacity of the woman is amazing,' Rosenthal says. 'I was her father's lawyer and her lawyer and business manager from 1968 to 1980, and she claimed that she never even knew I was an attorney! I was her champion, but she has now become the very thing she once fought against. In her case, there is always a high-minded purpose to cover the basest of schemes.'

After their separation, Tom took up full-time residence in Sacramento, where he planned his 1992 bid for the Senate seat occupied since 1969 by Alan

Cranston. Jane, meanwhile, continued to live in Santa Monica. Fonda's unprepossessing home, located one block from the beach and hidden from the street by a ten-foot-high hedge, is as eclectic as its owner. From the outside, the look is traditional: the lush grounds are overgrown with willows, rosebushes, and a towering white-barked eucalyptus she claims is, in terms of the trunk's circumference, the largest in the West. With its chimneys and slanting shingle roof, the house itself resembles a quaint English country cottage. In the garden, a hutch full of rabbits vies for attention with Fonda's frisky golden retriever, Spencer; Taxi the black labrador (who was once dognapped and then used in a series of robberies); and the family mutt, Scott.

Step inside and the ambience is, as Fonda puts it, 'Spanish mixed with California contemporary'. From a wall above the staircase, four striking Andy Warhol portraits of Jane stare out over the cavernous living room, with its skylights, soaring twenty-foot-high ceilings, white stucco walls and exposed timbers. Navajo rugs cover the bare wooden floors, and huge glass bowls spill over with fresh-cut flowers from the garden (Fonda employs a gardener and a live-in housekeeper).

The house is entirely solar heated ('We had trouble getting a building permit because we didn't have a heater'). There is no air conditioning – another luxury Fonda opposes on environmental grounds – and as a result the house is uncomfortably warm throughout the summer.

On a huge Parsons table are dozens of silver-framed photographs: of Vanessa at twenty; of Troy at sixteen; of Jane hamming it up with her *Nine to Five* co-stars Dolly Parton and Lily Tomlin; of Jane with her dad, and with Hayden and Polish Solidarity leader Lech Walesa. Another, even more arresting, memento of Fonda's political activism rests against one wall – a large portrait of farm labour leader Cesar Chavez against a backdrop of human skulls. At the head of the stairs, there is another reminder of the woman who lives here: an elegant carved-oak bureau piled high with running shoes.

Jane's continuing commitment to fitness may have saved her life in June 1989. During a hiking trip through Sequoia National Forest with Femmy DeLyser, the writer of Jane's last two fitness books, Fonda decided to forge ahead of DeLyser. 'I said, 'Follow me,' recalls Jane, 'and then took off – eight miles in the wrong direction with no food and no water.'

Jane was missing for some thirty hours before she was spotted and picked up by helicopter. 'It was a peak experience,' she said a couple of months later, curling up on the floor to show how she kept herself warm using only a thin thermal foil emergency blanket as overnight temperatures dipped below 40°F. 'I had always wondered how I'd behave if left to my own devices in the wilderness, and now I had the chance to find out. One way I kept calm was to imagine all my friends who would become hysterical in the same situation. Somehow that was reassuring. Now I know why I've been working out all these years – to be strong enough to get through something like that.'

Still, she remains concerned that her fitness-guru persona has begun to eclipse her acting career. 'My God, I thought, is this going to destroy my being thought of as an actress? You know what? No problem. Depending on who you are, I am a mature woman, a political activist, an athlete, an actress, a producer. God, come to think of it, I'd better slow down!'

As always, her work sustains her. Jane's two Oscars are nowhere in evidence among the memorabilia in her living room. They are enshrined – along with her Emmy for *The Dollmaker*, three People's Choice awards, several Golden Globes, and a wall of platinum records and awards from the video industry – in her office eight blocks away. With its floral chintz chairs, pink marble conference table, and mauve walls, Jane's office seems more suited to an interior designer than to one of Hollywood's most notorious rebels.

Yet Fonda concedes that her divorce from Hayden has been one of the most traumatic events in her life. 'To pretend that the ending of a seventeen-year marriage is not painful is to betray reality,' she concedes, pausing to weigh her words. 'I've never felt this kind of pain. It leaves you raw, vulnerable. Now, when you're faced with something that painful, you have two choices: you can go down, go under – just cave in out of fear of what it means to be single again – or you can say this is an opportunity to open doors that I've never even thought of opening in my life.'

To sort out her feelings, Jane returned to the analyst's couch. 'I've been working on myself,' she says. 'I never thought I'd see the day when I was "off to see my therapist". It's so Hollywood,' she notes wryly, apparently forgetting that she spent years in therapy and once publicly urged her father to see a psychiatrist.

Occasionally, she retreats to Laurel Springs Ranch in Santa Barbara. The property still encompasses Fonda's pricey, no-frills spa and the camp she and Hayden established for LA-area children. 'The air is something,' she sighs. 'I could stay there for months.'

Not that she is likely to find the time. On most days in Santa Monica, Fonda gets up at around six, has a light breakfast (usually cereal), and heads for her production company. Following the October 1989 release of *Old Gringo* (which proved to be a critical and commercial disappointment) and the more warmly received *Stanley and Iris* in early 1990, Jane has been zeroing in on two new projects: an English-language remake of the Spanish film *Women on the Verge of a Nervous Breakdown*, and the screen version of Neil Sheehan's best-seller about Vietnam, *A Bright Shining Lie* (which she would produce but not star in). She has also made plans to team up again with Dolly Parton and Lily Tomlin for a comedy called *Jury Duty*.

The key to success, Fonda insists, is happiness in one's personal life. 'If you're not happy there, it shows up everywhere else. Contrary to belief, I am not Wonder Woman. I lack confidence. I am vulnerable. But', she adds, 'I am also resilient, definitely a survivor.'

She hopes she has passed along these qualities to her children. Fonda describes Vanessa as 'intense, intellectual, analytical, independent, extremely forceful but emotional, too'. Conversely, she sees Troy, seventeen in 1990, as 'mellow, easygoing, and very funny'. Having been both the child of a famous parent and a famous parent herself, Fonda is sensitive to the unique pressures brought to bear on a celebrity's children. 'Some movie stars' kids are brought up to believe that "Oh my God, we've got to protect this national monument, this perfect human being," and you as the child know it ain't so. So I've tried to demystify the whole thing, to let my kids see my faults and insecurities. Not that I'm somebody everyone idolises, mind you. Vanessa and Troy have got all my baggage to lug around – the political controversy, the movie stardom, the Workout stuff.'

The divorce has not made things easier. 'Going through a divorce, to what extent do you allow your pain to be visible to a child?' she asks rhetorically. 'I'm not going to demolish the feelings they have for their father. No way. When you're really hurting, there's a tendency to do and say all kinds of things about the other parent. I'm a very stable person, but I was in agony when I realised how easy it would be to use the children as weapons. Oh, my Lord, what is going on? What are we doing to our children? As a parent, I have got to put the children first, to turn this trauma into something bearable and positive. I had to get well not only for myself but for my children.'

Even before she formally filed for divorce, Jane maintained that her children were benefiting from the split. 'It's like living with an alcoholic, where there's a problem but nobody's talking about it, where you are constantly waiting for the other shoe to drop. Sometimes it's better for the shoe to drop, if afterwards the child realises, "Hey, I'm not going to slip through the cracks. I still have a mother and father, and they still love me."' Troy, who divides his time between his father's apartment and the Santa Monica house, has "blossomed", says Jane, 'and I think it's because he's seen that I'm happier and his father is happier'.

Jane bristles at the notion that she may have to give up custody of her causes to Hayden. 'I was a political woman before I met Tom,' she says. 'I'll just be my own person now. My gut-level attraction is to grass-roots organisations rather than Democratic party politics. I don't want to lose my idealism. After seeing it from the perspective of a politician's wife,' she adds in a quick yet obvious swipe at Hayden, 'I'm more convinced than ever that citizens have got to do it themselves – politicians won't do anything unless they're pressured.' Even since the split, Fonda has remained on the steering committee of Campaign California, which Hayden chairs.

By the autumn of 1989, Jane had presented Tom with a take-it-or-leave-it offer of $5 million in cash. While he mulled it over, she wasted no time getting back into circulation. After dating handsome blond hairdresser Barron Matalon and Atlanta-based cable television mogul Ted Turner, Jane unveiled her new shape at a topless beach in the Caribbean. At the island resort of St Bart's, she was also photographed frolicking with the man she now described as 'my boyfriend', 35-year-old actor Lorenzo Caccialanza.

When *Old Gringo* had its star-studded première at New York's Ziegfeld Theater in early October, Jane was escorted by Caccialanza. Hours later, she found herself coping not only with negative reviews for the film but also with an unexpected family crisis. After a scuffle with police on New York's Lower East Side the morning after the première, Vanessa was arrested outside a heroin shooting gallery. When police tried to arrest her boyfriend, New York University student Thomas Feegal, for possession of heroin, sale of heroin, and possession of a hypodermic needle, Vanessa stepped in. 'She was abusive and she interfered with the arrest,' said Narcotics Captain Stephen Nasta. Vanessa was charged with loitering for the purpose of buying drugs, obstructing police officers, and disorderly conduct.

NARCS BUST FONDA'S KID screamed the full-page headline on the next morning's *New York Daily News*. The *Post* blared, JANE FONDA'S DAUGHTER IN DRUG BUST, and showed a front-page photograph of Vanessa in chains as she waited with other suspects to be booked. 'The whole thing is really sad,' said Captain Nasta. 'These are affluent people who should have everything going for them, and they come down here to shoot down their lives like this.'

Prophetically, Jane had earlier admitted to imagining 'worst-case scenarios' as Vanessa grew up: 'In spite of my best efforts, I'm a lousy parent, my daughter hates me, she's going to run away, become a drug addict, refuse to go to school.' The day of Vanessa's arrest, Jane cancelled her tour to promote *Old Gringo* in Europe and issued a terse statement: 'Vanessa is a good daughter and a serious student of whom I am very proud. And I stand behind her.' Jane, whose behaviour had caused her father so many uncomfortable moments, now found herself on the receiving end as a parent.

For Jane, Vanessa's arrest outside a drug den was only one more private crisis lived out in full public view. (The court agreed to drop the charges if Vanessa performed three months of community service and kept out of trouble for six months.) Not long after, Troy was arrested with seven other teenage boys on charges of vandalising phone booths and covering a car park with graffiti.

Meanwhile, Tom — not Jane — took the first formal step towards ending their marriage, filing for divorce on 1 December 1989. Jane countersued two weeks later. Under the terms of their agreement, Jane was awarded legal custody of Troy. Hayden, according to one source, received close to $10 million. By her 52nd birthday (21 December 1989), Jane seemed ready to begin again.

'I'm not as macho as several years before,' she said. 'In the old days I was very driven. Now I'm striving hard to control compulsive tendencies.'

It is not going to be easy. It never has been for Henry Fonda's passionate daughter, one of the most complex and controversial personalities of our time. From sparkling ingenue to sex symbol to revolutionary to fitness guru to chief executive to respected actress-producer, she has experienced more incarnations than any other public woman in memory.

Few individuals have inspired such extremes of opinion – from adulation to contempt – and that remarkable range of public regard mirrors the complex of paradoxes one faces in trying to sum her up.

From the day 'Lady Jane' arrived, her life has been a mind-spinning tangle of conflicts and contradictions. She is the tousle-haired sex symbol who went on to champion feminism; the Miss Army Recruiting of 1962 who rooted for the enemy during the Vietnam War; the chain-smoking, pill-popping bulimic who became the world's leading health and fitness advocate; the outspoken critic of cosmetic surgery who herself underwent eye lifts and breast implants; and, most jarringly, the virulent anti-capitalist who became a bottom-line-obsessed business mogul worth more than $60 million.

Over the years, each of Jane's causes and careers has evolved to fill a specific need in her life. (Facing the 1990s, Jane has hinted that she might embark on yet another crusade – this time as a sort of money-management guru for a whole new generation of working women.) From childhood, she craved attention – first from her mother, whose own demons made it impossible to love her daughter, and then from her father. Clearly, Jane's relationship with her father – a man adored by his daughter no less than by his public, and in personal terms remaining as remote as any other screen idol – was the most important in her life. Needing more affection and guidance than her father was able to give her, Jane sought both from a succession of men, at once both mentors and lovers. In the process, she finally gained her father's attention, even if it had to be to the point of outrage. Voutsinas, Vadim, Hayden – each would exert a profound influence on Jane for a time, and each would be discarded as Jane's focus changed.

Jane has been no less driven by her need for control. Roger Vadim has pointed out that, even when it came to mundane domestic matters, Jane was 'frighteningly efficient'. Once shed of her sex-object Barbarella image, Jane took complete charge of her political activities, her film role, and in time her far-flung business interests.

It may be difficult to pinpoint what makes Jane run, but run she has, from one commitment to another – movie projects, political and social causes, business enterprises – her public persona changing along the way like the protective colouring of a chameleon. Continually Jane has recharted her course, rechannelled her energies, reset her vectors. Yet she has also shown an ability to focus her energies with laserlike precision. From this ability to concentrate on many different things and do them all well, she has derived her power, a power that, according to those close to her, she guards jealously.

When trying to figure out Jane's motivation, one has to return to her complicated love–hate relationship with Henry. As with most women – perhaps more intensely for this innately intense woman – it was that father–daughter dynamic that taught Jane what to expect of men. For all their obvious differences, the men in Jane's life all exerted over her a degree of control her father never could (and never sought to) exercise. Initially, at least, she would defer to each of them, until her focus shifted and, with it, her allegiance. It may be more than passing coincidence that Jane's marriage to Tom Hayden, the lover most pervasively influential over her life, began to sour soon after Henry's death. Whether her father's death has freed Jane from all need for a male mentor remains to be seen. Perhaps now she will merely seek out another man – a significantly younger one this time – whom *she* can control.

However one tries to analyse Jane Fonda, what emerges from all these conflicting images is an American marvel. As an actress-producer, she is arguably the most powerful woman in the motion picture industry. She is incontrovertibly one of the wealthiest in the entire entertainment world, with an annual income of more than $20 million. She is also widely regarded as the founder of the home video industry, one of the world's most commercially successful authors, and the single most controversial figure Hollywood has ever produced.

Who is Jane Fonda, really? It is a question generations will debate. On one thing Citizen Jane's admirers and detractors can agree: if her life were a movie script, it would never get produced. Nobody would believe it.

Jane Fonda's Academy Awards and Nominations

(In each case, the winner is in italics)

1969 BEST ACTRESS NOMINEES

Geneviève Bujold *(Anne of the Thousand Days)*
Jane Fonda *(They Shoot Horses, Don't They?)*
Liza Minnelli *(The Sterile Cuckoo)*
Jean Simmons *(The Happy Ending)*
Maggie Smith (The Prime of Miss Jean Brodie)

1971 BEST ACTRESS NOMINEES

Julie Christie *(McCabe and Mrs Miller)*
Jane Fonda (Klute)
Glenda Jackson *(Sunday, Bloody Sunday)*
Vanessa Redgrave *(Mary, Queen of Scots)*
Janet Suzman *(Nicholas and Alexandra)*

1977 BEST ACTRESS NOMINEES

Anne Bancroft *(The Turning Point)*
Jane Fonda *(Julia)*
Diane Keaton (Annie Hall)
Shirley MacLaine *(The Turning Point)*
Marsha Mason *(The Goodbye Girl)*

1978 BEST ACTRESS NOMINEES

Ingrid Bergman *(Autumn Sonata)*
Ellen Burstyn *(Same Time, Next Year)*
Jill Clayburgh *(An Unmarried Woman)*
Jane Fonda (Coming Home)

1979 BEST ACTRESS NOMINEES

Jill Clayburgh *(Starting Over)*
Sally Field (Norma Rae)
Jane Fonda *(The China Syndrome)*
Marsha Mason *(Chapter Two)*
Bette Midler *(The Rose)*

1981 BEST SUPPORTING ACTRESS NOMINEES

Melinda Dillon *(Absence of Malice)*
Jane Fonda *(On Golden Pond)*
Joan Hackett *(Only When I Laugh)*
Elizabeth McGovern *(Ragtime)*
Maureen Stapleton (Reds)

1986 BEST ACTRESS NOMINEES

Jane Fonda *(The Morning After)*
Marlee Matlin (Children of a Lesser God)
Sissy Spacek *(Crimes of the Heart)*
Kathleen Turner *(Peggy Sue Got Married)*
Sigourney Weaver *(Aliens)*

Film Chronology

TALL STORY (Warner Bros, 1960)
Based on the novel *The Homecoming Game* by Howard Nemerov and the play *Tall Story* by Howard Lindsay and Russel Crouse.
Principal cast: Jane Fonda, Anthony Perkins, Marc Connelly, Ray Walston, Murray Hamilton, Anne Jackson, Tom Laughlin.
Produced and directed by Joshua Logan. Screenplay by J. J. Epstein.

WALK ON THE WILD SIDE (Columbia, 1962)
Based on the novel by Nelson Algren.
Principal cast: Jane Fonda, Laurence Harvey, Capucine, Barbara Stanwyck, Anne Baxter.
Produced by Charles K. Feldman. Directed by Edward Dmytryk.
Screenplay by John Fante and Edmund Morris.

THE CHAPMAN REPORT (Warner Bros, 1962)
Based on the novel by Irving Wallace.
Principal cast: Jane Fonda, Claire Bloom, Efrem Zimbalist, Jr, Shelley Winters, Glynis Johns, Cloris Leachman, Jack Cassidy, Ray Danton.
Produced by Richard D. Zanuck. Directed by George Cukor. Screenplay by Wyatt Cooper and Don M. Mankiewicz.

PERIOD OF ADJUSTMENT (MGM, 1962)
Based on the play by Tennessee Williams.
Principal cast: Jane Fonda, Jim Hutton, Tony Franciosa, Lois Nettleton, John McGiver, Jack Albertson.
Produced by Lawrence Weingarten. Directed by George Roy Hill.
Screenplay by Isobel Lennart.

IN THE COOL OF THE DAY (MGM, 1963)
Based on the novel by Susan Ertz.

Principal cast: Jane Fonda, Peter Finch, Arthur Hill, Angela Lansbury, Constance Cummings.
Produced by John Houseman. Directed by Robert Stevens. Screenplay by Meade Roberts.

SUNDAY IN NEW YORK (MGM, 1964)
Based on the play by Norman Krasna.
Principal cast: Jane Fonda, Rod Taylor, Cliff Robertson, Robert Culp, Jim Backus, Peter Nero, Jo Morrow.
Produced by Everett Freeman. Directed by Peter Tewksbury. Screenplay by Norman Krasna.

JOY HOUSE (MGM, 1964)
Principal cast: Jane Fonda, Alain Delon, Lola Albright.
Produced by Jacques Bar. Directed by René Clément. Screenplay by René Clément.

CIRCLE OF LOVE (Walter Reade-Sterling, 1965)
Based on the movie *La Ronde*, and the play *Reigen* by Arthur Schnitzler.
Principal cast: Jane Fonda, Maurice Ronet, Marie Dubois, Claude Giraud, Jean Sorel, Anna Karina, Catherine Spaak.
Produced by Robert and Raymond Hakim. Directed by Roger Vadim. Screenplay by Jean Anouilh.

CAT BALLOU (Columbia, 1965)
Based on the novel by Roy Chanslor.
Principal cast: Jane Fonda, Lee Marvin, Michael Callan, Dwayne Hickman, John Marley, Nat 'King' Cole, Stubby Kaye, Tom Nardini.
Produced by Harold Hecht. Directed by Elliot Silverstein. Screenplay by Walter Newman and Frank R. Pierson.

THE CHASE (Columbia, 1966)
Based on the novel and the play by Horton Foote.
Principal cast: Jane Fonda, Marlon Brando, Robert Redford, Angie Dickinson, James Fox, E. G. Marshall, Miriam Hopkins, Robert Duvall, Martha Hyer, Janice Rule.
Produced by Sam Spiegel. Directed by Arthur Penn. Screenplay by Lillian Hellman.

ANY WEDNESDAY (Warner Bros, 1966)
Based on the play by Muriel Resnick.
Principal cast: Jane Fonda, Dean Jones, Jason Robards, Rosemary Murphy.

Produced by Julius J. Epstein. Directed by Robert Ellis Miller. Screenplay by Julius J. Epstein.

THE GAME IS OVER (Royal-Marceau, 1966)
Based on the novel *La Curée* by Emile Zola.
Principal cast: Jane Fonda, Peter McEnery, Michel Piccoli, Tina Marquand.
Produced and directed by Roger Vadim. Screenplay by Jean Cau, Bernard Frechtman, and Roger Vadim.

HURRY SUNDOWN (Paramount, 1967)
Based on the novel by K. B. Gilden.
Principal cast: Jane Fonda, Michael Caine, Diahann Carroll, Faye Dunaway, John Phillip Law, Robert Hooks, Burgess Meredith, Madeleine Sherwood, George Kennedy, Jim Backus, Robert Reed.
Produced and directed by Otto Preminger. Screenplay by Horton Foote and Thomas C. Ryan.

BAREFOOT IN THE PARK (Paramount, 1967)
Based on the play by Neil Simon.
Principal cast: Jane Fonda, Robert Redford, Mildred Natwick, Charles Boyer, Herb Edelman, Sam Albertson.
Produced by Hal Wallis. Directed by Gene Saks. Screenplay by Neil Simon.

BARBARELLA (Paramount, 1968)
Based on the book by Jean-Claude Forest.
Principal cast: Jane Fonda, John Phillip Law, David Hemmings, Anita Pallenberg, Milo O'Shea, Claude Dauphin, Marcel Marceau.
Produced by Dino De Laurentiis. Directed by Roger Vadim. Screenplay by Terry Southern, Claude Brule, Jean-Claude Forest, Clement Wood, Tudor Gates, Villario Bonaceil, Brian Degas, and Roger Vadim.

SPIRITS OF THE DEAD (American International, 1969)
Based on stories by Edgar Allen Poe.
Principal cast: Jane Fonda, Peter Fonda, Brigitte Bardot, Alain Delon, Terence Stamp.
Produced by Les Films Marceau-Cocinor. Directed by Federico Fellini. Screenplay by Federico Fellini, Louis Malle, Roger Vadim, Bernardino Zapponi, and Daniel Boulanger.

THEY SHOOT HORSES, DON'T THEY? (Cinerama, 1969)
Based on the novel by Horace McCoy.

Principal cast: Jane Fonda, Michael Sarrazin, Gig Young, Susannah York, Red Buttons, Bruce Dern, Bonnie Bedelia.
Produced by Irwin Winkler and Robert Chartoff. Directed by Sydney Pollack. Screenplay by Robert E. Thompson.

KLUTE (Warner Bros, 1971)
Principal cast: Jane Fonda, Donald Sutherland, Roy Scheider, Charles Cioffi, Dorothy Tristan.
Produced and directed by Alan J. Pakula. Screenplay by Andy K. Lewis and Dave Lewis.

FTA (American International, 1972)
Principal cast: Jane Fonda, Donald Sutherland, Holly Near, Len Chandler.
Produced by Jane Fonda, Donald Sutherland, and Francine Parker. Directed by Francine Parker. Written by Jane Fonda, Donald Sutherland, Dalton Trumbo, Robin Menken, Rita Martinson, Michael Alaimo, Len Chandler, Pamela Donegan, and Holly Near.

STEELYARD BLUES (Warner Bros, 1972)
Principal cast: Jane Fonda, Donald Sutherland, Peter Boyle, Howard Hesseman.
Produced by Tony Bill and Michael and Julia Phillips. Directed by Alan Myerson. Screenplay by David S. Ward.

TOUT VA BIEN (NEW YORKER FILMS, 1973)
Principal cast: Jane Fonda, Yves Montand, Jean Pignol, Vittorio Caprioli.
Produced by Jean-Pierre Rassam. Directed by Jean-Luc Godard. Screenplay by Jean-Luc Godard and Jean-Pierre Gorin.

A DOLL'S HOUSE (Tomorrow Entertainment for ABC-TV, 1973)
Based on the play by Henrik Ibsen.
Principal cast: Jane Fonda, David Warner, Trevor Howard, Edward Fox, Delphine Seyrig.
Produced and directed by Joseph Losey. Screenplay by David Mercer.

INTRODUCTION TO THE ENEMY (IPC Films, 1974)
Documentary chronicling Jane Fonda's second trip to Vietnam.
By Jane Fonda, Tom Hayden, Haskell Wexler.

THE BLUEBIRD (Twentieth Century-Fox, 1976)
Based on the play by Maurice Maeterlinck.
Principal cast: Elizabeth Taylor, Jane Fonda, Ava Gardner, Cicely Tyson, Robert Morley, Will Geer, Mona Washbourne.

Produced by Paul Maslansky. Directed by George Cukor. Screenplay by Hugh Whitemore and Alfred Hayes.

FUN WITH DICK AND JANE (Columbia, 1977)
Principal cast: Jane Fonda, George Segal, Ed McMahon, Dick Gautier, Hank Garcia.
Produced by Peter Bart and Max Palevsky. Directed by Ted Kotcheff. Story by Gerald Gaiser. Screenplay by Jerry Belson, Mordecai Richler, and David Giler.

JULIA (Twentieth Century-Fox, 1977)
Based on the book *Pentimento* by Lillian Hellman.
Principal cast: Jane Fonda, Vanessa Redgrave, Jason Robards, Hal Holbrook, Maximilian Schell, Meryl Streep.
Produced by Richard Roth. Directed by Fred Zinnemann. Screenplay by Alvin Sargent.

COMING HOME (United Artists, 1978)
Principal cast: Jane Fonda, Jon Voight, Bruce Dern, Penelope Milford, Robert Carradine.
Produced by Jerome Hellman. Directed by Hal Ashby. Story by Nancy Dowd. Screenplay by Robert C. Jones and Waldo Salt.

COMES A HORSEMAN (United Artists, 1978)
Principal cast: Jane Fonda, James Caan, Jason Robards, George Grizzard, Richard Farnsworth.
Produced by Gene Kirkwood and Dan Paulson. Directed by Alan J. Pakula. Screenplay by Dennis Lynton Clark.

CALIFORNIA SUITE (Columbia, 1978)
Based on the play by Neil Simon.
Principal cast: Jane Fonda, Alan Alda, Bill Cosby, Michael Caine, Maggie Smith, Richard Pryor, Walter Matthau, Elaine May.
Produced by Ray Stark. Directed by Herbert Ross. Screenplay by Neil Simon.

THE CHINA SYNDROME (Columbia, 1979)
Principal cast: Jane Fonda, Jack Lemmon, Michael Douglas, James Hampton, Scott Brady, Peter Donat.
Produced by Michael Douglas. Directed by James Bridges. Screenplay by Mike Gray, T. S. Cook, and James Bridges.

THE ELECTRIC HORSEMAN (Columbia-Universal, 1979)
Principal cast: Robert Redford, Jane Fonda, Valerie Perrine, Willie Nelson, John Saxon.

Produced by Ray Stark. Directed by Sydney Pollack. Story by Shelly Burton, Paul Gaer, and Robert Garland. Screenplay by Robert Garland.

NINE TO FIVE (Twentieth Century-Fox, 1980)
Principal cast: Jane Fonda, Lily Tomlin, Dolly Parton, Dabney Coleman, Elizabeth Wilson, Sterling Hayden.
Produced by Bruce Gilbert. Directed by Colin Higgins. Story by Patricia Resnick. Screenplay by Patricia Resnick and Colin Higgins.

ON GOLDEN POND (ITC Films/IPC Films, 1981)
Based on the play by Ernest Thompson.
Principal cast: Katharine Hepburn, Henry Fonda, Jane Fonda, Dabney Coleman, Doug McKeon, William Lanteau.
Produced by Bruce Gilbert. Directed by Mark Rydell. Screenplay by Ernest Thompson.

ROLLOVER (Orion/IPC (Bruce Gilbert), 1981)
Principal cast: Jane Fonda, Kris Kristofferson, Hume Cronyn, Josef Sommer, Bob Gunton, Macon McCalmar, Ron Frazier.
Produced by Bruce Gilbert. Directed by Alan J. Pakula. Screenplay by David Shaber.

AGNES OF GOD (Columbia, 1985)
Based on the play by John Pielmeier.
Principal cast: Jane Fonda, Anne Bancroft, Meg Tilly.
Produced by Patrick Palmer and Norman Jewison. Directed by Norman Jewison. Screenplay by John Pielmeier.

THE MORNING AFTER (Lorimer Motion Pictures/American Filmworks, 1986)
Principal cast: Jane Fonda, Jeff Bridges, Raul Julia, Diane Salinger, Richard Foronjy, Geoffrey Scott.
Produced by Bruce Gilbert. Directed by Sidney Lumet. Screenplay by James Hicks.

OLD GRINGO (Columbia, 1989)
Based on the novel by Carlos Fuentes.
Principal cast: Jane Fonda, Gregory Peck, Jimmy Smits, Gabriella Roel, Pedro Armendariz, Jr.
Produced by Lois Bonfiglio. Directed by Luis Puenzo. Screenplay by Luis Puenzo and Aida Bortnik.

STANLEY AND IRIS (MGM, 1989)

Based on the novel *Union Street* by Pat Barker.

Principal cast: Jane Fonda, Robert De Niro, Swoosie Kurtz, Martha Plimpton.

Produced by Alex Winitsky and Arlene Sellers. Directed by Marty Ritt.

Screenplay by Irving Ravetch and Harriet Frank, Jr.

Work for Television

A STRING OF BEADS (NBC, 1961)
Based on a story by W. Somerset Maugham.
Principal cast: Jane Fonda, George Grizzard, Glenda Farrell, Roland Winters, Chester Morris.

FASCINATING WOMAN (segment of WNET's 'The Great American Dream Machine', 1973)

THE DOLLMAKER (ABC, 1985)
Based on the novel by Harriette Arnow.
Principal cast: Jane Fonda, Levon Helm, Susan Kingsley, Nick Cresswell.
Directed by Daniel Petrie.

Theatre Chronology

THE COUNTRY GIRL by Clifford Odets.
Omaha Community Theater, 1955.
Principal cast: Henry Fonda, Dorothy McGuire, Jane Fonda.

THERE WAS A LITTLE GIRL by Daniel Taradash.
Broadway, 1960.
Principal cast: Jane Fonda, Sean Garrison, Ruth Matteson.

INVITATION TO A MARCH by Arthur Laurents.
Broadway, 1960.
Principal cast: Jane Fonda, Eileen Heckart, Madeleine Sherwood, James MacArthur.

THE FUN COUPLE by Neil Jansen and John Haase.
Broadway, 1962.
Principal cast: Jane Fonda, Dyan Cannon, Bradford Dillman.

STRANGE INTERLUDE by Eugene O'Neill.
Broadway, 1963.
Principal cast: Geraldine Page, Ben Gazzara, Jane Fonda, Franchot Tone, Betty Field, Richard Thomas.

Notes

The following abbreviations are used in this section:

AMPAS	Academy of Motion Picture Arts and Sciences
AFI	American Film Institute
AP	Associated Press
CST	*Chicago Sun-Times*
CPD	*Cleveland Plain Dealer*
LAT	*Los Angeles Times*
LHE	*Los Angeles Herald Examiner*
LHJ	*Ladies Home Journal*
NYP	*New York Post*
NYT	*New York Times*
PI	Personal Interview
SEP	*Saturday Evening Post*
UPI	*United Press International*
VF	*Vanity Fair*
WP	*Washington Post*
WR	*Waterbury Republican*

Chapter 1

PAGE

1   'Being a movie star': PI.
3–4 'vigorously against her presence': WR, 24 Nov. 1987.
4   'Patriotism runs deep': AP, 23 Dec. 1987.
4   'I just watched': WR, 10 Mar. 1988.
4   'Thank you! Thank you!': *ibid.*
4   'Hooray for Waterbury': *ibid.*
4   'It's about time': *ibid.*
4–5 'If we are willing': *ibid.*
5   'We were supposed to finish': Rosenblum, 'Dangerous Jane', VF, Nov. 1988.
6   'a strong-willed patriotic American': WR, 17 Apr. 1988.
7   'Why do you think': interview with Barbara Walters on ABC's '20/20', 17 June 1988.
9   'more in the nature': Ben Wattenberg, syndicated column, 20 June 1988.
10   'To some of the guys': PI.
10   'This is what': PI.

Chapter 2

PAGE

11   'a Norman Rockwell childhood': PI.
11   'there were always': *ibid.*
12   'When I was about eleven': PI.
12   'All the while': PI.
12   'repulsive': Henry Fonda, *Fonda: My Life*, as told to Howard Teichmann, p. 29.
13   'Ricky': *ibid.*, p. 30.
13   'Shut up': PI.
14   'When this girl': Brooke Hayward, *Haywire*, pp. 184–5.
15   'the most loathsome': PI.
15   'I'd lean against the fence': Fonda, *My Life*, p. 65.
16   'I was visiting': *Time*, 16 Feb. 1970.
17   'was intoxicating': PI.
20   'straight from': PI.
20   MRS. F. S. BROKAW': NYT, 17 Sept. 1936.
21   'The Fondas went back': Hayward, p. 141.

23   'Frances was': *Time, ibid.*

24   'I was gardening': PI.

24   'Pancho was': Rosenblum.

26   'I always had': PI.

26   'got out and chased us': Hayward, p. 142.

27   'Hank could be': PI.

27   'We were all': PI.

28   'My father': Fonda, *My Life*, p. 168.

28   'Peter's childhood': PI.

28   'I didn't like': Fonda, *My Life*, p. 188.

28   'I used to look': PI.

Chapter 3

PAGE

30   'booted out': Fonda, *My Life*, p. 185.

31   'Our fathers': PI.

32   'We children would': Hayward, p. 237.

32   'We were eleven': PI.

34   'I didn't want': Vadim, *Bardot, Deneuve, Fonda*, p. 272.

34   'Oh, no': *ibid.*

35   'the only way': *Time*, 16 Feb. 1970.

Chapter 4

PAGE

36   'Hank can be rough': PI.

37   'everything I wanted': Fonda, *My Life*, p. 213.

38   'She put in': *ibid.* p. 219.

39   'the great leveller': PI.

40   'they said I would': PI.

40   'Jane was a leader': PI.

40   'I know': Rosenblum.

40   'Acting was': PI.

41   'he said "Thanks"': Vadim, *Bardot, Deneuve, Fonda*, p. 238.

41   'In one scene': Fonda, *My Life*, p. 239.

41   'pale, inquiring': *Time*, 16 Feb. 1970.

43   'She basically did': PI.

43 'socially promiscuous': PI.

43 'At Vassar': Rex Reed, 'Jane: Everybody Expected Me to Fall on My Face,' NYT, 25 Jan. 1970.

44 'And anyone': PI.

44 'But before I got': *Time*, *ibid.*

45 'I went to Paris': 'Three Faces of Fonda,' *Show Business Illustrated*, 28 Nov. 1961.

46 'Have you seen': Vadim, *Bardot, Deneuve, Fonda*, p. 209.

Chapter 5

PAGE

47 'For dessert': *Time*, 16 Feb. 1970.

47 'I bought Balenciagas': NYT, 25 Jan. 1970.

48 'When it came to thinking': *Newark Evening News*, 29 July 1960.

49 'Henry was warmth': PI.

49 'I could see': Alfred Aronowitz, 'Lady Jane', SEP, 23 Mar. 1963.

49 'she was with': *ibid.*

49 'My father would say': *ibid.*

49 'Finally one of the girls': Fonda, *My Life*, p. 265.

50 'I discovered': Rex Reed, NYT, 25 Jan. 1970.

Chapter 6

PAGE

53 'Attention, Hollywood!': Jack Gaver, UPI, 18 July 1959.

54 'It's wonderful': Hyman Goldberg, *New York Mirror*, 6 Sept. 1959.

54 'I was at': Leroy Arrons, WP News Service, 12 Aug. 1973.

55 'If you're Marilyn': Chicago Sunday *Tribune*, 11 Oct. 1959.

57 'I got consumed': Thomas Kiernan, *Jane: An Intimate Biography of Jane Fonda*, p. 117.

57 'I taught her': *ibid.*

58 'I'll murder anyone': AP, 15 Nov. 1959.

58 'I don't think you can': Tom Prideaux, *Life*, 22 Feb. 1960.

58 'I got so mad': *ibid.*

59 'There's a tremendous': Harry Harris, *Philadelphia Inquirer*, 5 Feb. 1961.

59 'I began to see': PI.

Chapter 7

60 'It was like the *Invasion*': PI.
61 'It took a lot of guts': New York *Herald Tribune*, 28 June 1960.
61 'I had her': *This Week*, 8 Jan. 1967.
61 'The minute I read it': *ibid.*
61 'There's a play': Sidney Fields, *New York Mirror*, 29 Aug. 1960.
61 'Hindrance?': *ibid.*
62 'In the beginning': UPI, 8 Nov. 1961.
62 'She got the part': *New York World Telegram*, 4 Feb. 1961.
62 'It made me feel': *ibid.*
62 'She was like someone': Hayward, p. 34.
63 'You're afraid': Aronowitz.
63 'Yeah, yeah. I always think': *ibid.*
64 'If Svengali': PI.
64 'Now she could': Kiernan, p. 131.
64 'Because I': AFI.
64 'You'd expect to find': Harry Harris, *Philadelphia Inquirer*, 5 Feb. 1961.
65 'Out of nerves': *ibid.*
65 'What I want to do': UPI, 8 Nov. 1961.
66 'There was a lot of stir': Hedda Hopper, *Chicago Tribune*, 6 July 1962.
66 'What a strange girl!': Michael Freedland, *Jane Fonda*, p. 63.
68 'All that baloney': Hopper, *ibid.*
68 'Cukor looked at me': LAT, 8 July 1962.
68 'it was George Cukor': *ibid.*
69 'Impeccable taste': *ibid.*, 26 Nov. 1962.
69 'extraordinarily impressed': *ibid.*
69 'an American original': Aronowitz.
69 'Now': NYT, 7 Oct. 1961.
70 'Don't mention Andreas': SEP, 23 Mar. 1963.
70 'Afterwards, I mean for': Kiernan, p. 141.
71 'Jane approached': PI.
71 'It was a great play': PI.

Chapter 8

74 'going to': Fonda, *My Life*, p. 287.
74 'I can't be that much': Aronowitz.

75 'Think of all the wonderful': Hopper, 8 July, 1962.

76 'Daddy': Vincent Canby, LAT, 1 July 1962.

76 'I'm between planes': SEP, 23 Mar. 1963.

76 'It was a time': *Time*, 16 Feb. 1970.

76 'I was a registered Republican': *ibid.*

77 'I could bite': Canby, *ibid.*

77 'Jane was simply great': *ibid.*

77 'I've just discovered': *New York Journal-American*, 3 June 1963.

77 'That son-of-a-bitch': Fonda, *My Life*, p. 288.

78 'But shortly before the party': Winters, pp. 470–1.

78 'So I guess': Jesse Zunser, *Cue*, 29 Feb. 1964.

78 'Who said anything': *ibid.*

78 'a consummate tease': *Motion Picture*, May 1964.

Chapter 9

PAGE

81 'caged animal': Haddad-Garcia, *The Films of Jane Fonda*, p. 105.

81 'There was no script': Haddad-Garcia, *ibid.*, p. 103.

82 'He was a classic': PI.

82 'How can you prove': LAT, 26 April 1964.

84 'My reputation': Vadim, *Bardot, Deneuve, Fonda*, p. 139.

84 'I went': Spada, p. 58.

85 'I was blocked': Vadim, *Bardot, Deneuve, Fonda*, p. 215.

85 'Any man in his right': *ibid.*

86 'always thought that to be happy': Spada, p. 58.

86 'I will be a character': Vadim, p. 238.

87 'I was supposed to be nude': Jim Bennett, *Sound Stage*, May 1965.

88 'It was': Vadim, *Bardot, Deneuve, Fonda*, p. 227.

Chapter 10

PAGE

92 'There we were on location': AP, 2 Dec. 1964.

93 'She's too young': Vadim, *Bardot, Deneuve, Fonda*, p. 244.

94 'When I left America': Chicago *Sun-Times*, 9 May 1971.

Chapter 11

Chapter 12

Chapter 13

Chapter 14

Chapter 15

Chapter 16

151   'I was so used to being': AMPAS archives.
152   'there was a': Collier and Horowitz, p. 268.
152   'I took off on my trip': CST, 9 May 1971.
154   'Yes, I could be': Colorado Springs *Sun*, 22 Apr. 1970.
154   'They won't arrest me': *ibid*.
155   'rage – rage that people feel': *Sunday Record*, 21 Aug. 1973.
156   'establishment': WP, 23 May 1970.
156   'in it': *ibid*.
156   'You think this is *fun*?': *ibid*.
158   'Dad and I': Fonda, *My Life*, p. 302.
158   'Jane, if I ever': *ibid*.
159   'I feel': Detroit *Free Press*, Dec. 1970.

Chapter 17

PAGE

160   'These women': *New York Sunday News*, 1970.
160   'I noticed in all': *ibid*.
160   'Being a movie star': PI.

Chapter 18

PAGE

168   'My position, not being,': *Miami Herald*, 24 Nov. 1970.
169   'grass, mescaline, and acid': *OMT*, Fayetteville, Ark., 5 Dec. 1970.
169   'the hardest thing for me': Detroit *Free Press*, 6 Dec. 1970.
169   'I am no longer a wife': *ibid*.
170   'She turned': Hayden, *Reunion*, p. 442.
173   'Because she can't do': *Philadelphia Inquirer*, 8 Oct. 1972.
173   'And so': *ibid*.
174   'I'm not a loser': NYT, 23 Feb. 1974.
174   'I was playing': NYT, *ibid*.

Chapter 19

PAGE

177   'I asked him': PI.
177   'He just played right': *ibid*.

178   'Perhaps': *Partisan Review*, 1966.

178   'a little fascist': Collier and Horowitz, p. 244.

178   'Tom gives': PI.

179   'the only ones who could': Collier and Horowitz, p. 266.

179   'Well': *ibid.*

180   'I went to': Hayden, *Reunion*, p. 446.

180   'Complicated relationships': *ibid.*

180   'Instead of ignoring': *People*, June, 1982.

180   'It was important that Jane': Hayden, *Reunion*, p. 447.

181   'To understand Tom and Jane': PI.

181   'Jane was still': *ibid.*

Chapter 20

PAGE

185   'we almost went fucking crazy': PI.

185   'It's difficult to put': PI.

185   'I was hung by that': UPI, 14 Apr. 1973.

187   'She's a': *Washington Star*, 14 Aug. 1972.

188   'Declared war or undeclared war': UPI, 18 July 1972.

188   'Was it': Hayden, *Reunion*, p. 450.

188   'she felt a lot more': WP, 12 Aug. 1973.

189   'The degree to which Jane': *ibid.*

189   'I want to have a child': Hayden, *Reunion*, p. 448.

189   'in the upper berth': *ibid.*, p. 452.

189   'I would literally empty': *Cosmopolitan*, Jan. 1985.

189   'There is a lot of sexual': WP, *ibid.*

190   'I keep asking': PI.

190   'Jane Fonda seemed': *Chicago Tribune*, 1 Apr. 1973.

190   'Jane has encased': *ibid.*

191   'And since she loved him': *ibid.*

191   'I have directed': *ibid.*

191   'Do we': Hayden, *Reunion*, p. 453.

192   'I remember sitting': PI.

193   'Will you, Jane': PI.

193   'I couldn't even consider': *Washington Star*, 1 Feb. 1974.

194   'I think that one': AP, NBC, April 1973.

194   'laughable. These were not': *ibid.*

195   'the rottenest': UPI, 6 Feb. 1974.

196 'You know': UPI, 20 Feb. 1975.
197 'Watergate has given us': *ibid.*

Chapter 21

PAGE

198 'I'm lucky': PI.
198 'A terrorist, a Maoist': Vadim, *Bardot, Deneuve, Fonda*, p. 316.
199 'couldn't care less': *New York Sunday News*, 28 Nov. 1976.
200 'for the assistance': *Christian Science Monitor*, 21 Sept. 1975.
201 'We worked together': PI.
201 'There is no law': *ibid.*
202 'false American dream': *Chicago Tribune*, 6 June 1976.
202 'Hide my falsies!': *ibid.*
203 'Jane was distraught': PI.
204 'What did the soldiers': NYT, 3 Feb. 1974.

Chapter 22

PAGE

205 'Lillian is a homely woman': *Newsweek*, 10 Oct. 1977.
205 'There's a lot about': NYT, 31 Oct. 1976.
206 'In the goodbye scene': *Newsweek, ibid.*
206 '"Oh," gushed Jane': *ibid.*
209 'All we wanted to do': AFI archives.
210 'Ron Kovic': *Rolling Stone*, 5 Nov. 1987.
210 'The result': *ibid.*

Chapter 23

PAGE

214 'teaches them how to be': PI.
215 'You can't propagandise': PI.
215 'She had a terrific': *The Soho Weekly News*, 22 Mar. 1979.
215 'People were actually going': *Rolling Stone*, 5 Nov. 1987.
216 'Jane was treated like a functionary': PI.

217 'People *want* to': NYT, 30 March 1981.
218 'I'm opposed to all forms': Andersen, *The New Book of People*, p. 40.
218 'Jane was scared': PI.
219 'It was at that point': PI.

Chapter 24

PAGE

220 'get the CED': PI.
221 'It would have been cheaper': PI.

Chapter 25

PAGE

224 'a high-minded purpose': PI.
224 'You have wrinkles': PI.
225 'She was reluctant': PI.
225 'the particular combinations': PI.
225 'Jane is an actress': *Fortune*, 20 Feb. 1984.
225 'violent': *ibid.*
225 'I shed no tears': *Us*, 13 May 1980.
226 'Well, it's about time': PI.
226 'I'm a big believer': PI.
226 'absolutely terrified': PI.
226 'some arrogant, upstart': PI.
227 'I think Katharine': PI.
227 'It was ludicrous': PI.
227 'We rendezvoused': PI.
227 '"Now you're talking"': PI.
227 'I remembered': PI.
227 'terrifying experience': PI.
227 'That's what is so scary': PI.
228 'I thought, Holy cow!': PI.
228 'I could see Katharine': PI.
228 'What I love about Katharine': PI.
228 'learned more from Katharine': PI.
228 'didn't know who he was': PI.
228 'They sat': PI.
229 'She put': PI.

229 'We never talked about the meaning': PI.

231 'a wealthy society-type': NYT, 30 Mar. 1981.

232 'trying to sort things out': PI.

233 'It was very, very touching': *People*, 30 Aug. 1982.

233 'There's no question about it': *ibid.*

233 'It handed down to me': PI.

Chapter 26

PAGE

235 'Tom always bragged': PI.

235 'It really irked Jane': PI.

236 'messing around': LHJ, 20 Jan. 1982.

237 'Every inflammatory remark': Hayden, *Reunion*, p. 478.

238 'We're really upset': NYP, 31 Mar. 1983.

238 'more productive at running people': *Newsweek*, 11 Apr. 1983.

238 'I've never been better': NYP, 15 Dec. 1983.

238 'I'm not particularly paranoid': *ibid.*

238 'Changed?': *Fortune*, 20 Feb. 1984.

240 'What I really hate': interview on 'Good Morning America', 1985.

240 'For men and women': PI.

240 'Sure I wish I was forty': PI.

241 'If they had': *Chicago Tribune*, 8 Sept. 1985.

241 'returned to a sense of the importance': *ibid.*

241 'Mommy!': *ibid.*

241 'I had a very long talk': *NY Daily News Magazine*, 14 Dec. 1986.

242 'His empathy for those women': Roger Ebert, 'Fonda as a Drunk':
       NYP, 23 Dec. 1986.

242 'I was so scared': *ibid.*

242 'Alex is a wreck': *NY Daily News Magazine*, 14 Dec. 1986.

242 'Most women's roles': *ibid.*

242 'The decision was made': *ibid.*

Chapter 27

PAGE

244 'I'm actually looking forward': *People*, 17 Dec. 1984.

244 'I'm really appalled': *ibid.*

245 'when I went to Mexico': PI.

245 'I told him I wanted': PI.

245 'It was very complicated': PI.

246 'You know': *Premier*, Nov. 1988.

246 'Whenever they talk': *ibid.*

246 'All you have to do': PI.

246 'Both were real gentlemen': PI.

246 'looks seamless': PI.

246 'absolutely blown away': PI.

247 'We were supposed to finish': Rosenblum.

247 'A thirty-five-year-old virgin': PI.

249 'People need scapegoats': PI.

249 'Bobby was one': PI.

250 'I wanted to work': PI.

250 'This story': PI.

250 'I don't believe': PI.

251 'The obvious mendacity': PI.

252 'Spanish mixed with California': PI.

252 'We had trouble': PI.

252 'I said, "Follow me,"': PI.

252 'It was a peak experience': PI.

252 'I had always wondered': PI.

253 'My God, I thought': PI.

253 'To pretend that the ending': PI.

253 'I've been working on myself': PI.

253 'The air is something': PI.

253 'If you're not happy': PI.

254 'Some movie stars' kids': PI.

254 'Going through a divorce': PI.

254 'It's like living': PI.

254 'I was a political woman': PI.

255 'worst-case scenarios': LHJ, Dec. 1986.

Bibliography

Andersen, Christopher. *The New Book of People*. Putnam, New York; 1985.
—— *Young Kate*. Henry Holt, New York; 1988.
Aronowitz, Alfred. 'Lady Jane,' *Saturday Evening Post*, 23 March 1963.
Bacon, James. *Hollywood Is a Four-Letter Town*. Henry Regnery, Chicago; 1976.
Brown, Peter H., and Pinkston, Jim. *Oscar Dearest*. Harper & Row, New York; 1987.
Cavett, Dick. *Cavett*. Harcourt Brace Jovanovich, New York; 1974.
Collier, Peter, and Horowitz, David. *Destructive Generation: Second Thoughts About the '60s*. Summit Books, New York; 1989.
Davis, Angela. *Angela Davis*. Random House, New York; 1974.
Fonda, Adfera. *Never Before Noon*. Weidenfeld, New York; 1987.
Fonda, Henry. *Fonda: My Life*, as told to Howard Teichmann. NAL Books, New York; 1981.
Fonda, Jane. *Jane Fonda's Workout Book*. Simon & Schuster, New York; 1981.
—— *Jane Fonda's Workout Book for Pregnancy, Birth and Recovery* (with Femmy DeLyser). Simon & Schuster, New York; 1982.
—— *Jane Fonda's Year of Fitness, Health & Nutrition*. Simon & Schuster, New York; 1984, 1985.
—— *Women Coming of Age* (with Mignon McCarthy). Simon & Schuster, New York; 1984.
—— *Jane Fonda's Workout Book* (paperback). Simon & Schuster, New York; 1986.
—— *Jane Fonda's New Workout & Weight-loss Program*. Simon & Schuster, New York; 1986.
—— *Jane Fonda's New Low Impact Workout & Weight-Loss Program*. Fireside/Simon & Schuster, New York; 1988.
—— *Jane Fonda's New Pregnancy Workout and Total Birth Program* (with Femmy DeLyser). Simon & Schuster, New York; 1989.
Ford, Dan. *Pappy: The Life of John Ford*. Prentice-Hall, Englewood Cliffs, N.J.; 1979.

Fredrik, Nathalie. *Hollywood and the Academy Awards*. Hollywood Awards Publications, Beverly Hills; 1969.

French, Philip. *The Movie Moguls*. Weidenfeld & Nicolson, London; 1969.

Haddad-Garcia, George. *The Films of Jane Fonda*. Citadel Press, Secaucus, N.J.; 1981.

Halliwell, Leslie. *Halliwell's Filmgoer's Companion*. Grafton Books, London; 1988.

Hayden, Tom. *Reunion*. Random House, New York; 1988.

——— *Trial*. Holt, Rinehart, New York; 1970.

Hayward, Brooke. *Haywire*. Alfred A. Knopf, New York; 1977.

Houseman, John. *Final Dress*. Simon & Schuster, New York; 1983.

Kael, Pauline. *Kiss Kiss Bang Bang*. Little, Brown, Boston; 1968.

Katz, Ephraim. *The Film Encyclopedia*. Putnam Publishing Group, New York; 1979.

Kelley, Kitty. *Elizabeth Taylor: The Last Star*. Simon & Schuster, New York; 1981.

Keylin, Arleen, and Bent, Christine, eds. *The New York Times at the Movies*. Arno Press, New York; 1979.

Kiernan, Thomas. *Jane: An Intimate Biography of Jane Fonda*. G. P. Putnam's Sons, New York; 1973.

Lambert, Gavin. *On Cukor*. G. P. Putnam's Sons, New York; 1972.

Logan, Joshua. *Movie Stars, Real People, and Me*. Delacorte, New York; 1978.

Mordden, Ethan. *Movie Star: A Look at the Women Who Made Hollywood*. St Martin's Press, New York; 1983.

Rosenblum, Ron. 'Dangerous Jane,' *Vanity Fair*, November 1988.

Shawcross, William. *Sideshow: Nixon, Kissinger and the Destruction of Cambodia*. Simon & Schuster, New York; 1987.

Spada, James. *Fonda: Her Life in Pictures*. Doubleday, New York; 1985.

Vadim, Roger. *Memoirs of the Devil*. Harcourt Brace Jovanovich, New York; 1976.

——— *Bardot, Deneuve, Fonda*. Simon & Schuster, New York; 1986.

Winters, Shelley. *Shelley II: The Middle of My Century*. Simon & Schuster, New York; 1989.

Index

288

297

298